Advance Praise for *The Credit Derivatives Handbook*

"This handbook on the rapidly developing and important market segment represented by credit derivatives will be useful to anyone requiring a comprehensive review and introduction to most aspects of this exciting new area, including innovations, design, pricing, and asset allocation. The editors are to be congratulated on this timely and valuable set of contributions featuring this important new class of financial instruments".

—**David E. Allen,** Professor of Finance, Edith Cowan University, Perth, Western Australia

"*The Handbook of Credit Derivatives* presents a rigorous examination of the design, pricing, and use of credit derivatives. It combines an impressive breadth of topics with in-depth analysis of individual topics. The result is a relevant and reliable source of information about credit derivatives for both investors and researchers."

—**Paul Brockman,** Matteson Professor of Financial Services, Department of Finance, University of Missouri-Columbia, Columbia, Missouri

"An impressive survey of current research in credit derivatives by academics and practitioners from around the world. It will be useful to those working outside the area who wish to gain a greater understanding of this topic and to those within the field who want to learn more about state-of-the-art research in credit derivatives."

—**Burt Porter,** Iowa State University, Ames, Iowa

"The book is an interesting compilation of several relevant themes in credit risk that range from CDS pricing and innovations to CDO pricing and their role in investment portfolios. Paul Ali and Greg Gregoriou have struck well the delicate balance between theoretical and empirical papers and also managed to include geographies beyond the United States."

—**Dr. Viral Acharya,** Professor of Finance and Academic Director of Private Equity Institute, London Business School, London

THE CREDIT DERIVATIVES HANDBOOK

Global Perspectives, Innovations, and Market Drivers

GREG N. GREGORIOU
PAUL U. ALI

EDITORS

New York   Chicago   San Francisco
Lisbon   London   Madrid   Mexico City
Milan   New Delhi   San Juan   Seoul
Singapore   Sydney   Toronto

1 2 3 4 5 6 7 8 9 0   DOC/DOC   0 9 8

ISBN: 978–0–07-154952–3
MHID: 0–07-154952–8

This publication is designed to provide accurate and authoritative information in regard to the subject
matter covered. It is sold with the understanding that neither the author nor the publisher is engaged in
rendering legal, accounting, futures/securities trading, or other professional service. If legal advice or
other expert assistance is required, the services of a competent professional person should be sought.
—*From a Declaration of Principles jointly adopted by a Committee*
of the American Bar Association and a Committee of Publishers

McGraw-Hill books are available at special quantity discounts to use as premiums and sales promo-
tions, or for use in corporate training programs. For more information, please write to the Director of
Special Sales, Professional Publishing, McGraw-Hill, Two Penn Plaza, New York, NY 10121–2298.
Or contact your local bookstore.

This book is printed on acid-free paper.

Library of Congress Cataloging-in-Publication Data

The credit derivatives handbook / [edited] by Greg N. Gregoriou and Paul Ali.
     p. cm.
  Includes index.
  ISBN-13: 978-0-07-154952-3
  ISBN-10:   0-07-154952-8
  1. Credit derivatives. I. Gregoriou, Greg N., 1956- II. Ali, Paul A. U.

HG6024.A3C753 2009

332.64'57—dc22   2008018185

C O N T E N T S

PART ONE

INNOVATIONS IN CREDIT DEFAULT SWAPS

Chapter 1

The Changing Face of Credit Default Swaps   3

Paul U. Ali and Jan Job de Vries Robbé

Chapter 2

Derivatives in Islamic Finance   15

Andreas A. Jobst

Chapter 12

**Pricing Forward-Starting Collateralized Debt
Obligations Using Dynamic Copula Processes   259**
Daniel Totouom and Margaret Armstrong

Chapter 13

**Identifying Systemic and Idiosyncratic Risk from Standardized
Single-Tranche Collateralized Debt Obligations   289**
Jorge A. Chan-Lau and Yinqiu Lu

Chapter 14

Default Contagion in Large Homogeneous Portfolios   303
Alexander Herbertsson

PART FOUR

ASSET ALLOCATION AND CREDIT DERIVATIVES

Chapter 15

An Asset Allocation Problem with Credit Derivatives   337

Francesco Menoncin

Chapter 16

Synthetic Collateralized-Debt-Obligation-Squared Pricing Methodologies   361

Dominique Guégan and Julien P. Houdain

Chapter 17

The Role of Credit and Credit Index Derivatives in Portfolio Management: Asset Allocation Issues and Opportunities   379

R. McFall Lamm, Jr.

ACKNOWLEDGMENTS

We would like to thank a handful of anonymous referees for reviewing and selecting the chapters for this book. We also thank Jeanne Glasser and the team at McGraw-Hill as well as Richard Rothschild and the production team at Print Matters. Each of the chapters in this book is the original work of the relevant author(s). We thank them for their contribution. Neither the editors nor the publisher can guarantee the accuracy of the chapters.

Greg N. Gregoriou is Professor of Finance in the School of Business and Economics at State University of New York (Plattsburgh). A native of Montreal Greg received his Bachelor of Arts in Economics from Concordia University in 1988. In 1991 he completed his MBA from the University of Quebec at Montreal (UQAM) and obtained his Graduate Diploma in Applied Management from McGill University. He then completed his PhD in finance at UQAM in the joint doctoral PhD program in Montreal (McGill University, Concordia, and HEC Montreal). He specializes in hedge funds, funds of hedge funds, and managed futures. He has published over 50 academic articles on hedge funds and managed futures in various peer-reviewed journals, such as the *Journal of Portfolio Management, Journal of Futures Markets, European Journal of Operational Research, Annals of Operations Research, Computers and Operations Research INFORS, Journal of Asset Management, Journal of Alternative Investments, European Journal of Finance, Journal of Derivatives Accounting, Journal of Financial Crime*, and *Journal of Wealth Management* and has written 20 book chapters. He is hedge fund editor and editorial board member for *Journal of Derivatives and Hedge Funds*, a London-based academic journal, and also editorial board member of the *Journal of Wealth Management* and the *Journal of Risk and Financial Institutions*. He is the co-author and co-editor of 24 books published by John Wiley & Sons, Elsevier Butterworth-Heinemann, McGraw-Hill, Palgrave-MacMillan, and Risk Books.

Paul U. Ali is an Associate Professor in the Faculty of Law, University of Melbourne, and a member of that Law Faculty's Centre for Corporate Law and Securities Regulation. Prior to becoming an academic, Paul was, for several years, a finance lawyer in Sydney. Paul has published widely on banking and finance law, corporate governance and institutional investment law, securitization law, and structured finance law. His most recent publications include *Innovations in Securitization* (The Hague, 2006), *International Corporate Governance after Sarbanes-Oxley* (Hoboken, NJ, 2006), *Opportunities in Credit Derivatives and Synthetic*

Securitization (London, 2005), and *Securitization of Derivatives and Alternative Asset Classes* (The Hague, 2005). In 2006 the Australian Federal Attorney General appointed Paul a member of the Personal Property Securities Review Consultative Group. Paul holds a S.J.D. from the University of Sydney.

CONTRIBUTORS

Margaret Armstrong has a Masters degree in mathematical statistics at the University of Queensland (Australia). Margaret moved to France where she received a doctorate in geostatistics (stochastic processes applied to natural resources) in 1980. Her research interests include financial analysis of mining and petroleum projects as well 3-dimensional (3D) spatial modeling. In 2001 she and Alain Galli started the quantitative finance group within the Ecole des Mines de Paris. Their research topics include commodities, real options and credit derivatives.

Jorge A. Chan-Lau is a senior economist in the Monetary and Capital Markets Department at the International Monetary Fund. He holds M.Phil. and PhD degrees in Economics and Finance from the Graduate School of Business, Columbia University, and a BS in Civil Engineering from Pontificia Universidad Catolica del Peru. He currently works on credit risk, financial markets, and financial stability and has published work on contagion, financial crises, credit derivatives, corporate restructuring, risk management, and institutional investors' asset allocation.

Jan Job de Vries Robbé is structured finance counsel at FMO, the Dutch Development Bank. He specializes in securitization and derivatives. He has extensive experience in structured finance, gained both in private practice (at De Brauw Blackstone Westbroek and Minter Ellison) and in-house (at NIBC and ANZ) in Europe and overseas. He regularly lectures on structured finance and is a visiting scholar at the University of Melbourne, where he lectures on securitization and derivatives. He has authored and edited various books on structured finance, including *Synthetic, Insurance and Hedge Fund Securitization* (2003), *Opportunities in Credit Derivatives and Synthetic Securitization* (2005), *Securitization of Derivatives and Alternative Asset Classes* (2005), and *Innovations in Securitization* (2006).

Pascal François is Associate Professor at HEC Montreal's Department of Finance. He holds a PhD from Sorbonne University and ESSEC Business

School. He is a member of the CREF scientific committee (Research Centre in E-Finance) based in Montreal. His research focuses on the pricing and the design of debt contracts, with a special emphasis on credit risk, capital structure, and corporate debt financing strategies. His publications appeared in the *Journal of Business*, the *Journal of Banking and Finance*, the *Financial Review,* and the *European Journal of Operational Research*. His book on derivatives (Dunod editions, 2005) was recently awarded the François-Albert Angers Prize.

Raquel M. Gaspar is assistant professor at ISEG, Technical University of Lisbon, since February 2006. She has a PhD in Finance from the Stockholm School of Economics (SSE); post-graduate studies in Risk Management and Derivatives from IDEFE, NOVAFORUM, and Instituto de Mercados de Capitais (IMC); a Masters in Applied Mathematics from ISEG; and undergraduate studies in Economics from Universidade Nova de Lisboa. Her research interests are in mathematical finance and concretely in credit risk, energy markets, portfolio optimization, and term structure models.

Hayette Gatfaoui obtained his PhD in 2002 at the University of Paris 1 Sorbonne. His PhD dissertation dealt with credit risk valuation in corporate bonds. Hayette is an associate professor at Rouen School of Management where he teaches fixed income, applied stock portfolio management, financial markets, financial mathematics as well as stochastic calculus, and quantitative method courses to postgraduate students. His main research areas are credit risk assessment, risk management, and modeling. He also does consulting in the portfolio performance measurement area for numerous financial firms and is also a member of the editorial board of the *Middle Eastern Finance and Economics Journal*.

Dominique Guégan is Full Professor in Mathematics in University Paris1—Panthéon—Sorbonne. She obtained her PhD (in Mathematics) in 1975 from the University of Grenoble (France). She has published seven books on mathematics, nonlinear time series, and chaos theory. She has also published over 55 articles in finance, probability, statistics, nonlinear time series, econometrics, and chaos theory, including the *Statistics and Probability Letters, Economic Letters, Econometrics Review, Journal of Statistical and Planning Inference,* and the *Journal of Applied Probability.* She has also contributed numerous book chapters for 10 edited books.

Marc Gürtler is Professor of Finance at the Technical University at Braunschweig. Before coming to Braunschweig in 2002, he was assistant professor of Finance at RWTH Aachen University. His fields of research interest are credit risk management, portfolio management, and international financial management.

Alexander Herbertsson is at present employed as researcher at Centre for Finance and Department of Economics at the School of Business, Economics and Law, belonging to Göteborg University. He holds a PhD in Economics from Göteborg University and has a Licentiate degree in industrial mathematics from Chalmers University of Technology and an MS in Engineering Physics from the same university. His main research field is default dependence modeling with a view towards pricing and hedging portfolio credit derivatives. Alexander has also done practical work in option pricing (implied volatility tree models) as a programmer and quantitative analyst in the Financial Engineering and Risk Management group at Handelsbanken Markets, Stockholm. He has taught mathematics courses at Chalmers University of Technology, in stochastic calculus for PhD students at the Department of Economics and also supervised several MS theses in Financial Mathematics.

Martin Hibbeln is research associate at the chair of Finance (since 2004), Technical University at Braunschweig. His fields of research interest are financial intermediation and credit risk management, the latter particularly with regard to concentration risk in credit portfolios. Furthermore, he works at the Volkswagen Bank GmbH on LGD modeling.

Julien P. Houdain is a Structured Credit Fund Manager at Legal & General IM. Before that he was a Structured Finance Quantitative Strategist at Fortis Investments, Paris. He had a very active participation to the pricing and the management of more than 30 bespoke CDO deals (Synthetic CDO, First to Default CDO, Single Tranche CDO, CDO Squared, CDO of ABS, CPPI with CDO Tranches and CDS Indexes). He developed market standard and proprietary models for the pricing of all types of CDO structures. He has also worked on trading long and short hedging strategies for CDO tranches, single-name CDS, and CDS indexes. He has published several internal articles on CDO pricing and hedging and made numerous presentations for clients, investors, and counter parties. He obtained his PhD (Business and Economics) from the École Normale Supérieure at Cachan-France in 2006.

Georges Hübner (PhD, INSEAD) is the Deloitte Professor of Financial Management and is cochair of the Finance Department at HEC— Management School of the University of Liège. He is Associate Professor of Finance at Maastricht University and Academic Expert at the Luxembourg School of Finance, University of Luxembourg. He is also an Affiliate Professor at EDHEC (Lille/Nice) and an Invited Professor at the Solvay Business School (Brussels). He has published numerous research articles in leading scientific journals including *Journal of Banking and Finance, Journal of Empirical Finance, Review of Finance, Financial Management,* and *Journal of Portfolio Management.* Georges Hübner was the recipient of the prestigious 2002 Iddo Sarnat Award for the best paper published in the *Journal of Banking and Finance* in 2001, and corecipient of the *Operational Risk & Compliance Achievement Award 2006* in the best academic paper category.

Andreas Jobst is a mid-career economist at the Monetary and Capital Markets Department (MCM) of the International Monetary Fund (IMF) in Washington, DC. His research focuses on structured finance, risk management, sovereign debt management, financial regulation, and time series econometrics. He previously worked at the Division for Insurance and Research at the Federal Deposit Insurance Corporation (FDIC), the Economics Department of the Deutsche Bundesbank, the Financial Markets Group (FMG) at the London School of Economics (LSE), the Center for Financial Studies (CFS) in Frankfurt/Main, the International Division of the European Central Bank (ECB), the Financial Institutions Division of the Bank of England, the Comisión Económica para América Latina y el Caribe (CEPAL) of the United Nations, the European Securitization Group of Deutsche Bank in London, and the Financial Services Group of the Boston Consulting Group (BCG). Mr. Jobst holds a PhD in Finance from the London School of Economics (LSE). He was also educated in Oxford, Cambridge, Leicester and Maryland, and holds the professional qualification of Accredited Asset Management Specialist (AAMS). Andy is a regular speaker at professional and academic conferences on risk management and structured finance. His most recent research was published in *Derivatives Use, Trading & Regulation, Managerial Finance, International Journal of Emerging Markets, Journal of Banking Regulation, Journal of Structured Finance, International Journal of Banking Law and Regulation, Journal of Operational Risk, Macroeconomics and Finance in Emerging Market Economies, The Securitization Conduit,* and *Euromoney.* He has also been one of the authors of the *Global Financial Stability Report* published by the Monetary and Capital Markets Department of the IMF (2005–2007).

Yinqiu Lu is an economist in the Monetary and Capital Markets Department at the International Monetary Fund. She holds a PhD in Economics from the City University of New York, an MA in economics from Fudan University, China, and a BA from Nanjing University, China. She currently works on credit derivatives, structured products, and sovereign asset and liability management.

Stephen J. Lubben is the Daniel J. Moore Professor of Law at Seton Hall University School of Law, in Newark, NJ, where he specializes in corporate reorganization. Professor Lubben joined Seton Hall after several years in practice with Skadden, Arps, Slate, Meagher & Flom in New York and Los Angeles, where he represented parties in chapter 11 cases throughout the United States.

Giovanni Masala is a researcher in mathematical methods for economy and finance at the Faculty of Economics in the University of Cagliari (Italy). He obtained his PhD in differential geometry from the University of Mulhouse (France) and his current research interests include mathematical risk modeling for financial and actuarial applications.

R. McFall Lamm, Jr. is the chief investment strategist for Deutsche Bank's Global Investment Management Group in London. His current responsibilities include asset allocation for DB's discretionary management business, advising large bank clients on portfolio strategy, and directly managing a boutique hedge fund portfolio. Dr. Lamm is a frequent speaker at conferences and events around the globe. He also writes market commentary that is disseminated worldwide and is often quoted in the news media. In addition, Dr. Lamm is an energetic writer having published numerous book chapters and professional articles in publications such as the *The Journal of Portfolio Management, The Journal of Economic Dynamics and Control,* and *The Journal of Alternative Investments*.

Francesco Menoncin is Associate Professor at Brescia University (Italy). He obtained his MA and PhD in Economics at Louvain-Le-Neuve

(Belgium). His fields of interests are stochastic programming, optimal portfolio rules, pension funds, and, in general, the link between actuarial and financial risks. He has published numerous papers in *Insurance: Mathematics and Economics, Annals of Operations Research, European Journal of Finance, Revue Economique,* and *International Economics.*

Massimiliano Menzietti is Professor of Life Insurance Mathematics in the University of Calabria (Cosenza). From 2002 to 2006 he was research fellow of the Department of Actuarial and Financial Science in the University "La Sapienza" of Rome. He graduated in economics from the University LUISS-Guido Carli of Rome. He obtained a PhD in Actuarial Science from University "La Sapienza" of Rome. His research has focused on actuarial mathematics of pension schemes, financial mathematics (specifically on actuarial model for credit risk), and automobile car insurance. He is now also working on actuarial mathematics and risk management of long term care insurance.

Marco Micocci is full Professor of Financial Mathematics and Actuarial Science at the University of Cagliari. From 1996 to 2001 he was Researcher of Financial and Actuarial mathematics at the University of Rome "La Sapienza." He has a degree in economics, a degree in banking, financial, and insurance science, and a degree in actuarial statistics. His fields of research are financial and actuarial management of pension funds, mathematical finance, and credit risk. He is author of over 60 publications (papers, articles, books) and is also a consultant actuary.

Antonio Nicolò, PhD, Universitat Autonoma de Barcelona, is currently Associate Professor at the University of Padua (Italy). His main research interests are in theoretical economics, namely, game theory, contract theory, and social choice. He was awarded in 2005 the Financial Management Association (FMA) European Conference Best Paper Award, for the paper "Credit Derivatives: Capital Requirements and Strategic Contracting" (with L. Pelizzon). In 2004 he won the M. Fanno Prize for young researchers of the M. Fanno Department of Economics (University of Padua). He is local organizer and Chair of the Scientific Committee of the 2007 Association of Southern European Economist Theorists (ASSET) meeting at Padua (Italy). His work includes papers published in the *Journal of Economic Theory, Games and Economic*

Behavior, Journal of Public Economic Theory Mathematical Social Sciences, and *Review on Economic Design*. During the last few years, he visited the Indian Statistical Institute, New Delhi Centre (2007), the Department of Economics, University of Rochester (2006), and the Center for Mathematical Studies in Economics & Mathematical Science, Kellogg's School of Management, Northwestern University (2005).

Sven Olboeter is a research associate at the chair of Finance (since 2006), Technical University at Braunschweig. His field of research interest is credit risk management particularly with regard to credit derivatives. Sven also works at the Volkswagen Bank GmbH on LGD modeling.

Mehmet Orhan is associate professor at the Economics Department of Fatih University, Istanbul. He is also the Director of Social Sciences Institute that is responsible from the coordination of several graduate programs. He has MA and PhD degrees from Bilkent University, Ankara, and has graduated from the Industrial Engineering Department of the same university. His main interest is econometrics, both theoretical and applied and has published numerous articles in Economics Letters, International Journal of Business, and Journal of Economic and Social Research. His theoretical research interests include HCCME estimation, robust estimation techniques, and Bayesian inference. His areas of interest are IPO performance in Turkey, hedge funds, venture capital, inflation and its uncertainty, tax revenue estimation, and international economic cooperation.

Loriana Pelizzon is Associate Professor of Economics at the University of Venice. She graduated from the London Business School with a doctorate in Finance. She also holds a degree from the University of Venice (Laurea in Business Administration). She was assistant professor in Economics at the University of Padova from 2000 until 2004. Her research interests are risk measurement and management, asset allocation and household portfolios, hedge funds, financial institutions, and financial crisis. Her work includes papers published in the *Journal of Financial and Quantitative Analysis, European Journal of Finance, Journal of Economics and Business,* and *Journal of Empirical Finance,* and she has presented at the Western Finance Association and European Finance Association. Pelizzon has been awarded the EFA 2005 Barclays Global Investor Award for the Best Symposium paper and FMA European Conference, 2005 best conference paper. She is participating in many research projects: NBER, FDIC, RTN, HCM, TACIS, ACE, MURST, PRIN, etc. She is a referee for the following journals: *JMCB, JFI, JEFM, JMFM, JB&F, RoF, JIFMIM, Journal of Macroeconomics, Risk Analysis, Research in Economics, RISEC,* and *Elsevier: Finance Publications.* In addition, she is a member of the Program Committee: European Finance Association Conferences, Coordinator of the EFA Doctoral Tutorial, and Member of the Teaching Committee of the PhD in Economics, University of Venice. She teaches financial economics and investments at the International Master in Economics and Finance Program and economics and financial economics at the undergraduate program. She has been awarded the Best Teacher 2006 at the Ca' Foscari University of Venice. She frequently advises banks and government agencies on risk measurement and risk management strategies.

François-Éric Racicot, PhD, holds a joint doctorate in Business Administration (Finance) from UQAM. He also holds an MS in Economics (Econometrics) from University of Montreal where he also received his BS in Economics (Quantitative Economics). He is associate Professor of Finance at the Department of Administrative Sciences of the University of Quebec, Outaouais (UQO). He was Professor of Finance at the Department of Strategic Business at the University of Quebec at Montreal. He is a permanent member of the Laboratory for Research in Statistics and Probability (LRSP) and a research associate at the *Chaire d'information financière et organisationnelle* located at School of Business (ESG)-UQAM. He is also a consultant in financial engineering for various financial institutions in Quebec. His research fields include the theory of fixed income securities, the theory of derivative products, the empirical analysis of hedge funds, and financial engineering. His research focuses on the development of new econometric techniques for correcting and detecting specification errors in financial models, especially in the context of estimating the alpha and conditional beta of hedge funds. This research should be useful, especially for improving the selection of hedge funds used in the construction of funds of funds. He has published numerous books on quantitative finance used at the graduate level in universities and also in financial institutions as well as several articles on empirical finance in international journals.

Thorsten Schmidt is assistant professor in financial mathematics at the University of Leipzig. He has a background in statistics and probability theory and is currently working on pricing and hedging credit risk, infinite-dimensional models, shot-noise effects, and incomplete information issues. His works cover moment estimators for MARCH models; the application of SDEs on Hilbert spaces, including Lévy random fields, to credit risk, in particular to CDOs, shot-noise models applied to equity, credit, and energy markets; and the use of nonlinear filtering theory for pricing corporate securities under noisy asset information.

M. Nihat Solakoglu is an assistant professor in the Banking and Finance Department of Bilkent University in Ankara, Turkey. He was an assistant professor in the Department of Management at Fatih University. Before joining Fatih University, he worked for American Express in the United States in international risk management, international information management, and information and analysis departments. He received his PhD in economics and Masters degree in statistics from North Carolina State University. His main interests are applied finance and international finance. His papers have been published in *Applied Economics, Journal of International Financial Markets, Institutions & Money,* and *Journal of Economic and Social Research.*

Raymond Théoret, PhD, holds a doctorate in Economics (financial economics) from by the University of Montreal. He is Professor of Finance at l'École des Sciences de la Gestion (ESG) of the University of Quebec, Montreal (UQAM). He was previously Professor in financial economics at *l'Institut d'Économie Appliquée* located at HEC Montreal. He was an economic and financial consultant at various financial institutions in Quebec and Secretary of Campeau Commission on the improvement of the situation of financial institutions in Montreal. He has published many articles and numerous books on financial engineering, computational finance, and asset pricing. Moreover, he is the founder of the DESS (Finance) pregramat UQAM and a co-founder of the Master in Applied Finance at the same university. He teaches portfolio management theory and computational finance. His research focuses on modeling hedge fund returns with specification errors. He is an associate member of the *Chaire d'information financière et organisationnelle* located at ESG-UQAM.

Daniel Totouom joined the Risk Management Group at BNP Paribas in Paris in March 2003. Since November 2005, he has been based in the London office within the Product Development and Quantitative Structuring

Group, where he is in charge of developing methodologies in the Exotic CDO field. Before joining the bank in 2003, Daniel was a Quantitative Analyst in Equity Derivatives at Goldman Sachs in London. He is a graduate from the Ecole Polytechnique in France and the Ecole des Mines de Paris and holds a MS degree in microelectronics.

PART ONE

Innovations in Credit Default Swaps

CHAPTER 1

The Changing Face of Credit Default Swaps

Paul U. Ali and Jan Job de Vries Robbé

ABSTRACT

Trading in credit default swaps, the most common type of credit risk transfer derivative, has grown explosively over the last decade. Much of this growth is attributable to the development of standardized market documentation for both "vanilla" and exotic variants of credit default swaps, the new source of liquidity provided by hedge funds, the inherent flexibility of credit default swaps, which allows for highly customized trades in credit risk geared to match the risk appetites of market participants, and rapid product innovation. This is well illustrated by three new types of credit default swaps, which form the subject of this chapter.

INTRODUCTION

The global market for credit derivatives and securitized products incorporating credit derivatives has grown explosively over the last decade. This rapid growth has been accompanied by an equally rapid level of innovation in that market, which has seen credit derivatives evolve beyond their original vanilla structures to reference complex financial assets, including securitized and other structured finance products, and also be incorporated into increasingly complex securitization structures

3

to deliver highly customized credit exposure to investors. Both the high levels of transaction volumes and the high degree of product innovation have benefited considerably from the standardization of documentation for credit derivatives under the supervision of the International Swaps and Derivatives Association (ISDA) and the continuing efforts of market participants to address operational risks.

However, the single most important factor for this expansion in transaction volumes—which has also enabled product innovation—is the inherent flexibility of credit derivatives, which has made it possible to customize the trading of credit risk to match the risk appetites of market participants. This is well illustrated by three new types of credit derivatives that form the subject of this chapter: credit default swaps on asset-backed securities, credit index derivatives, and loan-only credit default swaps. These credit derivatives are discussed on a stand-alone basis as distinct from their use in synthetic securitizations, for instance, in single-tranche structures (de Vries Robbé and Ali, 2005a; ibid., 2005b; ibid., 2006; Ali, 2007).

CREDIT DEFAULT SWAPS

Credit derivatives, in common with other over-the-counter derivatives, are privately negotiated bilateral contracts for shifting risk. In the case of credit derivatives, the risk being transferred under the derivative is credit risk, principally, the risk of nonperformance due to default or bankruptcy (de Vries Robbé and Ali, 2005a).

The credit default swap, particularly in its vanilla single-name and more recent credit index forms, is by far the most common type of credit derivative. It enables the parties to trade the credit risk of one or more entities—whether corporations or sovereign states—in isolation to the other risks associated with those entities. Basically, one party (known as the *protection seller*) agrees, in exchange for the payment to it of a fee by the other party (known as the *protection buyer*) to the credit default swap, to sell credit risk protection to the protection buyer in relation to certain debt instruments (known as *reference obligations*) of a third party (known as the *reference entity*) (de Vries Robbé and Ali, 2005a). In this manner, the protection buyer is able to transfer the credit risk, the subject of the credit default swap, to the protection seller.

The protection seller is obligated to make a payment to the protection buyer if a credit event occurs in relation to the reference entity during the term of the credit default swap. The credit events most commonly encountered in credit default swaps are the bankruptcy of the reference entity and the failure of the reference entity to make principal and interest payments on the reference obligations when due (de Vries Robbé and Ali, 2005a).

A credit default swap envisages two mutually exclusive possibilities. If no credit event occurs during the term of the credit default swap, the protection buyer will continue to pay the fee to the protection seller until the maturity of the credit default swap. If, however, a credit event does occur during the term of the credit default swap, the swap will terminate, with the protection buyer's obligation to pay the fee ceasing and the protection seller becoming obligated to make a payment to the protection buyer. The quantum of that payment will depend upon how the settlement of the credit default swap has been structured. In the case of a physically settled credit default swap, the protection seller will be obligated to purchase the reference obligations or other eligible substitute debt instruments of the reference entity for their full face value from the protection buyer (de Vries Robbé and Ali, 2005a). In contrast, in the case of a cash-settled credit default swap, the protection seller will be obligated to pay either an amount calculated by reference to the fall in value of the reference obligations or a fixed proportion of the face value of the reference obligations (de Vries Robbé and Ali, 2005a).

Stand-alone credit default swaps are typically physically settled, while the credit default swaps used in synthetic securitizations are normally cash settled (de Vries Robbé and Ali, 2005a). There is, however, now a trend in the case of stand-alone credit default swaps away from physical settlement. A key reason is that the difficulty with sourcing illiquid debt instruments for delivery under the swap may impact negatively upon the transfer of credit risk. Once a credit event occurs, the protection buyer—in the case of a physically settled credit default swap—must deliver the requisite debt instruments to the protection seller within the time period provided for in the contract terms. Failure to do so will cause the protection buyer to lose its right to obtain payment from the protection seller and, consequently, the benefit of credit risk protection under the credit default swap (*Deutsche Bank v. Ambac Credit Products*, 2006). Cash settlement also avoids the risk of there being a run on the debt instruments of a popular reference entity following a credit event.

In their simplest and, until recently, most common form, credit default swaps transfer the credit risk relating to single reference entities (these swaps are known as *single-name* credit default swaps). It is, however, eminently possible to structure credit default swaps to transfer the credit risk of multiple reference entities (*multiname* or *portfolio* credit default swaps) (de Vries Robbé and Ali, 2005a). In the case of a multiname credit default swap, the swap can be structured to terminate upon the first or any subsequent credit event with respect to any one of the reference entities (de Vries Robbé and Ali, 2005a). However, as with single-name credit default swaps, the majority of multiname credit default swaps are first-to-default swaps (de Vries Robbé and Ali, 2005a). It is also possible to structure credit default swaps to transfer the credit risk of all reference entities in a particular geographic region or market sector; these credit index derivatives are discussed below.

Credit Default Swaps on Asset-Backed Securities

The debt instruments referenced by credit default swaps have, to date, mainly comprised loans made to and debt securities issued by corporate and sovereign reference entities (de Vries Robbé and Ali, 2005a; Fitch Ratings, 2007). The last three years, in particular, have witnessed the extension of credit default swaps to more exotic reference obligations, including debt securities issued in structured finance transactions such as securitizations. This can be viewed as simply an incident of the increasing maturation of the global market for credit derivatives, with market participants designing products to permit the trading of credit risk in relation to an ever-wider range of debt instruments. It is also a consequence of the equally explosive growth in the global securitization market over the last decade.

The so-called asset-backed securities referenced by this new form of credit default swap are typically debt securities issued in cash securitizations. These cash securitizations are the most common form of securitization transaction and involve the issue of debt securities to fund the acquisition of diversified pools of income-generating assets where the cash flows generated by those assets are utilized to make principal and interest payments on the debt securities. The assets are isolated in an orphan entity, thus enabling the originator of the assets to transfer the credit risk (together with all other risks) of the assets to the orphan entity and permitting the originator to remove the assets from its balance sheet as well as, in the case of banks and other financial institutions, release the risk capital held against those assets. The assets involved in these cash securitizations are predominantly mortgage loans, credit card receivables, auto loans, and corporate loans.

Credit default swaps on asset-backed securities are, however, not only used to transfer the credit risk of the debt securities issued in cash securitizations but are also being employed increasingly to effect transfers of credit risk in relation to debt securities incorporating other credit default swaps or, in other words, in relation to funded credit default swaps. In a synthetic securitization, the proceeds of the debt securities issued by an orphan entity are used by that entity to collateralize the entity's sale of credit risk protection to, typically, a bank or other financial institution (again, the transfer of the credit risk of the reference obligations to the orphan entity permits the bank or other financial institution to release the risk capital held against those obligations) (de Vries Robbé and Ali, 2005a). The fees received by the orphan entity from its role as protection seller are used, in combination with the returns generated from the entity's investment of the proceeds from the issue of debt securities, to make interest payments on the debt securities (de Vries Robbé and Ali, 2005a). If during the term of the securities, a credit event occurs in respect of one or more of the credit derivatives entered into by the orphan entity, the payment obligations of the entity will be met out of the invested proceeds (de Vries Robbé and Ali, 2005a). The orphan entity's obligation to repay the principal amount of the debt securities to the investors is conditional upon no credit event occurring during the term of the debt securities, and accordingly, the issue of the debt securities by the orphan entity to the investors can be said to fund the orphan entity's obligations under its credit derivatives (de Vries Robbé and Ali, 2005a).

The credit default swap on asset-backed securities thus performs an important role in enabling the participants in securitizations to trade the credit risk of the debt securities issued in securitizations and also the credit risk of the underlying assets, whether these are the assets backing the securities or assets whose credit risk has been incorporated in those securities by credit derivatives (de Vries Robbé and Ali, 2005a; ibid., 2005b; de Vries Robbé, 2006; Parker, 2007). In particular, this swap enables market participants to synthesize credit exposure to debt securities that, due to those securities being illiquid, may be in short supply.

The development of credit default swaps on asset-backed securities has been greatly assisted by the publication by ISDA of contract templates dealing with the most common types of asset-backed securities referenced by those swaps (de Vries Robbé, 2006; Parker, 2007).

Among the key issues addressed in these templates is settlement. The debt securities issued in securitizations are illiquid, unlike the corporate and sovereign debt securities referenced by single-name credit default swaps. Physical settlement may be impracticable if the protection buyer cannot source sufficient reference obligations or eligible substitute obligations in the secondary market, and this lack of liquidity also makes cash settlement difficult as it will impede valuation (de Vries Robbé and Ali, 2005b; de Vries Robbé, 2006; Parker, 2007).

The first ISDA template (the so-called non-PAUG [pay-as-you-go] template) addresses this by allowing the protection buyer to elect physical settlement or synthetic delivery (where a total return swap synthesizing the total returns on the reference obligations is entered into by the parties on the termination of the credit default swap) in place of cash settlement (de Vries Robbé, 2006; Parker, 2007). This template is used mainly in the European credit derivatives market (de Vries Robbé, 2006; Parker, 2007).

The other ISDA templates (the "pay as you go" or PAUG templates) provide for an ongoing process of settlement during the term of the credit default swap with the protection seller being required to compensate the protection buyer for shortfalls suffered by the latter in relation to cash flows from the reference obligations until the termination of the swap (de Vries Robbé, 2006; Parker, 2007). PAUG settlement or physical settlement can be elected by the protection buyer in place of cash settlement for the Form I and CDO PAUG templates, while the Form II PAUG template provides only for PAUG settlement (de Vries Robbé, 2006; Parker, 2007). These three templates are mainly used in the U.S. credit derivatives market (de Vries Robbé, 2006; Parker, 2007).

Credit Index Derivatives

The second, major innovation in the global market for credit derivatives with which this chapter is concerned relates to credit index derivatives. This has involved the extension of the template for single-name credit default swaps first to multiple reference entities (as in the case of multiname credit default swaps) and then to reference entities in a geographic region or market sector as represented by a credit index (de Vries Robbé and Ali, 2005b). These credit indexes comprise the most liquid reference entities in a particular market (as determined by the extent to which such entities are referenced by single-name credit default swaps). The most important—and liquid—indexes are the CDS CDX and iTraxx credit indexes. The iTraxx credit indexes cover reference entities in Europe and Asia, while the CDX credit indexes cover reference entities in North America as well as in Africa, Asia, Eastern Europe, and the Middle East (Parker, 2007). Credit index derivatives have now surpassed single-name credit default swaps as the most widely traded form of credit derivative (Fitch Ratings, 2007).

Credit index derivatives are similar to multiname credit default swaps in that both involve the transfer of the credit risk of multiple reference entities. In the case of the latter, the credit risk transferred relates to the entities in a reference portfolio, while in the case of the former, credit risk is transferred in relation to all of the reference entities in a particular index. There is, however, a critical structural difference between these two types of credit derivatives. A multiname credit default swap involves only a single swap, while a credit index derivative is not a single swap but, instead, comprises a set of individual single-name credit default swaps referencing each of the entities that make up the relevant credit index (de Vries Robbé and Ali, 2005a; ibid., 2005b).

Even though a credit index derivative is a series of individual swaps, the parties cannot deal with one of those swaps in isolation from the other swaps (de Vries Robbé and Ali, 2005a; ibid., 2005b).

A single credit default swap can only be transferred or terminated together with an equal part of each other credit default swap forming part of the index transaction, as permitting the parties to deal with an individual credit default swap without also dealing with the other swaps would affect the weighting of the reference entities in the credit index derivative relative to their weightings in the relevant credit index (de Vries Robbé and Ali, 2005a; ibid., 2005b). That would lead to a mismatch between the credit index derivative and the credit index, meaning that the former would no longer transfer credit risk in respect of the market or region measured by the latter (de Vries Robbé and Ali, 2005a; ibid., 2005b).

In addition, the protection seller's obligation to make a payment to the protection buyer in respect of a credit index derivative is triggered by the occurrence of a credit event in relation to any one of the individual credit default swaps and not (as is the case with conventional index derivatives) by changes in the value of the credit index itself (de Vries Robbé and Ali, 2005a; ibid., 2005b).

Credit index derivatives, like stand-alone single-name and multi-name credit default swaps, are usually physically settled (de Vries Robbé and Ali, 2005a; ibid., 2005b). This may, however, pose difficulties for the protection buyer where the debt instruments of a reference entity in respect of which a credit event has occurred are illiquid (not all the debt instruments of the reference entities that make up a credit index are liquid, and those instruments could be far less liquid than the index itself). To address this issue, ISDA has developed a series of protocols under which the parties to a credit index derivative—as well as under other physically settled credit default swaps—can substitute cash settlement for physical settlement where the reference entity in question is bankrupt (de Vries Robbé and Ali, 2005a; ibid., 2005b; Rajan et al., 2007). Also, as noted above, there is now a trend away from physical settlement in the case of stand-alone credit default swaps.

Loan-Only Credit Default Swaps

Loan-only credit default swaps, the last of the three major innovations considered in this chapter, are similar to single-name credit default swaps. While single-name credit default swaps can also be used to transfer the credit risk of loans, the loans that are the subject of such swaps are typically unsecured loans of investment-grade reference entities (and are thus of equal priority ranking to the debt securities that are usually referenced by stand-alone single-name credit default swaps). Loan-only credit default swaps, in contrast, reference only secured and, more particularly, syndicated secured loans.

The main impetus for the development of a market for loan-only credit default swaps has come from the leveraged loan market, which had enjoyed strong growth (at least until the onset of the U.S. subprime crisis), due to the financing requirements of mergers and acquisitions (M&A) and leveraged buyout (LBO) transactions (Fitch Ratings, 2006; Maly, 2007). These swaps provide the same benefits for secured loans as single-name credit default swaps do for unsecured loans and debt securities (Fitch Ratings, 2006). Market participants can use them to hedge the credit risk of syndicated loans, as well as to create exposure to such loans, which has proven to be a particularly attractive feature of loan-only credit default swaps due to syndicated loans being generally less liquid than corporate debt securities (Bartlam and Artmann, 2007). Loan-only credit default swaps have also been given a major boost by the publication of contract templates by ISDA and the Loan Syndications and Trading Association and the launch of the CDS LCDX and iTraxx LevX credit indexes (Bartlam and Artmann, 2007).

In common with other stand-alone credit derivatives, stand-alone loan-only credit default swaps are typically physically settled (although, due to the secured nature of the reference obligations in the case of the latter, only loans of the reference entity having at least the same priority ranking as the reference obligations may be delivered in place of the reference obligations following the occurrence of a credit event).

Moreover, as with credit default swaps on asset-backed securities, important regional differences in relation to the legal structure of loan-only credit default swaps have emerged. Loan-only credit default swaps in the European market are designed to match credit exposure to particular reference obligations, and consequently, the prepayment of a syndicated secured loan prior to the maturity of the loan-only credit default swap referencing that loan will result in the cancellation of the swap (Fitch Ratings, 2006; Bartlam and Artmann, 2007; Maly, 2007) (unlike other credit default swaps that focus, instead, on the reference entity and that remain in force until their maturity or the earlier occurrence of a credit event, regardless of whether the reference obligations remain outstanding). In contrast, the loan-only credit default swaps used in the U.S. market are closer in structure to other credit default swaps. On the prepayment of the reference obligation, another secured loan of the reference entity can be substituted. These differences have been addressed in the latest template for European loan-only credit default swaps published by ISDA, which provides for such swaps to continue on the refinancing of the original reference obligations with the new loan being substituted as a reference obligation for the original loan unless the parties elect, on the inception of the swap, that the swap should be canceled on a refinancing (ISDA, 2007a; ibid., 2007b; ibid., 2008).

CONCLUSION

This chapter has provided an overview of three important innovations in the global market for credit derivatives. Two of these, credit default swaps on asset-backed securities and loan-only credit default swaps, well illustrate the potential of credit derivatives to trade the credit risk on an ever-expanding range of financial assets. The third product, the credit index derivative, is in many ways an extrapolation of the multiname credit default swap and allows market participants to trade credit risk in respect of entire markets or market segments.

Given the inherent flexibility of credit derivatives, it is no surprise that the development of new financial assets has been swiftly accompanied by the creation of new credit derivatives to hedge or synthesize credit exposure to those assets.

REFERENCES

Ali, P.U. (2007) Credit Derivatives. In P.U. Ali (ed), *Secured Finance Transactions*. London: Globe Law and Business.

Bartlam, M. and Artmann, K. (2007) Loan-Only Credit Default Swaps— The Story So Far, *Capital Markets Law Journal,* 2(3): 281–294.

de Vries Robbé, J.J. (2006) CDS of ABS: Structured Credit and Securitisation at the Cutting Edge. In J.J. de Vries Robbé and P.U. Ali (eds.), *Innovations in Securitisation*. The Hague: Kluwer Law International.

de Vries Robbé, J.J. and Ali, P.U. (2005a) *Opportunities in Credit Derivatives and Synthetic Securitisation.* London: Thomson Financial.

de Vries Robbé, J.J. and Ali, P.U. (2005b) The Continuing Evolution of the Structured Credit Market. *Journal of International Banking Law and Regulation,* 20(12): 628–632.

de Vries Robbé, J.J. and Ali, P.U. (2006) Synthetic CDOs: The State of Play. *Journal of International Banking Law and Regulation*, 21(1): 12–16.

Deutsche Bank AG v. Ambac Credit Products LLC and Ambac Assurance Corporation (2006) United States District Court, Southern District of New York (04 CIV 5594, 6 July).

Fitch Ratings (2006) Loan-Only Credit Default Swaps. Credit Policy— Special Report (31 May).

Fitch Ratings (2007) CDx Survey—Market Volumes Continue Growing while New Concerns Emerge. Credit Policy—Special Report (16 July).

International Swaps and Derivatives Association (2007a) Confirmation for Use with the Syndicated Secured Loan Credit Default Swap Standard Terms Supplement (22 May).

International Swaps and Derivatives Association. (2007b) Syndicated Secured Loan Credit Default Swap Standard Terms Supplement (22 May).

International Swaps and Derivatives Association (2008) Standard Terms Supplement and Confirmation for Credit Derivative Transactions on Leveraged Loan (12 March).

Maly, V. (2007) *Loan Credit Default Swaps. Securitization 2007.* London: Global Legal Group.

Parker, E. (2007) *Credit Derivatives.* London: Globe Law and Business.

Rajan, A., McDermot, G., and Roy, R. (2007) *The Structured Credit Handbook.* Hoboken, NJ: John Wiley & Sons.

CHAPTER 2

Derivatives in Islamic Finance

Andreas A. Jobst

ABSTRACT

Despite their importance for financial sector development, derivatives are few and far between in countries where the compatibility of capital market transactions with Islamic law requires the development of shariah-compliant structures. Islamic finance is governed by the shariah, which bans speculation, but stipulates that income must be derived as profits from shared business risk rather than interest or guaranteed return. This chapter explains the fundamental legal principles of Islamic finance and includes the presentation of a valuation model that helps illustrate the shariah-compliant synthetication of conventional finance through an implicit derivative arrangement. Based on the current use of accepted risk transfer mechanisms in Islamic structured finance, the chapter explores the validity of derivatives from an Islamic legal point of view and summarizes the key objections of shariah scholars that challenge the permissibility of derivatives under Islamic law. In conclusion, the chapter delivers suggestions for shariah compliance of derivatives.

INTRODUCTION

Financial globalization facilitates greater diversification of investment and enables risk to be transferred across national financial systems through derivatives. The resulting improvement in allocation of risks has made overall capital markets more efficient, while the availability of derivatives has increased liquidity in the underlying cash markets. Amid a compressed spread environment, lower risk premia have also encouraged investors to seek higher yields from emerging market assets as alternative investment. With increasingly market-determined emerging market interest rates and currencies, extension of emerging market yield curves, rapidly growing volume of international trade and capital flows, and increasing stock market activity, the local and foreign interest in emerging derivative markets is growing rapidly.

The development of derivative markets in emerging markets plays a particular role in this context as more institutional money is dedicated to emerging markets, which requires the availability of financial instruments to manage market, credit and interest rate risks in largely underdeveloped local capital markets. Derivatives in general are financial contracts whose inherent value derives from, and exists by reference to, a predetermined payoff structure of securities, interest rates, commodities, credit risk, foreign exchange or any other tradable assets, indices thereof and/or baskets of any combination of the above with varied maturities. Derivatives assume economic gains from both risk shifting and efficient price discovery by providing hedging and low-cost arbitrage opportunities.

While documentation standards and market practices that govern conventional derivative transactions in mature markets have reached a point of uniform application, derivative markets are still poorly developed in many emerging market countries due to the absence of enabling legal provisions and accounting standards specific to the trading and enforcement of derivative claims have inhibited a maturing of derivative markets.

Despite their importance for financial sector development, derivatives are few and far between in countries where the compatibility of capital market transactions with Islamic law requires the development of *shariah*-compliant structures. Islamic finance is governed by the shariah, which bans interest, short selling and speculation, and stipulates that income must be derived as profits from shared business risk rather than guaranteed return. Notwithstanding these religious constraints and legal uncertainty surrounding the enforceability of investor interest under Islamic jurisprudence, Islamic finance can synthesize close equivalents to equity, mortgages, and derivatives known in conventional finance. To this end, it relies on structural arrangements of asset transfer between borrowers and lenders to emulate traditional interest-bearing financial contracts.

This chapter explains the fundamental legal principles of Islamic finance, which includes the presentation of a valuation model that helps illustrate the shariah-compliant synthetication of conventional finance through an implicit derivative arrangement. Based on the current use of accepted risk transfer mechanisms in Islamic structured finance, this chapter explores the validity of derivatives from an Islamic legal point of view and evaluates key objections of shariah scholars challenging the permissibility of derivatives under Islamic law. In conclusion, the chapter delivers suggestions for shariah compliance of derivatives.

TYPES OF ISLAMIC FINANCE

Islamic finance substitutes the costly temporary use of assets for a permanent transfer of funds as a source of borrower indebtedness. While interest payments in conventional finance represent the contractible cost for funds tied to the amount of principal over a pre-specified lending period, the central tenet of the Islamic financial system is the prohibition of *riba*, which applies to any unlawful capital gain derived from the quantitative inequality of the counter values of exchange or sales contracts.[1,2] Riba is generally classified into unlawful advantage by way of excess (*riba al-fadl*) and deferment (*riba al-nasia*), respectively.[3] Islamic law derives

---

[1] The general consensus among Islamic scholars is that *riba* covers not only usury but also the charging of interest and any positive, fixed, predetermined rate of return that is guaranteed regardless of the performance of an investment (Iqbal and Tsubota, 2006; Iqbal and Mirakhor, 2006). Besides interest earnings [or usury (*riba*)] and money lending, Islamic law also prohibits (1) *haram* (sinful activity), such as direct or indirect association with lines of business involving alcohol, pork products, firearms, tobacco, and adult entertainment, (2) speculation, betting, and gambling (*maisir*), including the speculative trade or exchange of money for debt *without* an underlying asset transfer, (3) the trading of the same object between buyer and seller (*bay' al-inah*), as well as (4) preventable uncertainty (*gharar*), such as all financial derivative instruments, forward contracts, and futures agreements for speculative (rather than hedging) purposes.

[2] While the elimination of interest is fundamental to Islamic finance, *shariah*-compliant investment behavior also aims to eliminate exploitation pursuant to Islamic law. Riba applies to any transaction purporting to effect the profitable exchange of two or more species (*anwa*) that belong to the same genus (*jins*) and are governed by the same efficient cause (*illah*).

[3] The prohibition of *riba* is upheld if the rate of exchange between two objects is unity and no gain is permissible to either party and if deferred settlement is disallowed, which ensures that the transaction is settled on the spot by both parties.

from (1) the *shariah'ah* (or *shariah*), which comprises the *qur'an* and the sayings and actions of the Prophet *Mohammed* recorded in a collection of books known as the *sahih hadith* and (2) the *fiqh*, which represents Islamic jurisprudence based on a body of laws deducted from the shariah by Islamic scholars. The shariah is frequently characterized as Islamic religious law, which is binding upon Muslims as a matter of religious mandate and also may be incorporated into the secular law of a given jurisdiction (Jobst, 2007b; ibid., 2007d).

Since only interest-free forms of finance are considered permissible in Islamic finance, financial relationships between financiers and borrowers are not governed by capital-based investment gains but shared business risk (and returns) in lawful activities (*halal*). Any financial transaction under Islamic law implies *direct participation in asset performance*, which constitutes entrepreneurial investment that assigns to financiers clearly identifiable rights and obligations for which they are entitled to receive commensurate return in the form of state-contingent payments according to an agreed schedule and amount relative to asset performance.[4] The shariah does not object to payment for the use of an asset as long as both lender and borrower share the investment risk together and profits are not guaranteed ex-ante but accrue only if the investment itself yields income.

In light of moral impediments to "passive" investment and secured interest as form of compensation, shariah-compliant lending requires the replication of interest-bearing conventional finance via more complex structural arrangements of contingent claims subject to the intent to create of an equitable system of distributive justice and promote permitted activities (*halal*) and public goods (*maslaha*). The permissibility of risky capital investment without explicit interest earning has spawned three basic forms of Islamic financing for both investment and trade: (1) synthetic loans (*debt based*) through a sale–repurchase agreement or back-to-back sale of borrower or third-party-held assets, (2) lease contracts (*asset based*) through a sale–leaseback agreement (operating lease) or the lease of third-party acquired assets with purchase obligation components (financing lease), and (3) profit-sharing contracts (*equity based*) of future

---

[4] The underlying asset transfer of Islamic lending arrangements provides collateralization until the lender relinquishes ownership at the maturity date. In equity-based Islamic investments, lenders do not have any recourse unless premature termination enables the lender to recover some investment funds from the salvage value of project assets.

assets. As opposed to equity-based contracts, both debt- and asset-based contracts are initiated by a temporary transfer of existing assets from the borrower to the lender or the acquisition of third-party assets by the lender on behalf of the borrower.[5]

Islamic "loans" create borrower indebtedness from the purchase and resale contract of an (existing or future) asset in lieu of interest payments. The most prominent form of such a "debt-based" structural arrangement is the *murabaha* (*or murabahah*) ("cost-plus sale") contract. Interest payments are implicit in an installment sale with instantaneous (or deferred) title transfer for the promised payment of an agreed sales price in the future.[6] The purchase price of the underlying asset effectively limits the degree of debt creation. A *murabaha* contract either involves (1) the sale–repurchase agreement of a borrower-held asset ("negative short sale") or (2) the lender's purchase of a tangible asset from a third party on behalf of the borrower ("back-to-back sale"). The resale price is based on original cost plus a pre-specified profit markup imposed by the lender so that the borrower's future repurchase of the underlying asset or the sale of the asset to a third party to raise funds at the spot price involves a loss commensurate to the lender's profit ("loss-generating contract").

Different installment rates as well as delayed repayment and asset-delivery schedules for back-to-back sales and negative short sales, respectively create variations to the standard *murabaha* cost-plus sale. The most prominent examples are *salam* (deferred delivery sale), *bai bithaman ajil* (BBA) (deferred payment sale), *istina* (or *istisna, istisna'a*) (purchase order), *quard al-hasan* (benevolent loan), and *musawama* (negotiable sale). As opposed to the concurrent purchase and delivery of an asset in *murabaha*, asset purchases under a *salam*[7] or a *bai bithaman ajil*[8] contract

---

[5] In a debt-based *synthetic loan*, the borrower repurchases the assets from the lender at a higher price than the original sales price, whereas borrowers under a *leaseback agreement* repurchase the assets at the same price at the end of the transaction and pay quasi-interest in the form of leasing fees for the duration of the loan.

[6] The so-called commodity *murabaha* is a frequently used form of wholesale debt-based Islamic finance between a bank and its client to replicate short-term money market deposits and medium-term syndicated loans. Such a contract involves the sale on a deferred payment basis of a commodity, usually metals, at the market price plus an agreed profit margin to the borrower, who raises the required funds by immediately selling the asset to a broker or a financial institution.

[7] *Salam* contracts are mostly used in agricultural finance.

[8] A *bai bithaman ajil* (BBA) contract is primarily used for long-term financing and does not require the lender to disclose the profit margin.

allow deferred delivery or payment of *existing* assets. *Salam* closely syn-
thesizes a conventional futures contract and is sometimes also considered
an independent asset class outside the asset spectrum of *murabaha*
(Batchvarov and Gakwaya, 2006). An *istina* contract provides predelivery
(project) finance for *future* assets, such as long-term projects, which the
borrower promises to complete over the term of the lending agreement
according to contractual specifications. A *quard al-hasan* signifies an interest-free loan contract that is usually collateralized. Finally, a *muswama*
contract represents a negotiable sale, where the profit margin is hidden
from the buyer.[9]

Analogous to conventional operating and finance leases, *al-ijarah*
leasing notes[10] ("asset based") provide credit in return for rental payments[11] over the term of the temporary use of an (existing) asset, conditional on the future repurchase of the assets by the borrower.[12] The lease
cash flow is the primary component of debt service. The lessor (i.e., financier) acquires the asset either from the borrower[13] (*operating lease* or
"sale–leaseback"/"lease–buyback") or a third party at the request of the
borrower (*financing lease* or "lease–purchase") and leases it to the borrower (or a third party) for an agreed sum of rental payable in installments
according to an agreed schedule. The legal title of the asset remains with
the financier for the duration of the transaction. The financier bears all the

---

[9] This form of *murabaha* is only permitted for merchant banks, as in the case of *Kuwait Finance House*'s in-house car dealership.

[10] An *ijarah* lease fulfills the functions of either a finance or operating lease. It is increasingly used in aircraft finance by lessees in Islamic countries and in operating leaseback transactions, which combine conventional lending with Islamic investment. Note that Islamic scholars make no distinction between operating and financial leases as to the classification of profits from the use of assets against the prohibition of interest.

[11] However, rental payments and their adjustment to changing market conditions (for floating-rate financed assets) cannot be expressed by reference to an interest rate. Lessors pass down the risk of rate fluctuations by subjecting the rental payable to adjustments by reference to provisions in other documents [e.g., an adjustment letter linking rentals to London Interbank Offered Rate (LIBOR)] or by cross-reference to another non-Islamic lease signed at the same time and the same rentals.

[12] Besides the option to (re)purchase the asset, the lessee can be given the right to sublet the asset. Moreover, the terms of the lease must be clearly identified, and the lease needs to be renewed for every rental payment if the rent is linked to LIBOR or some other market interest rate.

[13] If the underlying assets were originally held by the borrower, this arrangement represents a leaseback agreement over the term of the financing agreement to the borrower, who has the option to acquire the equipment after the lease expires.

costs associated with the ownership of the asset, whereas the costs from the use of the asset have to be defrayed by the lessee.[14, 15]

If the *ijarah* transaction is a financing lease (*ijarah wa iqtina*), such as an *Islamic mortgage*, the repayment through lease payments might also include a portion of the agreed resale price (in the form of a call option premium), which allows borrowers to gradually acquire total equity ownership for a pre-determined sales price.[16] If the lessee does not exercise the call option at maturity, the lender disposes of it in order to realize the salvage value (put option).[17] In an operating lease, the asset is returned to the borrower for the original sale price or the negotiated market price[18] unless otherwise agreed.[19] In this case, the lender's put option represents a repurchase obligation[20] by the borrower (at the current value of outstanding payments), which is triggered upon certain conditions, such as delinquent payments or outright default.

In Islamic *profit-sharing contracts* (equity based), lenders (i.e., investors) and borrowers (i.e., entrepreneurs) agree to share any gains of profitable projects based on the degree of funding or ownership of the asset by each party. In a trustee-type *mudharaba* (or *mudarabah*) financing contract, the financier (*rab ul maal*) provides all capital to fund an investment, which is exclusively managed by the entrepreneur (*mudarib*) in accordance with agreed business objectives. The borrower shares

---

[14] Possible ways of ijarah-compliant relief of the responsibility for the maintenance and insurance of leased assets by the lessor are (1) the lessor agrees to perform insurance and maintenance and to an increase of rental payments to recover insurance premium and appointment of lessee or third party as agent to acquire the insurance in return for a fee commensurate to the insurance markup or (2) the lessor appoints the lessee or third party to discharge these duties for a fee. The degree of transfer of maintenance responsibility is reflected in the lease payments.

[15] Also note that in a head-lease–sublease *ijara* transaction the legal title remains with the borrower, who leases the assets to the lender. This form of asset retention implies similar counterparty risk as with some types of debt-based Islamic finance (see below) unless the borrower enters into a guarantee agreement to repay the exercise price of the transferred asset on a dissolution event.

[16] This structural feature has been applied especially in Islamic mortgage deals in the United States.

[17] In Figure 2.1, the temporary retention of asset ownership by lender in a lease contract represents a put option with a strike price on the present value of transferred assets.

[18] In contrast, debt-based contracts require a higher repurchase price, which includes quasi-interest payments.

[19] The temporary transfer of stock ownership from borrower to lender pursuant to a repurchase agreement within a lease contract implies full collateralization if its value at the time of transfer equals the present value of the borrowed amount repayable at some future date. The lower the present value of the reference asset being funded by the contract is, the lower the degree of collateralization will be.

[20] The repurchase obligation insulates the lender from the performance of the underlying asset.

equity ownership with the financier (i.e., a call option on the reference assets) and might promise to buy out the investor after completion of the project. At the end of the financing period, the entrepreneur repays the original amount of borrowed funds only if the investment was sufficiently profitable. Profits are distributed according to a pre-agreed rate between the two parties. Investors are not entitled to a guaranteed payment and bear all losses unless they have occurred due to misconduct, negligence, or violation of the conditions mutually agreed by both financier and entrepreneur.[21] The equity participation and loss sharing in a *musharaka* (or *musharakah/musyarakah*) contract is similar to a joint venture, where both lender/investor and borrower (or asset manager/agent) jointly contribute funds to an existing *or* future project, either in form of capital or in kind, and ownership is shared according to each party's financial contribution. Although profit sharing is similar to a *mudharaba* contract, losses are generally borne according to equity participation.

Overall, the different basic types of Islamic finance combine two or more contingent claims to replicate the risk–return trade-off of conventional lending contracts or equity investment *without* contractual guarantees of investment return or secured payments in reference to an interest rate as time-dependent cost of funds. Such arrangements may become complicated in practice, once they are combined to meet specific investor requirements under Islamic law (El-Qorchi, 2005).

IMPLICIT DERIVATIVES: IDENTIFICATION AND EVALUATION

Islamic Finance and Put–Call Parity

From an economic point of view, "creditor-in-possession"-based lending arrangements of Islamic finance replicate interest income of conventional lending transactions in a religiously acceptable manner. The concept of *put–call parity*[22] illustrates that the three main types of Islamic finance

---

[21] This equity-based arrangement implies a nonrecourse debt feature (see Figure 2.1).

[22] The relationship between the put and call values of a European option on a non-dividend paying stock of a traded firm can be expressed as $PV(E) + C = S + P$. $PV(E)$ denotes the present value of a risky debt with a face value equal to exercise price E, which is continuously discounted by $\exp(-rT)$ at a risk-free interest rate r over T number of years. In our case of a lending transaction, the share price S represents the asset value of the funded investment available for the repayment of terminal value E.

FIGURE 2.1

Pay-off profile of all three basic forms of Islamic finance

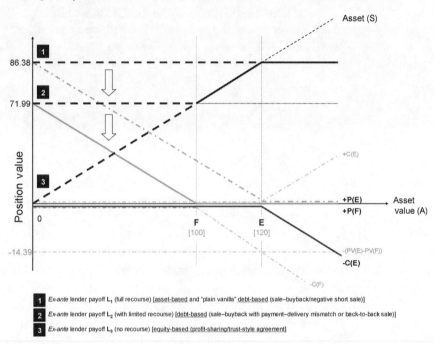

1   *Ex-ante* lender payoff **L₁** (full recourse) [asset-based and "plain vanilla" debt-based (sale–buyback/negative short sale)]

2   *Ex-ante* lender payoff **L₂** (with limited recourse) [debt-based (sale–buyback with payment–delivery mismatch or back-to-back sale)]

3   *Ex-ante* lender payoff **L₃** (no recourse) [equity-based (profit-sharing/trust-style agreement]

represent different ways to recharacterize conventional interest through the attribution of economic benefits from the (temporary) use and original ownership of an existing or future (contractible) asset (see Figure 2.1).

In *asset-based* Islamic finance for investment or trade, the borrower leases from the lender one or more assets A valued at S, which have previously been acquired from either the borrower or a third party. The lender entitles the borrower to (re-)gain ownership of A at time T by writing a call option $-C(E)$ with time-invariant[23] strike price E subject to the promise of full repayment of E [via a put option $+P(E)$] plus an agreed premium in the form of rental payments over the investment period. This arrangement amounts to a *secured* loan with *fully collateralized* principal (i.e., full recourse). The present value of the lender's ex-ante position at

---

[23] This assumption contrasts with asset-based contracts that function as financing leases (e.g., Islamic mortgages), where the borrower reduces E by gradually acquiring complete equity interest over the duration of the transaction (see below).

maturity is $L_1 = S - C(E) + P(E) = \text{PV}(E)$,[24] which equals the present value of the principal amount and interest of a conventional loan.

In a more realistic depiction, the combination of a put and call option on the same strike price represents a *series of individual (and periodically extendible) forward contracts* on asset value S over a sequence of rental payment dates t, so that

$$L_1' = S_T - \left(\frac{\sum_{t=1}^{T-1} C_{t,t+1}(E) - \sum_{t=1}^{T-1} P_{t,t+1}(E)}{\prod_{t=1}^{T} \left[\left(1 + r_f\right)\left(1 + \lambda\right) \right]^t} \right) = \underbrace{E\left[\left(1 + r_f\right)\left(1 + \lambda\right) \right]^{-T}}_{\text{PV}(E)} \quad (2.1)$$

where r_j and λ denote the risk-free interest rate analog and the market price of risk[25] implicit in the pre-specified repayment of the lending transaction. Overall, the put–call arrangement of *asset-based Islamic lending implies a series of cash-neutral, risk-free (forward) hedges of credit exposure.* Since poor transparency of S in long-dated contracts could make the time value of $+P(E)$ appear greater than its intrinsic value, long-term Islamic lending with limited information disclosure would require a high repayment frequency to ensure efficient investor recourse. In *debt-based* Islamic finance, borrower indebtedness from a sale–repurchase agreement ("cost-plus sale") of an asset with current value $\text{PV}(E)$ implies a premium payment to the lender for the use of funds over the investment period T and the same investor payoff L_2 as asset-based Islamic finance.[26]

In Islamic profit-sharing (*equity-based*) agreements, the lender receives a payout in accordance with a pre-agreed disbursement ratio only if the investment project generates enough profits to repay the initial investment amount and the premium payment at maturity T. Since the lender bears all losses, this equity-based arrangement precludes any recourse in the amount $+P(E)$ in absence of enforceable collateral. In the

---

[24] The lease payments received from the borrower wash out in this representation.

[25] We assume unity between the individual risk premium and the market price of risk in this case; i.e., the underlying asset is perfectly sensitive to changes of the market risk premium.

[26] However, some debt-based financing with deferred payment of future claims on existing assets (*salam*), pre-delivery finance for future assets (*istina*), or the deferred cost-plus sale of a third-party-held asset imply counterparty and market risks from lost recovery value, which could translate a lower strike price F on the call or put option, respectively.

simplest case, the discrete form ex-ante payoff of an investor with 100% equity interest would be

$$L_3 = S_T - \frac{\sum_{t=1}^{T-1} C_{t,t+1}(E)}{\prod_{t=1}^{T} \left[\left(1 + r_f\right)\left(1 + \lambda\right)\right]^t} = \underbrace{E\left[\left(1 + r_f\right)\left(1 + \lambda\right)\right]^{-T}}_{\mathrm{PV}(E)}$$

$$- \frac{\sum_{t=1}^{T-1} P_{t,t+1}(E)}{\prod_{t=1}^{T} \left[\left(1 + r_f\right)\left(1 + \lambda\right)\right]^t} \qquad (2.2)$$

The lender payoff L_1'' from a "rent-to-buy" asset-based financing lease, which is particularly prominent in Islamic mortgage finance, is similar to payoff L_3 above. In such contracts, borrowers gradually acquire all of the equity interest S as part of their periodic rental payments while renting the portion of the asset the lender still owns. Therefore, the strike price E of a sequence of individual put–call-based forward contracts declines over time as the partial equity ownership of borrowers increases until they eventually acquire the underlying asset at maturity T, so that

$$L_1'' = S_T - \left(\frac{\sum_{t=1}^{T-1} C_{t,t+1}\left(E - tE/T\right) - \sum_{t=1}^{T-1} P_{t,t+1}\left(E - tE/T\right)}{\prod_{t=1}^{T}\left[\left(1 + r_f\right)\left(1 + \lambda\right)\right]^t} \right)$$

$$= \underbrace{E\left[\left(1 + r_f\right)\left(1 + \lambda\right)\right]^{-T}}_{\mathrm{PV}(E)} - \frac{\sum_{t=1}^{T-1} P_{t,t+1}\left(tE/T\right)}{\prod_{t=1}^{T}\left[\left(1 + r_f\right)\left(1 + \lambda\right)\right]^t} \qquad (2.3)$$

Application of the Black–Scholes–Merton Framework

The representation of lender payoffs under put–call parity permits the identification and exact valuation of all constituent components of Islamic finance contracts as balance sheet identities within the standard Black–Scholes–Merton (BSM) framework of capital-structure-based *option pricing theory* (OPT) (Black and Scholes, 1973; Merton, 1973; ibid., 1974). In the following section, we show how to derive the fair market price of Islamic lending transactions if the underlying collateral conforms to a lognormal asset process.[27] In particular, this approach allows us to characterize the implicit interest rate of Islamic lending as a result of the premium payments (i.e., periodic rental or lease payments) received by the lender in return for the call position on assets held by the borrower in Islamic finance.

According to Merton's reduced-form model, a firm's outstanding liabilities constitute a bankruptcy level (*default threshold*). Owners of corporate equity in leveraged firms hold a call option on the firm value after outstanding liabilities have been paid off. They also have the option to default if their firm's asset value (*reference asset*) falls below the present value of the notional amount of outstanding debt (*strike price*) owed to bondholders at maturity. So, corporate bond holders effectively write a European put option to equity owners, who hold a residual claim on the firm's asset value in non-default states of the world. Bond holders receive a put option premium in the form of a credit spread above the risk-free rate in return for holding risky corporate debt due to the limited liability of equity owners. The value of the put option is determined by the duration of debt claim, the leverage of the firm, and asset-price volatility.

The BSM approach assumes that the firm's debt consists of a zero-coupon bond B with a notional value F and a maturity term of T periods. The firm's outstanding liabilities constitute the bankruptcy level, whose standard normal density defines the *distance to default* relative to the firm value. This capital-structure-based evaluation of contingent claims on firm performance under the risk neutral measure implies that a firm defaults if its asset value is insufficient to meet the amount of debt owed to bondholders at maturity. Conversely, if the distance to default is positive and the asset value of the firm exceeds the bankruptcy level, the call option held by equity holders on firm value has intrinsic value (in addition to its time value until the maturity of debt). The same logic can be readily applied to pricing singular Islamic finance transactions.

The BSM model assumes that market price S of the underlying asset evolves following the stochastic differential equation of asset-price dynamics

$$\frac{dS_t}{S_t} = r_S dt + \sigma dW_t \tag{2.4}$$

---

[27] Note that the use of the BSM framework appeals to universal recognition, but fails to generate accurate option prices in times when extreme outcomes occur amid periods of high volatility unless the normality assumption of asset price dynamics underpinning the "default trigger" of the distance to default measure (see below) is altered.

with drift r_s and diffusion defined by a standard *geometric Brownian motion* (GBM) $\Delta W_t \sim \varphi(0, \Delta t)$ with Wiener process $z \sim \varphi(0, \sigma)$ of instantaneous asset value change. After application of Ito's lemma, the discrete form analog of Equation (2.4) for initial value S_0 can be written as a lognormal asset process

$$\ln S_t - \ln S_0 \sim \phi \left[\frac{\ln S + (r_S - \sigma_S^2/2)t}{\sigma_S^2 \sqrt{t}} \right] \tag{2.5}$$

where $\varphi(.)$ is the standard normal density function. Equation 2.5 defines the physical probability distribution of the end-of-period value S_T,

$$S_T \sim S_0 \exp \left[\left(r_S + \frac{\sigma_S^2}{2} \right) T + \sigma_S \sqrt{T} z \right] \tag{2.6}$$

based on

$$S_t = S_0 \exp \left[\left(r_S + \frac{\sigma_S^2}{2} \right) t + \sigma W_t \right] \tag{2.7}$$

Analogous to firm leverage $d = De^{-rt}/V$ as the ratio of the discounted face value of outstanding debt D and the asset value V of the firm in the original BSM, we define the default barrier as the ratio $b = Ee^{-r_f t}/S$ of the future repayment amount E, discounted at the risk-free rate of return r_f, and asset value S.[28] Hence, the expected (*physical*) probability of default [or *expected default frequency* (EDF)] $P_t = \Pr(S \leq Ee^{-r_f t})$ $\approx \Pr(\ln S \leq \ln Ee^{-r_f t}$ at time t is defined as

$$P_t = \Phi \left(\frac{\ln Ee^{-r_f t} - \left[\ln S_t - \left(r_S - r_{div} + \sigma_S^2/2 \right)t \right]}{\sigma_S \sqrt{t}} \right)$$
$$= \Phi \left(\frac{\ln b + \left(r_S - r_{div} + \sigma_S^2/2 \right)t}{\sigma_S \sqrt{t}} \right) \equiv \Phi(-d_1) = 1 - \Phi(d_1) \tag{2.8}$$

---

[28] The *repayment obligation* is defined as the discounted future value of repayment E of face value F and all coupon values in line with the conventional application of BSM.

with an internal rate of return r_{div} (*dividend yield*), the standard normal cumulative distribution function $\Phi(.)$, and the distance to default (DD) measure

$$d_t \equiv \frac{\ln\left(S_t / Ee^{-r_f t}\right)+\left(r_S - r_{div} + \sigma_S^2/2\right)t}{\sigma\sqrt{t}}$$

$$= \frac{\ln(-b)+\left(r_S - r_{div} + \sigma_S^2/2\right)t}{\sigma\sqrt{t}} \tag{2.9}$$

whose probability density $\Phi(d_1) = 1 - P_t = \Pr(S \geq Ee^{-r_f t}) \approx \Pr(\ln S \geq \ln Ee^{-r_f t})$ defines the *survival probability*.

We expand Equations (2.8) and (2.9) under the risk-neutral measure to take into account the asset-specific spread $\mu_s - r_f$ for the market price of risk, in addition to the continuous time risk-neutral return r_f, which compensates for expected default. Thus, the *risk-neutral* probability of default is

$$P_t^Q = 1 - \Phi\left(\Phi^{-1}\left(\Phi(-d_1)\right) + \frac{\left(\mu_S - r_f\right)\sqrt{t}}{\sigma_S}\right)$$

$$= \Phi\left(-\left(\Phi^{-1}\left(\Phi(-d_1)\right) + \frac{\left(\mu_S - r_f\right)\sqrt{t}}{\sigma_S}\right)\right) \tag{2.10}$$

based on the revised DD measure

$$d_1' = \Phi^{-1}\left(\Phi(-d_1)\right) + \left(\mu_S - r_f\right)\sqrt{t}/\sigma_S \tag{2.11}$$

According to the continuous time capital asset pricing model (CAPM),

$$\mu_S - r_f = \beta\lambda \tag{2.12}$$

with asset beta

$$\beta = \frac{\text{cov}\left(r_S, r_m\right)}{\sigma_m^2} = \frac{\rho_{S,m}\,\sigma_S}{\sigma_m} \tag{2.13}$$

where r_s and r_m denote the continuous time rate of return on the asset and a comparable market portfolio, σ_s and σ_m are the volatility of the asset return and the return of the market portfolio, $\rho_{s,m}$ is the correlation between both asset and market returns and *market risk premium*

$$\lambda = \mu_m - r_f \tag{2.14}$$

where μ_m denotes the continuous time expected rate of return on the market portfolio. Thus, the combination of Equations (2.12) to (2.14) yields

$$\frac{(\mu_S - r_f)}{\sigma_S} = \frac{\beta\lambda}{\sigma_S} = \frac{\rho_{S,m}\lambda}{\sigma_m} = \rho_{S,m} \, SR \tag{2.15}$$

where the market Sharpe ratio $SR = \lambda/\sigma_m$, i.e., the excess return per unit of market volatility for the market portfolio. After substituting (2.15) into (2.11), so that

$$d'_1 = \Phi^{-1}\left(\Phi(-d_1)\right) + \rho_{S,m} \, SR\sqrt{t} \tag{2.16}$$

where $\rho_{S,m}$ is estimated as the square root of the residual sum of squares (R^2) of the linear regression of asset returns on market returns

$$r_S = \alpha + r_m + \varepsilon \tag{2.17}$$

with constant α and error term ε.

If these conditions hold, default occurs if the asset value S falls below the repayment value E and the call option on future repayment E

$$C(E) = S_t e^{-\mu_1 t} \Phi(d'_1) - E e^{-\mu_2 t} \Phi(d'_2) \tag{2.18}$$

represents the fair market value of each rental or lease payment in debt- and asset-based contracts or the periodic profit payout in equity-based Islamic transactions at each time period t, where $\mu_1 = (1 + r_{div})(1 + \mu_S - r_f) - 1$ and $\mu_2 = (1 + r_f)(1 + \mu_S - r_f) - 1$ are the internal rate of return and the risk-free rate under the risk-neutral measure, respectively, and $d'_2 = d'_1 - \sigma_s\sqrt{t}$.

Application of Adapted BSM to Put–Call Parity

Since the present value $PV(E) = Ee^{-\mu_z t}$ and asset price S at time t are given, we can solve for $P(E) = PV(E) + C(E) - S_t$ under put–call parity, and identify all components of an Islamic transaction, given

$$C(E) = \frac{Ee^{-\left[\left(1+r_f\right)\left(1+\mu_S\right)-1\right]t} - P(E)}{\left[\Phi(d_1) - b\Phi(d_2)\right]^{-1} - 1} \qquad (2.19)$$

which implies the declining positive correlation of the call option value $C(E)$ and Islamic debt $PV(E) - P(E) = S_t - C(E)$ as $t \to T$. We finally derive the annual, continuously compounded interest rate as

$$r' = \frac{E}{\sqrt[T]{S_t - C(E)}} - 1 \qquad (2.20)$$

Given the lack of suitable market prices in Islamic finance, the current asset price S (and attendant return r_S and volatility) σ^2_S) can also be derived from a *mark-to-market* (MTM) exercise, internal audits or some other verification process. Similarly, the continuous time rate of return r_m and the volatility σ^2_m of the market portfolio needs to be obtained from a pool of reference obligations, such as publicly quoted Islamic funds or other investments, which serve as pricing benchmark.

Numerical Example

We calculate the conventional rate of return r' under the risk-neutral measure for a notional amount of $F = 100$ of issued debt with future repayment $E = 120$ and a tenure T of five years, discounted in continuous time at $\mu_2 = (1 + r_f)(1 + \mu_S) - 1 = (1.05 \times 1.015) - 1 = 6.575\%$, so that present value $PV(E) \approx 86.38$ and $PV(E) \approx 71.99$ of full repayment and partial repayment of the principal amount only (see Figure 2.1). We assume risk-neutral return $\mu_S = 6.5\%$, standard deviation $\sigma_m = 10\%$ of market returns, and cov $(r_S, r_m) = 0.005$, so that asset beta $\beta = 0.5$, $\rho_{S,m} = 1/3$, and $SR = 0.3$. For asset value $S_0 = 100 = F$ (assuming that the firm is fully leveraged and firm value at inception $t = 0$ is equivalent to the notional amount F) and a standard deviation σ_S of 15%,[29] the fair market price of the Islamic lending contract would be 89.93, which implies an annual interest rate of $r' = 6.18\%$ according to our OPT-based valuation model if we assume dividend yield $r_{div} = 0\%$.

ISLAMIC FINANCE AND STRUCTURED FINANCE

Based on the above put–call parity replication of state-contingent payoffs of underlying asset performance, any form of Islamic finance could be considered a structured finance transaction, which contains implicit derivative elements with unilateral deferral of settlement and a double coincidence of obligations.

Structured finance encompasses all financial instruments—other than individual (basic or exotic) derivative contracts—that serve to hedge any activity beyond the scope of conventional forms of on-balance sheet securities (debt, bonds, equity). They either (1) combine traditional asset classes with contingent claims, such as derivative claims on commodities, currencies, or receivables from other reference assets, or (2) replicate traditional asset classes through synthetication or new financial instruments (Jobst, 2007a). Structured finance offers the issuers enormous flexibility to create securities with distinct risk–return profiles in terms of maturity structure, security design, and asset types, which allows issuers to provide enhanced return at a customized degree of diversification commensurate to an individual investor's appetite for risk. Hence, structured finance contributes to a more complete capital market by offering any mean-variance trade-off along the efficient frontier of optimal diversification at lower transaction cost. However, the increasing complexity of the structured finance market and the ever growing range of products being made available to investors invariably create challenges in terms of efficient assembly, management, and dissemination of information.

The flexible nature of structured finance straddles the indistinct boundary between traditional fixed income products, debentures, and equity on one hand and derivative transactions on the other hand. Notwithstanding the perceivable ostensible difficulties of defining structured finance, a *functional*

---

[29] Empirically, the value of the assets of the firm can be estimated by discounting the expected cash flows from the assets at the cost of capital.

and *substantive* differentiation informs a useful demarcation between the most salient properties of structured and conventional forms of finance as regards the role of Islamic finance. The following definition reflects such a proposition if we compare two cases:

1. Investment instruments are motivated by the *same or similar financial objective* from both the issuer's and the investor's point of view, but are *dissimilar* in that they *differ in legal and functional implementation*. They also might require a *different valuation*.[30]

2. Investment instruments are motivated by the *same or similar financial objective* and are *substantively equivalent* (i.e., they share a close equilibrium price relation); they *differ in legal form, transaction structure, and/or security design*, necessitating a different valuation.

In the second case appeals to the characteristics of Islamic finance, which fall squarely within the domain of structured finance instrument whenever religious constraints require the replication of conventional interest-bearing assets through structural arrangements of two or more contingent claims in the form of "implicit derivatives." Although both Islamic and conventional finance are *in substance equivalent to conventional finance* and yield the same lender and investor payoffs at the inception of the transaction, they require a different valuation due to dissimilar transaction structures (and associated legal enforceability of investor claims) and/or security design.

---

[30] In the first case, *pure credit derivatives* are clear examples of structured products, which allow very specific and capital-market-priced credit risk transfer. Credit insurance and syndicated loans share the same financial objective; however, they do *not* constitute an arrangement to create a new risk–return profile from existing or future reference assets. In the same vein, *mortgage-backed securities* (MBSs) and (*Pfandbrief*-style) covered mortgage bonds represent different functional and legal methods of securitization with the same financial objective. Although both refinancing techniques convert homogenous pools of mortgage claims into negotiable securities, they represent two distinct forms of debt securities issued on the same type of underlying reference asset: Either off-balance sheet (*asset-backed securitization*) or on-balance sheet securitization. Whereas originators of Pfandbrief issues retain securitized assets on their balance sheet, issuers of MBSs sell assets to a separate legal entity (such as trust, fund, and corporation), commonly referred to as a *special-purpose vehicle* (SPV), which refinances the acquisition of the assets by issuing debt (e.g., bonds or commercial paper) or equity claims on these reference assets.

EXPLICIT DERIVATIVES IN ISLAMIC STRUCTURED FINANCE: CREDIT RISK TRANSFER

There is wide agreement that derivatives with the option of unilateral deferment (and attendant contingency risk), such as delayed payment contracts on existing assets (*salam*) or purchase order murabaha contracts on future assets (*istina*), concur with shariah principles. However, the deferment of obligations of *both* parties to a future date is tantamount to a debt exchange without underlying asset transfer, which implies the possibility of profit taking and excessive uncertainty (*gharar*) of a kind that is not permissible under Islamic law. However, the prevalence of shariah-compliant securitized issuance (in combination with hedging transactions) demonstrates the possibility of mutual risk transfer mechanisms with a view to foster *halal* in the spirit of distributive justice and the consideration of public interest (*maslaha*).

In conventional structured finance, the two major asset classes of *capital market-based risk transfer* (except loan sales, asset swaps, and natural hedges through bond trading) include *asset securitization* (which is mostly used for funding purposes) and *credit derivative* transactions (as hedging instruments), which permit issuers to devise almost an infinite number of ways to combine various asset classes in order to both transfer asset risk between banks, insurance companies, other money managers and nonfinancial investors in order to achieve greater transformation and diversification of risk.

Since most Islamic financial products are based on the concept of asset backing, the economic concept of asset securitization is particularly amenable to the basic tenets of Islamic finance. Asset securitization describes the process and the result of issuing certificates of ownership as pledge against existing or future cash flows from a diversified pool of assets (reference portfolio) to investors. It registers as an alternative, capital-market-based refinancing mechanism to diversify external sources of asset funding in lieu of intermediated debt finance based primarily on the risk assessment of securitized assets. The implicit risk transfer of securitization not only helps issuers improve their capital management but also allows issuers to benefit from enhanced liquidity and more cost-efficient terms of high-credit quality finance without increasing their on-balance sheet liabilities or compromising the profit-generating capacity of assets. Investors in securitization have a wider choice of high-quality investments at their disposal, whose market valuation engenders greater overall efficiency and liquidity of capital markets. The tradability of securitized asset risk also facilitates the synthetic assembly and dynamic adjustment of asset portfolios via secondary markets according to investor preferences (Jobst, 2006a; ibid., 2006b).

In the wake of rapid growth of the Islamic finance sector,[31] structured finance instruments have been receiving increasing attention in Islamic countries owing in large part to enabling capital market regulations, a favorable macroeconomic environment, and financial innovation aimed at establishing shariah compliance. As one form of structured finance, Islamic securitization transforms *bilateral risk sharing* between borrowers and lenders in Islamic finance into the *market-based refinancing* of one of the three broad types of Islamic finance (asset, debt, and equity based) as reference asset. In its basic concept, Islamic securitization allows originators to sell existing or future revenues from lease receivables (asset-based), "sale-back profit" (debt-based) or private equity from a portfolio of Islamic-acceptable assets to a *special-purpose vehicle* (SPV),[32] which refinances itself by issuing unsecured securities to market investors that assume the role of a "collective financier" whose entrepreneurial investment does not involve guaranteed, interest-based earnings. In this context, investors represent the "capital market corollary" to a singular lender in ordinary Islamic finance. Irrespective of religious conditions, Islamic securitization offers the same economic benefits conventional structured finance purports to generate, such as the active management of designated asset portfolio due to greater control over asset status, enhanced asset-liability management, and term structure transformation, as well as the isolation of certain assets in order to make them self-financing at a fair market rate (see Box 2.1).

Although the religious prohibition of the exchange of debt and the required conferral of ownership interest to participate in business risk still

---

[31] The outstanding stock of shariah assets worldwide has been increasing by an average of 15 percent a year since 2003 and has stood at about $500 billion at the end of 2006, about half of which is held by Islamic banks. Global volume could increase even faster in response to surging demand from Muslim investors flocking to the growing number of competing Islamic investment products.

[32] In conventional securitization, an SPV is set up solely for the purpose of the securitization and might be a trust, limited liability company, partnership, or a corporation. In Islamic securitization, the objectives set out in the constitutional documents of the SPV also must not infringe on the prohibition of *riba* and *haram* under Islamic law.

B O X   2.1

East Cameron Gas Sukuk: Credit risk transfer and commodity hedging in Islamic finance

The first Islamic securitization transaction in the United States demonstrates the shariah-compliant use of derivatives in structured finance. In July 2006, East Cameron Partners (ECP), an independent oil and gas exploration and production firm located in Houston, Texas, raised $165.67 million from the issuance of a *sukuk al-musharaka* backed by natural oil and gas royalties.

Its two-tier securitization structure, which was designed by arrangers Beirut-based Bemo Securitization (BSEC) and Merrill Lynch, consists of a "purchaser SPV" (incorporated in Delaware), which acquires the underlying assets, and an "issuer SPV," registered in the Cayman Islands, which funds the asset purchase by issuing investment trust certificates (sukuk notes). The relationship between both SPVs is governed by a "funding agreement," which includes periodic funding repayments and the transfer of net profits. The funding agreement aims at materializing the ". . . contribution of the 'issuer SPV' (as a *musharek*) and (ii) conveying to the 'issuer SPV' a certain risk and reward profile, which is passed on to the sukuk note holders . . ." (see www.sirajcapital.com) pursuant to the following provisions: (1) the purchase of *overriding royalty interest* (ORRI) from the originator for $113.84 million, (2) the payment of the development plan for $38.28 million, (3) the funding of the reserve account with an initial balance of $9.5 million, and (4) the purchase of natural gas put options for $4.05 million in a specific hedge agreement with an outside party. The commodity price hedge as part of the funding agreement to protect investor interest is remarkable in the context of Islamic finance. The hedge constitutes a shariah-compliant obligation (*iltizam*), since it confers true commercial value (rather than speculative interest).

Overall, shariah compliance of the transaction is established by the uncertainty of cash flows from the asset performance of permissible real economic activity with identified and direct investor participation, which does not imply the payment or receipt of any interest guarantee. While deferrals are possible, in the default event, investors have recourse to the underlying assets and can force the sale of the cash-flow-generating assets. However, legal risk from Islamic jurisprudence could affect the legal enforceability of the funding arrangement and the asset control of investors.

poses challenges to the development of Islamic securitization, the gradual acceptance of Islamic investment certificates, so-called *sukuk* bonds, represents a successful attempt to overcome these impediments based on the adequate interpretation and analogical reasoning of shariah principles applied in Islamic finance. Sukuks are shariah-compliant and tradable asset-backed, medium-term notes,[33] which have been issued internationally by governments, quasi-sovereign agencies, and corporations after

---

[33] "Investment sukuk are certificates of equal value representing undivided shares in ownership of tangible assets, usufructs and services, or (in the ownership of) the assets of particular projects or special investment activities (AAOIFI Standard No. 17)."

their legitimization by the ruling of the Fiqh Academy of the Organization of the Islamic Conference in February of 1988.[34] Over the last five years, the sukuk has evolved as the most popular form of securitized credit finance within capital-market-based Islamic structured finance, reconciling the concept of securitization *and* principles of the shariah law on the provision and use of financial products and services in a risk-mitigation structure subject to competitive pricing.[35] The Accounting and Auditing Organization of Islamic Finance Institutions (AAOIFI) currently recognizes 14 different types of sukuks, which are traded on the Scripless Securities Trading System (SSTS)[36] in Malaysia. Gross securitized issuance of these Islamic debt securities has nearly quadrupled over the past two years, rising from $7.2 billion in 2004 to over $27 billion in 2006—but still only little more than one tenth of conventional securitized issuance of asset-backed securities (ABS) in emerging markets over the same time period. During the first half of 2007, greater standardization triggered a further uptick of issuance volume to more than $10 billion. According to recent market reports governments and corporations will raise about $30 billion in sukuk over the next three years, bringing the size of the Islamic securitization market to $100 billion.

Sukuk notes convey *equity* interest to (capital market) investors in the form of a *call option* on partial or complete ownership of underlying reference assets, including the right to some calculable rate of return as a share of profit (*secondary notes*) and the repayment of the principal amount (*primary notes*). Sukuks ". . . operate similarly to mortgage pass-throughs except investors own a portion of the underlying . . ." (Thetgyi, 2006, p. 1) assets, which collateralize debtor repayments. However, the scrutiny of securitized collateral is more complicated and less accurate when there is a requirement for shariah compliance of assets. Most Islamic finance products require issuers to originate their own Islamic-acceptable

---

[34] Although there is no formal obligation of compliance associated with the ruling, it carries considerable weight with most Islamic financial institutions.

[35] Only appropriate Islamic bodies, so-called shariah boards, may adjudicate the shariah compliance of the terms of any sukuk issuance.

[36] The SSTS is a system operated by the Bank Negara Malaysia's (BNM's) real-time gross settlement/delivery-versus-payment system through which sovereign and unlisted corporate bonds are registered, cleared, and settled via the *Real-Time Electronic Transfer of Funds and Securities* (RENTAS), Malaysia's scripless book-entry securities trading and funds transfer system. The SSTS also maintains securities accounts for financial institutions.

assets (rather than buy asset pools in the market) due to the absence of eligible collateral assets.[37] Moreover, the comparative paucity of historical data on defaults hinders reliable estimates for recovery rates used in pricing and rating tranched products and leads rating agencies to use very conservative assumptions, especially if lender credit scoring and infrastructure are not up to the standards usually sought by the rating agencies.

ASSESSMENT OF DERIVATIVES IN ISLAMIC FINANCE

Discussion of Current Legal Opinion

Amid weak reliance on capital market financing in many Islamic countries, risk transfer mechanisms, be it sukuk issuance or hedging tools, are subject to several critical legal impediments that impact on the way derivatives redress perceived market imperfections and financing constraints. While implicit derivatives are essential to the replication of interest through profit generation in Islamic finance (see above), and thus are not deemed objectionable on religious grounds, the explicit use of derivatives remains highly controversial.

In the implicit derivative transaction underlying basic Islamic finance, definite performance preserves equitable risk sharing consistent with shariah principles of unsecured entrepreneurial investment due to certain asset delivery—without objectionable zero-sum gains. The sequence of periodic and maturity-matched put–call combinations (see above) coupled with the bilateral nature and asset backing replicate the *definite performance* element of a conventional forward, eliminating unilateral gains from favorable price movements (e.g., in-the-money appreciation of option premia). By virtue of holding equal and opposite option positions both creditor and debtor are obliged to honor the terms of the contract irrespective of changes in asset value, without the opportunity of the creditor (debtor) to cash in on a higher (lower) asset price relative to the contractual agreed repayment amount through asset sale to a third party at the maturity date. Although a matched pairing of simultaneously issued option positions would normally cause contingency risk on the

---

[37] This would make Islamic ABS a secondary tool and not a primary tool to service and/or underwrite third-party financial institutions; however, it holds the prospect of restructuring non-shariah-compliant assets into permissible investments.

delivery of the underlying asset (when actual obligations are not certain) similar to conventional forward contracts, this is not the case in Islamic lending because creditors hold legal title to the underlying asset (asset backing). Nonetheless, in a multilateral setup with many market participants, only options, which offer the right (but not the obligation) to sell or buy an asset at an agreed strike price until the maturity date, cater for contingent scenarios.

Nonetheless, the forward element of Islamic lending contracts involves troubles of dual coincidence and counterparty risk due to a high degree of privately negotiated customization. Parties to a forward agreement need to have an identical match in both the contrary direction of price movement of the underlying asset or commodity as well as the timing and the amount of delivery. Moreover, a forward contract elevates risk of the counterparty defaulting on an obligation beyond actual default risk in circumstances when the spot price of the underlying asset falls below the forward price (i.e., the originally agreed upon price) prior to maturity, rendering the contract out of the money. While the nondefaulting party possesses a legal alternative, the process of seeking contractual enforcement can be lengthy, cumbersome, and expensive, especially in areas of conflicting legal governance as a matter of form (commercial law vs. Islamic law).

These obvious shortcomings of forwards create the economic rationale of futures, which are standardized forward contracts with respect to size, maturity, and quality, and thus avert the prerequisite of double coincidence but appear to contravene shariah principles. Future contracts limit counterparty risk through MTM[38] pricing, which requires margin calls from the party that is out of the money. However, contingency risk to both parties due to nonperformance still resides with these derivative claims. Cash-settled margin calls typically serve to mitigate the counterparty risk of futures. Since the absence of underlying asset transfer would render MTM pricing unacceptable under Islamic law, a shariah-compliant solution to this problem could be the marginal adjustment of repayment

---

[38] Marked-to-market pricing defines the process of constantly monitoring the variations to contingencies (e.g., market conditions, micro- and macroeconomic indicators, price volatility, quality considerations, or political risk) pertaining to a forecasted spot price (i.e., expected future price) of an asset on a specified delivery date in order to price a derivative contract. For instance, if the asset price falls below (increases above) the contracted strike price, a call option would be "out of the money" ("in the money").

amounts in response to any deviation of the underlying asset value from the pre-agreed strike price at different points in time throughout the term of the transaction.

In conventional finance, options cover the contingency risk of actual asset delivery in return for the payment of an upfront, nonrefundable premium. Unlike a futures contract, holding a call option implies the right (but not the obligation) to acquire the underlying asset and replaces the obligation to deliver, which could otherwise only be met by the purchase of the underlying asset at the prevailing spot price. Therefore, options not only serve to hedge adverse price movements, but they also cater for contingencies regarding the delivery or receipt of the asset and offer the opportunity to take advantage of favorable price movements.

While the elimination of contingency risk is desirable under Islamic law, the assurance of definite performance by means of options (which imply a zero-sum proposition) is not considered acceptable. An important objection to derivatives from the perspective of shariah compliance is that they are valued by reference to the sale of a nonexistent asset or of an asset not in the ownership (*qabd*) of the seller at the time of closing, which negates the *hadith* "sell not what is not with you." Shariah principles require creditors (or protection sellers) to actually own the reference asset at the inception of a transaction. The absence of a legalistic cause (*illah*) leading to contingency risk in forwards and futures has led commentators to dispute their general permissibility under Islamic law. That said, the probability of failure to deliver in absence of asset ownership might have been more relevant in the past when then simple, primitive, and unorganized capital markets implied considerable counterparty risk on contractual performance.

Futures (and options) still continue to be rejected by a majority of scholars on the grounds that a purchase or sale cannot be realized for a potential date and that they almost never involve delivery by both parties. In fact, " . . . in most futures transactions delivery of the commodities or their possession is not intended" (Usmani, 1996), which would invalidate these contracts under shariah law. Often parties to the contract reverse the transaction and cash settle the price difference only, which transforms a derivative contract into a paper transaction without the element of a genuine sale. Besides the lack of asset ownership at the time of sale, other concerns shared by a majority of Islamic scholars about shariah compliance of derivatives have centered on (1) the selection of reference assts that are nonexistent at the time of contract; (2) the requirement of *qabd*, i.e., taking possession of the item prior to resale; (3) mutual deferment of both sides of the bargain, which reduces contingency risk but turns a derivative contract into a sale of one debt for another; and (4) excessive uncertainty or speculation that verges on gambling, resulting in zero-sum payoffs of both sides of the bargain (Kamali, 2007).

Although Khan (1995) claims that even in the contemporary form of futures trading, "some of the underlying basic concepts as well as some of the conditions for such trading are exactly the same as [the ones] laid down by the Prophet [Mohammed (*sallallâhu 'alayhi wasallam*)] for forward trading," he attests to the associated risk of exploitation and speculation, which belie fundamental precepts of the shariah.[39] For the same reasons, several scholars also consider options in violation of Islamic law. Nonetheless, in one of the most comprehensive studies on the subject so far, Kamali (2001) found that "there is nothing inherently objectionable in grating an option, exercising it over a period of time or charging a fee for it, and that options trading like other varieties of trade is permissible *mubah*, and as such, it is simply an extension of the basic liberty that the *qur'an* has granted."

Legal Uncertainty

Derivative transactions in Islamic financial systems are beset by legal uncertainty from the heterogeneous assessment of shariah compliance, which entails procedural and substantive difficulties. The absence of practical and hard-wired guidance on shariah compliance affects the legal integrity and restitution interest of parties to derivative transactions. Islamic jurisprudence is not definite or bound by precedent and still lacks of homogeneous interpretation and universal recognition. Legal opinions of Islamic courts may deviate from previous decisions made by other shariah scholars. Since Islamic law itself is divided in different juristic schools of thought (*madhahib*), which provide guidance on the interpretation (*ijtihaad*) or analytical reasoning (*qiyas*) of the general principles of the shariah, there is no consistent ruling of Islamic courts on the religious compliance of the eligibility of certain assets and transaction structures for

---

[39] Khan (1995) substantiates the permissibility of futures contracts based on "clear sayings" of Prophet Mohammed, which stipulate that a forward trade (*salaf*) should be completed for a specific quantity, specific weight and for a specific period of time—much like a modern-day futures contract.

securitization. For instance, even though the *hanbali* school is dominant in Saudi Arabia, a shariah board has considerable discretion in the interpretation of Islamic law and may choose any other school of thought to inform their decision-making process. Therefore, it its hardly surprising that the adjudication of derivatives under Islamic law varies greatly and differs in terms of individual interpretations of the shariah and the fundamental understanding of the economic purpose of the respective instrument (and transaction structure) under discussion. The resultant inconsistency of legal opinions has raised doubts about the general permissibility of derivative instruments in Islamic finance, which bear the potential of flouting the shariah ban on speculation and capital gains without underlying asset transfer.

Investor Protection

Islamic investors are concerned with not only the compliance of derivative transactions with the shariah but also their legal enforceability under contract law. So from an investor's perspective, Islamic derivatives need to satisfy *two* legal regimes: applicable commercial law as well as Islamic law. Eventually, the question of whether Islamic law governs a transaction by *substance* or *form* determines the investment risk from religious encroachment on the economic logic of the security design and the legal enforceability of commercial interests. If shariah compliance is treated as a *matter of substance* and upholds in spirit what was created in form (as defined by commercial law), the violation of any religious precepts is likely to temper investor interest and affect liquidity, but would not preclude legal enforceability of investor claims. However, if Islamic law is the governing law as a *matter of form* (i.e., the transaction is governed solely by shariah law), the opinion of shariah courts could override commercial legal concepts and re-qualify the legal nature of derivative contracts. For instance, the ex-post-facto legal interpretation of certain security features carries the possibility of bankruptcy courts or insolvency officials in Islamic jurisdictions to invalidate post-default settlement protocols under commercial law or "recharacterize" a derivative transaction as speculation or debt exchange without transfer of legal title to the lender, which, in turn, interferes with the premise of asset transfer in Islamic finance. Either outcome would undermine the economic purpose of derivatives, compromise investor protection, and upset the carefully constructed profit-and-loss sharing amongst investors, which effectively defines the transaction structure. Such legal uncertainty is amplified by that fact that bankruptcy and dispute resolution processes of Islamic securities are largely untested due to scarcity of default cases.

Possibilities to Establish Shariah Compliance of Derivatives

Contingent claims are present in a great variety of business and financial transactions. Risk diversification through derivatives increases stability at all levels of the financial system and enhances general welfare. Derivatives also contribute to continuous price formation and supplement cash markets at lower funding cost as alternatives to trading underlying assets. As a critical element of capital market development, derivatives ensure an efficient transmission of funds from lender to borrowers while enhancing sound financial planning and financial stability.

The heterogeneity of scholastic opinion about the shariah compliance of derivatives is largely motivated by individual interpretations of the shariah and different knowledge about the mechanics of derivative structures. Many policy makers, market participants, and regulators are frequently unfamiliar with the intricate mechanics and the highly technical language of many derivative transactions, which hinders a more comprehensive understanding and objective appreciation of the role of derivatives in the financial system. While Islamic regulators have a natural interest to err on the side of caution when attempting to resolve religious impediments to the use of derivatives under Islamic jurisdiction, they have come to realize the necessary importance of developing derivative markets. The absence of suitable risk transfer mechanisms under Islamic law stymies local capital market development and deprives market participants of an array of benefits and advantages in terms of adequate liquidity and risk management.

In principle, futures and options may be compatible with Islamic law if they (1) are employed to address genuine hedging demand on asset performance from direct ownership interest, (2) disavow mutual deferment without actual asset transfer, and (3) eschew avertable uncertainty (*gharar*) as prohibited sinful activity (*haram*) in a bid to create an equitable system of distributive justice in consideration of public interest (*maslaha*). Shariah-compliant derivatives would also maintain risk sharing between contract parties by forgoing the zero-sum proposition of many conventional derivative transactions in favor of win–win situations from changes in the value of the reference asset without mutual deferment.

For instance, the issuance of stock options to employees would be an ideal candidate for a shariah-compliant derivative. By setting incentives for higher productivity firm owners reap larger corporate profits that offset the marginal cost of greater employee participation in stock price performance. However, the de facto application of many derivative contracts is still objectionable, mainly because of the possibility of speculation and the absence of entrepreneurial investment violate of the tenets of distributive justice and equal risk sharing subject to religious restrictions on the sale and purchase of debt contracts as well as profit taking without real economic activity and asset transfer.

CONCLUSION: THE PROSPECTS OF ISLAMIC DERIVATIVES

Recent efforts of regulatory consolidation and standard setting have addressed economic constraints and the legal uncertainty imposed by Islamic jurisprudence and poorly developed uniformity of market practices on the use of derivative structures. Therefore, market inefficiencies caused by heterogeneous prudential norms and diverse interpretations of shariah compliance are expected to dissipate in the near future. In the area of banking regulation, the first signs of supervisory harmonization emerged in 2002, when central banks and national monetary authorities of Islamic countries inaugurated the Islamic Financial Service Board (IFSB) in Malaysia as an international standard-setting body to ensure stability and soundness of Islamic financial services industry by developing innovative, or using current, international finance standards coherent with shariah principles and harmonization of practices within the Islamic finance service industry.[40] Moreover, the IFSB has established a taskforce for the development of supervisory guidelines related to shariah-compliant capital market transactions, including the regulatory governance of sukuk.

---

[40] On March 15, 2005, the IFSB issued exposure drafts of prudential standards on risk management and capital adequacy for the Islamic financial service industry, and preparations are underway to issue an exposure draft of standards on corporate governance by the end of 2005. In April 2005 the IFSB also started preparing standards on the supervisory review process as well as transparency and market discipline.

At the same time, private sector initiatives, such as an Islamic primary market project led by Bahrain-based International Islamic Financial Market (IIFM) in cooperation with the International Capital Markets Association (ICMA), have resulted in the adoption of a memorandum of understanding on documentation standards and master agreement protocols for Islamic derivatives. Further work is also being done on issues regarding the tradability of sukuk and the standardization of Islamic treasury murabahah contracts. Moreover, greater importance of the Accounting and Auditing Organization of Islamic Finance Institutions (AAOIFI), the General Council for Islamic Banking and Finance Institutions (GCIBFI), and the Islamic International Rating Agency (IIRA) will add consistency to shariah rulings, while the retention of conventional finance market practice and the supremacy of a bankable governing law as a matter of form remain essential to maintain investor confidence in a rapidly growing structured finance market.

In addition, national solutions are gaining traction. While the IIFM was still working on the development of a *Master Agreement for Islamic Derivatives*, for which it had established an alliance with the International Swaps and Derivative Association (ISDA) in summer 2006, Malaysia's only fully-fledged Islamic banks, Bank Islam Berhad and Bank Muamalat Malaysia Berhad had already broken new ground by agreeing to execute a derivative master agreement for the documentation of Islamic derivative transactions in November 2006 (Jobst, 2007c). This standardization initiative was sponsored by the Malaysian Financial Market Association (Persatuan Kewangan Malaysia) with the participation from both Islamic and conventional Malaysian banks in a bid to create more liquidity and enhance transparency with a view to elevate Malaysia's aspirations of becoming a center of Islamic finance as the largest sukuk market in the world, while more specific regional initiatives provide a valuable platform for drawing further attention to derivatives as an important element of local capital market development.

As Islamic finance comes into its own and companies turn to means of hedging their exposures more efficiently, financial institutions in Bahrain, Kuwait, and Malaysia have been gearing up for more shariah-compliant financial instruments and structured finance—both on the asset and liability side. Financial innovation will contribute to further development and refinement of shariah-compliant derivative contracts. For instance, the development of Islamic derivatives bodes well for the Islamic insurance (*takaful*) industry,[41] whose shariah compliance has traditionally resulted in overdependence on equity and real-estate investment, restricting the potential of risk diversification from a wider spectrum of available assets.

ACKNOWLEDGMENTS

The views expressed in this paper are those of the author and should not be attributed to the International Monetary Fund, its Executive Board, or its management. Any errors and omissions are the sole responsibility of the author.

REFERENCES

Batchvarov, A. and Gakwaya, N. (2006) *Principles and Structures of Islamic Finance*. Merrill Lynch, European Structured Finance, ABS (8 September), London.

Black, F. and Scholes, M. (1973) The Pricing of Options and Corporate Liabilities. *Journal of Political Economy*, 81(3): 637–54.

El-Qorchi, M. (2005) Islamic Finance Gears Up. *Finance and Development*, International Monetary Fund (IMF), 42(4) December: 46–9.

International Financial Law Review (2007) June.

Iqbal, Z. and Tsubota, H. (2006) Emerging Islamic Capital Markets. *Islamic Finance Review*, Euromoney Handbook, London: Euromoney Institutional Investor PLC, 5–11.

Iqbal, M. and Mirakhor, A. (2006) *An Introduction to Islamic Finance—Theory and Practice*. Hoboken, NJ: John Wiley & Sons.

Jobst, A.A. (2006a) Asset Securitisation: A Refinancing Tool for Firms and Banks. *Managerial Finance*, 32(9): 731–760.

---

[41] The concept of takaful is similar to mutual insurance. Customers pay a certain amount of finances into a collective pool of funds and withdraw money when a claim is made. Administrators of takaful insurance charge a shariah-compliant fee in the form of a "donation" and distribute any funds left over at the end of the year among the original contributors.

Jobst, A.A. (2006b) Sovereign Securitization in Emerging Markets. *Journal of Structured Finance*, 12(3): 2–13.

Jobst, A.A. (2007a) A Primer on Structured Finance. *Journal of Derivatives and Hedge Funds*, 13(2): 199–213.

Jobst, A.A. (2007b) The Prospects of Islamic Securitization. *Islamic Finance News*, 4(25): 13–15.

Jobst, A.A. (2007c) Islamic Securitization. Islamic Banking, *Al Eqtisadiah* (10 June), Saudi Arabia: Riyadh, 15.

Jobst, A.A. (2007d) The Economics of Islamic Finance and Securitization. *Journal of Structured Finance*, 13(1):1–12.

Kamali, M.H. (2001) *Islamic Commercial Law—An Analysis of Futures and Options*. Cambridge, UK: Islamic Text Society.

Kamali, M.H. (2007) Commodity Futures: An Islamic Legal Analysis. *Thunderbird International Business Review*, 49(3): 309–339.

Khan, M.F. (1995) Islamic Futures and Their Markets. Research Paper, No. 32, Islamic Research and Training Institute, Islamic Development Bank, Jeddah, Saudi Arabia, 12.

Merton, R. (1973) Theory of Rational Option Pricing. *Bell Journal of Economics and Management Science*, 4(1): 141–183.

Merton, R. (1974) On the Pricing of Corporate Debt; the Risk Structure of Interest Rates. *Journal of Finance*, 29(2): 449–470.

http://www.sirajcapital.com/images/Sukuk%20Insider%20001.pdf

The Accounting and Auditing Organization of Islamic Finance Institutions (AAOIFI), (2005), Accounting, Auditing & Governance Standard for Islamic Financial Institutions 2004, 5th edition (Financial Accounting Statements), Bahrain.

Thetgyi, O. (2006) First Sukuk Backed by Shariah-Compliant Receviables in Works. *Securitization News*, February 20

Usmani, M.T. (1996) Futures, Options, Swaps and Equity Investments. *New Horizon*, No. 59. London: Institute of Islamic Banking and Insurance, 10.

CHAPTER 3

Credit Derivatives and the Resolution of Financial Distress

Stephen J. Lubben

INTRODUCTION

Following at least a decade of adjustment, chapter 11 of the United States Bankruptcy Code seems to have stabilized around a relatively efficient system that has become the starting point for discussion of corporate reorganization around the world (Jacoby, 2006). When corporations the size of Global Grossing or Kmart can reorganize in less than two years, with total professional costs of less than 1 percent of assets, complaints about the expense or delay associated with chapter 11 seem outdated and uninformed (LoPucki and Doherty, 2007). Instead, all indications are that chapter 11 as currently practiced is a relatively efficient and cheap means of redeploying a bankruptcy firm's assets.

The combination of low interest rates and plentiful liquidity has meant that only a few large companies have filed for chapter 11 relief in the past few years. However, at the very moment that the United States appears headed for a new round of large chapter 11 cases, chapter 11 is changing again. With the growth of credit derivatives, corporate reorganization threatens to become much more complex. The advent of credit derivatives could well mean that the present efficiency of chapter 11, which many trace to secured creditors' increased sophistication within chapter 11, may be coming to a quick end. Furthermore, the effects of these new instruments could extend to the "shadow" period before chapter 11.

The growth of credit derivatives could well impede the negotiation of workouts, as well as prenegotiated or prepackaged bankruptcy plans, inasmuch as the party with the real risk of loss will often be unknown. Similarly, credit derivatives may ultimately discourage out-of-court restructurings or at least place artificial time limits on the length of such negotiations while simultaneously increasing the incidence of involuntary bankruptcy filings. In general, creditors may no longer behave in predictable ways; previously unheard of creditors may appear on the scene, demanding a voice in the proceedings, and the debtor's true stakeholders may be subject to dispute.

Does this support call for legislative intervention in the credit derivative markets? Hardly, but as the remainder of this chapter explains, in coming years the changing nature of chapter 11 will present new challenges for bankruptcy judges and the professionals who negotiate reorganizations. For those in other jurisdictions, contemplating chapter 11–like systems of their own, one of the main concerns here is that a key feature of chapter 11 is its ability to change along with the changing financial markets.

CHAPTER 11 TODAY

As is well known, the key features of chapter 11 are creditor voting and debtor control. Formally, the Bankruptcy Code provides that two thirds of claims (by amount) in a class must vote to approve a plan and, in addition, that a flat majority (by head count) in a class must also vote in favor of the plan. Poised against the creditor's voting power is the debtor's exclusive right to propose a reorganization plan, at least at the outset of the case. Beyond these formal powers, the parties have an array of informal powers, like the debtor's ability to threaten liquidation under chapter 7, which mandates the appointment of a trustee and the piecemeal liquidation of the debtor, and the creditors' ability to seek the appointment of a trustee or examiners.

Finding an appropriate balance of debtor and creditor power, and thus ensuring an efficient reorganization, has been a key concern of American corporate reorganization since the late nineteenth century (Lubben, 2004). However, in recent years, creditors, especially secured creditors, have had increasing input into the crucial decisions that face a financially distressed company. Often using the powers that come to them as post-petition lenders under the Bankruptcy Code, senior creditors now prevent the kind of elongated cases that came to typify American corporate reorganization in the 1980s (Baird and Rassmussen, 2002). Indeed, while many academic commentators, especially in finance, seem to suppose that bankruptcy practice is static, modern chapter 11 practice features the frequent replacement of managers by outside restructuring experts and the going concern sales of companies that fail to reorganize on the senior lender's timetable. These lenders understand how to use their power in chapter 11, and the bankruptcy courts, especially in key jurisdictions like Delaware, New York, and Chicago, are inclined to defer to agreements reached in out-of-court bargaining among the parties and their sophisticated professionals (Skeel, 2003). While it can be argued that the pendulum has swung too far in the direction of lender control, it is beyond debate that today's chapter 11 is decidedly centered on senior creditor control (Lubben, 2005; Westbrook, 2005).

CREDIT DERIVATIVES AND THE PREBANKRUPTCY PERIOD

The most important credit derivative instrument is the credit default swap, also known as a *single-name* credit default swap. This type of swap is a contract covering the risk that a specified debtor defaults. One party (the *protection seller*) acquires the credit risk associated with a debt or class of debts in exchange for an annual fee from the other counterparty (the *protection buyer*). The debtor on the referenced obligation is not a party to the swap and in most cases is unaware of the transaction.

If the reference obligation goes into default, the protection buyer receives a payment meant to compensate it for its losses. More specifically, the protection seller's payment obligation is triggered by the occurrence of a "credit event" with regard to a specified class of obligations incurred by the reference entity. Commonly used credit events include bankruptcy,[1] failure to pay,[2] and restructuring.[3] The bankruptcy trigger includes both traditional chapter 7–style bankruptcy as well as chapter 11.

In the North American and European corporate markets these events typically must occur with respect to "borrowed money"—effectively any obligation owed to a voluntary creditor of the reference entity or its subsidiaries, assuming the parent guaranteed the subsidiaries' obligations, in excess of the $1 million and $10 million limitations built into the definitions of failure to pay and restructuring, respectively.

Most often the swap will call for *physical settlement* upon the occurrence of a credit event, meaning that the buyer will deliver a defaulted bond to the seller in exchange for payment of the full face value of the bond. The types of obligations that can be delivered to settle the swap are typically set forth in the documentation, although market practice does tend to give the protection buyer a choice within a range of debt instruments. This gives rise to the so-called cheapest-to-deliver option in a triggered swap, namely, the ability of a buyer to maximize recovery under the swap by purchasing the least valuable debt instrument that will satisfy the contractual provisions of the swap. In the North American and European corporate markets, swaps regularly allow for the delivery of any bond or loan issued by the reference entity, provided that, among other things, the obligation is not subordinated, i.e., not bearer paper with a maturity of less than 30 years from the settlement date.

Given these terms, credit derivatives may ultimately discourage out-of-court restructurings or at least place artificial time limits on the length of such negotiations while simultaneously increasing the incidence of involuntary bankruptcy filings. More generally, they may create perverse

---

[1] 2003 ISDA Credit Derivative Definitions, Section 4.2.

[2] 2003 ISDA Credit Derivative Definitions, Section 4.5. *Failure to pay* is defined, in part, as the failure of the reference entity to make payments in an aggregate amount of not less than the payment requirement. *Payment requirement* is a term that the parties can define; otherwise, it defaults to obligations of at least $1 million. See 2003 ISDA Credit Derivative Definitions, Section 4.8(d).

[3] 2003 ISDA Credit Derivative Definitions, Section 4.7. The restructuring must relate to debt in excess of the default requirement, which is set at $10 million unless the parties agree otherwise. 2003 ISDA Credit Derivative Definitions, Section 4.8(a). The definition of *restructuring* is not uniform among jurisdictions; for example, in the North American corporate market the definition is usually modified—and thus referred to as *modified restructuring*—by electing additional limitations on the maturity and transferability of the debt that can be delivered under the swap. 2003 ISDA Credit Derivative Definitions, Section 2.32.

incentives for parties to prefer outcomes that maximize the value of their swap position as opposed to the underlying investment in the debtor.

Credit default swaps often have a relatively short duration, and they expire without value to the protection buyer if no credit event occurs before maturity. Thus, as maturity dates approach on outstanding credit default swaps, protected creditors will have an increasing disincentive to work with the debtor on the terms of a restructuring arrangement that might not be announced or consummated until after the creditors' swaps have terminated. More generally, the protection buyer faces the risk that any workout could extend the underlying debt obligation beyond the duration of the swap.

Creditors will have every incentive to trigger the swap by filing an involuntary bankruptcy petition against the debtor, illustrating the important point that *bankruptcy* is the one credit event that can be controlled by many credit buyers. Moreover, the push to remove restructuring triggers from swaps in the North American market might solve the problem of how to interpret these clauses, but it will generate increased incentives to push the company into chapter 11, as the protection buyer will receive no protection benefits from agreeing to an out-of-court workout.

The increased incidence of credit risk transfer will also exacerbate creditor conflicts.

Restructuring agreements, including prepackaged chapter 11 plans, are most often negotiated with the debtor's largest creditors and then submitted to all creditors for consideration. However, the largest creditors are presumably the creditors most likely to have hedged their default risk. While it was undoubtedly always true that big bondholders are unlike small bondholders, the growth of credit derivatives may swell this gap, as large bondholders now agree to riskier reorganization plans or other similar terms that result solely from the downside protection these large bondholders have by virtue of their swap positions.

In short, negotiations on the event of bankruptcy can be expected to become increasingly complex and opaque (Skeel and Partnoy, 2007). In large part this is the result of the design of the credit protection markets, which expressly seek to allow banks and other lenders the ability to offload credit risk without alerting their customers of this fact and incurring the resulting reputation costs. However, this lack of transparency creates obvious and severe information asymmetries that may hinder pre-bankruptcy negotiation and planning, a serious problem after the 2005 amendments to the Bankruptcy Code make it increasingly difficult for a debtor to enter chapter 11 without such planning.

One likely response to this development is a return to coercive exchange offers, which may be used to force the "true" stakeholders of a firm to reveal themselves. Of course, this move might also further encourage involuntary bankruptcy petitions, with the attendant risk of an unplanned filing in an unfavorable jurisdiction.

CREDIT DERIVATIVES IN CHAPTER 11

The rapid growth of the credit derivatives market has recently led to supply-and-demand problems upon default. For example, after the recent chapter 11 filing of automotive parts manufacturer Delphi Automotive, $2 billion of bonds were said to be in circulation when it filed for bankruptcy, but the notional amount of outstanding derivatives of more than $20 billion initially had the explicable, although still strange, effect of driving up the market prices of the bonds just as Delphi filed for chapter 11. International Swaps and Derivatives Association (ISDA) has stepped in to mitigate this problem through a series of "protocols," which were successfully deployed not only in the Delphi case but also in connection with other recent chapter 11 cases.

Essentially these protocols use an auction mechanism to set a price for the debtor's bonds and then use that price to allow settlement of index credit default swaps without need for actual delivery of bonds. Removing index swaps from the mix reduces, but does not eliminate, the supply-and-demand effects on the bond markets. In the future it is expected that these problems will be solved by a move away from physical settlement of swaps, although the need for accurate, transparent markets in postdefault debt will remain if these swaps are to be settled.

If we assume that postdefault bond markets will return to a state of pretty good efficiency, the growth of credit default swaps and other credit protection represents a conundrum for chapter 11. In such a market a hedged senior creditor looses its ability to arbitrage, and its recovery in the chapter 11 case becomes essentially fixed. No matter what the lender does, they will not expect to alter their recovery in chapter 11 sufficiently to receive more or less than what the swap will pay them. Participation would simply mean incurring the positive costs of participation. Even if we assume that bond markets are somewhat inefficient, the protection buyer would have to assume a degree of inefficiency sufficient to clear their participation costs.

To the extent that recent commentators correctly identify senior creditor control as the lynchpin of a newly efficient chapter 11 process, any trend toward creditor passivity threatens to undermine the very basis of this putative reform. If we assume that the most concentrated creditors are the creditors most likely to hedge their positions, the growth of credit derivatives could plainly reverse the trend toward creditor control. More generally, if large creditors disengage from the chapter 11 process, the only check on debtor, shareholder, and management overreaching will be the bankruptcy court. The risk of a return to the debtor-controlled chapter 11 cases of the 1980s looms large.

Exceptions to this analysis exist, of course, because of the so-called cheapest-to-deliver option and the potential that the protection buyer has superior information about the reference debtor, a reasonable possibility in this example because the buyer is also a bank lender. However, this seems to be a rather slim basis for assuming that senior lender behavior in chapter 11 is not about to change dramatically.

Additionally, it is not clear that many protection sellers have any interest or desire to participate in chapter 11 cases. For example, some hedge funds purportedly sell credit protection as an easy way to generate income from the periodic fees paid by the seller. They likely have little interest in the underlying debt, and thus, even if they could take the place of senior lenders, it is not clear they will do so. More to the point, most hedge funds and private equity firms have no more experience with chapter 11 than the bank lenders of the late 1970s and early 1980s.

Somewhat more optimistically, it may be that protection sellers will aggregate large blocks of a reference debtor's bonds and thus represent a new source of creditor control in chapter 11. If smaller bondholders begin to use the swap settlement process as a market for exiting defaulted positions (a distinct possibility if supply and demand effects continue to drive up prices), there could be a mitigating trend at work in large chapter 11 cases. Furthermore, the possibility of reduced intraclass conflicts among bondholders, some of whom have bought at par and some of whom have bought in through the high yield markets, would be an unambiguous good in chapter 11 negotiations.

Likewise, the increasing transferability of bank loans may also moderate the problems of creditor passivity, inasmuch as the protection seller is more likely to be directly subrogated to the rights of the original creditor if that creditor's claim can be used to settle a swap. In this way, the increased transferability of claims might provide a market solution for the problem of creditor passivity. Of course, as the credit default swaps market continues to expand, other creditors with transfer restrictions on

their claims, such as trade creditors and contract creditors, might counter-
act this correction.

The implications for increased creditor passivity for chapter 11 are
manifold. Most obviously, the loss of senior lender control in chapter 11
could result in a power vacuum that returns corporate reorganization to
the debtor-controlled days of the past. Howerver, this seems unlikely,
given the academic vitriol directed against lingering cases like Eastern
Airlines (Lubben, 2005). The 2005 amendments to the Bankruptcy Code,
particularly those that limit the debtor's time in chapter 11, can be seen
as Congress' fix for the problems of cases like Eastern—albeit about
10 years too late.

Perhaps the bigger difficulty that may well arise as a result of senior
creditor passivity turns on the tremendous growth in second lien lending
in the United States (Baird and Rasmussen, 2006). The relationship
between the senior and second lender is set forth in a detailed intercreditor agreement, which typically provides for the second lien holders' consent to a wide variety of senior lender decisions, such as allowing the use
of the lenders' cash during chapter 11. This senior lender control may
become problematic if the lender ceases to have any real economic interest in the debtor. The second lender may have an option to buy out the
senior lender, but it may not be alerted to the need to exercise this option
until the senior lender has made key decisions in the chapter 11 case.

In addition, the potential turnover in the debtor's debt holders,
moving from a mix of buyers with varying incentives to a pool of speculative buyers, may reduce intraclass conflicts, but it will also increase
the overall risk tolerance of the creditors voting on the debtor's plan.
While not necessarily a bad thing, this could lead to riskier plans and,
consequently, higher refiling rates.

Whether repeated chapter 11 cases are suboptimal is the subject of
much debate (Lubben, 2007). It is plausible that two short chapter 11
cases might be preferable to a single, protracted chapter 11 case, which
may have greater indirect costs. The real issue is one of disclosure: If
chapter 11 plans increasingly become more speculative, driven by either
the increasing detachment of creditors or the aggregation of debt in the
hands of speculators, both in turn driven by the spread of credit default
swaps, courts will have to ensure that the remaining creditors understand
the plan under consideration and the risk the plans entails. Of course, this
assumes that the bankruptcy courts are themselves able to fully digest the
increasingly complex terms contained in modern reorganization plans.

The biggest risk to chapter 11 comes from the risk that the debtor's business will decline beyond the point of rescue while the parties debate, and litigate, the issues of who gets to participate in the debtor's reorganization and who gets to make key decisions during the reorganization. Recent disclosures that swaps may have been assigned without needed consents present one obvious point for litigation—to determine the identity of the debtor's stakeholders.

Debates about the enforceability of intercreditor agreements, the interpretation of terms of swaps, the conduct of ISDA settlement protocols, and the settlement of swaps that do not require physical delivery also may be points of contention. It is not clear that the bankruptcy court would have jurisdiction to hear these disputes, which largely involve nondebtor parties, yet the failure to resolve these issues quickly could leave the debtor unable to reorganize. These problems could be further compounded if the debtor's chapter 11 filing causes follow-on insolvencies of financial institutions, which fail as a result of their exposure to the debtor.

CONCLUSION

Overall, it seems probable that credit default swaps will alter the current chapter 11 landscape, especially in the larger cases where the most common recent trend is senior lenders leading the debtor through a reorganization largely designed by that lender. Instead, these creditors may loose their incentives to engage in such active participation, thus ceding the field to speculative debt buyers or, much less optimistically, the debtor's management. In either case the potential for riskier plans that seek to maximize the debtor's value will be the likely result. Courts should be aware of this potential, but they should not necessarily seek to stop it, as it is uncertain that this result is less desirable than the other likely option for a distressed firm: liquidation.

REFERENCES

Baird, D. and Rasmussen, R. (2002) The Four (or Five) Easy Lessons of Enron. *Vanderbilt Law Review,* 55(6): 1787–1810.

Baird, D. and Rasmussen, R. (2006) Private Debt and the Missing Lever of Corporate Governance. *University of Pennsylvania Law Review,* 154(5): 1209–1251.

Jacoby, M. (2006) Fast, Cheap, and Creditor-Controlled: Is Corporate
    Reorganization Failing?. *Buffalo Law Review,* 54(2): 401–438.

LoPucki, L.M. and Doherty, J.W. (2007) The Determinants of
    Professional Fees in Large Bankruptcy Reorganization Cases
    Revisited. UCLA School of Law, *Law-Econ Research Paper* No.
    06–16. Available at SSRN: http://ssrn.com/abstract=906184.

Lubben, S. (2004) Railroad Receiverships and Modern Bankruptcy
    Theory. *Cornell Law Review,* 89(6): 1420–1475.

Lubben, S. (2005) The "New and Improved" Chapter 11. *Kentucky Law
    Journal* 93(4): 839–866.

Lubben, S.J. (2007) Delaware's Irrelevance. *Seton Hall Public Law
    Research Paper* No. 967892. Available at SSRN:
    http://ssrn.com/abstract=967892.

Skeel, D. (2003) Creditors' Ball: The "New" New Corporate
    Governance in Chapter 11. *University of Pennsylvania Law Review,*
    152(2): 917–951.

Skeel, D. and Partnoy, F. (2007) The Promise and Perils of Credit
    Derivatives. *University of Cincinnati Law Review,* 75(3):
    1019–1051.

Westbrook, J.L. (2005) The Control of Wealth in Bankruptcy. *Texas Law
    Review,* 82(4): 795–862.

CHAPTER 4

Asymmetric Information and Opacity in Credit Derivatives Markets

Antonio Nicolò and Loriana Pelizzon

ABSTRACT

Credit derivatives provide banks with a whole range of flexible instruments for transferring loan risk, but they also create new informational problems. One distinctive aspect of credit derivatives markets is that they are a liquid but opaque forum for secondary market trading of banking assets, since credit derivative contracts are often not observable by third parties. We argue that the opacity of these markets is a fundamental element to consider. Most traditional instruments to mitigate asymmetric information problems cannot be used due to this fact. In this chapter we show how contracts already traded in the existing market could be used to reduce the informational problems.

INTRODUCTION

Credit derivatives provide banks with a whole range of flexible instruments for selling loans and transferring loan risk, but they also create new informational problems; therefore their effect on the efficiency of financial markets cannot be taken for granted. Asymmetry of information takes the form of adverse selection problems and/or moral hazard problems and affects the relations between lenders and borrowers as well as between risk buyers and sellers. This double asymmetric information (between lenders and borrowers and between lenders and risk buyers) not only influences the design of optimal contracts in credit derivatives markets, but it also affects the access to the financing markets.

One distinctive aspect of credit derivatives markets is that they are a liquid but opaque forum for secondary market trading of banking assets, since credit derivative contracts are often not observable by third parties. As the recent subprime crisis has highlighted, the opacity of these markets is a fundamental element in order to understand how they operate and to observe their effects on social welfare. Most traditional instruments to mitigate asymmetric information problems cannot be used due to this fact. For Josef Ackermann (the CEO of Deutschebank), an important reason for the current credit market turmoil is opaqueness: "As long as nobody knows where the risks are, people are very reluctant to buy some of these assets because they think they could be toxic."[1] In this chapter we investigate the problem faced (because of asymmetric information in the credit risk transfer market) by a bank that needs to signal its quality but, at the same time, satisfy minimum capital requirements. This problem is more interesting than it would appear at first glance because banks cannot signal their own type by freely varying the quantity of insurance, which is a standard solution for an insurance contract. Consequently, retaining a large portion of credit risk can be too costly because of the presence of capital constraints. Moreover, we assume that credit derivatives trades are not made public (i.e., credit derivatives are private contracts and outside investors are unable to observe all the credit derivatives positions of the banks), so the bank cannot make a commitment to a specific partial protection level to signal its type. In fact, any protection buyer purchasing partial protection for its loans with a protection seller can, at the same time, hedge the rest with another protection seller without the first being informed. The design problem requires the selection of a contract that balances the issuer's desire to transfer credit risk against capital cost that the bank faces if it retains part of the risk under the constraint that credit derivatives are private contracts.

Our goal is to study a menu of contracts presented in the literature and traded in the market to solve the adverse selection problem given

---

[1] *Financial Times*, September 5, 2007.

(1) the presence of capital constraints and (2) the fact that credit derivative contracts are not publicly observable.

The overall structure of our model is as follows. We assume that banks are of different types and vary in their ability to screen borrowers, and we further presume that there exist *high*-type banks that are able to screen their borrowers and choose only "good" loans and *low*-type banks that are unable to do so. In our model there is a one-to-one relation between a bank's ability and the riskiness of its credit portfolio (i.e., banks of diverse types have different loan pools). Risk buyer do not know the true type of the risk seller (simply from the "bank" now on) and therefore face an adverse selection problem. The bank is subject to minimum regulatory capital requirements. As frequently claimed in the literature, we assume that even for banks, capital at risk is costly as a result of asymmetric information [see Dewatripont and Tirole (1993), and Froot and Stein (1998)] or because of capital requirements [see Gorton and Winton (1998)]. This induces the bank to prefer to hold risk-free rather than risky assets even if it is risk neutral and to attribute a cost to the capital at risk required by loans.

The definition of minimum capital requirements is important in our analysis. Much of the initial activity in the credit risk transfer market was in response to inconsistencies in the regulatory framework for bank capital allocation (see Jones, 2000). In this paper we want to avoid this aspect and are concerned solely with capital requirements that prevent regulatory arbitrage and help to reduce the probability of bank default. The less intrusive capital adequacy rule suggested by regulators in pursuit of this objective is that banks hold a level of capital at risk at least enough to cover the value at risk (VaR) of their risky portfolio, where VaR is the maximum unexpected loss of bank asset portfolio given a certain confidence level.[2]

In order to solve the adverse selection problem, we consider a sample of contracts that have already appeared in the literature on security design. Namely, we concentrate on a menu of contracts that is quite new in the literature of financial innovation and is based on a basket of loans characterized by different maturities: a first-to-default basket and a plain vanilla credit default swap conditioned on the default of the first asset. The first-to-default basket is a financial contract in which the bank pays a premium to the risk buyer in exchange for a contingent payment by

---

[2] See Basel Committee on Banking Supervision (1999; 2005).

the counterpart if any of the underlying assets defaults. A plain vanilla conditioned on the default of the first asset is a commitment to buy, at a fixed price, an insurance contract (a credit default swap) on the rest of the basket after the first default. For sake of simplicity, we call this menu of contracts the first-to-default (FTD) menu. With an FTD menu, the bank is signaling its type by committing to buying "new" insurance in case of default and therefore showing that its credits have a low probability of default. We demonstrate that the FTD menu can solve the adverse selection problem. We also investigate the moral hazard problem where the probability of default of commercial loans may also depend on the intensity of monitoring and then show that the FTD menu provide the incentives to the bank in order to exert a monitoring activity.

The chapter is organized as follows. The next section describes the related literature. In the section after that, we present the basic model, and we analyze the benchmark case with symmetric information. Then, in the final three sections, we consider the asymmetric information case, investigate the moral hazard case, and conclude the chapter.

RELATED LITERATURE

The vast development in credit derivative markets has received the attention of both regulators and policy makers. Most international and national supervisors have published reports on the topic [e.g., International Monetary Fund (2002), Bank for International Settlement (2003; 2005; 2007)]. These reports are rather similar in tone. On one hand, they emphasize the benefits of credit derivatives in terms of risk sharing and diversification gains, and on the other hand, there is common concern that credit derivatives may have implications for financial stability. In creating new markets for credit risk, credit derivative instruments may (1) have an impact on asymmetric information problems existing between borrowers and lenders and (2) create new problems in the credit markets.[3] However, only few papers have considered the impact of the use of credit derivatives on banker's incentives.

Batthacharya and Chiesa (2007) show that monitoring incentives are provided through capital when aggregate risk matters, while Parlour

---

[3] See Kiff et al. (2003) for a review of almost all the potential implications of credit risk transfer markets because of the asymmetric information problems in the credit markets.

and Plantin (2007) consider the effect of credit risk transfer on relationship banking. The latter concentrate on the optimal mix of equity, bonds, and loans and show that liquidity effects can arise endogenously in credit derivative markets when banks are net protection buyers. Morrison (2005) demonstrates that if credit derivative trades are not published, the bank cannot make an ex-ante commitment to a specific protection level and then have a moral hazard incentive to fully hedge their exposition and therefore cease to monitor. This behavior has the negative effect of causing disintermediation and thus reducing welfare; however, Nicolò and Pelizzon (2007) illustrate that this is not the case if a binary credit default basket product is used as a signaling contract.

Even ignoring the capital requirement issue and the contract observability problem, the theoretical literature on credit derivatives and asymmetries of information problem is limited and borrows from optimal contract design to solve the adverse selection problem. In their model, DeMarzo and Duffie (1999) include general securities whose payoffs may be contingent on arbitrary public information such as collateralized debt obligation (CDO) contracts. DeMarzo and Duffie focus on liquidity problems with asymmetric information. They argue that the sharing process allows the bank to concentrate the "lemon's premium" on the small first-loss or equity tranche and create a relatively large, low-risk senior tranche. Also, the bank's retention of the subordinate tranche reduces the total lemon's premium by creating an incentive for the bank to align its interests with those of the risk buyer. Nicolò and Pelizzon (2007) consider this kind of contract design and show that CDO contracts are first best contracts under Basel I,[4] but they are not optimal under the new capital requirements introduced by Basel II or when a buyer cannot credibly commit to retain part of the risk because credit derivatives are private contracts.

Duffee and Zhou (2001) demonstrate that the problem of adverse selection may be overcome by drawing up credit derivatives with a smaller maturity than that of the underlying asset.[5] The key assumption in their model is the hypothesis that the bank's information advantage changes over the time and, in particular, is greater close to the maturity date of the loan. One of the contracts we present is similar in spirit to the

---

[4] See Basel Committee on Banking Supervision (1988).
[5] See Basel Committee on Banking Supervision (1988).

one proposed by Duffee and Zhou (2001). Nevertheless our approach is different because we do not assume that the bank's information advantage decreases over time or that there is perfect observability of credit derivative contracts.

THE MODEL

Assumptions

Let us consider a market where there is a bank operating in the local loan market that may hedge its exposure in the over-the-counter (OTC) credit derivative market by selling credit risk to other banks (protection sellers). By definition, the OTC market is characterized by private contracts; i.e., details of trades are not made public.

Banks and risk buyers are both risk neutral, and for simplicity, the riskless interest rate is zero. The bank belongs to one of two different types: high-type (denoted by h) and low-type (denoted by l). Both types vary only with respect to the quality of their loan pools for the credit risk on which the bank seeks protection. The quality of the pools is assumed to depend on borrowers' ability to repay loans. The probability of loan default depends on the ability of the bank to discern its borrowers, and therefore is lower for a high-type bank than for a low type. Let p_i for $i = \{h,l\}$ be the probability of success for loans repayment, then $0 < p_l < p_h < 1$, where p_l and p_h are the probability of loan success held by a low-type and a high-type bank, respectively.

The model incorporates three dates: 0, 1, and 2. On date 0, the bank makes two commercial loans with fixed size: I_1 and I_2. I_1 matures on date 1, while I_2 matures on date 2. Both credit lines can default only at the maturity date and are uncorrelated. Making a loan of amount I a bank $i = h, l$ obtains an expected profit $\pi_i = p_i(1 + \mu)I_i - I_i$, where μ is the interest rate, which is the same for both types. Hence, risk buyers cannot infer banks' types from the interest rate. Moreover, we assume that $\mu \le 1$; this assumption allows us to simplify the analysis while undermining the generality of our results. We assume that $\pi_h > \pi_l > 0$; that is, both types of loans have nonnegative net present value (NPV).

The bank is subject to capital requirements based on a VaR rule; i.e., its capital has to be at least equal to the amount of the largest unexpected loss that occurs with probability equal or lower than α. We assume that $p_h < \alpha$. Therefore, in order to issue loans the bank has to hold a buffer of capital called *capital at risk*. In line with the literature mentioned above, we assume that there is a positive unitary cost of capital denoted by ρ; this makes the bank's concern with risk management endogenous even if the bank is risk neutral.

We now focus on the case in which banks use credit derivatives in order to reduce capital requirements and therefore the cost of capital. The credit derivatives market is characterized by the presence of different types of contracts. At time 0, the bank offers to sell its credits to the risk buyers. Since there are many risk buyers we assume that the bank has full bargaining power.[6] At the time of the proposal, the bank's type is private information. The bank may offer a number of different contract menus:

1. Two plain vanilla credit default swaps (CDS), both of which hedge against a single name, I_1 and I_2 (for sake of brevity, the *CDS basket*);

2. An FTD basket and a plain vanilla CDS contract over I_2 conditioned on the default of the first asset I_1 (the *FTD menu*). The FTD basket is a financial contract in which the bank pays a premium to the risk buyer in exchange for a contingent payment by the counterpart if asset I_1 or I_2 defaults. In case the asset I_1 defaults the contract ends. The other contract in the menu is a commitment at time $t = 0$ to buy, at a fixed price, a plain vanilla contract on I_2 at time $t = 1$, conditional on the default of the first asset, I_1.

In our model, the credit event is identified with a failure to pay at the maturity date. The *credit event payment* is defined as the difference between the nominal value plus the accrued interest and the recovery value of the defaulted loan. For simplicity, we assume here that the recovery value is equal to zero, so that the credit event payment will be equal to the nominal value plus the accrued interest of each loan [$I_1(1 + \mu)$ in $t = 1$ and $I_2(1 + \mu)$ in $t = 2$]. Moreover, all the cash flows (including payment of the premiums) occur at the maturity of the contracts. Finally, let $0 < q < 1$ be the percentage of high-quality banks.

---

[6] We assume that protection sellers are not subject to capital requirements because, as in line with empirical evidence, they are largely insurance companies or hedge funds.

The Benchmark Case: Symmetric Information

When the buyer's type is common knowledge, then the lowest premium that a risk-neutral seller is willing to accept, in order to hedge the credit risk of an amount $I_j(1 + \mu)$ by means of a plain vanilla contract, is

$$\Phi_i(I_j) = (1 - p_i)I_j(1 + \mu) \text{ with } \Phi_i(I_j) \neq (1 - p_i)I_j(1 + \mu) \qquad (4.1)$$

The expected profits of a buyer of quality $i = h, l$ are

$$
\begin{aligned}
p_i(I_j) &= \mu I_j - \Phi_i(I_j) + \rho(\min(0, \mu I_j - \Phi_i(I_j)) \text{ with} \\
\pi_i(I_j) &\neq \mu I_j - \Phi_i(I_j) + \rho(\min(0, \mu I_j - \Phi_i(I_j))
\end{aligned}
\qquad (4.2)
$$

Since by assumption the NPV of the loans is positive for both types $i = h$, l, it follows that the capital requirement constraint is never binding. Hence,

$$\pi_i(I_j) = \mu I_j - \Phi_i(I_j) \text{ with } i = h, l \text{ and } j = 1, 2. \qquad (4.3)$$

The other possibility is that the protection buyer buys a CDS basket that covers both the loans. Given our assumption about correlation among loans, the premium that a risk-neutral seller is willing to accept is simply

$$\Phi_i(I_1 + I_2) = \Phi_i(I_1) + \Phi_i(I_2) \, i = h, l. \qquad (4.4)$$

It is straightforward to show that, with complete information, the full-coverage CDS basket (as well as full-coverage plain vanilla contracts) is a first-best contract.

ASYMMETRIC INFORMATION

Pooling Equilibrium

In pooling equilibrium, the minimal premium that a risk-neutral seller is willing to accept in order to sign a plain vanilla contract that hedges the counterpart against the credit risk of the loan I_j is

$$\Omega(I_j) = q(1 - p_h)I_j(1 + \mu) + (1 - q)(1 - p_l)I_j(1 + \mu) \text{ with } j = 1, 2. \qquad (4.5)$$

Signing a full-coverage plain vanilla credit derivative, a buyer of type i obtains the following expected profit:

$$\pi_i(I_j) = \mu I_j - \Omega(I_j) \text{ with } i = h, l \text{ and } j \text{ 5 } 1, 2. \qquad (4.6)$$

As usual, it is easy to find a pooling equilibrium. In particular, there exists a pooling perfect Bayesian equilibrium such that buyers of both types sign plain vanilla credit derivative contracts. The seller's beliefs are as follows: If a full-coverage plain vanilla contract (or a full-coverage CDS basket) is offered, then the buyer is a high type with probability q, and if any contract different than a full-coverage plain vanilla (or a full-coverage CDS basket) is offered, then the buyer is a low type with probability 1. High-type banks' profits are lower than their profits in a game with complete information, and the lower the number of high-type banks in the market, the stronger is the incentive to signal their own type. In the next section we analyze separating equilibria.

Separating Equilibriums

In this section we prove the existence of separating equilibriums such that at time zero, a high-type bank buys the FTD menu presented above and the low-type bank buys full-coverage plain vanilla contracts.

In order to overcome the multiplicity of perfect Bayesian equilibria, we only consider separating equilibria that satisfy the intuitive criterion proposed by Cho and Kreps (1987) for a signaling game (denoted CK perfect Bayesian equilibria).

With the FTD menu a bank signals its own type by accepting a stochastic payment for the insurance. The bank will pay a new premium to insure against a second default if and only if a default of one of the assets has already occurred. In this way, a high-type bank signals its own type with a contract that provides partial coverage such that it is not the amount of coverage but the amount of the payment (i.e., the premium paid for the insurance) that varies across different states of the world. Again, since the probability of having a first default is higher for low type (since $1 - p_l > 1 - p_h$), then there exists a premium large enough to deter low types to sign an FTD menu.[7]

---

[7] This is a typical signaling device in the literature on asymmetric information. For instance, in Diamond (1993) a borrower can decide to execute a (inefficient) short-term contract in order to signal that he is not afraid to turn again to the credit market.

Assuming that a protection buyer can only propose either an FTD menu or a CDS basket credit derivative contract, the following proposition holds:

Proposition 4.1: *If $\mu \geq [(1 - p_l) I_1 + (1 - p_l p_h) I_2]/[p_l (I_1 + p_h I_2)]$ or $\rho < (p_h - p_l)/p_l$, then there exists a unique CK separating perfect Bayesian equilibrium such that*

1. *High-type buyers sign an FTD basket contract, paying a premium, $\hat{\Psi}_{0,h}(I_1, I_2) = (1 - p_l)(I_1 + p_h I_2)(1 + \mu)$, and a plain vanilla contract on I_2 conditioned on the credit I_1 default, paying a premium $(1 - p_h) I_2(1 + \mu)$.*
2. *Low-type buyers sign full-coverage plain vanilla derivative contracts and pay the fair premium.*

   The seller's beliefs are such that the buyer is a high-type bank with probability 1 if and only if it offers an FTD menu with $(1-p_l)(I_1 + p_h I_2)(1 + \mu)$.

Proof: See the Appendix.

The premium paid at time $t = 1$ to hedge loan I_2 in case of I_1 default is equal to the fair premium for the high types. In fact, we restrict our analysis to renegotiation-proof contracts. In a separating equilibrium only high-type banks sign an FTD menu. Therefore, at time $t = 1$ in the case of I_1 default, there is complete information on the buyer type, and therefore, the unique renegotiation-proof premium that the buyer pays to hedge asset I_2 is equal to $(1 - p_h)I_2(1 + \mu)$.[8]

The capital requirement induced by an FTD menu can be positive or zero, depending on the level of the interest rate. As we show in the Appendix, if $\mu \geq [(1 - p_l) I_1 + (1 - p_l p_h) I_2]/p_l(I_1 + p_h I_2)$, then profits are large enough to pay the premium of the plain vanilla credit default swap on I_2 when I_2 defaults, and therefore, there is no capital requirement. If $\mu < [(1 - p_l) I_1 + (1 - p_l p_h) I_2]/p_l(I_1 + p_h I_2)$, then the high-type bank

---

[8] We may have different separating contracts if the premium paid at time $t = 1$ can be larger than $(1 - p_h)I_2(1 + \mu)$. If we assume that a buyer can commit at time $t = 0$ to pay a premium larger than $(1 - p_h)I_2(1 + \mu)$ to the seller in order to insure I_1 in case of I_2 default, then there exists equilibriums in which buyer's profits are higher. Consistently with the assumption that the buyer has full bargaining power, we assume that these contracts would be renegotiated.

that signs the FTD menu faces a positive cost of capital. Therefore, it chooses to not hedge the loss it faces in the worst state of the world (when I_1 defaults and it has to hedge again credit I_2) if and only if $\rho < (p_h - p_l)/p_l$. When $\mu < [(1 - p_l) I_1 + (1 - p_l p_h) I_2]/p_l (I_1 + p_h I_2)$ and $\rho > (p_h - p_l)/p_l$, the cost of capital is sufficiently high that high-type banks would prefer to hedge the unexpected loss. The high-type bank has no incentive to over-insure its portfolio issuing more than one FTD menu. Purchasing insurance is costly for a high-type bank, and this type of strategy increases profits only if the bank reduces its capital requirements. For the same reason, the high-type bank has no incentive to over-insure its portfolio using a CDS basket. The effect would be a reduction of expected profits since anyone buying that insurance contract is assumed to be a low-quality bank.

Low-type banks do not over-insure their exposure because the overall cost of purchasing any of the contracts (either CDS or FTD menus) is equal to their expected profits. Our separating equilibrium does not require that outsiders know that a bank has not secretly hedged its portfolio using other contracts. When a high-type bank buys an FTD menu, it commits to buy a plain vanilla contract at time $t = 1$ in case of default of the first asset. This commitment is ex-post incentive compatible as a result of the continuous application of capital requirements, because of the presence of a capital requirement constraint also at date 1.

The FTD menu is a costly contract for the high-type banks since they pay an insurance premium that is higher than the fair premium. In particular, the premium paid at time $t = 0$ is $(1 - p_l)(I_1 + p_h I_2)(1 + \mu)$ while the fair premium of a first-to default contract is equal to $(1 - p_h)$ $(I_1 + p_h I_2)(1 + \mu)$. Hence, an FTD menu is not a first best contract when $\rho = 0$. Moreover neither the premium paid at time $t = 0$ nor the premium eventually paid at time $t = 1$, depend on the unitary cost of capital ρ. Again, this occurs since we have assumed that buyers can privately sign credit derivatives and therefore the cost of capital does not influence the self-selection constraint of the low-type banks.

A SIMPLE MODEL WITH MORAL HAZARD AND ADVERSE SELECTION

Until now we have considered a model of adverse selection, where the asymmetry between the buyers' types rises by their different abilities in the screening activity. In many cases, however, the probability of default of commercial loans may also depend on the intensity of the monitoring activity exerted by the bank that has these loans in its portfolio. Therefore, it is also interesting to analyze how full-coverage credit derivative influences the level of monitoring.

We consider here the case in which the bank that grants the loans affects their probability of default by means of its monitoring activity. We consider the simplest model in which the effort in monitoring activity takes just two values, $\{e_l, e_h\}$ with $e_l < e_h$. We assume, without loss of generality, that $e_l = 0$ and $e_h = \bar{e}$ and that $c_i(0) = 0$, $c_j(\bar{e}) = \bar{c}$, where $c_j(e)$ simply denotes the cost for the buyer i of monitoring at level e. We also assume that $p_k(e) > p_k(0)$ and $p_j(e) < p_h(0)$; that is, the monitoring activity is effective in reducing the probability of default, but it cannot overcome the adverse selection problem. Finally, we make the assumption that the monitoring activity is "loan specific," that is, the probability of default of each loan in a basket is affected only by the effort that the buyer exerts in monitoring this specific credit.[9] The introduction of a moral hazard problem in our framework is relevant when

1. The asymmetric information between risk buyer and the bank of a credit derivative keeps the seller from monitoring the credits hedged by the credit derivative contract.
2. Monitoring activity is Pareto efficient:

$$(p_i(\bar{e}) - p_i(0))(1 + \mu)I_j > \bar{c} \text{ for both } i = h, l \text{ and } j = 1, 2. \quad (4.7)$$

When these two conditions hold, it is worth analyzing the impact of credit derivative issue on the probability of default of the underlying credits, since it clearly affects the social welfare and therefore the regulatory design.

The timing of the game is as follows: First a buyer proposes a contract to the seller in order to hedge its credits. Then, after the contract is signed, the buyer decides the level of effort to exert in the monitoring activity.

From this we easily see the following remark.

Remark: If buyer i signs a plain vanilla contract that hedges the total amount of the underlying credit, then in equilibrium, $e_i = 0$.

---

[9] Note that this assumption is in line with the previous assumption that credits I_1 and I_2 are not correlated.

As regards the FTD credit derivative, the same conclusion does not hold necessarily. In fact, since the monitoring activity reduces the probability of default of credit I_1, it reduces as a consequence the probability of paying a new premium to hedge credit I_2.

In fact, the following proposition is easily proved.

Proposition 4.2: *If*

$$\bar{c} < \left[p_h(\bar{e}) - p_h(0) \right] \left\{ \mu I_1 + \left[1 - p_h(0) \right] I_2 \right\} \tag{4.8}$$

then the bank that signs an FTD basket contract exerts the efficient level of monitoring activity with respect to the credit I_1.

Proof: See the Appendix.

Condition (4.8) simply compares the cost of monitoring with the benefit in the monitoring activity, where $[1 - p_h(0)]I_2$ is the premium paid to hedge credit I_2 in the separating equilibrium when credit I_1 defaulted and high-type buyers have full bargaining power.

We conclude that FTD basket credit derivatives not only have a different informative content with respect to plain vanilla contracts, but they also provide more incentive to the buyer in order to exert a monitoring activity, even in case of full coverage of the underlying loan pools.[10]

CONCLUSION

A major concern of both policy makers and regulators is the effect of credit derivatives on the performance of credit markets. We show that the existence of a credit derivatives market together with capital requirements for credit risk induces an adverse selection problem because low-type banks may cover their exposure with credit derivatives. Hence, the introduction of a credit derivatives market does not necessarily always benefit the economy and increase social welfare.

---

[10] This results holds even if the protection buyers commits at date 0 to buy protection at date 1 conditional on the first default. As mentioned before, this is ex-post-facto incentive compatible because of capital requirements constraints. This differentiates our paper from Morrison (2005), who assumes that banks cannot commit at time $t = 0$ to trade a specific credit derivative contract at time $t = 1$.

The use of classical signaling contracts able to solve the problems that arise from the opacity of the loan portfolios of banks is precluded in such market because (1) the retention of a part of the risk increases banks' capital requirements and (2) credit derivatives are private contracts and are not explicitly made public by banks. This last point makes the use of contracts based on partial coverage more difficult because risk-retention buyers are unable to commit to a specific level of protection that is ex-post-facto incentive compatible.

Our main result demonstrates when the cost of capital is not too high, there may nonetheless exist a separating equilibrium where high-type banks signal their own type by signing the FTD menu. We believe this result is particularly interesting for two main reasons. First, because it suggests a potential contract design that is able to solve the adverse selection problem when Basel II is implemented. Second, it shows that theoretical predictions may change whether credit derivative contracts are publicly observable or not. Since the assumption that contracts are not publicly observable seems much more plausible given the recent subprime crisis, our result suggests that the analysis of the presence of private contracts in the credit market may deserve further investigation.

APPENDIX

Proof of Proposition 4.1

The high-type buyer offers a FTD contract that satisfies the following maximization problem:

$$\max_{\Psi_h(I_1,I_2)} \mu(I_1 + I_2) - \Psi_h(I_1,I_2) - (1 - p_h)\Phi_h(I_2) +$$
$$\rho(\min(0, \mu(I_1 + I_2) - \Psi_h(I_1,I_2) - \Phi_h(I_2))) \tag{4.9}$$

such that

$$\Psi_h(I_1,I_2) + (1 - p_h)\Phi_h(I_2) - (1 - p_h)(1 + \mu)(I_1 + I_2) \geq 0 \tag{4.10}$$

$$\mu(I_1 + I_2) - \Psi_h(I_1,I_2) - (1 - p_h)\Phi_h(I_2) +$$
$$\rho(\min(0, \mu(I_1 + I_2) - \Psi_h(I_1,I_2) - \Phi_h(I_2))) \leq \tag{4.11}$$
$$\mu(I_1 + I_2) - (1 - p_l)(1 + \mu)(I_1 + I_2)$$

Condition (4.10) is the participation constraint for the seller, and condition (4.11) is the incentive compatibility constraint for the low-type buyer. It is straightforward to note that the buyer wants to minimize the premium. Since the equilibrium is separating and the buyer has full bargaining power, at time $t = 1$ the premium paid to hedge I_2 in case of h default is[11]

$$\hat{\Psi}_h(I_1, I_2) = (1 - p_h)I_2(1 + \mu) \tag{4.12}$$

Case 1
Let us assume that

$$\mu(I_1 + I_2) \geq \Psi_h(I_1, I_2) - \Phi_h(I_2) \tag{4.13}$$

Substituting (4.12) into condition (4.10) and into condition (4.11), it is easy to check that condition (4.11) is more binding. Hence, in equilibrium,

$$\Psi_h(I_1, I_2) \geq (1 - p_l)(I_1 + p_h I_2)(1 + \mu) \equiv \hat{\Psi}_h(I_1, I_2) \tag{4.14}$$

The buyer's expected profits are

$$\mu(I_1 + I_2) - (1 - p_l)(I_1 + p_h I_2)(1 + \mu) - (1 - p_h)(1 - p_h)I_2(1 + \mu) \tag{4.15}$$

and therefore the high-type buyer prefers to sign a FTD as a high type rather than sign a plain vanilla contract as a low type if

$$\mu(I_1 + I_2) - (1 - p_l)(I_1 + p_h I_2)(1 + \mu) - (1 - p_h)(1 - p_h)I_2(1 + \mu) \geq$$
$$\mu(I_1 + I_2) - (1 - p_l)(1 + \mu)(I_1 + I_2) \tag{4.16}$$

that is,

$$(p_h - p_l)I_2(1 + \mu)(1 - p_h) > 0 \tag{4.17}$$

---

[11] Equivalently, if the plain vanilla over I_2 conditioned on I_2 default is signed at time $t = 0$, the buyer cannot credibly commit to pay a premium higher than $\hat{\Psi}_h (I_1, I_2) = (1 - p_h)I_2 (1 + \mu)$. In fact, given its bargaining power, it is able to renegotiate the terms of the contract at time $t = 1$.

which holds by assumption. Finally, we have to check under which condition assumption (4.13) holds true. Substituting $\hat{\Psi}_h (I_1, I_2)$ and $\Phi_h (I_2)$ in (4.13), we obtain the following condition:

$$\mu \geq \frac{(1 - p_l)I_1 + (1 - p_h p_l)I_2}{p_l(I_1 + p_h I_2)} = \hat{\mu} \qquad (4.18)$$

Equilibrium beliefs are consistent with the equilibrium strategies and out-of-equilibrium beliefs satisfy the intuitive criterion. For any separating equilibrium where the high-type offers an FTD contract with $[\Psi_h (I_1, I_2), \Phi_h (I_2)]$ such that $\Psi_h (I_1, I_2) > \hat{\Psi}_h (I_1, I_2)$, there exists a deviating proposal $[\Psi'_h (I_1, I_2), \Phi h (I_2)]$ with $\Psi_h (I_1, I_2) > \Psi'_h (I_1, I_2) \geq \hat{\Psi}_h (I_1, I_2)$ such that, by the intuitive criterion, a seller has to assign probability 1 that the proposer is a high-type bank.

Case 2

If condition (4.18) does not hold, then the low-type bank that deviates and signs a FTD contract can draw up a credit derivative contract in order to hedge its position. Let X be the amount a low-type bank receives in case of credit I_l default, and let $(1 - p_l)X$ be the premium paid in equilibrium to hedge X. To avoid the cost of capital, the low type signs a credit derivative contract such that

$$\mu(I_1 + I_2) - \Psi_h(I_1, I_2) - (1 - p_h)I_2(1 + \mu) + X - (1 - p_l)X = 0 \qquad (4.19)$$

that is,

$$X = \frac{(1 - p_l)(I_1 + p_h I_2)(1 + \mu) + (1 - p_h)I_2(1 + \mu) - \mu(I_1 + I_2)}{p_l} \qquad (4.20)$$

Since the low-type banks pay a fair premium, it turns out that the incentive-compatible constraint is the same as in Case 1.

Hence, in equilibrium, high-type banks decide to not hedge their position if and only if the expected cost of capital is lower than the cost of hedging, that is, if

$$\rho(1 - p_l)(I_1 + p_h I_2)(1 + \mu) + (1 - p_h)I_2(1 + \mu) - \mu(I_1 + I_2) \le$$
$$(p_h - p_l)\frac{(1 - p_l)(I_1 + p_h I_2)(1 + \mu) + (1 - p_h)I_2(1 + \mu) - \mu(I_1 + I_2)}{p_l} \quad (4.21)$$

that is, only if

$$\rho \le \frac{p_h - p_l}{p_l} \quad (4.22)$$

Finally, the usual arguments apply to verify the consistency of the beliefs and the uniqueness of the *CK* equilibrium.

Proof of Proposition 4.2

The premium paid at period 1 in the separating equilibrium by high-type partners is

$$\Psi_{1,h}(I_2) = (1 - p_h(0))I_2 \quad (4.23)$$

Let $\Psi_{0,h}(I_1, I_2)$ be the premium paid at period zero in the separating equilibrium by high-type buyers.[12] The expected profit in case of no monitoring on credit I_1 is

$$p_h(0)\mu(I_1 + I_2) - \Psi_{0,h}(I_1, I_2) - (1 - p_h(0))\Psi_{1,h}(I_2) \quad (4.24)$$

while the expected profit in case of monitoring on credit I_l is

$$(p_h(\overline{e}))\,\mu I_1 + p_h(0)\,\mu I_2 - \Psi_{0,h}(I_1, I_2) - (1 - p_h(\overline{e}))_{1,h}(I_2) - \overline{c} \quad (4.25)$$

The high-type buyer decides to monitor I_l if and only if quantity $(4.24) \ge$ quantity (4.24), that is,

$$\big((p_h(\overline{e}) - p_h(0)\big)\,\big(\mu I_1 + \Psi_{1,h}(I_2)\big) \ge \overline{c} \quad (4.26)$$

Finally, note that since the result only depends on $\Psi_{1,h}(I_2)$, it holds for both Case 1 and Case 2 of Proposition 4.2.

REFERENCES

Bank for International Settlement (2003) Credit Risk Transfer: Committee on the Global Financial System. Working paper, Basel, Switzerland.

Bank for International Settlement (2005) Credit Risk Transfer: Committee on the Global Financial System. Working paper, Basel, Switzerland.

Bank for International Settlement (2007) Bank for International Settlement, International Banking and Financial Market Developments. *BIS Quarterly Review*, Basel, Switzerland.

Basel Committee on Banking Supervision (1988) International Convergence of Capital Measurements and Capital Standards. Basel, Switzerland.

Basel Committee on Banking Supervision (1999) A New Capital Adequacy Framework: Consultive Paper. Basel, Switzerland.

Basel Committee on Banking Supervision (2005) International Convergence of Capital Measurements and Capital Standards: A Revised Framework. Basel, Switzerland.

Bhattacharya, S. and Chiesa, G. (2007) Risk Transfer, Lending Capacity and Real Investment Activity. Working paper, Department of Economics, University of Bologna.

Cho, I.K. and Kreps, D.M. (1987) Signaling Games and Stable Equilibriums. *Quarterly Journal of Economics*, 102(2): 179–221.

DeMarzo P. and Duffie, D. (1999) A Liquidity-Based Model of Security Design. *Econometrica*, 67(1): 65–99.

Diamond, D. (1993) Seniority and Maturity of Debt Contracts. *Journal of Financial Economics,* 33(3): 341–368.

Dewatripont M. and Tirole, J. (1993) The Prudential Regulation of Banks. Boston, MA: MIT Press.

Duffee, G.R. and Zhou, C. (2001) Credit Derivatives in Banking: Useful Tools for Managing Risk? *Journal of Monetary Economics*, 48(1): 25–54.

Froot K. and Stein, J. (1998) Risk Management, Capital Budgeting and Capital Structure Policy for Financial Institutions: an Integrated Approach. *Journal of Financial Economics*, 47(1): 55–82.

Gorton G. and Winton, A. (1998) Liquidity Provision, The Cost of Bank Capital and the Macroeconomic. NBER working paper, Cambridge, MA.

Jones D. (2000) Emerging Problems with the Basel Capital Accord: Regulatory Capital Arbitrage and Related Issues. *Journal of Banking and Finance*, 24(1): 35–58.

Kiff, J, Michaud, F.L., and Mitchell, J. (2003) Instruments of Credit Risk Transfer: Effects on Financial Contracting and Financial Stability. Working paper, National Bank of Belgium, Brussels, Belgium.

International Monetary Fund (2002) Global Financial Stability Report. A Quarterly Report on Market Developments and Issues, Washington, D.C.

Morrison A. (2005) Credit Derivatives, Disintermediation and Investment Decisions. *Journal of Business,* 78(2): 621–647.

Nicolò, A. and Pelizzon, L. (2007) Credit Derivatives, Capital Requirements and Opaque OTC Markets. Univeristy Ca' Foscari of Venice working paper, Venice, Italy.

Parlour, C. and Plantin, G. (2008), Loan Sales and Relationship Banking, *Journal of Finance* (forthcoming 2008).

The Role of Macro and Country-Specific Factors on the Use of Credit Derivatives: Sovereign Credit Default Swap Market

Mehmet Orhan and M. Nihat Solakoglu

ABSTRACT

Credit derivatives are instruments that assist banks in managing their credit risk. This chapter examines the credit derivatives market and investigates how macro and country-specific factors affect the sovereign credit default swap market size through balanced panel data analysis. We find that GDP growth, current account deficit, exchange rates, volatility of interest rates, and nonperforming loan ratio are important determinants of sovereign credit default swap quotes.

INTRODUCTION

An important role played by financial intermediaries is to facilitate the flow of funds between lenders and borrowers. In this traditional type of lending practice, financial institutions (namely, banks) originate the credit, fund the credit, and also manage the credit risk associated with this type of lending. Given the size of the credit market, both credit risk and the management of credit risk are important for financial institutions.

In its simplest form *credit risk* can be defined as the inability of a borrower to repay some or all the principal and/or interest payment of a loan. If there are numerous borrowers with a decline in their ability to pay in an asset portfolio of a financial institution, the cost of borrowing will increase for borrowers. At the same time, financial institutions with this type of portfolio should expect to encounter a higher cost of funding (Batten and Hogan, 2002). As a result, it is imperative for lenders to keep their asset portfolio's credit quality constant or at least try to prevent its deterioration. One method to do this is to have financial guarantees with the lending contract such as letters of credit or bond insurance. Another method can be the asset securitization, i.e., combining assets with similar risk for the purpose of selling to manage credit risk (Broll et al., 2002). For emerging markets credit derivatives can be considered as the last option to manage credit risk.

In this chapter, we investigate the role of country-specific factors on the number of sovereign credit default swap (CDS) quotes on major emerging market economies, where *emerging markets* are defined as the emerging CDS markets. In addition, a brief examination of an emerging market (i.e., Turkey) is included with respect to the credit market and its use of credit derivatives. The remainder of the chapter is organized as follows: The next section provides a brief overview of credit derivatives market, and in the section after that there is a brief discussion of Turkish credit market, including the use of credit derivatives. The last three sections of the chapter provide information on the data sources and the methodology used, discuss the results, and present our conclusions and suggestions for further research.

CREDIT DERIVATIVES: A BRIEF OVERVIEW

Credit derivatives allow financial institutions to manage their credit exposure to existing lending contracts. These derivatives have been part of the over-the-counter (OTC) market since the early 1990s and their importance has been increasing yearly.[1] According to the Bank for International Settlements (BIS) (2007), at the end of 2006, the notional amounts of OTC derivatives market was approximately $415 trillion,[2] a 39.5 percent

---

[1] International Swaps and Derivatives Association publicly introduced credit derivatives in 1992 (Skinner and Townend, 2002).

[2] Over-the-counter derivatives market activity in the second half of 2006, BIS, Monetary and Economic Department, May 2007.

increase relative to the prior year. Although credit derivatives are a small part of the total OTC derivatives market, their growth outperforms their expectations. For example, the British Bankers Association (BBA) (2006) Credit Derivatives Report indicates that the market size is expected to be around $20 trillion by the end of 2006. However, BIS reports show that CDSs, part of the credit derivatives market, has reached to $28.8 trillion in notional amounts outstanding at the end of 2006, a 107 percent increase compared to the previous year.

Credit derivatives, as indicated earlier, are financial instruments that allow banks to manage credit risk either by trading in some risk or all the risk in a credit asset without transferring the underlying asset. These instruments derive their value from an existing lending contract with a positive level of risk that affects the borrowers' ability to pay. In a credit derivative, the protection buyer, the financial institution with the lending portfolio, buys a credit derivative instrument from the protection seller that requires a premium payment. By using a credit derivative instrument, the financial institution can separate credit origination, credit funding, and management of credit risk from each other. The lender through the use of a credit derivative instrument preserves the quality of the lending portfolio and hence the cost of funding. The seller of the protection can share the return without actually originating and funding the credit. In other words, credit risk and returns are diversified among banks and other financial and/or nonfinancial institutions without transferring the underlying assets (Hirtle, 2007; Batten and Hogan, 2002).[3] Diversification of risk and return is one reason why the protection seller actually sells protection for a premium. Another reason is the incremental return that a nonbank institution can get by transacting in credit derivatives market.[4]

Credit derivatives are different from traditional lending contracts with financial guarantees because derivatives contracts can incorporate one or many credit events other than default. A *credit event* is a trigger that starts the implementation process imbedded in the credit derivative

---

[3] Also see http://www.credit-deriv.com/introduction%20to%20credit%20derivatives%20article%20by%20Vinod%20Kothari.pdf

[4] By accepting additional risk, a nonbank firm, such as an insurance firm, can benefit from higher returns offered in the lending market in which they cannot operate legally. Although it is not often mentioned in the literature, one should note that protection buyer replaces credit risk from an existing lending contract with a risk on the protection seller. See http://www.credit-deriv.com/introduction%20to%20credit%20derivatives%20article%20by%20Vinod%20Kothari.pdf for more details.

contract. A contract can be based on one event or a series of events and parties can agree on the events themselves using standard credit events provided by International Swaps and Derivatives Association (ISDA). These events are bankruptcy, merger, cross-acceleration, cross-default, downgrade, failure to pay, repudiation, and restructuring. Credit derivatives can be categorized as single-name or multiname credit derivatives. While single name credit derivatives indicate the existence of one lending contract, multi-name credit derivatives include a portfolio of lending contracts. The portfolio can either be static or dynamic in nature and in the former case lending contracts of the portfolio remain fixed. Although constituents of the dynamic portfolio can change, total value of reference portfolio remains fixed (Batten and Hogan, 2002).[5]

There are several instruments used to manage credit exposure of a loan contract. The most common is the CDS. A CDS contract, as shown in Figure 5.1, includes three parties: the borrower (generally a corporation),

F I G U R E   5.1

Example of CDS contract

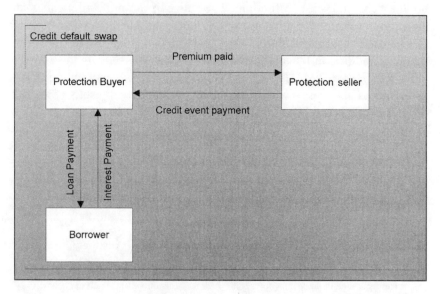

---

[5] Also see http://www.credit-deriv.com/introduction%20to%20credit%20derivatives%20article%
    20by%20Vinod%20Kothari.pdf

the protection buyer (generally the bank), and the protection seller (a bank, a hedge fund, an insurance company, etc).

The protection buyer extends credit to the borrower in return for interest payments. To remove the credit risk associated with the loan off the balance sheet, the protection buyer enters into a CDS contract with the protection seller. Therefore, the protection buyer transfers credit risk to the protection seller and pays a premium, which is generally expressed as basis points of the notional value of the contract. The original loan value and term do not have to match with the CDS contract's term and notional value.[6] If within the CDS contract term, the credit event or events defined in the contract occur, the protection seller makes the credit event payments. If no event occurs, the seller of the protection will benefit from the premium payment.[7] According to the *BBA Credit Derivatives Report* (2006), single-name CDS contracts are the largest product in the credit derivatives market with almost 33 percent of the market share. At the end of 2006, the notional amounts outstanding reached to $28.8 trillion, with about 66 percent of the contracts being single-name instruments (Bank for International Settlements [BIS] report).[8] Other credit derivatives instruments are credit-linked note, credit-spread instrument, and total return swaps [for details, see Batten and Hogan (2002)].

Credit derivatives may also be used to provide insurance against sovereign defaults. Although a small part of the credit derivatives market, sovereign CDS contracts have been traded actively on major emerging markets. It can be argued that the emergence of CDS contracts on emerging market bonds are responsible for the demise of the Brady bond futures contracts traded on the Chicago Mercantile Exchange (CME) by being a better alternative hedging tool (Carr and Wu, 2007; Skinner and Nuri, 2007).

Given that credit derivatives assist banks to diversify their credit risk, it should be plausible to argue that credit derivatives reduce bank risk and hence lead to an increase in the supply of credit. However, this does not have to be the case. For example, Instefjord (2005) identifies the conditions under which banks will play the risk acquisition game more aggressively. Faced with a richer set of tools to manage risk than before, banks can unnecessarily undertake more risk than they should, which will

---

[6] For example, original loan can be for $80 million for an eight-year term, but the notional value of the CDS contract can be for $50 million for five years.

[7] A CDS contract can be seen as a put option as well. See Skinner and Townend (2002).

[8] Over-the-counter derivatives market activity in the second half of 2006, BIS, Monetary and Economic Department, May 2007.

certainly cause a higher risk level. Duffee and Zhou (2001) also indicate that credit derivatives will not necessarily make banks better at managing their credit risk. However, Hirtle (2007) finds some support that the supply of credit increases as banks manage their credit risk through credit derivatives. Nevertheless, this result does not hold for all lending types and the benefits seem to flow mostly to large corporations.

Although credit derivatives are powerful in managing credit exposure for banks, their use does not seem to be that widespread. For example, in 2003, out of 345 U.S. banks, only 19 reported using credit derivatives. The total net notional amount of credit derivatives was only 2.73 percent of the total loans of these banks. In addition, the protection buyers seem to have larger fractions of commercial and industrial loans as well as foreign loans than nonusers of protection (Minton et al., 2005). Moreover, at the end of 2005, Hirtle (2007) cites that only 33 banks reported any credit derivatives use and that the usage is clustered among the largest banks. Similarly, in Germany, as reported by Düllmann and Sosinska (2007), the CDS market is narrow and concentrated mostly in large and internationally active firms; however, the authors can only find three German banks as reference entities.

For emerging markets, the importance of credit derivatives increased after 1999, and CDS contracts led as the instrument of choice, with hedge funds being the major actors (Ranciere, 2001). In addition, the most liquid credit derivatives instrument in emerging markets is considered to be the sovereign CDS contracts.[9] Sovereign CDS contracts, although important for emerging markets, are a small fraction of the global CDS market. For example, at the end of December of 2006, out of $18.8 trillion notional amounts outstanding, only about $1 trillion can be considered as sovereign CDS contracts. In addition, in 2002, out of 137,653 CDS quotes, only approximately 7 percent are considered to be sovereign CDS quotes. Moreover, sovereign-linked CDS contracts seem to be on lower credit quality assets (Packer and Suthipongchai, 2003).

AN EMERGING MARKET OVERVIEW: TURKEY

As an emerging market, sovereign CDS quotes for Turkey are reported as 380 in 2003 (half year) and 475 in 2002 by Packer and Suthipongchai (2003). Based on their data, excluding 2002 and 2003, there seems to be

---

[9] The OTC derivatives market activity in the second half of 2006, BIS, Monetary and Economic Department, May 2007.

a large positive growth in the number of sovereign quotes for Turkey as well as most other emerging economies. In addition, markets that have the largest sovereign CDS quotes in our sample are Brazil and Mexico. While Argentina and Philippines were high in the list in 2000, the number of quotes declines sharply over time.[10] From 2000 to 2003, South Africa and Colombia appear to have an increasing trend in terms of the number of quotes. For example, while the number of quotes was 94 in 2000 for South Africa, it has risen to 683 in 2003. For these countries, the underlying asset for CDS contracts seems to be sub-investment grade. That is, it has BB and/or below ratings (Packer and Suthipongchai, 2003).

A closer look at the banking sector in Turkey reveals that total credit extended almost tripled between the end of 2002 and mid–2005. In addition, about 90 percent of the credit is directed towards the private sector, which can be considered as the main source of credit risk. However, as a lagging indicator of loan quality, the ratio of nonperforming loans to gross loans displays a declining trend—from 17.6 percent in 2002 to 5.4 percent in mid–2005—implying declining credit risk (Başçı, 2006).[11] Nonetheless, this decline coupled with stable economic growth in Turkey and abroad, can be misleading to conclude that credit risk is not of importance to the Turkish financial sector and to macro stability.[12] The share of credit to the household sector, though still small in absolute value, is increasing for the majority of emerging economies and shifting the credit risk exposure for the banking sector. Overall, credit risk may increase for the banking sector in emerging economies as a result of this shift. Factors such as greater diversification of risks among a large number of household borrowers or higher profit from household lending can lead to a decline in credit risk. However, lower levels of bankruptcy protection, lower levels of implicit or explicit guarantees, and even lower levels of experience and knowledge of the lending institution can cause an increase in credit risk (Moreno, 2006).

---

[10] The reason should be clear for Argentina as total defaulted debt of Argentina in November of 2001 was around US$82 billion.

[11] For the entire banking sector, the ratio of nonperforming loans to gross loans was approximately 3.8 percent in June 2007. Out of all total loans, about 53 percent were mid- to long-term loans. (Monthly Bulletin, Banking Regulation and Supervision Agency, August, 2007).

[12] As reported by Fitch (Fitch Ratings, 2007), this low default environment along with tighter spreads causes ratings quality to drop. For example, in 2006, about 40 percent of the global credit exposure is for below investment grade. The share of below-investment-grade contracts was 18, 24, and 31 percent in 2003, 2004, and 2005, respectively. See CDx Survey: Market Volumes Continue Growing While New Concerns Emerge, 2007, http://www.fitchratings.com.

Based on the Banking Regulation and Supervision Agency (BDDK) report (2007), the use of derivative instruments by the banking sector focuses mostly on forward contracts and swap transactions in Turkey. These transactions consist of approximately 70 percent of the total derivatives transactions in June 2007, including the transactions of nearly 50 banks operating in Turkey. The analysis of financial statements for 15 banks trading on the Istanbul Stock Exchange (ISE) with respect to credit derivatives use and total derivatives use provide some useful information, though limited for the use of credit derivatives.[13] We present descriptive banking statistics for the 15 banks in Table 5.1.

First, the ratio of total credit to total assets is increasing. This can be attributed to the positive economic outlook, but it can also impact credit quality as new credits are extended to lower quality assets as indicated by Başçı (2006). There seems to be a decline in the ratio of nonperforming loans to total credit as mentioned earlier. Although the value of derivatives transactions increases over time the ratio of risk derivatives to total derivatives displays a declining trend.[14] Out of 15 banks, only one bank reported the use of credit derivatives, particularly credit default swap, to manage their credit risk. However, it is easy to argue that even this was limited in use. When grouped with similar sized banks, one distinguishing feature for the banks that indicates the use of credit derivatives is the

TABLE 5.1

Banking Statistics in Turkey

	2007*	2006	2005
Total credit / total assets	51.5%	46.5%	42.4%
Non-performing loans / total credit	3.8%	3.8%	5.0%
Risk-derivatives / total derivatives†	0.4%	0.7%	4.9%

*First six months of 2007.
†Risk derivatives are the derivatives used to avoid risk from value changes, from cash flow, and from investments.
Source: Istanbul Stock Exchange – individual financial statements

[13] Only 15 bank stocks are traded on Istanbul Stock Exchange (ISE), which is the main source of information for the financial tables. In addition, we accessed verbal statements of each bank that summarize year-end financial information for the relevant year through the ISE web site.
[14] Ratio of total derivatives to total assets increased from 16 percent to nearly 26 percent from 2005 to 2007 (first half), while ratio of risk derivatives to total derivatives declines from 4.9 to 0.7 percent for the same period.

higher total credits to total assets ratio. For example, for the first half of 2007, total credits to total assets ratio is 70 percent for the banks that indicate they use credit derivatives. On the other hand, this ratio, as reported in Table 5.1, is much lower for all banks, and it is around 51.5 percent, on average. In addition, the use of derivatives is the highest among this group. Existence of foreign owners in control is another distinguishing factor. This finding, the lack of widespread use of credit derivatives, is consistent with Minton et al. (2005), Hirtle (2007), and Düllmann and Sosinska (2007), who find that the use of credit derivatives is not widespread among banks.[15]

DATA AND METHODOLOGY

Empirical studies examining the relationship between the macroeconomic factors and the volume of activity in the credit derivatives markets is inconsistent to the best of our knowledge. However, there are studies along these lines such as Pesaran et al. (2006) that propose a model to explain the credit losses contingent on the macroeconomics, which distinguishes between default due to systematic vs. idiosyncratic (or firm-specific) shocks. Their model allows for simulation experiments on the effect of changes in observable macroeconomic dynamics on credit risk. The macroeconomic variables used include gross domestic product (GDP), inflation, the level of short-term interest rates, exchange rates, equity prices (when applicable), and real money balances. Rapid changes in these variables may lead to the default of the firms under credit risk. In a similar study, Pesaran and Schuermann (2003) use macroeconomic indicators of output (GDP), price level (Consumer Price Index [CPI]), nominal money supply, exchange rates, and interest rates as macroeconomic factors to consider that influence the credit risk.

Furthermore, Figlewski et al. (2006) model the effect of macroeconomic factors on corporate default and credit rating transitions. The authors incorporate firm specific factors of credit rating history and classify macroeconomic factors. The first category includes general macroeconomic factors such as long-term interest rate, unemployment rate, inflation, stock market return, and output (economic activity). The second

---

[15] Moreno (2006) reports in Annex Table 6 the answers provided by some emerging economies to questions on credit risk transfer instruments. Out of 18 economies, only five countries report the use of credit derivatives instruments, some in limited quantities. These countries are Phillippines, Singapore, Thailand, Venezuela, and Czech Republic.

category accounts for the direction of the economy and includes real GDP growth, growth in industrial production, and change in unemployment. The third category includes deviation from potential economic activity, capacity utilization, and industrial production deviation from the trend and these factors that represent the measures of economic slack.[16] Finally, the fourth category of factors includes corporate credit spreads and overall default rate for corporate bonds. Patro et al. (2002) use regression analysis to explain foreign exchange exposures driven by macroeconomic variables. The variables used by the authors in their regression are exports to GDP ratio, imports to GDP ratio, CPI inflation rate, government surplus to GDP ratio, tax revenues to GDP ratio, and the change in the logarithm of the country's credit ratings.

Our intention is to mark the macroeconomic factors that have impact on the concentration of sovereign CDSs and to include the basic macroeconomic factors of output and inflation. We use GDP growth to represent output and CPI to represent inflation. Furthermore, we use additional indicators such as the real interest rate, current account balance (as percentage of the GDP), the exchange rate as calculated by local currency per U.S. dollar, volatility of interest rates as calculated by the standard deviation of monthly interest rates within a year, and nonperforming loans as percentage of total gross loans. Moreover, there are two country-specific factors: the credit rating and the use of International Monetary Fund (IMF) credits.

We use regression analysis [Equation (5.1)] to evaluate the impact of the above-mentioned factors to credit derivatives in emerging markets. The model is as follows:

$$\text{CDS}_{it} = + \beta_0 + \beta_1 \text{OUT}_{it} + \beta_2 \text{INF}_{it} + \beta_3 \text{RIR}_{it} + \beta_4 \text{XCH}_{it} + \beta_5 \text{CAB}_{it} \\ + \beta_6 \text{IMF}_{it} + \beta_7 \text{RAT}_{it} + \beta_8 \text{VOLIR}_{it} + \beta_9 \text{NPL}_{it} + \varepsilon_{it} \tag{5.1}$$

where i and t represent individual country and time, respectively. The variables are defined as

CDS = The concentration of quotes on sovereign CDSs
OUT = Output measured by GDP growth
INF = Inflation measured by the CPI

---

[16] This study may suffer from multicollinearity since some economic indicators used in the model can behave similarly

RIR = Real interest rate

XCH = Exchange rate

CAB = Current account balance as percentage of the GDP

IMF = Use of the IMF credit

RAT = Year-end average of Moody's and Standard & Poor's ratings from Credit Trade transactions

VOLIR = Volatility of interest rates calculated using 12 monthly interest rates for the relevant year in a country

NPL = The ratio of nonperforming loans with respect to total gross loans

The CDS and RAT data sets are from the *BIS Quarterly Review*.[17] All the other series are taken from the official web site of the World Bank (Global Development Finance and World Development Indicator databases), except the XCH series is taken from the International Financial Statistics of the IMF. All series are annual and the coverage is from January 2000 to December 2003 for Brazil, Mexico, Japan, Philippines, South Africa, Colombia, China, Korea, Poland, Venezuela, Turkey, Malaysia, Argentina, Thailand, and Russia. Missing observations were replaced by linear interpolation.

ESTIMATION RESULTS

We pooled the panel data for estimation following Patro et al. (2002), who suggested that the use of the panel approach allows pooling data across countries in order to improve estimation efficiency. The estimation results are listed in Table 5.2 for least squares, fixed effects and random effects models.[18] The Lagrange multiplier (LM) test presented at the bottom of Table 5.2, indicates that ordinary least squares (OLS) should be preferred over generalized least squares (GLS). In addition, low values of Hausman χ^2 test statistics suggest that random effects model, not fixed effects model, should be used. However, based on the LM test, the correct specification is given by the OLS, and the Hausman χ^2 test loses its significance.[19]

---

[17] Packer and Suthipongchai (2003).

[18] Results did not change significantly when Japan is excluded from the sample.

[19] The null hypothesis states no correlation; thus low values of the Hausman's χ^2 test suggest statistical preference for a random effects model specification. It suggests that the differences between firms are not just parametric shifts of the regression function, and hence it is more appropriate to view firm-specific constant terms as randomly distributed across firms.

T A B L E   5.2

Estimation Results

Variables	Coefficients for Models		
	Least Squares	Fixed Effects	Random Effects
GDP growth	−29.5184*	−48.4618[†]	−39.1987[†]
	(12.8356)[‡]	(15.8092)	(13.0911)
Inflation	−7.1657	−9.3856	−8.4744
	(5.5559)	(12.0056)	(6.8872)
Real interest rate	2.8509	−8.8076	0.3718
	(5.3306)	(15.3699)	(7.2849)
Current account Deficit (% of GDP)	−30.7059[†]	−25.2731	−29.1020*
	(10.5574)	(30.1798)	(14.6468)
Use of IMF credit[§]	0.0061	0.0049	0.0071
	(.0072)	(.0097)	(.0075)
Rating	−12.8476	−17.9497	−15.7744
	(20.8198)	(56.0607)	(27.7732)
Volatility of interest rates	−726.0432[¶]	−1315.2083	−982.7709*
	(366.5244)	(830.9867)	(476.7392)
Exchange rates	−0.3402*	−0.0453	−0.2420
	(0.1549)	(0.2614)	(0.1868)
Nonperforming loans	−19.6451[†]	−15.1116	−17.0602[¶]
(% of gross loans)	(6.2898)	(21.4104)	(8.9731)
Constant	1193.5879[†]	−	1254.8362[†]
	(233.2861)	−	(296.6352)
Adjusted R^2	0.3553	−	−
Lagrange Multiplier Test	2.67		
Hausman χ^2	3.76		

[†] Represents 1% level of significance.
* Represents 5% level of significance.
[¶] Represents 10% level of significance.
[§] Times 10.$^{-6}$
[‡] Standard errors are presented in parentheses.

Hence, there does not seem to be additional country-specific factors that can be captured neither through fixed effects nor through random effects in the specification.

Based on the results presented under the Least Squares column of Table 5.2, the main economic indicators of output growth and current account deficit are significant. In addition, volatility of interest rates, ratio of nonperforming loans and exchange rates are significant at the 10 percent level. It is striking to see that ratings do not have any significance in explaining the number of CDS quotes on sovereign CDS, which may be caused by the shift towards below investment grade CDS contracts due to low default environment.[20]However, even if we consider the crisis period only to replicate the analysis,[21] ratings do not appear to be a significant determinant for the number of sovereign CDS quotes. Thus, the level of ratings does not seem to be a factor for the protection seller in the sovereign CDS market.

As expected, the current account deficit has a negative effect on the number of quotes. A higher current account deficit implies that the likelihood of observing a crisis in the near future increases and hence creates a risk for protection seller. A negative coefficient on interest rate volatility can be interpreted similarly. A volatile environment for interest rates indicates an unstable environment in the country, whether the source of volatility is from within or outside the country. In addition, a worsening in the credit quality in an economy, as proxied by a lagging indicator of ratio of nonperforming loans to total gross loans, causes a decline in the number of sovereign CDS quotes. A depreciating currency against the U.S. dollar, by creating an imbalance in trade, leads to a decline in the number of quotes as it also signals future problems for the economy. In addition, we find that an increase in economic activity, as represented by GDP growth, leads to a decline in the number of quotes on sovereign CDS. A growing economy suggests low default environment and hence lower need for credit protection.

CONCLUSION

After a brief overview of the credit derivatives market in general and a close look at Turkey, we examine the relationship between macro and country-specific factors on the number of sovereign quotes for some emerging CDS markets for sovereign CDS contracts. The CDS contracts are used to take off the balance sheet the credit risk associated with a lending portfolio. Hence, macroeconomic factors, by influencing

---

[20] See Başçı (2006) and Fitch report on CDx market.
[21] Years 2000 and 2001 are identified as the crisis period due to the global economic downturn and September 11. Results are not reported as it was not significantly different.

the probability of observing credit events, should have an impact on the number of quotes.

Our results indicate that economic activity, current account deficit, exchange rates, volatility of interest rates, and ratio of nonperforming loans to total gross loans are important determinants. Surprisingly, ratings of the countries do not appear to be significant in determining the number of quotes in a sovereign CDS market. This can be attributed to the positive attitude for credit risk due to low default environment especially after 2001.

The findings of this study can be improved by using more recent and detailed data on sovereign CDSs. However, given the narrow and concentrated market for credit derivatives, it is not easy to overcome this data problem in the near future.

REFERENCES

Başçı, E. (2006) Credit Growth in Turkey: Drivers and Challenges. *BIS Papers*, No 28: 363–375.

Batten, J. and Hogan, W. (2002) A Perspective on Credit Derivatives. *International Review of Financial Analysis*, 11(3): 251–278.

British Bankers Association (2006) *BBA Credit Derivatives Report*.

Banking Regulation and Supervision Agency (2007), *Monthly Bulletin*, No. 28.

Bank for International Settlement (2007) *OTC Derivatives Market Activity in the Second Half of 2006*. Monetary and Economic Department.

Broll, U., Pausch, T., and Welzel, P. (2002) Credit Risk and Credit Derivatives in Banking. Universitaet Augsbur, *Institute for Economics, Discussion Paper Series*, No. 228.

Carr, P. and Wu, L. (2007) Theory and Evidence on the Dynamic Interactions between Sovereign Credit Default Swap and Currency Options. *Journal of Banking and Finance*, 31(8): 2383–2403.

Duffee, G.R. and Zhou, C. (2001) Credit Derivatives in Banking: Useful Tools for Managing Risks? *Journal of Monetary Economics*, 48(1): 25–54.

Düllman, K. and Sosinska, A. (2007) Credit Default Swap Prices as Risk Indicators of Listed German Banks. *Financial Markets Portfolio Management*, 21(3): 269–292.

Figlewski, S., Frydman, H. and H. Liang, W. (2006) Modeling the Effect of Macroeconomic Factors on Corporate Default and Credit Rating Transitions. *NYU Stern Finance Working Paper*, No. FIN–06–007.

Fitch Ratings (2007) *CDx Survey: Market Volumes Continue Growing While New Concerns Emerge* (www.fitchratings.com).

Hirtle, B. (2007) Credit Derivatives and Bank Credit Supply. *Federal Reserve Bank of New York Staff Reports*, No. 276: 1–36.

Instefjord, N. (2005) Risk and Hedging: Do Credit Derivatives Increase Bank Risk? *Journal of Banking and Finance*, 29(2): 333–345.

Kothari, V. (2002) Introduction to Credit Derivatives. *Credit Derivatives and Synthetic Securitization,* www.credit-deriv.com.

Minton, B.A., Stulz, R., and Williamson, R. (2005) How Much Do Banks Use Credit Derivatives to Reduce Risk? *NBER Working Paper Series*, 11579:1–39.

Moreno, R. (2006) The Changing Nature of Risks Facing Banks. *BIS Papers*, No 28: 67–98.

Packer, F. and Suthiphongchai, C. (2003) Sovereign Credit Default Swaps. *BIS Quarterly Review*, December: 79–88.

Patro, D. K., Wald, J.K., and Wu, Y. (2002) Explaining Exchange Rate Risk in World Stock Markets: A Panel Approach. *Journal of Banking and Finance*, 26(10): 1951–1972.

Pesaran, M.H. and Schuermann, T. (2003) Credit Risk and Macroeconomic Dynamics. *Medium Econometrische Toepassingen*, 11(1): 27–32.

Pesaran, M.H., Schuermann, T., Treutler, B-J., and Weiner, S. M. (2006) Macroeconomic Dynamics and Credit Risk: A Global Perspective. *Journal of Money Credit and Banking*, 38(5): 1211–1262.

Ranciere, R.G. (2001) Credit Derivatives in Emerging Markets. *IMF Policy Discussion Paper*, September 2001.

Skinner, F.S. and Nuri, J. (2007) Hedging Emerging Market Bond and
    the Rise of the Credit Default Swap. *International Review of
    Financial Analysis*, doi:10.1016/j.irfa.2007.06.004 (in press).

Skinner, F.S. and Townend, T.G. (2002) An Empirical Analysis of Credit
    Default Swaps. *International Review of Financial Analysis*, 11(3):
    297–309.

PART TWO

Pricing Credit Default Swaps

CHAPTER 6

Pricing Credit Derivatives with a Copula-Based Actuarial Model for Credit Risk

Giovanni Masala, Massimiliano Menzietti, and Marco Micocci

ABSTRACT

In this chapter we present a model for the valuation of some multiname credit derivatives. Pricing methods use standard techniques of risk-neutral valuation, while the risk of the underlying credit portfolio uses both traditional tools of credit risk valuations of actuarial kind and more recent ones like copula functions for modeling the dependence structure between the debtors [see, for example, Masala et al. (2004)]. Several numerical applications conclude the chapter.

INTRODUCTION

Credit derivatives are financial contracts whose payoff is contingent on the creditworthiness of some counterparty. As pointed out in Mashal and Naldi (2002) and Meneguzzo and Vecchiato (2002), they have become the main tool for transferring and hedging credit risk in recent years. The most complicated of such instruments are the multiname credit derivatives. These instruments are not quoted since market prices are not available. Furthermore, we do not possess closed forms for their pricing and must use Monte Carlo simulation procedures to correctly model multiple defaults.

A dependence structure using copula methods was first set up by Li (2000). In his paper, the author considers time-until-default for each debtor and models their dependence structure through a Student's t copula, while other studies consider a copula dependence structure [Cherubini and Luciano (2002), Cherubini (2004), Galiani (2003), and Gregory and Laurent (2002)]. Li describes a default for a single debtor through the so-called survival function $S(t) = \Pr\{T > t\}$, which represents the probability that this counterpart attains age t and T is the time-until-default. In addition, the survival function is linked to the hazard rate function $h(t)$ in the following way:

$$S(t) = e^{-\int_0^t h(u)\,du}$$

Li (2000) also assumes that the hazard rate function is constant; $h(t) = h$ implying that the survival time is exponentially distributed with constant parameter h. Other features of this model are the following: Credit migrations at the end of the time horizon are not taken into account and recovery rates in default situations are assumed deterministic. This model has been used by Mashal and Naldi (2002) with the intent on pricing particular multiname credit derivatives such as nth-to-default baskets. Additionally, their model is a hybrid of the well-known structural and reduced form approach for modeling defaults.

After simulating a large number of multivariate times-until-default, one deduces a payoff for our derivative. Finally, the pricing is estimated using standard risk-neutral pricing technology (by assuming complete markets and a no-arbitrage hypothesis). The credit risk model for the underlying portfolio developed in Masala et al. (2004) follows a general credit risk framework: Hazard rates are random variables whose values follow gamma distributions coherently with Credit Risk Plus (Credit Suisse, 1997), Micocci (2000), Bürgisser et al. (2001), and Menzietti (2002). Recovery rates themselves are supposed to be stochastic as in Gupton et al. (1997), and following a Beta distribution, moreover, credit migrations are allowed. This feature becomes very important when we treat credit derivatives whose payoff depends on credit spread.

The chapter is structured as follows: The next section presents the model for default and credit migration; the section is divided in subsections dealing with the problems of time-until-default, the hazard rate function, recovery rates, credit migration, exposure valuation, and loss distribution. The final two sections introduce a basket of credit derivatives with numerical applications and conclude the chapter.

THE MODEL FOR DEFAULT AND CREDIT MIGRATION

Time until Default

We address the risk of default using different methods, which is modeled in all the approaches to credit risk. In our model, following Li (2000), Mashal and Naldi (2002), Meneguzzo and Vecchiato (2002), we define a new random variable; the survival time from now to the time of default or the time-until-default for an exposure. Time-until-default can be modeled as the survival time in life insurance.[1] We denote this random variable as T_0, and we assume several properties: It must take only positive values; it is continuous and has a density function $f_0(t)$ we assume is continuous. We denote as $F_0(t)$ its distribution function:

$$F_0(t) = \Pr\{T_0 \le t\} = \int_0^t f_0(u)\,du \text{ with } F_0(0) = 0 \text{ and } F_0(\infty) = 1.$$

The exposure survival function $S(t)$ gives the probability that the exposure survives for t years and can be expressed through the hazard rate function $h(t)$ as

$$S(t) = e^{-\int_0^t h(u)\,du}.$$

If τ is the time horizon and $h(t) = h$ for $t \in [0,\tau]$, then we have $f_0(t) = h \cdot e^{-h \cdot t}$ and the time-until-default follows an exponential distribution with parameter h. Assuming constancy, the hazard rate can be estimated from the one-year default probability (or for a different time horizon) as follows:

---

[1] See Pitacco (2000).

$$ {}_s q_t = 1 - e^{-h \cdot s} \Rightarrow h = -\frac{ln\left(1 - {}_s q_t\right)}{s} \tag{6.1} $$

$$ q_t = 1 - e^{-h} \Rightarrow h = -ln\left(1 - q_t\right). \tag{6.1a} $$

The Hazard Rate Function and the Recovery Rate

The relationship between the distribution function of survival time and the hazard rate function represents the default process by modeling the hazard rate function. Therefore, for our model we require the value of the hazard rate, which can be found in three different ways:

The hazard rate estimation: Using the expression (6.1) or (6.1a) and the default frequency from rating agencies, we can calculate the hazard rate each year.

From market data:[2] In the market price of defaultable bonds, a credit spread curve is implied, and if we assume a deterministic value for the recovery rate, a specific credit spread implies a value for default probability and for the hazard rate.

Within a structural model framework using the Merton option theoretical approach (1974): In this case the default probability equals the probability that the firm's asset value goes under the liabilities value.

Each approach has identical drawbacks and the solution proposed to avoid these difficulties is a copula function approach presented in Li (2000), Schönbucher and Schubert (2001), Frey and McNeil (2002), and Mashal and Naldi (2002). The individual (marginal) survival probabilities of the debtors are taken from an intensity-based approach, and the dependency is obtained with an appropriate copula function. Such a solution is not feasible in case we do not possess market prices of defaultable financial instruments for the same debtor. For this kind of exposure a different solution is to employ the rating agencies default probability for single exposure and to use a copula function for the dependence structure. In this case we can

---

[2] See Jarrow and Turnbull (1995), Das and Tufano (1996), Duffie and Singleton (1997; 1999), Jarrow et al. (1997), Lando (1998), and Hull and White (2000).

model the heterogeneity of default frequencies between debtors of the same rating class, assuming that the default probability is not deterministic but stochastic.

In our model we assume the hazard rate for a debtor in a given rating class is constant each year but the value is not the expectation of historical default frequencies for its class but a random variable following a gamma distribution with two parameters α and β and a density function $u(h_i)$.[3] The gamma distribution choice is typical in an insurance framework where its parameters α_k, β_k are typical for each rating class k (estimated with maximum likelihood or moments method).

The hazard rate mean and variance for debtor i are equal to

$$E(H_i) \equiv \bar{H}_i = \frac{\alpha_k}{\beta_k} = \mu_k \qquad \text{var}(H_i) = \frac{\alpha_k}{\beta_k^2} = \sigma_k^2$$

Thus the time-until-default for debtor i, $T_0^{(i)}$, conditional on a value h_i for hazard rate, is exponentially distributed with parameter h_i:

$$f_0^{(i)}(t)\Big|_{h_i} = h_i \cdot e^{-h_i \cdot t}.$$

The default will occur if $T_0^{(i)} < \tau$ with τ time horizon for the evaluation; therefore, the probability of default for debtor i, conditional on a value h_i is

$$p_{Di}\Big|_{h_i} = \Pr\left\{T_0^{(i)} < \tau \Big|_{h_i}\right\} = 1 - e^{-h_i \cdot \tau}.$$

In case of default we assume the immediate recovery of the exposure with a random rate R_i on exposure face value, associated to debtor i. The exposure value V_i after default should be

$$V_i\Big|_{T_0^{(i)} < \tau, R_i = r_i} = N_i \cdot r_i$$

where N_i is the face value of the exposure.

---

[3] The assumption that the hazard rate is a random variable explains the risk heterogeneity of default frequency for rating classes published by rating agencies. However, it can be used if we adopt a hazard rate structure inferred from market data to introduce random noise. Indeed, even in reduced-form models, the hypothesis of a constant hazard rate for a time horizon of one year or more is not realistic.

In terms of representing the recovery rate uncertainty we assume [as Gupton et al. (1997) using CreditMetrics] that it follows a beta distribution and choose the parameters such that R_i stays within the bounds of 0 to 1, which is coherent with the recovery rate. In order to have random values within the required bounds, we set $v = 1$. If the expectation and variance of recovery rate distribution are known, the parameters p and q can be estimated with the moments method. The random recovery rate and recovery risk are important features of the model (1) because only a few models introduce such a risk aspect and (2) because of the possible introduction of correlation between recovery rates of different counterparts.

The Credit Migration and the Exposure Valuation

The main feature of our proposal is the inception of credit migration in the framework of an intensity-based model with a copula function dependence structure. We assume that in t_0 the debtor is in the k th rating class and that at each time horizon the debtor could end in $K + 1$ different states—in default or in a survival case in one of the K rating classes. If the arrival class is better (worse) than k, then we obtain an upgrading (downgrading). Obviously, it is possible that the class is identical to the original one with the final rating class influencing the exposure value.

To model credit migration, we assume that information on credit quality could be inferred from time-until-default: A high value implies that the default is not likely and the debtor is in a "good" rating class; however, a low value implies the default is near and the debtor should be ranked in a "bad" rating class. The time-until-default model follows an exponential distribution, and the value it assumes is used to evaluate whether the default is incurred. Subsequently, if the exposure survives the same value could be used to estimate migrations. In other words, we represent default process and credit migration with the same marginal distribution for time-until-default.

We obtain this result fixing K bounds over the time-until-default distribution.[4] If $T_0^{(i)}$ assumes a value within 0 and the first bound (which is equal to time horizon τ), the debtor defaults. If $T_0^{(i)}$ assumes a value within

---

[4] The idea to model the migrations with bounds on some specific distribution was first proposed by Gupton et al. (1997) in CreditMetrics with bounds on the asset return distribution (normal distribution), whereas in Menzietti (2002) in a CreditRisk+ framework they used bounds on risk factor distribution (gamma distribution).

the first and the second bound, the debtor ends in the "worst" rating class. If $T_0^{(i)}$ value crosses the K th bound, then we place the debtor in the "best" rating class. In order to define the K bounds we need the default probability as well as the probabilities of switching in other rating classes. These probabilities are included in the transition matrices that rating agencies publish, which can be produced even in a KMV–Merton-type model (Kealhofer, 2003a).

We denote with p_{ki} the probability of remaining in class k for counterpart i at the end of the time horizon. This probability depends on the initial rating class, which is the information known for each debtor. We must also find two bounds $S_k^{(i)}$ and $S_{k+1}^{(i)}$ such that the unconditional probability that $T_0^{(i)}$ assumes a value within the bounds is p_{ki}. The density probability function $\delta(t)$ of time-until-default T is $\delta(t) = \alpha \beta^\alpha / (\beta + t)^{\alpha + 1}$ (see Masala et al. 2004).

Elementary calculus yields the following:

$$
s_1 = \left(\frac{1 - p_D}{\beta^\alpha} \right)^{-1/\alpha} - \beta
$$

and

$$
s_{k+1} = \left(\frac{-p_k + \beta^\alpha (\beta + s_k)^{-\alpha}}{\beta^\alpha} \right)^{-1/\alpha} - \beta \tag{6.2}
$$

hence the bounds can be determined recursively.

The Loss Distribution

The exposure valuation at time t is obtained as present value of cash flows [the same solution is adopted in CreditMetrics by Gupton et al. (1997)]. We assume that the spot and forward zero curves for each rating class are known. Furthermore, we presuppose one-year time horizons ($t_0 = 0$; $t_1 = 1$); if the exposure survives, then its value depends on forward rate term structure, cash flows, and the arrival state χ, while if default occurs, then the exposure value will be

$$
V_{i,1} \Big|_{T_0^{(i)} < \tau, R_i = r_i} = N_i r_i.
$$

Let us denote with $\mathbf{y} \in R^m$ the random vector representing uncertainties that can affect the value (such as the hazard rate, ratings, and the recovery rate). We also presume that the distribution of $\mathbf{y}$ in R^m has density $p(\mathbf{y})$. Thereafter, we find the value of the exposure conditional to $\mathbf{y}$, $V_i(\mathbf{y})$, and it is possible to calculate the loss (or gain):

$$L_i(\mathbf{y}) = V_i(\mathbf{y}^*) - V_i(\mathbf{y})$$

with $V_i(\mathbf{y}^*)$ being the exposure value if the credit characteristics (i.e., the rating) do not change.

We now examine a model for a portfolio of n exposures. In this case each scenario $\mathbf{y}$ is obtained from n gamma distributions for the hazard rate (with specific characteristics for each rating class), then from a random vector of n time-until-default (with marginal exponentially distributed) we evaluate the single exposures and calculate portfolio value and consequent loss for the specific scenario. We denote with $\mathbf{x} = (x_1, \ldots, x_i, \ldots, x_n)^{\mathbf{T}}$ the vector of the quotas held for each exposure (it belongs to the set of available portfolios $X \subset R^n$), with $\mathbf{L}(\mathbf{y}) = (L_1(\mathbf{y}), \ldots, L_i(\mathbf{y}), \ldots, L_n(\mathbf{y}))$ the vector of the loss functions for single debtors, and we assume that in $t_0, x_i = 1$ $(i = 1, \ldots, n)$. The loss function will be

$$L(\mathbf{x},\mathbf{y}) = \sum_{i=1}^{n} L_i(\mathbf{y}) \cdot x_i = \mathbf{L}(\mathbf{y}) \cdot \mathbf{x} \qquad (6.3)$$

The implication for a portfolio of n debtors is that we must generate scenarios for time-until-default from a multivariate distribution function.[5] Therefore, we have the following Equation (6.4):

$$F_0(t_1, \ldots, t_i, \ldots, t_n) = \Pr\left\{ T_0^{(1)} \le t_1, \ldots, T_0^{(i)} \le t_i, \ldots, T_0^{(n)} \le t_n \right\} \qquad (6.4)$$

Copula functions are useful for generating scenarios from this type of multivariate distribution. In addition, numerous models use a copula function approach to represent the dependence structure of a credit portfolio. We anticipate that the copulas we use capture two features of the

---

[5] The hazard rates are generated from n independent gamma marginal distributions, because they express risk heterogeneity in each rating class for which we assume no reciprocal influence.

dependence relationship in the joint distribution: the correlation level and tail dependence.

A number of specifications are required for correlation levels. For example, if we have two debtors A and B, the individual default probability in a fixed time horizon (respectively, P_{DA}, P_{DB}) and the joint default probability $P_{DA,DB}$ in the same time horizon, then the linear default correlation coefficient is by definition (Lucas, 1995)

$$^{(D)}\rho_{A,B} = \frac{P_{DA,DB} - P_{DA} \cdot P_{DB}}{\sqrt{P_{DA} \cdot \left(1 - P_{DA}\right) \cdot P_{DB} \cdot \left(1 - P_{DB}\right)}}$$

However, if there are more than two debtors, we can construct a correlation matrix A whose elements a_{ij} are the linear default correlation between debtors i and j.[6]

KMV–Merton-type models and CreditMetrics link the default correlation between each pair of debtors with the correlation of debtors' asset returns $^{(R)}\rho_{A,B}$ (included in the correlation matrix R) (Gupton et al. 1997; Kealhofer, 2003a; ibid., 2003b). Li (2000) proposes a more general definition of correlation, the survival time correlation, which can be calculated as follows:

$$^{(T)}\rho_{A,B} = \frac{\mathrm{Cov}\left(T_0^{(A)}, T_0^{(B)}\right)}{\sqrt{\mathrm{Var}\left(T_0^{(A)}\right) \cdot \mathrm{Var}\left(T_0^{(B)}\right)}} = \frac{E\left(T_0^{(A)} \cdot T_0^{(B)}\right) - E\left(T_0^{(A)}\right) \cdot E\left(T_0^{(B)}\right)}{\sqrt{\mathrm{Var}\left(T_0^{(A)}\right) \cdot \mathrm{Var}\left(T_0^{(B)}\right)}}.$$

Li demonstrates that if we use this concept of correlation and a bivariate normal copula function for the dependence structure, then the correlation parameter $^{(T)}\rho_{A,B}$ is equal to the asset correlation between the two debtors $^{(R)}\rho_{A,B}$. This result has been extended to t-copulas by Mashal and Naldi (2002) and Meneguzzo and Vecchiato (2002).

In our applications, we use Student's t copula with different degrees of freedom (we can modify the probability of extreme events). For

---

[6] In the case of two debtors, we can reach the probabilities of all elementary events by using the linear correlation coefficient. If we had more than two debtors, this would not be possible. With n debtors we have 2^n joint default events and only $n(n-1)/2$ correlations plus n individual default probabilities and the constraint that these probabilities must sum up to 1. Therefore, the correlation matrix produces the bivariate marginal distribution but not the full distribution (Schönbucher, 2003).

standard definitions of copulas, see Nelsen (1998), while algorithms for generating pseudo-casual numbers from a Student's t copula can be found in Meneguzzo and Vecchiato (2002). The copula-based algorithm evaluates the loss distribution of our credit portfolio, which is linked to the modeling of the multivariate distribution function (6.4).

The main steps are as follows:

• First, we must determine the marginal distributions, namely, time-until-default distribution for each debtor. As pointed out, marginal distributions are exponential distributions whose parameter is a random number extracted from a gamma distribution.

• Second, we generate pseudo random $n$tuples from a Student's t copula. Each random $n$tuples represents a simulated time-until-default for each debtor.

• Third, for each simulation and for each debtor, we examine the simulated time-until-default.

• If it is less than 1, we conclude that this debtor has defaulted. In this case, we extract a random recovery rate from a beta distribution (whose characteristics have been previously revealed). We then determine the value of this credit at the end of our time horizon;

• Otherwise, no default has occurred. The simulated value is compared with migration bounds so that we can determine the new rating class. We then evaluate the value of this credit at the end of our time horizon.

• Fourth, for each simulation, we calculate the portfolio value at the end of the time horizon by summing the values of each credit.

• Finally, we deduce the portfolio loss for each simulation.

In the next section we present an example of the method previously described with a credit portfolio of 10 debtors applied to credit derivatives pricing.

CREDIT DERIVATIVES

Underlying Basket Description

In this section we apply the model presented in the previous sections to a portfolio of 10 exposures ($n = 10$). We assume that for each exposure we know the (1) rating using the Standard & Poor's scale,[7] (2) the face value, (3) the coupon rate, and (4) the time to maturity. The value in t_0 is calculated using the term structure of spot rate in Table 6.1. The exposure characteristics are reported in Table 6.2 with all amounts expressed in euros.

The portfolio value in t_0 is 40,873,635 euros with a face value of 37,500,000 euros. The time horizon is five years (more precisely 5 one-year

T A B L E   6.1

Term structure of spot rates

Rating class	Spot Rates							
	$\delta(0,1)$	$\delta(0,2)$	$\delta(0,3)$	$\delta(0,4)$	$\delta(0,5)$	$\delta(0,6)$	$\delta(0,7)$	$\delta(0,8)$
AAA	2.96%	3.25%	3.71%	4.21%	4.59%	4.65%	4.70%	4.74%
AA	3.00%	3.29%	3.76%	4.25%	4.63%	4.70%	4.75%	4.79%
A	3.06%	3.36%	3.84%	4.37%	4.76%	4.83%	4.88%	4.92%
BBB	3.54%	3.78%	4.22%	4.72%	5.09%	5.15%	5.20%	5.23%
BB	4.88%	5.14%	5.52%	6.14%	6.59%	6.66%	6.71%	6.75%
B	5.35%	5.61%	6.31%	7.13%	7.61%	7.71%	7.77%	7.82%
CCC	14.15%	14.08%	14.05%	13.38%	12.97%	12.93%	12.89%	12.86%

T A B L E   6.2

Exposure characteristics

Debtor	Rating	Face Value	Coupon rate	Maturity	$V_0(i)$
1	AAA	7,000,000	6.75%	7	7,679,930
2	AA	3,000,000	8.25%	5	3,432,805
3	A	3,000,000	7.25%	6	3,259,974
4	BBB	2,500,000	9.00%	5	2,846,401
5	BB	2,000,000	9.25%	6	2,135,505
6	B	3,000,000	13.00%	5	3,319,387
7	CCC	2,000,000	13.75%	5	2,068,537
8	AA	5,000,000	10.75%	8	6,726,162
9	BB	6,000,000	6.75%	5	5,785,908
10	B	4,000,000	7.75%	5	3,619,026

---

[7] The basic rating scale of Standard & Poor's has seven rating classes decreasing from AAA to CCC.

subperiods). The term structure of forward rates used for exposure valuation in t_1, t_2, t_3, t_4, t_5 is extrapolated from the term structure of spot rate (we do not present them for sake of brevity). The expected value in t_5 is 53,165,091 euros. The recovery rates are extrapolated from a beta distribution with $p = 1.4612$ and $q = 1.3966$; these values ensure a recovery rate expectation equal to 0.5113 and a standard deviation equal to 0.2545.[8] Obviously, is it possible to assume that each exposure has different beta distributions. For simplicity we assume here the same distribution for each one. The previous data for rates and recoveries allow us to calculate the single exposure values conditional on rating state in t_i. If default occurs, then we calculate the expected value. Numerical values are not reported for sake of brevity.

The expected hazard rates are extrapolated from one-year default probabilities included in a S&P-style transition matrix. Such a matrix is used also for migration probabilities over one year. Despite the criticisms on rating agencies transition matrices, we use these data from rating agencies for the following reasons:

1. We assume that market data are not complete.
2. It is very difficult to use market data to find implicit migration frequency; so in the reduced form approach it is difficult to implement a multinomial[9] model for credit risk.[10]
3. In the context of the Merton-type model it is possible to model the credit migration but with the hypothesis of a normal copula dependence structure.
4. We model the heterogeneity of default frequency between debtors of the same rating classes assuming that the default probability is not deterministic but stochastic.

Conversely, it is possible to use default probabilities inferred from intensity-based models; however, in this case the transition matrix should be specially constructed—a possible direction for future model implementation. For the transition matrix M we use the expected hazard rates displayed in Table 6.3. We made the identical settlement to the original S&P matrix to guarantee various coherence features.[11]

---

[8] These values are reported by Carty and Lieberman (1996) for a senior unsecured bond.
[9] The multinomial model is the model that includes rating migrations, and the binomial model is the model with only default risk.
[10] See Jarrow et al. (1997) and Bielecki and Rutkowski (2003) for examples of intensity-based multinomial models.
[11] For more details see Gupton et al. (1997) and Gordy (2000).

T A B L E   6.3

Transition matrix and hazard rates

| Initial rating | Rating at Year End | | | | | | | | |
	AAA	AA	A	BBB	BB	B	CCC	Default	$E(h_i)$
AAA	0.9067	0.0833	0.0068	0.0016	0.0012	0.0002	0.0001	0.0001	0.0001
AA	0.0070	0.9055	0.0779	0.0064	0.0016	0.0012	0.0002	0.0002	0.0002
A	0.0019	0.0227	0.9092	0.0552	0.0074	0.0026	0.0004	0.0006	0.0006
BBB	0.0005	0.0033	0.0595	0.8690	0.0530	0.0117	0.0012	0.0018	0.0018
BB	0.0003	0.0014	0.0067	0.0773	0.8053	0.0884	0.0100	0.0106	0.0107
B	0.0002	0.0011	0.0024	0.0043	0.0648	0.8345	0.0407	0.0520	0.0534
CCC	0.0001	0.0002	0.0022	0.0130	0.0238	0.1124	0.6504	0.1979	0.2205

In order to simulate hazard rate values, we use gamma parameters with a method of moments. The standard deviation for each rating class is assumed to be equal to a quota of expected values with different quotas for each class. The value of such quotas is coherent with the statistical analysis of Gordy (2000); however, the trend from one class to the next has been somewhat smoothed to have a more regular shape. The expectation, standard deviation, and parameters for the hazard rate of each rating class are reported in Table 6.4.

The bounds that determine state transitions have been calculated using expression (6.3) with the probabilities included in the transition

T A B L E   6.4

Hazard rate data

Rating	μ_k	σ_k	α_k	β_k	σ_k/μ_k
AAA	0.0001	0.00014	0.51020	5101.79	1.40
AA	0.0002	0.00026	0.59172	2958.28	1.30
A	0.0006	0.00072	0.69444	1157.06	1.20
BBB	0.0018	0.00180	1.00000	555.06	1.00
BB	0.0107	0.00853	1.56250	146.62	0.80
B	0.0534	0.03204	2.77778	52.02	0.60
CCC	0.2205	0.11026	4.00000	18.14	0.50

matrix M and the vector of expected hazard rates for each rating class $\bar{1} = (\mu_1, \ldots, \mu_7)$.

Finally, we require data regarding the correlation between each pair of exposures. We reiterate that the linear correlation between the time-until-default of two different debtors is equal to the linear correlation between the asset return of the two counterparts.[12] This information is usually not easy to extrapolate; therefore, the solution that has been proposed in the literature[13] is to use the linear correlation between the equity of each debtor as a proxy variable. The correlation matrix R is specified in Table 6.5.

Some Multiname Credit Derivatives

Put Option on Basket Portfolio

As a first application we consider a put option with strike price K and multiperiodal time horizon (five years, $T = 5$). The portfolio value at time T is indicated by V (estimated with the procedure explained in the previous section). The payoff is then simply

T A B L E   6.5

Correlation matrix between debtors

	1	2	3	4	5	6	7	8	9	10
1	1.00	0.45	0.45	0.45	0.15	0.15	0.15	0.15	0.15	0.10
2	0.45	1.00	0.45	0.45	0.15	0.15	0.15	0.15	0.15	0.10
3	0.45	0.45	1.00	0.45	0.15	0.15	0.15	0.15	0.15	0.10
4	0.45	0.45	0.45	1.00	0.15	0.15	0.15	0.15	0.15	0.10
5	0.15	0.15	0.15	0.15	1.00	0.35	0.35	0.35	0.35	0.20
6	0.15	0.15	0.15	0.15	0.35	1.00	0.35	0.35	0.35	0.20
7	0.15	0.15	0.15	0.15	0.35	0.35	1.00	0.35	0.35	0.20
8	0.15	0.15	0.15	0.15	0.35	0.35	0.35	1.00	0.35	0.20
9	0.15	0.15	0.15	0.15	0.35	0.35	0.35	0.35	1.00	0.20
10	0.10	0.10	0.10	0.10	0.20	0.20	0.20	0.20	0.20	1.00

---

[12] See the section The Model for Default and Credit Migration and Li (2000).
[13] Merton (1974) has a standard solution, adopted from the CreditMetrics model [see Gupton et al. (1997)] and from the KMV model (see Kealhofer, 2003a, 2003b).

$$P = \text{Max}\left(K - V; 0\right)$$

The pricing of the option is performed using standard risk-neutral pricing technology (complete markets framework). This implies that the value of the option is the expected discounted payoffs (under the risk-neutral measure F). The general formula is the following:

$$S = E^F\left[e^{-\int_0^T r(s)\,ds}\, P\right] \tag{6.5}$$

where $r(s)$ represents the risk-free spot curve. As no closed forms are available, we perform a Monte Carlo simulation by simulating N portfolio values at time T (we take here $N = 10{,}000$). In numerical applications, we consider different values of strike prices. At first, we use different degrees of freedom ($d = 3$ and $d = 10$) and obtain the results displayed in tabular format in Table 6.6 as well as in a graphical format in Figure 6.1.

T A B L E   6.6

Put value for different strike prices and different tail fatness

Strike	$d = 3$	$d = 10$
45,000,000	48,603	18,496
46,000,000	74,615	34,761
47,000,000	112,968	62,042
48,000,000	165,540	105,574
49,000,000	245,245	172,052
50,000,000	363,940	266,961
51,000,000	527,868	405,349
52,000,000	753,941	618,124
53,000,000	1,058,635	911,070
54,000,000	1,476,008	1,336,967
55,000,000	2,046,773	1,919,774

and graphically:

F I G U R E   6.1

Put value for different strike prices and different tail fatness

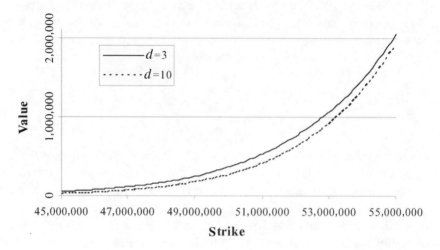

We observe in Table 6.6 that the price obtained with fat tails ($d = 3$) dominates the price with low tails ($d = 10$). In the first case, extreme credit events have a stronger impact. Nevertheless, the difference reduces as strike price increases. We then examine the sensibility of the migrations, and the results are displayed in Table 6.7 and graphically displayed in Figure 6.2.

T A B L E   6.7

Put value for different strike prices with (or without) migrations

Strike	Migrations	No Migrations
45,000,000	48,603	37,049
46,000,000	74,615	54,993
47,000,000	112,968	85,758
48,000,000	165,540	130,236
49,000,000	245,245	190,831
50,000,000	363,940	284,083
51,000,000	527,868	419,043
52,000,000	753,941	612,745
53,000,000	1,058,635	878,839
54,000,000	1,476,008	1,257,922
55,000,000	2,046,773	1,815,539

F I G U R E   6.2

Put value for different strike prices with (or without) migrations

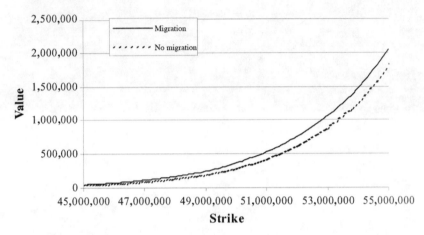

We observe that allowing migrations increases the price of the derivative. We then investigate the situation in the absence of correlation (independence hypothesis). The results are displayed in Table 6.8 and graphically in Figure 6.3.

T A B L E   6.8

Put value for different strike prices with (or without) correlation

Strike	Correlation	Independent
45,000,000	48,603	23,863
46,000,000	74,615	40,870
47,000,000	112,968	67,713
48,000,000	165,540	114,748
49,000,000	245,245	189,698
50,000,000	363,940	294,214
51,000,000	527,868	464,632
52,000,000	753,941	721,107
53,000,000	1,058,635	1,061,336
54,000,000	1,476,008	1,514,079
55,000,000	2,046,773	2,131,606

Put value for different strike prices with (or without) correlation

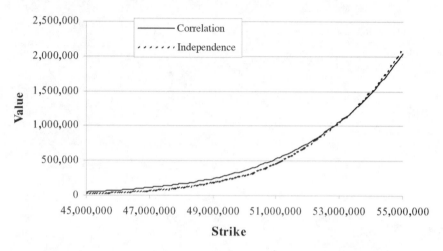

We observe that the price with no correlation dominates the price with correlation only for high values of strike prices. Indeed, a positive correlation between debtors increases the probability of extreme portfolio values.

First-to-Default Option

The first-to-default option is a contract where the protection buyer pays a periodic premium S to the protection seller and the protection seller pays the protected buyer at the time of the first default in the basket the nonrecovered part of the defaulted credit. The contract ends at the predetermined maturity (if no default occurs) or at the time of the first default.

Pricing techniques use standard risk-neutral pricing technology (complete markets framework). We require that the expected discounted payments of premia equal the expected payment of the insurance (under the risk-neutral measure F) [see Mashal and Naldi (2002)]. The general pricing formula requires solving the following equation:

$$E^F\left[\sum_{k=0}^{T} e^{-\int_0^k r(s)\,ds} Sl_{\tau(1)>k} - e^{-\int_0^{\tau(1)} r(s)\,ds} VN\left(1-R_{(1)}\right)\cdot l_{\tau(1)<T}\right]=0 \quad (6.6)$$

where S is the premium, VN is the notional value of the defaulted credit, $R_{(1)}$ is the recovery rate of the defaulted credit, $\tau_{(1)}$ is the first default time, $l_f(x)$ is the counting function, and $r(t)$ is the risk-free rate curve. As no closed pricing forms are available, we set up a Monte Carlo simulation. We obtain the following results with varying degrees of freedom and take into account the independence situation and absence of migrations ($T \le 5$) in Table 6.9.

The premium calculated with 10 degrees of freedom (Table 6.9) dominates the premium calculated with 3 degrees of freedom. Taking into consideration fatter tails (i.e., decreasing degrees of freedom), more extreme joint credit events are allowed; thus the price requested to buy/sell protection decreases. We also observe that migrations influence marginally the price of the derivative. Finally, we perform a correlation sensibility test, and the results are displayed in Table 6.10. We observe that the option value is decreasing with respect to the correlation.

T A B L E   6.9

Premium for different first-to-default options

	$T = 1$	$T = 2$	$T = 3$	$T = 4$	$T = 5$
$d = 3$	303,905	425,285	471,865	499,392	520,299
$d = 10$	363,637	450,977	497,057	524,083	543,412
$d = 3$ (independent)	366,643	487,030	539,862	565,302	583,465
$d = 3$ (no migration)	306,871	413,301	466,865	496,577	511,019
$d = 3$ (independent, no migration)	328,036	447,610	502,066	530,991	548,894

T A B L E   6.10[14]

Premium correlation sensibility

Correlation	Premium
0%	327,285
10%	312,988
20%	302,665
30%	273,896
40%	256,005
50%	218,718

---

[14] We consider $T = 1$, and we assume the same correlation between each pair of debtors.

We can explain this property by simple no-arbitrage argument. If the correlation between the debtors is null (assuming a flat term structure for CD premia), it is possible to perfectly hedge a short position on a first-to-default contract by holding a long position on each credit reference of the basket. Upon default, the payment required on the first-to-default contract will be compensated by the positive cash flow on the corresponding single counterpart. In addition, with no correlation, the default of one debtor will not influence the credit spreads of the other credits in the portfolio. Conversely, the higher the correlation, the higher the probability of multiple defaults and, hence, the lower the degree of protection (thus the premium required lowers). Moreover, we observe that the mean first-to-default time is increasing with respect to correlation and graphically obtain Figure 6.4. Thus, the discounted payoff decreases with respect to correlation.

Collateralized Debt Obligation (CDO)

As Sanchez (2004) states, "This kind of product consists in a tranche structure on a portfolio of credit default names. The protection seller promises to cover the range of collateral losses defined by a particular tranche, and receives periodic premia payments in exchange." Because various structures are possible, we consider a simpler form, "a percentile basket derivatives." The protection seller will compensate the protection buyer for the losses registered on certain portfolios of credit names, up to

F I G U R E   6.4

First time until default (TUD)

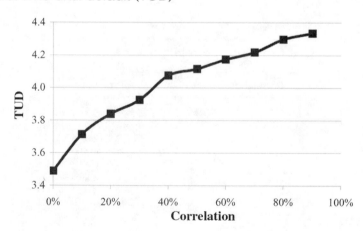

the first α percent. In our application we consider the following payoff at the end of each subperiod j:

$$P_j = \text{Max}\left(L_j - \alpha E(V_j); 0\right) \tag{6.7}$$

where L_j is the simulated loss, $E(V_j)$ is the expected portfolio value, and $\alpha \in (0, 1)$. Pricing results are derived using Monte Carlo simulation. We obtain the following results (Table 6.11) with varying degrees of freedom and by taking into account the independence situation and absence of migrations. We also perform a correlation sensibility test and the results are displayed in Table 6.12.

T A B L E   6.11

Premium for different collateralized debt obligations

α	$d = 3$	$d = 3$ (independent)	$d = 10$	$d = 3$ (no migrations)	$d = 10$ (no migrations)
1%	1,731,820	1,770,030	1,760,100	1,544,160	1,587,780
5%	1,294,740	1,267,740	1,264,440	1,031,960	1,006,820
10%	668,076	606,218	584,084	541,194	497,862

T A B L E   6.12

Premium correlation sensibility[15]

Correlation	Premium
0%	90,684
10%	97,922
20%	113,426
30%	116,243
40%	82,785
50%	73,917

---

[15] We consider $T = 1$, $\alpha = 10$ percent, and we assume the identical correlation between each pair of debtors.

We finally consider the following tranche structure determined by the two bounds Γ and Δ (fraction of the expected loss of the portfolio, as a percentage). Denoting L_j the simulated loss in the scenario j, we define the following payoff:

$$L_j^{\Gamma,\Delta} = \begin{cases} 0 & \text{if } L_j < \Gamma \\ L_j - \Gamma & \text{if } \Gamma < L_j < \Delta \\ \Delta - \Gamma & \text{if } L_j \geq \Delta \end{cases}$$

The seniority of the tranche is defined by the relative location of the thresholds Γ and Δ. If $\Gamma = 0$, the tranche is called an *equity tranche*; if $\Gamma > 0$ and $\Delta < \sum_{i=1}^{N} VN_i$, the tranche is called a *mezzanine tranche*; finally, if $\Delta = \sum_{i=1}^{N} VN_i$, the tranche is called a *senior tranche*.

Using Monte Carlo simulation, pricing assumes that the expected value of discounted payoffs equals the expected value of discounted premia, and we obtain the following results by assuming the different hypotheses in Table 6.13.

CONCLUSION

According to the results, we observe that our pricing model is sensible to correlation, credit migrations, and tail fatness. Credit migrations generally increase derivative values, especially in multiperiod time horizons: small

T A B L E   6.13

Premium for different collateralized debt obligations with tranches structure

Tranche	$d = 3$	$d = 10$	Independent	No Migrations
0%–3%	942,007	923,058	968,028	909,503
3%–6%	446,077	524,316	542,607	439,717
6%–9%	247,310	242,499	258,537	207,065
9%–12%	130,121	131,296	105,179	114,642
12%–15%	69,167	58,987	61,854	50,223
15%–20%	44,536	41,277	32,418	30,940
20%–100%	15,144	20,569	11,355	9,536

impact on first-to-default. Tail fatness lowers first-to-default basket of derivatives value (due to the increasing probability of extreme events). The opposite conclusion is reached in the other two applications. Increasing correlations lowers first-to-default basket derivative value, and independence provides lower results but values do not increase monotonically (a maximum value is attained). Finally, we point out that our model is able to tackle hard-to-price different types of basket credit derivatives.

REFERENCES

Bielecki, T. and Rutkowski, M. (2003) Dependent Default and Credit Migrations. *Applicationes Mathematicae*, 30(2): 121–145.

Bürgisser, P., Kurth, A., and Wagner, A. (2001) Incorporating Severity Variations into Credit Risk. *Journal of Risk*, 3(4): 5–31.

Cherubini, U. (2004) Pricing Swap Credit Risk with Copulas. EFMA 2004 Basel Meetings Paper. Available at SSRN: http://ssrn.com/abstract=485603.

Cherubini, U. and Luciano, E. (2002) Pricing and Hedging Vulnerable Credit Derivatives with Copulas. EFA 2003 Annual Conference, Paper No. 738. Available at SSRN: http://ssrn.com/abstract=424882.

Credit Suisse (1997) Credit Risk+. A Credit Risk Management Framework. Technical document, New York City, NY.

Frey, R. and McNeil, A. (2002) VaR and Expected Shortfall in Portfolios of Dependent Credit Risks: Conceptual and Practical Insights. *Journal of Banking and Finance*, 26(2–3): 1317–1344.

Galiani, S. (2003) Copula Functions and Their Application in Pricing and Risk Managing Multiname Credit Derivative Products. Master Thesis, Kings College, London.

Gordy, M.B. (2000) A Comparative Anatomy of Credit Risk Models. *Journal of Banking and Finance*, 24(1): 119–149.

Gregory, J. and Laurent, J.-P. (2002) Basket Default Swaps, CDOs, and Factor Copulas. Working paper, ISFA Actuarial School, University of Lyon, Lyon, France.

Gupton, G., Finger, C., and Bhatia, M. (1997) CreditMetrics. Technical document, J.P. Morgan, New York.

Hull, J. and White, A. (2000) Valuing Credit Default Swaps I: No Counterparty Default Risk. *The Journal of Derivatives,* 8(1): 29–40.

Jarrow, R.A., Lando, D., and Turnbull, S.M. (1997) A Markov Model for the Term Structure of Credit Risk Spreads. *Review of Financial Studies,* 10(2): 481–523.

Kealhofer, S. (2003a) Quantifying Credit Risk I: Default Prediction. *Financial Analysts Journal,* 59(1): 30–44.

Kealhofer, S. (2003b) Quantifying Credit Risk II: Debt Valuation. *Financial Analysts Journal,* 59(3): 78–92.

Lando, D. (1998) On Cox Processes and Credit Risky Securities. *Review of Derivative Research,* 2(2–3): 99–120.

Li, D.X. (2000) On Default Correlation: A Copula Function Approach. *Journal of Fixed Income,* 9(4): 43–54.

Lucas, D.J. (1995) Default Correlation and Credit Analysis. *Journal of Fixed Income,* 5(1): 32–41.

Mashal, R. and Naldi, M. (2002) Pricing Multiname Credit Derivatives: Heavy Tailed Hybrid Approach. Working paper, Columbia Business School, New York.

Masala, G., Menzietti, M., and Micocci, M. (2004) A Copula-Based Actuarial Model for Credit Risk. Deptartment of Economics Science, 137, University of Rome, "LUISS—Guido Carli."

Meneguzzo, D. and Vecchiato, W. (2002) Copula Sensitivity in Collateralised Debt Obligations and Basket Default Swaps Pricing and Risk Monitoring. Working paper, Intesa Bank, Milan, Italy.

Menzietti, M. (2002) Modelli di Portafoglio per la Gestione del Rischio di Credito: Proposta di un Modello Attuariale Generalizzato. PhD thesis on Actuarial Science, University of Rome, "La Sapienza."

Merton, R.C. (1974) On the Pricing of Corporate Debt: The Risk Structure of Interest Rates. *Journal of Finance,* 2(2): 449–470.

Micocci, M. (2000) M.A.R.C.: An Actuarial Model for Credit Risk. XXXI International Astin Colloquium, Rome, Italy.

Nelsen, R.B. (1998) *An Introduction to Copulas*. Lecture Notes in Statistics 139. New York: Springer-Verlag.

Pitacco, E. (2000) Matematica e Tecnica Attuariale delle Assicurazioni sulla Durata di Vita. Trieste, Italy: Lint Editoriale.

Sanchez, L.G. (2004) Pricing Basket of Credit Derivatives and CDO in Factor Models Framework. Master's Thesis, University of Zurich, Switzerland.

Schönbucher, P.J. and Schubert, D. (2001) Copula-Dependent Default Risk in Intensity Models. Working paper, Bonn University, Germany.

CHAPTER 7

Asset Dynamics Estimation and Its Impact on CDS Pricing

Pascal François and Georges Hübner

ABSTRACT

Implementation of a structural model for credit risk requires the estimation of underlying asset dynamics. Three techniques are commonly used for parameter estimation: The system-of-equations approach (Ronn and Verma, 1986), the iterative approach (Vassalou and Xing, 2004), and the maximum likelihood approach (Ericsson and Reneby, 2005). Using an example with real data, we challenge these three techniques (1) for their in-sample estimation of asset value and volatility and (2) for their impact on out-of-sample credit default swap pricing. There is a strong consensus regarding asset value estimation, but the system-of-equations approach yields more unstable volatility estimates in sample. Yet, credit default swap price forecasts based on this method are the most accurate. The level of estimated asset value, independent of the estimation method, affects the pricing error.

INTRODUCTION

This chapter addresses the implementation of a structural model for pricing credit default swaps (CDS). Specifically, we challenge three techniques commonly used for parameter estimation: Ronn and Verma (1986) approach, Vassalou and Xing (2004) iterative method (aka KMV method), and maximum likelihood method. These three methods have in common that they use a time series of stock prices to extract the dynamics of asset value and volatility. The nonlinear relation between equity value and asset value is captured by the Merton model (1974), which works with a crude, yet easy to implement, view of the firm's liabilities.

The pricing model then needs to be adapted when it comes to CDS. In particular, the assumption of default only upon maturity is no longer applicable to a five-year credit derivative with interim (defaultable) payments. A general pricing formula for CDS is derived from the no-arbitrage principle. We present a simple extension of the Merton (1974) model with a constant default barrier that accounts for early default during the life of the contract. We then review the three methods of asset dynamics estimation. Then, we gauge the impact of the estimation method on the out-of-sample pricing of CDS using a simple example on real data.

Credit default swaps are still by far the most actively traded credit derivatives (see Figure 7.1).

F I G U R E   7.1

Credit derivative products

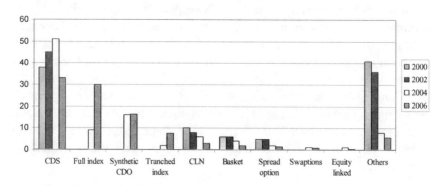

The histograms represent the market share (in percentage) of major credit derivatives.
Source: British Bankers Associations, *Credit Derivatives Report*, 2006.

Credit default swap payoffs

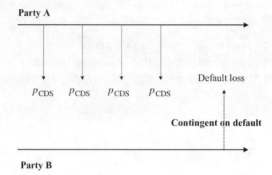

In a CDS agreement, the protection buyer (party A) pays the protection seller (party B) a fixed periodic amount, while B pays A an agreed
amount upon default of the reference obligation. Usually, this amount is
the loss in market value due to default. Figure 7.2 represents the payoffs
typically involved in CDS.

The pricing problem is to set the premium p_{CDS} such that the value of
the swap is nil at contract inception. Typically, most CDS have a three- to
five-year maturity.

NO-ARBITRAGE PRICING OF CDS

This section derives the CDS premium under very general conditions.
Specifically, we only assume that markets are arbitrage free. The value of
the default-free discount bond with face value $1 and maturity t is denoted
by $P(t)$. The reference obligation underlying the CDS has face value F,
maturity T, and pays n coupons c at dates t_i, $i = 1, \ldots, n$ with $t_n = T$. Its
current market price is denoted $\tilde{p}(c, F, T)$. Default of the issuer is the
random date θ.

The absence of arbitrage ensures the existence of an equivalent
probability measure Q under which asset prices discounted at the risk-free
rate are martingales. In other words, the no-arbitrage price of a security g
with promised payment $f(t)$ at date t is

$$g = \mathrm{E}_Q \left[\exp\left(-\int_0^t r_u \, du \right) f(t) \right],$$

where $(r_u)_{u \geq 0}$ stands for the risk-free rate process.

In the absence of arbitrage, the holder of the underlying corporate debt and the CDS replicates a long position in the equivalent riskless bond. That is,

$$\tilde{P}(c,F,T) + \sum_{i=1}^{n} \mathrm{E}_Q \left(\exp\left(-\int_0^{t_i} r_u \, du \right) P_{cds} \, l_{\theta > t_i} \right) = c \sum_{i=1}^{n} P(t_i) + FP(T)$$

where $L_{1 > ti}$ is the indicator function for the event $\theta > t_i$. The CDS premium therefore verifies that

$$P_{cds} = \frac{c \sum_{i=1}^{n} P(t_i) + FP(T) - \tilde{P}(c,F,T)}{\sum_{i=1}^{n} \mathrm{E}_Q \left(\exp\left(-\int_0^{t_i} r_u \, du \right) l_{\theta > t_i} \right)}$$

The denominator can be made more explicit using a change of probability measure. Specifically, let Q_{ti} denote the t_i-forward probability measure.[1] We obtain

$$P_{cds} = \frac{c \sum_{i=1}^{n} P(t_i) + FP(T) - \tilde{P}(c,F,T)}{\sum_{i=1}^{n} P(t_i) Q_{t_i}(\theta > t_i)}$$

In other words, determination of CDS premia requires knowledge of three items:

1. The term structure of risk-free discount bonds $P(t_i)$
2. The value of the underlying $\tilde{P}(c, F, T)$
3. The term structure of default probabilities (under the t_i-forward probability measure) $[Q_{t_i}(\theta > t_i)]$.

---

[1] Under Q_{ti}, forward prices of all securities with delivery date t_i are martingales. For more details on the t-forward probability measure, see Brigo and Mercurio (2001), for instance.

In what follows, we will assume that the term structure of risk-free discount bonds (item 1) is known. Our attention is therefore focused on building a model of credit risk that allows for determining items 2 and 3.

THE STRUCTURAL MODEL OF CREDIT RISK

In this section, we present the structural approach for modeling credit risk, as developed initially by Merton (1974) and currently implemented by KMV-Moody's among others. The variable driving the event of default is the value of the issuer's assets, denoted by V. It is assumed that V follows a lognormal diffusion under the risk-neutral probability measure

$$\frac{dV_t}{V_t} = r\,dt + \sigma\,dW_t$$

where σ is the constant volatility of the returns on the firm's assets, r is the constant risk-free rate, and $(W_t, t \geq 0)$ is a standard Brownian motion accounting for the business risk of the firm.[2]

The issuer will default if the value of its assets falls below K at date T. In other words,[3] $\theta = \inf\{t \geq 0 : V_t = K\}$.

Upon default, it is assumed that creditors will recover a fraction α of the debt nominal. This framework allows for closed-form formulas for credit derivatives and their underlying coupon-bearing bond.

The value for the underlying coupon-bearing bond is given by

$$\tilde{P}(c,F,T) = Fe^{-rT}\left[\Phi(z_1^n) - \left(\frac{K}{V}\right)^{2r/\sigma^2 - 1}\Phi(z_2^n)\right]$$

$$+ \alpha F\left[\left(\frac{K}{V}\right)^{2r/\sigma^2}\Phi(z_3) - \frac{V}{K}\Phi(z_4)\right]$$

$$+ \sum_{i=1}^{n} ce^{-rt_i}\left[\Phi(z_1^i) - \left(\frac{K}{V}\right)^{2r/\sigma^2 - 1}\Phi(z_2^i)\right]$$

---

[2] A structural model for credit risk that prices credit derivatives with stochastic interest rates can be found in François and Hübner (2004).

[3] The assumption of a constant default threshold is consistent with a firm that maintains the same debt level over an infinite horizon. Alternatively, Collin-Dufresne and Goldstein (2001) propose a default threshold that captures a targeted capital structure.

with

$$z_1^i = \frac{1}{\sigma\sqrt{t_i}}\left[\ln\tfrac{V}{K} + (r - \tfrac{\sigma^2}{2})t_i\right] \qquad z_2^i = \frac{1}{\sigma\sqrt{t_i}}\left[\ln\tfrac{K}{V} + (r - \tfrac{\sigma^2}{2})t_i\right]$$

$$z_3 = \frac{1}{\sigma\sqrt{T}}\left[\ln\tfrac{K}{V} + (r + \tfrac{\sigma^2}{2})T\right] \qquad z_4 = \frac{1}{\sigma\sqrt{T}}\left[\ln\tfrac{K}{V} - (r + \tfrac{\sigma^2}{2})T\right]$$

where $\Phi(.)$ stands for the cumulative normal distribution function. Similar results with alternative default barriers are derived in Black and Cox (1976), Longstaff and Schwartz (1995), or Briys and de Varenne (1997), for instance.

When it comes to single-name plain-vanilla CDS written on the company's total debt, the reference obligation corresponds to the company's aggregate debt. Hence, we have that $F = M$ and $c = 0$. Quoted as a spread in basis points, the CDS premium, paid on a quarterly basis and expressed annually, is given by

$$P_{cds} = \frac{e^{-r\frac{n}{4}}\left(\Phi(-z_1^n) + (K/V)^{2r/\sigma^2 - 1}\,\Phi(z_2^n)\right) - \alpha\left((K/V)^{2r/\sigma^2}\,\Phi(z_3) + \frac{V}{K}\Phi(z_4)\right)}{1/40000 \sum_{i=1}^{n} e^{-r\frac{i}{4}}\left(\Phi(z_1^i) - (K/V)^{2r/\sigma^2 - 1}\,\Phi(z_2^i)\right)}, \qquad (7.1)$$

and

$$z_1^i = \frac{1}{\sigma\sqrt{i/4}}\left[\ln\tfrac{V}{K} + (r - \tfrac{\sigma^2}{2})\tfrac{i}{4}\right] \qquad z_2^i = \frac{1}{\sigma\sqrt{i/4}}\left[\ln\tfrac{K}{V} + (r - \tfrac{\sigma^2}{2})\tfrac{i}{4}\right]$$

$$z_3 = \frac{1}{\sigma\sqrt{n/4}}\left[\ln\tfrac{K}{V} + (r + \tfrac{\sigma^2}{2})\tfrac{n}{4}\right] \qquad z_4 = \frac{1}{\sigma\sqrt{n/4}}\left[\ln\tfrac{K}{V} - (r + \tfrac{\sigma^2}{2})\tfrac{n}{4}\right]$$

and n denotes the number of quarters within time to maturity.

Equation (7.1) is not explicit unless the unobservable parameters are characterized. These are

1. The current value of the issuer's assets (V)
2. The volatility of the issuer's asset returns (σ)
3. The issuer's default threshold (K)
4. The recovery rate (α)

The next section describes several methods that address the issue of parameter estimation.

ESTIMATION OF ASSET VALUE DYNAMICS

Implementation methods share the common feature that they rely on the information extracted from a time series of stock prices to estimate V and σ jointly.

System of Equations

This is the most direct and simple method. In the structural approach, there is a functional relation that links the current stock price S with the current value of assets V. Considering that the issuer's total debt can be aggregated as a discount bond with face value M and duration D, the stock price appears as a European call option on V with strike price M and maturity D. Furthermore, the volatility on stock price returns, σ_S, can be expressed from the volatility on the asset returns. We can therefore estimate the parameters V and σ by solving a system of two equations.

First, compute the historical volatility on stock price returns. That is, for a collection $S(t_i)$ of stock prices observed at dates t_i, $i = 0, \ldots, m$, define stock returns as

$$R(t_i) = \ln \frac{S(t_i)}{S(t_{i-1})},$$

and estimate σ_S with

$$\hat{\sigma}_S = \sqrt{\frac{1}{m}\left[\sum_{i=1}^{m}(R(t_i) - \bar{R})^2\right]}$$

where $\bar{R}$ is the average value of stock returns. Then, estimates for V and σ are the values that simultaneously solve the following two equations:

$$\begin{cases} S = V\Phi(d_1) - Me^{-rD}\Phi(d_2), \\ \hat{\sigma}_S = \sigma\frac{V}{S}\Phi(d_1), \end{cases}$$

with

$$d_1 = \frac{1}{\sigma\sqrt{D}}\left[\ln\frac{V}{M} + \left(r + \frac{\sigma^2}{2}\right)D\right],$$

$$d_2 = \frac{1}{\sigma\sqrt{D}}\left[\ln\frac{V}{M} + \left(r - \frac{\sigma^2}{2}\right)D\right].$$

This approach, initially proposed by Ronn and Verma (1986), is appealing for its simplicity. However, the repeated use of the method often yields unstable results.

Iterative Approach

We start by setting $\sigma = \hat{\sigma}_S$, computed as previously. Using this initial value for σ, a collection $V(t_i)$ of asset values at dates t_i, i = 0, ..., m, is obtained by inverting the formula for $S(t_i)$. Compute the volatility on asset returns

$$\sigma = \sqrt{\frac{1}{m}\left[\sum_{i=1}^{m}(R_V(t_i) - \bar{R}_V)^2\right]}$$

where

$$R_V(t_i) = \ln\frac{V(t_i)}{V(t_{i-1})}$$

where $\bar{R}_v$ (t_i is the average value of asset returns.

We repeat the procedure until the values of σ from two consecutive iterations converge (a tolerance level must be specified). The estimate for V is simply the inversion of the formula for S using the final value of σ. Vassalou and Xing (2004) apply this method with daily data from the past 12 months.

Maximum Likelihood

The starting point of this method is to observe a time series of realized asset values: $V(t_1)$, $V(t_2)$, ..., $V(t_m)$. According to Merton's (1974) model, the process for asset return is normally distributed with mean μ and standard deviation σ. Parameters μ and σ can be inferred from maximizing the probability of observing the sequence $V(t_1)$, $V(t_2)$, ..., $V(t_m)$ in the right order. In practice, we only observe a sequence of realized stock prices: $S(t_1)$, $S(t_2)$, ..., $S(t_m)$. But since

$$\frac{dS}{dV} = \Phi(d_1)$$

the goal is to maximize the following log-likelihood function

$$L = -\frac{m}{2}\ln(2\pi\sigma^2\theta) - \frac{1}{2}\sum_{i=1}^{m}\frac{\left(R_V(t_i) - (\mu - \frac{\sigma^2}{2})\theta\right)^2}{\sigma^2\theta}$$
$$- \sum_{i=1}^{m}\ln V(t_i) - \sum_{i=1}^{m}\ln\Phi(d_{1i}),$$

where $\theta = t_i - t_{i-1}$. Once again, the value for V is obtained by inverting the formula for S using the estimated value of σ. Ericsson and Reneby (2005) show how to apply the maximum likelihood approach to estimate parameters for different structural models of credit risk.

EMPIRICAL IMPACT

The three estimation methods are applied to the five-year CDS written on Disney Corp. The sample period is May 2002 to September 2003. This is a period of turbulent times (high premia and frequent trading in the second half of 2002) followed by quieter moments (lower premia and more infrequent trading after the second half of 2003). The variety of market conditions allows for challenging the robustness of our horse race exercise. Figures 7.3 and 7.4, respectively, plot the CDS mid-quotes as well as the CDS relative spreads over the sample period.

The sample period comprises 231 days of quotes.[4] The average five-year CDS premium on Disney is 100.71 bps. Standard deviation is 34.46 bps. The average relative spread is 11.84%. Standard deviation is 5.98%.

Figure 7.5 plots the evolution of the stock price over the sample period.

---

[4] Credit default swaps data are provided by the brokerage services company GFI. We ignored dates for which only the bid or only the ask was available

F I G U R E 7.3

Disney five-year CDS premia mid-quotes: May 2002 to September 2003

The premia, expressed in basis points, are computed as the average of the bid and offer prices.
Source: GFI.

F I G U R E 7.4

Disney five-year CDS premia relative spreads May 2002 to September 2003

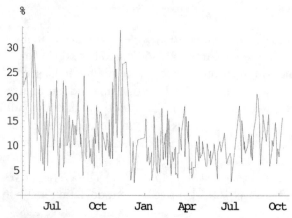

The spreads, expressed in percentage, are computed as the difference between the offer and the bid prices divided by the mid-quote.
Source: GFI.

F I G U R E   7.5

Disney stock price May 2002 to September 2003

Reported values are closing prices at the New York Stock Exchange (NYSE).
Source: Yahoo Finance.

The challenge of the structural approach is to extract information conveyed in the dynamics of stock price in order to explain the dynamics of CDS quotes. Inspection of Figures 7.3 and 7.5 shows the relevance of this exercise. The strong negative correlation between the two graphs indicates informational consistency between the stock and the CDS markets.

Parameter Estimation

Estimation is performed with a rolling estimation window of 12 months. Regarding M and D, that is, the aggregate debt level and duration, respectively, a common approach is to set $D = 1$ year and to consider that M equals debt due in one year plus half of long-term debt [see KMV Corporation (2002)]. These accounting data are obtained from Mergent Online on a quarterly basis. We transform them into daily data using linear interpolation. The interest rate is the 10-year T-Bond rate observed daily (source: St. Louis Fed). Note that convergence of the iterative approach is fast. With a tolerance level set at 10^{-5}, no more than three iterations are needed. Vassalou and Xing (2004) obtain similar conclusions.

FIGURE 7.6

Estimated asset value May 2002 to September 2003

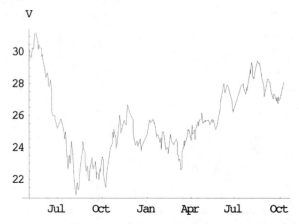

Estimates are plotted using the maximum likelihood approach. Other methods yield indistinguishable results.

The three methods reach a very strong consensus on the estimation of asset value. As a matter of fact, the relative difference between the three estimates never exceeds 0.004 percent over the whole sample period. Figure 7.6 plots the estimated asset value.

The difference between V and S looks stable over time, indicating that the firm adjusts the debt level to maintain a target leverage.

Regarding volatility estimation, the iterative and the maximum likelihood approaches yield very similar results, while the system-of-equations method produces more volatile estimates, as shown in Figure 7.7.

This empirical finding supports the theoretical result of Duan et al. (2004), who highlight the equivalent statistical properties of KMV and maximum likelihood estimates.

Pricing Performance

Forecasts on CDS premia are derived using Equation (7.1). For each day of quote, asset value and asset return volatility are estimated using the three methods and the currently observed stock price. The interest rate is the 10-year T-Bond rate. Moody's rating is used to calibrate the expected recovery rate. At the beginning of the sample period (May 2002), Moody's rating for Disney was A3. On October 19th, rating was downgraded to Baa1, but the company was on watch since August 2nd.

Estimated volatility: May 2002 to September 2003

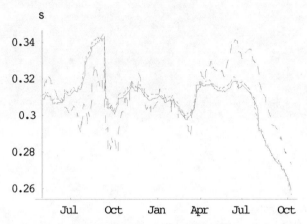

Estimates using the system-of-equations method are plotted with the long-dashed line, estimates using the iterative method are plotted with the short-dashed line, and estimates using the maximum likelihood approach are plotted with the straight line.

Moody's computed average recovery rates (in percent) are given in Table 7.1

Hence, for the first three months of the sample period (May to July), we compute the expected recovery rate a as the average recovery rate over the five-year horizon for the A-rating category, that is, $\alpha = 0.4956$. Thereafter, we do the same computation using the Baa-rating data, which yields $\alpha = 0.4548$. Finally, the default threshold K is calibrated for each quote on day j so as to minimize the squared pricing error on the preceding (day $j - 1$) mid-quote.

T A B L E   7.1

Average senior unsecured recovery rates by rating prior to default, 1982–2005

	Years Prior to Default				
	1	2	3	4	5
A	46.4	54.9	50.3	47.7	48.4
Baa	48.1	46.4	47.3	44.1	41.5

F I G U R E   7.8

CDS premia forecasts: May 2002 to September 2003

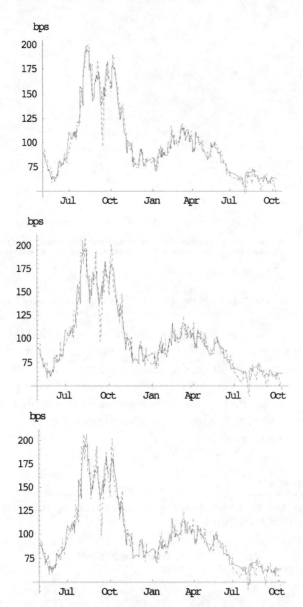

For all three graphs, real CDS premia are plotted with the straight line. Forecasted CDS premia are plotted with the dashed line. Asset dynamics are estimated using the system-of-equations method (top graph), the iterative method (middle graph), and the maximum likelihood approach (bottom graph).

Figure 7.8 reports the time series of CDS forecasts resulting from the three asset dynamics estimation methods.

For all three methods, the fitting exercise is more difficult during the episode of peaking spreads (August 2002 to November 2002). In quieter periods, the out-of-sample pricing performance is improved. Surprisingly enough, forecasts using the system-of-equations method seem to be the most accurate. This is confirmed by the following statistics on the pricing error.

Let $p_{cds}(k)$ and $\hat{p}_{cds}(k)$ denote the observed and predicted CDS premium on quoting day k. The root-mean-square error (RMSE) is defined as

$$\text{RMSE} = \sqrt{\frac{1}{230}\sum_{k=1}^{230}\left[p_{cds}(k) - \hat{p}_{cds}(k)\right]^2}$$

The average absolute error (AAE) is defined as

$$\text{AAE} = \frac{1}{230}\sum_{k=1}^{230}\frac{\left|p_{cds}(k) - \hat{p}_{cds}(k)\right|}{p_{cds}(k)}$$

We also report the percentage of occurrence when forecasted CDS premium falls within the bid–ask spread or within enlarged bid–ask spreads. Table 7.2 summarizes the statistics on the pricing error.

As is apparent from the table below, even though the system-of-equations method yields unstable in-sample volatility estimation, its out-of-sample pricing performance is substantially better than those induced by the other two estimation methods.

T A B L E   7.2

Pricing error statistics

	System of Equations	Iterative Approach	Maximum Likelihood
RMSE (bps)	7.84	9.21	9.17
AAE (%)	5.66	6.81	6.87
∈ [bid − ask] (%)	58.70	49.13	49.57
∈ [0.95 bid − 1.05 ask] (%)	88.70	80.00	77.39
∈ [0.90 bid − 1.10 ask] (%)	96.52	92.17	93.91

ANALYSIS OF THE PRICING ERROR

In this section, we investigate the relation between the pricing error and the model inputs. The pricing error on quoting day k is defined as

$$\sqrt{\left[p_{cds}(k) - \hat{p}_{cds}(k) \right]^2}$$

Figure 7.9 plots the evolution of the pricing error over time.

The big pricing failures typically occur in the period of high premia. However, the estimation method of asset dynamics has little impact on the evolution of the pricing error. Also note that in all three cases, the change in expected recovery value (that occurs in the beginning of August) seems to have a negative impact on the pricing error.

Next, we investigate the relation between the pricing error and the estimated asset value and volatility. Results for asset value are reported in the scatter plots in Figure 7.10. Results for volatility are reported in the scatter plots in Figure 7.11.

The pricing model seems to be more prone to error when asset value is low, and this finding holds for all three estimation methods. As far as volatility is concerned, the scatter plots show no clear relation with the pricing error. Again, the estimation method of asset dynamics does not seem to introduce a bias in the pricing performance of the model.

We verify this conjecture with regression analysis. Our goal is to detect whether the absolute value of the pricing error is related to firm value or asset volatility. Thus we cannot use the observed pricing error, but we also cannot use traditional statistical inference on the squared errors. Under the null hypothesis of a random pricing error, the standardized squared error follows a chi-square distribution. Thus, to get standard normal variables, we transform the squared error into a normalized squared error (NSE) through the following transformation:

$$\text{NSE} = \Phi^{-1}\left(\chi\left(\frac{\text{SE} - \overline{\text{SE}}}{\sigma_{\text{SE}}} \right)^2 \right),$$

where $\Phi(.)$ and $\chi(.)$ denote the cumulative distribution functions (CDF) of the standard normal distribution and the chi-square distribution with 1 degree of freedom, respectively.

F I G U R E   7.9

Pricing error: May 2002 to September 2003

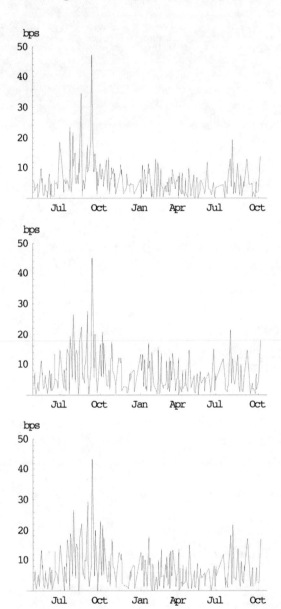

Asset dynamics are estimated using the system-of-equations method (top graph), the iterative method (middle graph), and the maximum likelihood approach (bottom graph).

F I G U R E   7.10

Pricing error and estimated asset value

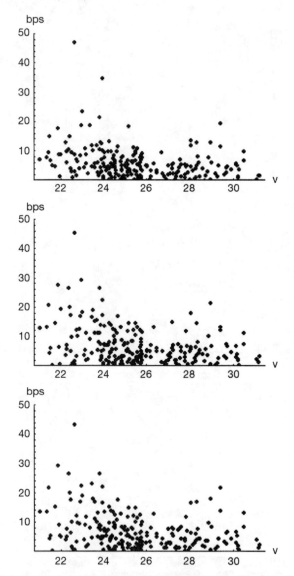

Asset dynamics are estimated using the system-of-equations method (top graph), the iterative method (middle graph), and the maximum likelihood approach (bottom graph).

Pricing error and estimated volatility

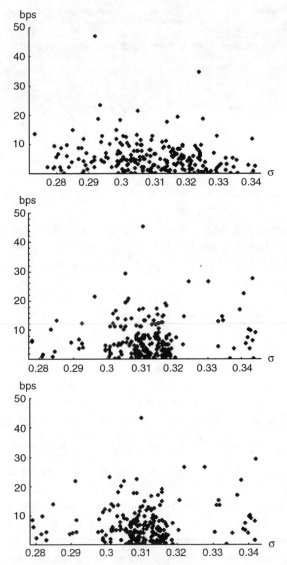

Asset dynamics are estimated using the system-of-equations method (top graph), the iterative method (middle graph), and the maximum likelihood approach (bottom graph).

T A B L E   7.3

Correlation and regression summaries

| | Correlation | | | Regression | | |
Method	System of Equations	Iterative Approach	MLE	Adjusted R^2	Value	Sigma
System of Equations	1			7.18%	−0.122***	−4.15
Iterative Approach	0.83	1		5.49%	−0.116***	−0.41
Maximum Likelihood	0.85	0.97	1	5.18%	−0.219***	0.83

The correlation and regression analyses of the pricing errors are summarized in Table 7.3.

The first method, which produces pricing errors that are least correlated with the other two, also displays the largest negative dependence with asset value. Altogether, the statistical findings confirm the visual impression from the graphical analysis.

CONCLUSION

We have presented and challenged the three most common approaches in estimating asset dynamics for structural models of credit risk. The challenge consisted in comparing the in-sample estimates of asset value and volatility as well as the out-of-sample pricing of CDS. As far as in-sample results are concerned, all three methods yield similar estimates of asset value. By contrast, there is a strong consensus between the KMV and the maximum likelihood approach in estimating volatility, a finding supported by theory, whereas the system-of-equations method provides more unstable volatility estimates.

This higher instability favors the system-of-equations method when it comes to pricing CDS out of sample. As a matter of fact, in periods of strong fluctuations of CDS prices, most recent stock price movements are insufficiently captured by the other two methods, resulting in higher pricing errors. By contrast, the system-of-equations method amplifies volatility estimates, which helps the model better match observed CDS prices. These findings are, of course, based on a small sample and therefore call for a more comprehensive validation. Yet they shed an interesting light on the conflicting purposes of in-sample and out-of-sample estimations when applying structural models of credit risk.

REFERENCES

Black, F. and Cox, J. (1976) Valuing Corporate Securities: Some Effects of Bond Indenture Provisions. *Journal of Finance,* 31(2): 351–367.

Brigo, D. and Mercurio, F. (2001) *Interest Rate Models: Theory and Practice.* New York: Springer Verlag, Springer Finance.

Briys, E. and de Varenne, F. (1997) Valuing Risky Fixed Rate Debt: An Extension. *Journal of Financial and Quantitative Analysis,* 32(2): 239–248.

Collin-Dufresne, P. and Goldstein, R. (2001) Do Credit Spreads Reflect Stationary Leverage Ratios? *Journal of Finance,* 56(5): 1929–1957.

Duan, J.-C., Gauthier, G., and Simonato, J.-G. (2004) On the Equivalence of the KMV and the Maximum Likelihood Methods for Structural Credit Risk Models. Working paper, HEC Montréal.

Ericsson, J. and Reneby, J. (2005) Estimating Structural Bond Pricing Models. *Journal of Business,* 78(2): 707–736.

François, P. and Hübner, G. (2004) Credit Derivatives with Multiple Debt Issues. *Journal of Banking and Finance,* 28(5): 997–1021.

KMV Corporation (2002) Modeling Default Risk. Technical report. San Francisco, CA.

Longstaff, F. and Schwartz, E. (1995) A Simple Approach to Valuing Risky Fixed and Floating Rate Debt. *Journal of Finance,* 50(3): 789–819.

Merton, R. (1974) On the Pricing of Corporate Debt: The Risk Structure of Interest Rates. *Journal of Finance,* 29(2): 449–470.

Ronn, E. and Verma, A. (1986) Pricing Risk-Adjusted Deposit Insurance: An Option Based Model. *Journal of Finance,* 41(4): 871–895.

Vassalou, M. and Xing, Y. (2004) Default Risk in Equity Returns. *Journal of Finance,* 59(2): 831–868.

CHAPTER 8

A Unified Approach to the Theory of Default Risk and Credit Derivatives

François-Éric Racicot and Raymond Théoret

ABSTRACT

In this chapter, we show that the theories related to the pricing of credit derivatives have revived approaches to option pricing that prevailed prior to the Black and Scholes (B&S) breakthrough. The precursors to the B&S model recently regained their popularity as a result of Derman and Taleb (2005) and Haug (2007), which are based on the introduction of a risky rate in the differential equation of B&S. First, we revise the classical default risk models and their foundations, similar to the concept of a rare event and a Poisson distribution. Thereafter, we show how these models are related to the most recent ones. Finally, we consider the pricing of the major categories of credit derivatives. We pay particular attention to the credit default swap (CDS) and show the relevance of the Longstaff et al. (2003) model to price this credit derivative.

INTRODUCTION

Asset pricing models of options operate in a risk-neutral world. For instance, the value of a European call is the discounted value, at the risk-free rate, of the risk-neutral expectation of the option final payoff. This is the usual procedure to compute option prices since the appearance of the seminal model developed by Black and Scholes (1973). Prior to this, the models used to compute option prices incorporated risk premiums.[1] For instance, Samuelson's (1965) model for valuing a warrant focused on the growth rate of the option and of the underlying prices as inputs. Nonetheless, these growth rates incorporate a risk premium, which depends on the average investor's degree of risk aversion.

The procedure used to compute option prices before B&S was initiated by Bachelier at the beginning of the 20th century and is thought by many today to be obsolete; this is not the case. To compute option prices in the context of credit risks, researchers go back to Bachelier's procedure. For example, consider the Merton (1974) model, which aims to compute the equity value of a firm threatened with possibility of bankruptcy. Equity is viewed as a call whose price is computed by using the B&S formula in which the risk-free rate is replaced by the rate that incorporates the risk premium.[2] In the omega computation[3] (an investment performance measure), we also use an interest rate shifted by the risk premium to compute the price of the put used to value the risk of the investment. We thus revert to the option pricing models prior to B&S. As we will observe in this chapter, credit derivative pricing models are based on the estimation of risk premiums, a critical input for valuing these derivatives.

There exist two main categories of models to measure credit risk. The objective of these models is to compute a yield spread between a risky and risk-free bond. These two categories are (1) the structural models and (2) the reduced form model. The structural models consider the evolution of the value of a firm as a diffusion process. In these models, default occurs when the value of the firm falls below the debt value or another barrier. The reduced form model is a contingent claim model used to compute the probability of default. These models make a link between the firm value and the default. The default is an unpredictable event that follows a Poisson process and gives rise to a sudden decrease in firm value. To paraphrase Gatheral (2006), ". . . basically, you estimate an intensity for the arrival of default (possibly as a function of time, possibly as a stochastic process, possibly as a function of other things)." According

---

[1] For further details on these models, see Haug (1998; 2007).

[2] Gatheral (2006).

[3] Kazemi et al. (2004).

to this approach, bankruptcy is not a progressive process as in structural models. Finally, hybrid models share the features of both structural and reduced form models. The aim of this article is to present credit risk models that have strongly influenced the literature and to apply them to the most popular credit derivatives.

A SIMPLE MODEL OF CREDIT RISK[4]

A financial institution has at its disposal a historical series on the losses of its portfolio of loans. The expected value of the credit loss (CL), denoted by $E(CL)$, depends upon three factors:

1. The probability of default on every loan. It is a Bernoulli variable taking the value of 1 if there is default or 0 otherwise, and its expected value is equal to the probability of default.
2. The exposure to credit risk. If we link the creditor to the borrower, the exposure to a given borrower stands for the amount loaned.
3. The loss rate on a loan which is equal to $(1 - t_{rc})$, where t_{rc} denotes the recovery rate when there is default. The loan losses are equal to

$$CL = \sum_{i=1}^{N} b_i \times EC_i \times t_{pi} \qquad (8.1)$$

Here N is the number of granted loans; b_i, a Bernoulli variable that takes the value of 1 if there is default and 0 otherwise; EC_i, the amount of the loan granted to the ith borrower; and t_{pi}, the loss rate on the loan i that is equal to $(1 - t_{rci})$. The expected value of the loss is, therefore,

$$E(CL) = \sum_{i=1}^{N} E(b_i) \times EC_i \times t_{pi} = \sum_{i=1}^{N} p_i \times EC_i \times t_{pi} \qquad (8.2)$$

We assume that the expected value of the loss on a loans portfolio has been estimated to $15 million and the standard deviation of this portfolio losses are $10 million. The worst loss that may occur with a probability of

---

[4] In this section, we follow Jorion's (2003; 2005) approach. See also: Racicot and Théoret (2006), Chapter 18.

99 percent on an annual basis, assuming the loss distribution follows a normal law, is 2.33 × \$10 million = \$23.3 million.[5] The unexpected loss is then \$23.3 − \$15 = \$8.3 million,[6] which is the capital-at-risk (CaR) the financial institution must maintain to hedge its loans.

The return required by a financial institution on a loan must be sufficient to cover the expected loss and a normal remuneration for the CaR. An institution taking into account only the expected value of the losses to price its loans would therefore underestimate the return on its loans.

The risk-neutral pricing only takes into account the expected value of the losses to compute the return on the loans. However, the risk-neutral probabilities are not equal to the objective probabilities, also called *physical probabilities*. Risk-neutral probabilities, computed with the observed prices of the derivatives, are indeed contaminated by risk premiums, which incorporate the degree of risk aversion of the average investor. These probabilities therefore incorporate an implicit premium for the CaR. The objective probabilities do not incorporate such a premium, and therefore, we add an explicit remuneration for the CaR when resorting to objective probabilities.

We can state the expected value of the credit loss of a portfolio in a more formal way by resorting to integral calculus. $E(CL)$ may then be written as

$$E(CL) = \int \left(b \times EC \times t_p \right) \times f\left(b, EC, t_p \right) \times \left(db \times EC \times t_p \right) \quad (8.3)$$

If the three variables are independent, we may write

$$E(CL) = \int bf(b)\, db \times \int EC\, f(EC)\, dEC \times \int t_p f\left(t_p \right) dt_p \quad (8.4)$$

which is the product of the expected values of the three variables:

$$E(CL) = prob(default) \times E(EC) \times E\left(t_p \right) \quad (8.5)$$

For instance, if the default probability is 3 percent, the exposure is \$200 million, and the recovery rate is 40 percent, the expected value of the loss is $E(CL) = 0.03 \times \$200 \times (1 - 0.40) = \$2.8\ million.$

---

[5] It is the relative value of the portfolio VaR.
[6] It is the absolute value of the portfolio VaR.

F I G U R E   8.1

The CaR

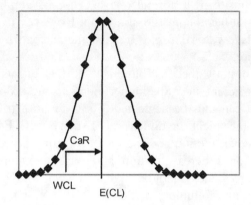

The worst credit loss at the c confidence level may be defined implicitly as follows:

$$\int_{-\infty}^{WCL} f(x)\, dx = 1 - c = \alpha \tag{8.6}$$

where $f(x)$ is the density function of the losses. The WCL variable is drawn at Figure 8.1. For instance, if c is equal to 95 percent, we search for the WCL, which is the superior boundary of the surface equal to 5 percent, under the density function of the losses, comprised between $-\infty$ and the value of WCL. The CaR, or unexpected loss, is equal to $CaR = WCL - E(CL)$.

Given that credit risk relies extensively on the notion of a rare event and on the Poisson distribution, we dedicate the next two sections to these notions.

NORMAL EVENTS AND RARE EVENTS

Merton (1992) and Neftci (2000) have established a clear distinction between a normal and a rare event and have demonstrated that in the former case, only the two first moments are important while in the latter case, higher order moments must also be considered.

Let h be a time interval equal to dt. An event is said to be *normal* if its amplitude decreases with h. Moreover, the probability of such an event does not depend upon h; i.e., it is not equal to 0 when $h \to 0$ and as such is why such an event is viewed as normal. The profile of a rare event is the opposite of a normal one because its amplitude does not decrease with h; it has the profile of a jump. However, its probability of occurrence tends towards 0 as $h \to 0$ and is the reason why such as event is considered rare.

In order to study the distribution of normal events, the first two moments are sufficient since the higher moments are proportional to the square of h and can thus be neglected. The normal distribution may be used to analyze the stochastic dimension of such events. For instance, the geometric Brownian motion and the mean-reverting process rely on the normal distribution. Whereas, the third and fourth moments of rare events are proportional to h and cannot be neglected when studying such events; since they are similar to jumps, the Poisson distribution seems relevant in the study of such events.

Neftci (2000) shows how the Poisson process can be incorporated in a binomial tree.[7] If the price of a stock is only dependent for normal events, then the up (u) and down (d) movements of the stock price may be written as follows:

$$u = e^{\sigma\sqrt{h}} \tag{8.7}$$

$$d = e^{-\sigma\sqrt{h}} \tag{8.8}$$

where σ is the standard deviation of the stock return. The probability of an up movement may be chosen as

$$p = \frac{1}{2}\left(1 + \frac{\alpha}{\sigma}\sqrt{h}\right) \tag{8.9}$$

with α being the growth rate of the stock price. We notice that when $h \to 0$, $p \to 1/2$, therefore justifying the choice of this constant as the

---

[7] Das (2000) shows how to introduce jump processes in a hexanomial tree that also takes into account skewness and kurtosis. It should also be noted that this approach, due to Cox et al. (1979), may be improved in terms of efficiency. For instance, Rouah and Vainberg (2007) show how to implement the Leisen–Reimer binomial tree, a much more efficient method than the standard binomial tree. Further work could be done to adapt new numerical methods in our context.

upward probability insofar as h is very small.[8] These values of u, d, and p are associated with normal events. Indeed, the importance of upward and downward movements tends to decrease as $h \to 0$. However, the probability of such events does not cancel as $h \to 0$; it tends instead toward the constant $1/2$.

For rare events, we state the following assumptions regarding the three parameters u, d, and p. We assume that the upward movement u depends upon the importance of the jump. The parameter d is equal to $d = e^{\theta h}$ and is related to the absence of jumps. Moreover, the probability p of a jump is equal to λh. The parameters λ and θ must be calibrated according to the importance and the probability of the rare event. The jump movement being a constant, does not depend upon h, a characteristic of a rare event. Moreover, the probability of the rare event tends to 0 as $h \to 0$.

THE POISSON DISTRIBUTION[9]

Similar to the hypergeometric distribution, the Poisson distribution is a particular form of the binomial. Let n be the number of drawings and p the probability to observe a rare event. We make n tend to ∞, and p then tends to 0 under the constraint that np remains finite and tends to λ. We thus obtain the density function of the Poisson's law:

$$\binom{n}{r} p^r q^{n-r} = f_r = e^{-\lambda} \frac{\lambda^r}{r!} \qquad r = 0, 1, 2, \ldots \qquad (8.10)$$

with $\lambda > 0$. The first four moments of this distribution are the following:

$$\mu_1 = \mu_2 = \mu_3 = \lambda \qquad (8.11)$$

$$\mu_4 = \lambda + 3\lambda^2 \qquad (8.12)$$

When the events are normal, the binomial distribution tends toward the normal form. If the events are rare, the binomial distribution tends

---

[8] For instance, in their binomial interest rate model, Black et al. (1990) assume that the upward probability and the downward probability are equal to $1/2$.

[9] For more details, see Stuart and Ord (1994).

toward the Poisson form. When $\lambda \to \infty$, the Poisson distribution tends toward the normal form.

How can we compute λ? A simple method is provided by Dixit and Pindyck (1994). Let us denote by $E(T)$ the expected value of the time required for the happening of a jump. For instance, $E(T)$ is equal to 10 implies that one jump occurs on average once every 10 years. According to the density function of the Poisson distribution, the probability for an absence of jumps is

$$f_0 = e^{-\lambda} \frac{\lambda^0}{0!} = e^{-\lambda} \tag{8.13}$$

The probability that the first event occurs in the interval $(T, T + dT)$ is

$$f_1 = e^{-\lambda} \frac{\lambda^1}{1!} = \lambda e^{-\lambda} \tag{8.14}$$

so $E(T)$ is equal to

$$E(T) = \int_0^\infty \lambda T e^{-\lambda T}\, dT = \frac{1}{\lambda} \tag{8.15}$$

The ratio $\left(\dfrac{1}{\lambda}\right)$ stands for the mean time interval between two jumps.

If $\lambda = 0.2$, it implies that there is a jump once every five years. Hence, if there is one jump every five years, λ will be equal to 0.2.

CREDIT RISK IN THE FRAMEWORK OF THE B&S DIFFERENTIAL EQUATION[10]

We would like to make the distinction between a risk-free bond and a bond that involves credit risk in the B&S differential equation framework. We first derive the differential equation of the price of a bond without default risk. This approach is similar to the one employed for introducing jump (such as a default) processes in the B&S differential equation.

---

[10] In writing this section, we followed the approach of Wilmott (2000). See also Racicot and Théoret (2006), Chapter 18.

Let us assume that the interest rate, denoted by r, follows an Itô process:

$$dr = u(r, t)\, dt + w(r, t)\, dz \tag{8.16}$$

The value of the bond assumes the form $V(r, t, T)$, t being the present time and T, the expiration time of the bond. In order to construct the differential equation of $V(.)$, we must hedge this bond to a bond with a different maturity since the interest rate is not a traded asset.[11] We thus have at our disposal two bonds, V_1 and V_2, that differ only by their maturity. Their respective maturities are T_1 and T_2. We construct the following hedging portfolio:

$$\Pi = V_1 - \Delta V_2. \tag{8.17}$$

Resorting to the Itô's lemma, we obtain the differential equation of this portfolio:

$$
\begin{aligned}
d\Pi = {} & \frac{\partial V_1}{\partial t}\, dt + \frac{\partial V_1}{\partial r}\, dr + \frac{1}{2} w^2 \frac{\partial^2 V_1}{\partial r^2} \\
& dt - \Delta \left(\frac{\partial V_2}{\partial t}\, dt + \frac{\partial V_2}{\partial r}\, dr + \frac{1}{2} w^2 \frac{\partial^2 V_2}{\partial r^2}\, dt \right)
\end{aligned}
\tag{8.18}
$$

In this equation, the only risk factor is the interest rate because there is no credit risk yet. The coefficient of dr is

$$\left(\frac{\partial V_1}{\partial r} - \Delta \frac{\partial V_2}{\partial r} \right)$$

To remove risk from the portfolio, it suffices to cancel the term. We thus obtain the following value for Δ, i.e., the delta of the hedge:

$$\Delta = \frac{\partial V_1 / \partial r}{\partial V_2 / \partial r} \tag{8.19}$$

---

[11] For a plain-vanilla call, we resort to its underlying, the stock, a traded asset, to hedge it.

By choosing this value for Δ, we remove all uncertainty from the portfolio, and by replacing Δ by its value given by Equation (8.19) in Equation (8.18), we have

$$d\Pi = \left[\frac{\partial V_1}{\partial t} + \frac{1}{2} w^2 \frac{\partial^2 V_1}{\partial r^2} - \left(\frac{\partial V_1 / \partial t}{\partial V_2 / \partial t} \right) \left(\frac{\partial V_2}{\partial t} + \frac{1}{2} w^2 \frac{\partial^2 V_2}{\partial r^2} \right) \right] dt \quad (8.20)$$

As this portfolio is without risk, its return must be equal to the risk-free rate r, that is,

$$d\Pi = r\Pi dt \quad (8.21)$$

Substituting Equations (8.17) and (8.19) in Equation (8.21), we have

$$d\Pi = r\Pi\, dt = r\left[V_1 - \left(\frac{\partial V_1 / \partial t}{\partial V_2 / \partial t} \right) V_2 \right] dt \quad (8.22)$$

Equating Equations (8.20) and (8.22), we find

$$\left[\frac{\partial V_1}{\partial t} + \frac{1}{2} w^2 \frac{\partial^2 V_1}{\partial r^2} - \left(\frac{\partial V_1 / \partial t}{\partial V_2 / \partial t} \right) \left(\frac{\partial V_2}{\partial t} + \frac{1}{2} w^2 \frac{\partial^2 V_2}{\partial r^2} \right) \right] dt$$
$$= r\left[V_1 - \left(\frac{\partial V_1 / \partial t}{\partial V_2 / \partial t} \right) V_2 \right] dt \quad (8.23)$$

By regrouping at left the terms containing V_1 in Equation (8.23) and at right those containing V_2, we have

$$\frac{\partial V_1 / \partial t + 1/2\, w^2\, \partial^2 V_1 / \partial r^2 - rV_1}{\partial V_1 / \partial r} = \frac{\partial V_2 / \partial t + 1/2w^2\, \partial^2 V_2 / \partial r^2 - rV_2}{\partial V_2 / \partial r} \quad (8.24)$$

In Equation (8.24), the term on the left depends upon T_1 and not upon T_2, and the opposite is true for the term on the right. This may be possible only if both sides are not related to T. Removing the indices in Equation (8.24), we have

$$\frac{\partial V / \partial t + 1/2\, w^2\, \partial^2 V / \partial r^2 - rV}{\partial V / \partial r} = a(r,t) \qquad (8.25)$$

We apply the following Girsanov transformation:

$$a(r,t) = w(r,t)\lambda(r,t) - u(r,t) \qquad (8.26)$$

By substituting (8.25) in (8.24), we obtain the differential equation of the price of the bond:

$$\frac{\partial V}{\partial t} + \frac{1}{2}\, w^2\, \frac{\partial^2 V}{\partial r^2} + (u - \lambda w)\frac{\partial V}{\partial r} - rV = 0 \qquad (8.27)$$

We note that Equation 8.27 is identical to B&S except for the coefficient of $\partial V/\partial r$ which is equal to $(\mu - \lambda w)$ and not to r. Indeed, the interest rate, which is the underlying value of V, is not traded. Therefore, the drift of the interest Equation (8.16) remains in the differential equation of V. The Girsanov transformation also does not eliminate the market price of risk λ, which is multiplied by w, the interest rate volatility. When the option underlying is not traded, risk reappears in the differential equation of B&S.

To find a unique solution to differential Equation (8.27), we must impose a final condition and two other boundary conditions. The final condition is $V(r, T, T) = 1$, i.e., the bond price is 1 at its expiration date. The boundary conditions depend upon u and w. If a coupon $K(r,t)$ is cashed inside the interval dt, Equation (8.27) becomes

$$\frac{\partial V}{\partial t} + \frac{1}{2}\, w^2\, \frac{\partial^2 V}{\partial r^2} + (u - \lambda w)\frac{\partial V}{\partial r} - rV + K(r,t) = 0 \qquad (8.28)$$

We now introduce default risk in the analysis. The default probability between t and $(t + dt)$ is $p\, dt$. Let Z be the value of the zero coupon bond without default risk and with the same maturity as the bond with default risk. The value V of the risky bond is then written as

$$V = e^{p(T-t)}Z. \qquad (8.29)$$

The yield to maturity of the risky bond is

$$-\frac{\log\left(e^{-p(T-t)}Z\right)}{T-t} = -\frac{\log Z}{T-t} + p. \qquad (8.30)$$

Default risk thus adds a spread p to the yield of the risky bond, which as a result is the foundation of credit derivatives models.

Wilmott (2000) considers this model as a part of the Poisson processes. Nothing occurs during a certain time, and suddenly there is a change of state. To quote Gatheral (2006, p. 74), "There is no observable or latent variable which triggers the default event, it just happens." The B&S differential equation modified by a process of λ intensity contains a λ spread added to the term that stands for the discount rate in this equation. By analogy, default risk transforms differential Equation (8.27) as follows:

$$\frac{\partial V}{\partial t} + \frac{1}{2} w^2 \frac{\partial^2 V}{\partial r^2} + (u - \lambda w) \frac{\partial V}{\partial r} - (r + p) V = 0 \qquad (8.31)$$

The probability of default has thus been added to the coefficient of the last term of the differential equation[12] and is no longer the risk-free rate appearing in the B&S formula, but rather the risky rate. This reverts back to the derivative pricing approaches prior to B&S.

Why do we add the probability of default p in differential Equation (8.31)? Because the arbitrage portfolio Π is only hedged for the fluctuations of the interest rate risk, it is not protected against default risk. For this reason, a premium is added to r in the last term of differential Equation (8.31), which is necessary to remunerate default risk.

Instead of considering p as fixed, we may view it as a random variable. Its stochastic equation is

$$dp = \gamma \, dt + \delta \, dz_2 \qquad (8.32)$$

---

[12] As explained in Haug (2007), researchers have recently found that a derivative is only weakly dependent upon the underlying asset even in a B&S framework and that the supply and demand of options also influence option prices. Racicot and Théoret (2006, Chapter 2) have presented an example showing how a supply-and-demand model might fix the price of a derivative in a dynamic context.

We know that the stochastic process followed by the interest rate is

$$dr = u\, dt + w\, dz_1 \tag{8.33}$$

ρ stands for the correlation between the Brownian motions z_1 and z_2. V depends now upon three variables: t, r, and p. With the help of Itô's lemma, we find the new differential equation of V:

$$\frac{\partial V}{\partial t} + \frac{1}{2} w^2 \frac{\partial^2 V}{\partial r^2} + \frac{1}{2} \delta^2 \frac{\partial^2 V}{\partial p^2} + \rho w \delta \frac{\partial^2 V}{\partial r \partial p} + (u - \lambda w) \frac{\partial V}{\partial r}$$
$$+ \gamma \frac{\partial V}{\partial p} - (r + p) V = 0 \tag{8.34}$$

with the final condition $V(r, p, T) = 1$.[13]

THE MERTON MODEL AND ITS EXTENSIONS

Merton (1974)[14] proposed a model based on the firm's financial leverage to explain the risk premium on its bonds. The model is innovative because it resorts to the B&S equation to model this risk premium. The Merton (1974) model remains a popular method to explain credit risk.

Let us assume that a firm has issued n stocks and its balance sheet contains a zero coupon bond issue whose face value is $\$F$. The global market value of the bonds is presently B_0 ($B_0 < F$), and the price of the firm stock is S_0. The current market value of this firm is thus $V_0 = B_0 + nS_0$. Let V_T be the market value of the firm at the expiration date of the bonds and B_T,[15] the market value of these bonds at expiration. At the expiration date, two events may occur: (1) The firm can repay the face value of its bonds. We then have ($V_T > F$). The debt is thus repaid and the stockholders' cash is the residual value of the firm, i.e., ($V_T - F$). (2) The firm cannot repay the face value of its bonds; the firm then files for bankruptcy and the creditors take possession of the firm, and the stockholders receive nothing.

---

[13] For more details on this approach, see: Wilmott (2000), Chapter 55.
[14] For further details on this model, see: Racicot and Théoret (2005), Chapter 11.
[15] If the firm is solvent when its bonds expire, the market value of the bonds (B_T) is then obviously equal to F, the face value of these bonds.

We transpose this reasoning in terms of option theory. By lending to the firm, the creditors have acquired this firm and have sold a call to the stockholders. Indeed, the creditors of this firm will become its owners. If the firm goes bankrupt, then stockholders will exercise their calls at the expiration of the bonds if the firm can repay the face value of the issued bonds.

Depending on whether the firm is solvent at the expiration of the bonds, their value is equal to the corresponding equations:

$$B_T = V_T \quad if\ V_T < F$$
$$B_T = F \quad if\ V_T > F$$

We can combine these two equations as follows:

$$B_T = MIN(F, V_T) \tag{8.35}$$

This expression implies that B_T is equal to the minimum of the two values in the parentheses, F or V_T. If F is greater than V_T, the firm is then insolvent at the expiration of the bonds, and their market value is equal to the value of the firm. Otherwise, if F is less than V_T at the expiration of the bonds, the firm is then solvent, and the market value of the bonds is equal to their face value.

This last equation may be rewritten as

$$B_T = V_T - MAX(V_T - F, 0) \tag{8.36}$$

Indeed, if V_T is greater than F, the maximum is then equal to $(V_T - F)$ at the right of this equation, and B_T is then equal to F. Otherwise, if V_T is less than F, the maximum is 0, and B_T is then equal to V_T.

At this point the call appears, and we write the following:

$$C_T = MAX(V_T - F, 0) \tag{8.37}$$

In this expression, C_T denotes the terminal value of a call on the value of the firm whose strike is F.

By substitution, we get

$$B_T = V_T - C_T \tag{8.38}$$

Discounting back this equation to time 0, we have

$$B_0 = V_0 - C_0 \tag{8.39}$$

According to this equation, the creditors control the market value of the firm, that is, V_0, but have sold a call $(-C_0)$[16] to its stockholders. This is in line with our previous statement, which may seem suspect initially: The creditors, and not the stockholders, are the owners of the company. However, these owners are very restricted since they have sold a call to the stockholders of the company.

We can also express the market value of the bonds issued by a firm in terms of puts. We return to the equation used to write the market value of the bonds in terms of calls:

$$B_T = \text{Min}\left(V_T, F\right) \tag{8.40}$$

This equation may be rewritten as follows

$$B_T = F - \text{Max}\left(F - V_T, 0\right) \tag{8.41}$$

We know that

$$P_T = \text{Max}\left(F - V_T, 0\right) \tag{8.42}$$

In this expression, P_T denotes the value of a put written on the value of the firm, whose strike is F.

By substitution, we find finally

$$B_T = F - P_T \tag{8.43}$$

and by discounting this equation to the present (0),

$$B_0 = Fe^{-r_f t} - P_0 \tag{8.44}$$

To bring back F to the present, we discount it continuously at the risk-free rate (r_f).

---

[16] In this equation, $(+C)$ denotes a long position in a call, i.e., the investor has bought this option; $(-C)$ denotes a short position in a call and is associated to the sale of the option.

This equation provides another interpretation regarding the relation existing between the creditors and the stockholders of a firm. Under this new perspective, the stockholders remain the owners of the firm. They borrow the present value of F and purchase a put from the creditors to protect themselves against the risk related to the debt. Without buying this option, the stockholders would not have a limited liability. This put represents an insurance policy for the stockholders, and if, at the expiration of the bonds, the firm value is less than the face value of bonds, then the stockholders will exercise their put option and release the firm to its creditors.

The probability that the firm defaults is obviously equal to the probability to exercise the put, that is, $N(-d_2)$. The previous equation, which relates the market value of the debt to the value of a put, allows writing

Price of a risky bond = price of a risk-free bond − price of a put

or alternatively,

Price of a risky bond = price of a risk-free bond − risk premium

The risk premium on a bond is similar to that of a put. Risky bonds involve a discount when compared to risk-free bonds, of which the amount changes with respect to the function of factors that influence the price of this put.

We know that the price of a European put is equal to

$$P = Fe^{-r_f t} N(-d_2) - VN(-d_1) \tag{8.45}$$

Substituting the value of this put in the equation of the price of a risky bond, that is,

$$B = Fe^{-r_f t} - P \tag{8.46}$$

we have

$$B = Fe^{-r_f t}\left[1 - N(-d_2) + \frac{VN(-d_1)}{Fe^{-r_f t}}\right] \tag{8.47}$$

Let us replace the expression in brackets by K. We have

$$B = Fe^{-r_f t} K \qquad (8.48)$$

where K is the discount factor of a risky bond. This factor is used to discount the risk-free bond value to obtain the risky bond value, and it is simple to derive the risk premium of a bond from this last equation, expressed in terms of yield. As the composition of interest rates is assumed continuous, the yield of the risky bond (r_B) is equal to the following expression:

$$r_B = \left(\ln \frac{F}{B} \right) \times 100 \qquad (8.49)$$

The risk premium of the bond is thus equal to

$$risk\ premium = \left(r_B - r_f \right) \times 100 \qquad (8.50)$$

We illustrate these equations by the following example. The market value of a firm is equal to $40 million, and the face value of its debt amounts to $39.5 million with its debt expiring in one year. The risk-free rate is 10 percent and the volatility of the assets return of the firm is 0.4, and we calculate the risk premium on the bonds of this firm.

The debt of this firm is obviously risky, and its financial leverage, at 79 (i.e., 39.5/0.5), is very high with the risk premium on the stock of this company being substantial. This will reveal the computation of this risk premium with the B&S equation.

To compute the value of the put incorporated in the debt, we resort to a program written in Visual Basic, which appears at Table 8.1. With the data of our problem, the put value is $5.61.

The value of the risk-free debt is $39.5e^{-0.02} = 38.71$.

As the value of the risky debt is equal to the difference between the risk-free debt and the value of the put, we obtain $38.71 - 5.61 = 33.09$. The yield of the risky bonds is then equal to

$$r_B = \left(\ln \frac{38.71}{33.09} \right) \times 100 = 17.67\%.$$

T A B L E   8.1

Visual basic program for the price of a European put

```
Function PutOptionBS(s, x, T, rf, sigma)
Num = Log(s/x) + (rf + 0.5 * sigma ^ 2) * T
d1 = Num / (sigma * Sqr(T))
PutOptionBS = −s * Application.NormSDist(−d1) + _
x * Exp(−T * rf) * Application.NormSDist(−d1 + sigma * Sqr(T))
End Function
```

According to our expectations, the risk premium on such bonds is high and is equal to $17.67\% - 2\% = 15.67\%$

The risk premium is strongly dependent upon the face value of the debt and upon the volatility of the asset returns of the firm. Figure 8.2 shows these relationships, and we notice the high sensitivity of the risk premium to the volatility of the asset returns.

Black and Cox (1976) have modified the Merton model to allow the firm bankruptcy before the expiration of the debt. Their model is thus considered as a "stopping time" model, which is used to price American options. In their model, the value V of the firm is given by the following differential equation:

$$dV_t = V(r - \kappa)dt + V\sigma\,dz \tag{8.51}$$

with κ the continuous dividend payment rate. The interest rate is fixed, which may be regarded as a weakness of this model, whose main thrust is to model credit risk. Contrary to the Merton model (1974), the time at

F I G U R E   8.2

Several determinants of the risk premium

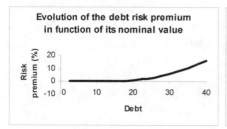

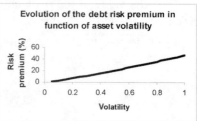

which the bankruptcy happens is not fixed at the expiration of the debt but is a function of time. The period τ when default occurs is modeled by the following equation:

$$\tau = \inf\{t > 0 : V(t) \leq K(t)\} \tag{8.52}$$

where *inf* means "infimum."[17] We thus search for the closest period for which the value of $V(t)$ falls below the barrier $K(t)$, which triggers the bankruptcy. Several authors prefer to write the former equation as follows:

$$\tau = \min\{t > 0 : V(t) \leq K(t)\} \tag{8.53}$$

The Black and Cox model allows accounting for several categories of debts that differ by their repayment seniority. Longstaff and Schwartz (1995) added more realism to the Black and Cox model by making the interest rate stochastic while adapting Vasicek's (1977) interest rate model.

In addition to the structural model just presented, Merton (1976) has also proposed a default reduced form model. In this model, when the jumps occur, the stock price changes from S to JS. If the jump is negative, for instance when a firm is threatened with bankruptcy, then J is in the range from 0 to 1. Otherwise, if the jump is positive, then J is greater than 1. A jump process superimposed on a Brownian motion may be written as

$$dS = \alpha S\, dt + \sigma S\, dz + (J - 1)\, S\, dq \tag{8.54}$$

with S, the stock price; α, the growth rate of the stock price; dt, the time step; and d_z, a Wiener process.[18] The dq takes a value of 1 if a jump occurs and 0 otherwise. Merton (1976) found an analytic solution to the option price V when J follows a lognormal distribution. Let γ be the total proportion of the S volatility explained by the jumps. The formula of a European call may then be written in the presence of jumps:[19]

$$c = \sum_{i=0}^{\infty} \frac{e^{-\lambda T}(\lambda T)^i}{i!} c_i\left(S, X, T, r, \delta, \sigma_i\right) \tag{8.55}$$

---

[17] That is the greatest lower bound.
[18] Racicot and Théoret (2006) show how to estimate a jump process with mean reversion applied to the exchange rate. The EViews code is provided by the authors.
[19] A very good reference on this subject is Haug (1998; 2007).

with c_i, the value of a European call as given by the B&S equation for such a call, and T, the maturity of the call. The standard deviation of the stock return that appears in the formula is equal to

$$\sigma_i = \sqrt{z^2 + \varphi^2 \left(\frac{i}{T} \right)} \qquad (8.56)$$

with $\varphi = \sqrt{\gamma \sigma^2 / \lambda}$ and $z = \sqrt{\sigma^2 - \lambda \varphi^2}$. As we can see, the price of a European call with jumps is equal to the weighted average of the value of the calls over every jump. The weights are the probabilities related to every jump. This formula assumes an infinite number of jumps, but in practice, we resort to a limited number of jumps because this formula converges quickly.

The results of the B&S equation with jumps do not differ sensitively from those related to the formula without jumps when the call is in the money. However, when the option is out of the money, the price of a call computed with the B&S equation with jumps is greater than the plain-vanilla call for relatively short maturities for the option. This is in line with the studies demonstrating that the B&S formula underestimates out-of-the-money calls. The presence of jumps may provide an explanation to the smile phenomenon observed on the options market. If a certain of amount of kurtosis is added within the distribution of the underlying returns, the Poisson process gives more value to out-of-the-money options.

The Merton equation can be simplified if we assume there is only one jump and the value of the underlying asset goes to 0 at the start of this jump. In this case, the differential equation is

$$\frac{\partial V}{\partial t} + \frac{1}{2}\sigma^2 S^2 \frac{\partial^2 V}{\partial S^2} + (r - \delta) S \frac{\partial V}{\partial S} - (r + \lambda) V = 0 \qquad (8.57)$$

This equation is identical to the B&S differential equation except for the last term where the risk-free interest rate is shifted by the intensity rate of the Poisson process, i.e., λ. The value of a European call is then computed resorting to the B&S formula with a greater interest rate since it is then equal to $(r + \lambda)$. According to Merton (1976), since the price of the call is an increasing function of the interest rate, a call written on a stock that is confronted to a positive probability of complete ruin is worth more than a call for which this probability is nil. According to Merton, this result corroborates Samuelson's conjecture on this subject, a result that is not obviously a priori. Moreover, an increase in interest rate gives way to a decrease in the value of a put. "A put said risky is thus worth less than a risk-free put, what is also not an obvious result a priori" (Gatheral, 2006, p.78).

DYNAMIC MODELING OF THE PROBABILITY OF DEFAULT: THE PROBABILITIES OF TRANSITION[20]

Before introducing transition matrices, it is important to make a distinction between a bond's promised yield and a bond's expected yield. The promised yield of a bond is its maturity yield, also called the *internal rate of return,* with the further assumption that the default rate of the bond's cash flows is zero. The bond issuer is solvent and will pay with certainty the coupons and the face value of the bond.

We now assume that the default rate is not zero and would like to calculate the expected yield of a one-year bond whose annual coupon rate is C and whose face value is VN. The probability that the issuer will not default during the year is equal to π, while λ stands for the recovery rate of the face value if there is default. The expected cash flow for the bond at the end of the year is thus $[\pi(1 + C)VN + (1 - \pi)\lambda F]$. Since we know the bond price P, we can compute the expected yield $\bar{r}$:

$$\bar{r} = \frac{\pi(1+C)VN + (1-\pi)\lambda F}{P} - 1 \tag{8.58}$$

The expected yield is less than the promised yield because it relies on the postulate that all of the bond cash flows will be repaid with certainty. At equilibrium, the expected yield must be proportional to the probability of default and to the unrepaid proportion of the bond's cash flows, whereby these two factors represent the risk of the bond. The more important these two risk factors are, the higher the expected yield should be.

The firms issuing bonds are given a credit rating by a rating agency, such as, Moody's and Standard & Poor's. We assume here that there exist only four credit ratings reported in an order of increasing risk: A, B, C,

---

[20] To write this section, we resort to Jorion (2003; 2005).

T A B L E   8.2

Transition matrix

$$\Pi = \begin{bmatrix} \pi_{AA} & \pi_{AB} & \pi_{AC} & 0 \\ \pi_{BA} & \pi_{BB} & \pi_{BC} & 0 \\ 0 & 0 & 0 & 1 \\ 0 & 0 & 0 & 1 \end{bmatrix}$$

and D, the last rating being related to credit default. We use these quotes to define the transition matrix that appears at Table 8.2.

The π_{ij} are the probabilities that, in a given period, the bond transits from rating i to rating j. These are conditional probabilities because the initial rating is i. To illustrate this point, we introduce numbers in the transition matrix (Table 8.2). As they are probabilities, the numbers of every line must sum to 1.

According to the matrix of Table 8.3, if the rating of a firm is A, the probability that it remains at A in one period is 0.98. Moreover, there is a probability that this firm moves to B in one period, conditionally to its A rating in the current period. According to the transition matrix, it is impossible that a firm rated A in the current period moves to the C or D ratings in the next period.

We further assume that the periods are in years, and we compute the cumulative probability that a firm rated i at the end of the first year moves to j at the end of the second year. We presume that the probabilities of transition follow a Markov chain. In other words, the transitions from one rating to another are independent from one period to the other since only the current values are relevant in a Markov process.

T A B L E   8.3

Transition matrix of a firm

	A	B	C	D
3	0.98	0.02	0	0
4	0.03	0.92	0.02	0.03
5	0.01	0.12	0.7	0.17
6	0	0	0	1

We consider the firm rated B in Table 8.3 and compute the probability that it defaults at the end of the second year. There are three ways for it to be in default at the end of the second year. First, it may have shifted to rating A at the end of the first year and be in default at the end of the second year. The probability of such a shift is[21]

$$p\left(D_2|A_1\right) \times p\left(A_1\right) = 0.03 \times 0 = 0.$$

In Table 8.3, there is a probability of 0.03 that the firm moves from B to A at the end of the first year. However, if it is really in this position at the end of the first year, it can no longer default at the end of the second year.

There are two other ways for B to be in default at the end of the second year. Second, it may have remained at rating B at the end of the first year before migrating to D at the end of the second year. Third, it may have migrated to C at the end of the first year to default at the end of the second year. The probability of these three moves is thus

$$\left[p\left(D_2|A_1\right) \times p\left(A_1\right)\right] + \left[p\left(D_2|B_1\right) \times p\left(B_1\right)\right] + \left[p\left(D_2|C_1\right) \times p\left(C_1\right)\right]$$
$$= \left(0 \times 0.03\right) + \left(0.03 \times 0.92\right) + \left(0.17 \times 0.02\right)$$
$$= 0.031$$

This computation corresponds to the transitory (marginal) probability for the firm rated B at year 1 to be in default at year 2. The cumulative probability is obtained by adding to this transitory probability the one related to its default at year 1, that is, 3 percent according to Table 8.3. The cumulative probability is thus 6.1 percent.

There is an easy method to compute cumulative probabilities for every year. Indeed, to compute the cumulative probabilities of the second year, it suffices to square the transition matrix, i.e., multiply this matrix by itself. Table 8.4 gives the corresponding transition matrix Π^2.

As can be seen in the Π^2 matrix, the cumulative probability that the firm rated B defaults at the end of the second year is 6.1 percent, which is the former result. This probability is equal to the probability of the first year to which is added the transitory probability of the second year. To

---

[21] We use Bayes rule, i.e., $p(D_2|A_1) = p(A_1 \cup D_2)/p(A_1)$.

T A B L E   8.4

Squared transition matrix

	A	B	C	D
10	0.961	0.038	0.0004	0.0006
11	0.0572	0.8494	0.0324	0.061
12	0.0204	0.1946	0.4924	0.2926
13	0	0	0	1

obtain the cumulative probabilities of the third year, it suffices to raise the transition matrix to the cubic power.

The marginal probabilities of each year, i.e., the variations of the cumulative probabilities, differ with the ratings. The marginal probabilities of the high ratings increase with time. However, the marginal probabilities of the low ratings increase during the first years and tend to decrease thereafter. For Jorion (2007) this profile is associated to a survival effect or a mean reverting process. A firm that has a low rating and that gets through its first years has more chances to survive thereafter. Hence, there will be a decrease of its marginal probability of default afterward.

The first advantage of the transition matrix is to inform about probabilities of default. The second is to compute the expected cash flows of a loans portfolio for estimating its C-VaR,[22] that is, the "credit VaR." The C-VaR is the worst loss on a fixed-income securities portfolio or a loans portfolio for a given confidence level and horizon.

Let us assume a bond with a given annual coupon equal to C. There exist four credit ratings, the last one being associated to default. The payoff vector of this bond defined over the possible states of the world (the credit ratings) depends upon whether we are at or before the expiration date. If $(t < T)$, the payoffs vector of the bond, one for each state of the world, is the following:

$$\Psi_t = \begin{bmatrix} C \\ C \\ \lambda \\ 0 \end{bmatrix}$$

---

[22] We resort to a hyphen to make the distinction between C-VaR and CvaR; this last acronym is reserved for conditional VaR.

We assume that the payoff is equal to λ if the rating is C and 0 if the rating is D. Otherwise, we are at expiration ($t = T$), and the payoffs vector is then

$$\Psi_T = \begin{bmatrix} 1+C \\ 1+C \\ \lambda \\ 0 \end{bmatrix}$$

To calculate the expected payoff, we add a vector that indicates the state of the world in which the firm is initially. For instance, it may take the following form:

$$E_0 = \begin{bmatrix} 1 \\ 0 \\ 0 \\ 0 \end{bmatrix}$$

According to this vector, the firm is initially in the first state and is rated A. The expected payoff for the bond is thus the following:

$$E\left[\Psi_t\right] = E_0 \Pi^t \Psi_t \tag{8.59}$$

with Π the transition matrix.

We further elaborate our analysis and compute the maximal loss for a bond with a given probability, i.e., the C-VaR of this bond. We assume that the bond maturity is one year and that it may take only four values V_i at the end of the year, i being the state of the world. The expected value of V is $V_m = \sum_{i=1}^{4} p_i V_i$, with p_i, the probability of state i. In addition, the standard deviation of V is computed as follows: $\sigma_V = \sqrt{\sum_{i=1}^{4} p_i (V_i - V_m)^2}$.

As $\sigma^2_x = E(X^2) - [E(X)]^2$, the standard deviation may be rewritten as follows: $\sigma_V = \sqrt{\sum_{i=1}^{4} p_i V_1^2 - (V_m)^2}$. If we assume a Gaussian distribution for V, the C-VaR for a 95 percent confidence level is equal to $C - VaR = V_m - 1{,}65\sigma_V$. However, the payoffs of the debt are not assumed to be normally distributed. The losses on loans possess a distribution similar to the payoff of a short put, where the distribution is leptokurtic and has negative asymmetry.

Cuthbertson and Nitzsche (2001) provide another method to compute the expectation of a bond payoff and its standard deviation at the end of a year. A bond is rated A initially and it expires in n years with an annual coupon of C. We compute the expected payoff and standard deviation at the end of the first year.

We assume the transition matrix contains only the ratings, A, B, and C, with C being associated to default. The transition matrix assigns probabilities to the firm issuing the bond for these three ratings. As we value the bonds at the end of the first year, we have the term structure of the forward rates from year 2 to year n. Let us consider the A rating. For this rating, we must have the forward rate f_{12}, that is, the discount rate that prevails from the end of the first year to the end of the second. We must also have the forward rate f_{13}, that is, the discount rate that prevails from the end of the first year to the end of the third year, and so on until $f_{1,n-1}$. The term structure of these rates also changes with the ratings because risky ratings will have forward rates shifted by higher risk premiums.

At the end of the first year, the firm may still be rated A or may have migrated to ratings B or C. If it is rated A, then the value of the bond is

$$V_{A,A} = C + \frac{C}{1+f_{12}} + \frac{C}{\left(1+f_{13}\right)^2} + \frac{C}{\left(1+f_{14}\right)^3} + \cdots + \frac{C}{\left(1+f_{1n}\right)^{n-1}} \quad (8.60)$$

We repeat the calculation for $V_{A,B}$ and $V_{A,C}$, making sure to change the term structure of the forward rates to account for the risk premiums that differ from one rating to the other.

We then value the expected payoffs of the bond and its standard deviation at the end of the first year as

$$V_{m,A} = \sum_{i=1}^{3} p_i V_i \quad (8.61)$$

where the p_i are drawn from the transition matrix. Besides, the standard deviation is computed as follows:

$$\sigma_{m,A} = \sqrt{\sum_{i=1}^{3} p_i V_i^2 - V_{m,A}^2} \qquad (8.62)$$

We also compute the C-VaR for a confidence level of 95 percent as follows: $C - VaR = V_m - 1{,}65\sigma_v$. The calculation is not reliable because the distribution of the losses of a risky debt involves (as in the payoff distribution of a short put) negative asymmetry and a high level of kurtosis. A solution to this problem is to use a multiple higher than 1.65 to compute the C-VaR for a confidence level of 95 percent. We may also resort to the Cornish−Fisher expansion to correct for this.

CREDIT DERIVATIVES

Credit derivatives are contingent claims whose payoffs are related to the credit situation of a firm or of a sovereign entity. The credit derivatives market is relatively new since its origins go back to the beginning of the 1990s. The traditional derivatives provide a protection against market risks, i.e., against the fluctuations of the price of securities and interest rates. Moreover, credit derivatives provide a protection against credit events likely to give rise to losses for investors, as the payment default by the issuer of a bond. The payoff of a credit derivative may be related linearly or nonlinearly to a credit event or to an indicator of credit risk. These instruments are over-the-counter securities, sold by financial institutions.

For Myhre (2003), the advent of credit derivatives may be explained in part by the international banking regulation established by the Basle committee in 1988. According to this regulation, every granted loan receives a weight of 100 percent to estimate the regulatory capital. However, if the bank is hedged by credit derivatives, the weight is reduced to 20 percent; therefore, resorting to credit derivatives allows banks to save capital.

Table 8.5, drawn from Jorion (2007), gives the composition of the credit derivatives market in 2003.

Credit Default Swaps

As shown in Table 8.5, CDSs clearly dominate the credit derivatives market. In a classical swap, counterparty A pays to counterparty B a fixed

T A B L E   8.5

Composition of the credit derivatives market 2003

Category	Percent of notional values
Credit default swap	73%
Synthetic securitization	22%
Credit linked notes	3%
Total return swap	1%
Credit spread options	1%
Total	100%

Source: Jorion (2007)

amount per period, similar to an option or insurance premium, and if default occurs, counterparty A receives nothing. Otherwise, if the loan granted by counterparty A defaults, B pays to A the face value of the loan reduced by its value on the secondary market.

The payoff of a CDS is equal to the following amount:

$$Payoff = notional\ value \times Q \times I(EC) \tag{8.63}$$

where the notional value is the amount of the loan; Q is the payment by unit of notional value and $I(EC)$ is the indicator function, which takes the value 1 if defaults occurs and 0 otherwise.

There is a variant to the classical credit swap that is, the pure credit swap. In this variant, the hedger, say A, pays to B the LIBOR to which is added a spread related to the risk of the loan hedged by the swap. This payment is effective as long as there is no default. When default occurs, this payment is terminated. Moreover, B pays the LIBOR to A over all the duration of the loan independently of the default of payment. This interest rate multiplies the notional amount, which stands for the value of the loan. This amount is said to be notional because it is not paid. As in all swaps, its value is zero initially, in the sense that the expected value of the net discounted cash flows is zero.

Jorion (2007) observes that credit swaps are embedded in many financial securities. For example, buying a risky bond is equivalent to buying a risk-free bond and selling a CDS.[23]

Longstaff et al. (2003) provide a simple example of a CDS. On January 22, 2007 an investor interested in hedging against credit risk purchases

---

[23] For the engineering of a risky bond, see Neftci (2004), Chapter 16.

a five-year protection against the default of bonds whose yield is 7.75 percent with expiry date of April, 1 2007. The investor has 10,000 bonds and the face value of each bond is $10,000. The notional value of this investor position is therefore $10 million. The credit swap provides full protection of the notional value of the bonds. The spread is 169 basis points (1.69 percent). Hence, the premium is $A/360 \times 169$ basis points per quarter, where A stands for the number of days in a quarter. Hence, the quarterly payment of the buyer of this credit swap is $A/360 \times (10 \times 10^6$ dollars$) \times 0.0169 = A/360 \times 169{,}000$ dollars. In case of default, the investor delivers its 10,000 bonds to the seller of the swap and receives in exchange an amount of $10 million.

The Longstaff et al. (2003) Model and the Premium of the Credit Swap

Longstaff et al. (2003) have proposed a reduced form model that involves an analytical solution and aims to compute the premium of the credit swap (spread). This model contains two key variables that follow a stochastic process: r_t, the risk-free interest rate, and λ_t, the default intensity, which is modeled by a Poisson process. The owner of the credit swap retrieves a fraction equal to $(1 - w)$ of the face value of the bond in case of default.

As r_t and λ_t follow independent stochastic processes, it is not necessary to specify the risk-neutral dynamics of the interest rates. The value $D(t)$ of the risk-free zero coupon bond is given by the following equation:

$$D(T) = E\left(e^{-\int_0^T r_t \, dt} \right) \tag{8.64}$$

Moreover, the default intensity follows a risk-neutral dynamics:

$$d\lambda = (\alpha - \beta\lambda) \, dt + \sigma\sqrt{\lambda} \, dz \tag{8.65}$$

Yields spreads follow a mean reverting process and show conditional heteroskedasticity. The square root process maintains λ_t in R^+. The probability p_t of no default until time T is equal to

$$p_t = e^{-\int_0^T \lambda_t \, dt} \tag{8.66}$$

Besides, the density function of the probability of time-until-default is

$$
\lambda_t e^{-\int_0^t \lambda_s \, ds} \, dt \tag{8.67}
$$

It is simple to note down the value of the corporate bonds and the credit swap premium as simple expectations in a risk-neutral world. We assume the corporate bond whose credit risk we want to analyze pays a continuous coupon c. The price of this corporate bond, denoted by $OC(c, w, T)$, is then

$$
\begin{aligned}
OC(c, w, T) = E\left(c \int_0^T e^{-\int_0^t (r_s + \lambda_s) \, ds} \, dt \right) + E\left(e^{-\int_0^T (r_t + \lambda_t) \, dt} \right) \\
+ E\left((1-w) \int_0^T \lambda_t e^{-\int_0^t (r_s + \lambda_s) \, ds} \, dt \right)
\end{aligned} \tag{8.68}
$$

This expression for the price of a risky corporate bond is easy to understand. The first term on the right-hand side (RHS) is the present value of the coupons promised by the bond. As in the Merton (1976) model, we note that default risk shifts the discount rate r by the coefficient of default intensity λ. The second term on the RHS of this equation is the present value of promised principal, while the third term is the present value of retrieved amounts in the event of a default.

Let s be the premium paid by the buyer of the credit swap. Let us assume first that λ is not stochastic. The present value of the premium received by the buyer of the swap, denoted by $P(s, t)$, is equal to

$$
P(s, T) = E\left(s \int_0^T e^{-\int_0^t (r_s + \lambda) \, ds} \, dt \right) \tag{8.69}
$$

Moreover, the expected value of the losses borne by the seller of the swap, denoted by $PR(w, T)$, is equal to

$$
PR(w, T) = E\left(w\lambda \int_0^T e^{-\int_0^t (r_s + \lambda) \, ds} \, dt \right) \tag{8.70}
$$

To compute the premium s, it suffices to equalize $P(s, t)$ and $PR(w, T)$. We then easily find:

$$s = \lambda w \qquad (8.71)$$

Let us assume that the loss is total when the default occurs, that is, w is equal to 1. The premium of the credit swap is then equal to λ, which measures the intensity of default in the Poisson distribution. In the preceding example, s was equal to 0.169, implying that one default is expected at about every six years (1/0.169).

However, if λ follows a stochastic process as in the model of Longstaff et al. (2003), the results are different. $P(s, t)$ is then equal to

$$P(s,T) = E\left(s\int_0^T e^{-\int_0^t (r_s + \lambda_s)\,ds}\,dt \right) \qquad (8.72)$$

and $PR(w, T)$ is

$$PR(w,T) = E\left(w\int_0^T \lambda_t e^{-\int_0^t (r_s + \lambda_s)\,ds}\,dt \right) \qquad (8.73)$$

To fix the premium s at its fair value, the expected value of the premium paid by the buyer of the swap, that is, $B(.)$, must be equal to the expected value of the losses borne by the seller of the swap, that is, $PR(.)$. The expected value of the net cash flow of the swap is then zero. To compute the premium s of the credit swap, it thus suffices to equalize $P(.)$ and $PR(.)$ and to isolate s:

$$s = \frac{E\left(w\int_0^T \lambda_t e^{-\int_0^t (r_s + \lambda_s)\,ds}\,dt \right)}{E\left(\int_0^T e^{-\int_0^t (r_s + \lambda_s)\,ds}\,dt \right)} \qquad (8.74)$$

The premium s may then be viewed as the weighted present value of $\lambda_t w$.

For Duffie (1999), the premium s stands for the yield spread over the risk-free rate that a floating rate corporate bond must pay to be sold at parity. For Longstaff et al. (2003), we can resort, as a first proxy for s, to the yield spread between a corporate bond and a government bond with identical maturities and coupons.

The Longstaff et al. (2003) model involves an analytical solution. We can write the price OC of a corporate bond as

$$
\begin{aligned}
OC(c,w,T) = c\int_0^T D(t)A(t)e^{B(t)\lambda}dt + D(T)A(T)e^{B(t)\lambda} \\
+ (1-w)\int_0^T D(t)\left[C(t)+H(t)\lambda\right]e^{B(t)\lambda}dt
\end{aligned}
\tag{8.75}
$$

where λ is the current value of the intensity of the Poisson process and

$$
A(t) = e^{[\alpha(\beta+\phi)/\sigma^2]t}\left(\frac{1-\kappa}{1-\kappa e^{\phi t}}\right)^{2\alpha/\sigma^2}
\tag{8.76}
$$

$$
B(t) = \frac{\beta-\phi}{\sigma^2} + \frac{2\phi}{\sigma^2\left(1-\kappa e^{\phi t}\right)}
\tag{8.77}
$$

$$
C(t) = \frac{\alpha}{\phi}\left(e^{\phi t}-1\right)e^{[\alpha(\beta+\phi)/\sigma^2]t}\left(\frac{1-\kappa}{1-\kappa e^{\phi t}}\right)^{2\alpha/\sigma^2+1}
\tag{8.78}
$$

$$
H(t) = e^{\left\{[\alpha(\beta+\phi)+\phi\sigma^2]/\sigma^2\right\}t}\left(\frac{1-\kappa}{1-\kappa e^{\phi t}}\right)^{2\alpha/\sigma^2+2}
\tag{8.79}
$$

$$
\phi = \sqrt{2\sigma^2 + \beta^2}
\tag{8.80}
$$

$$
\kappa = \frac{\beta+\phi}{\beta-\phi}
\tag{8.81}
$$

The analytical solution for the premium s of the credit swap is the following:

$$
s = \frac{w\int_0^T D(t)\left[C(t)+H(t)\lambda\right]e^{B(t)\lambda}\,dt}{\int_0^T D(t)A(t)e^{B(t)\lambda}\,dt}
\tag{8.82}
$$

Total Return Swap

We assume that a bank has granted a loan for an amount of $100 million at an interest rate of 6 percent and to hedge against it acquires a total return swap (TRS). In such a swap, the bank pays two amounts to its counterparty: (1) a fixed amount F, which stands for the interests of the loan; (2) the change in the value of the loan denoted by P. The payment of the bank is thus equal to

$$Payment = F + \frac{P_t - P_{t-1}}{P_{t-1}} \tag{8.83}$$

If the value of the loan decreases, the bank will thus receive compensation. Moreover, the bank receives the LIBOR shifted by a spread. Let us assume that the sum of these two percentages is 6 percent and further assume that the value of the loan has decreased by 5 percent. The bank will then have to pay 1 percent ($6\% - 5\%$) to its counterparty and will receive 6 percent with its net return being 5 percent. This percentage will compensate the bank for the fall of the value of the loan that it has granted.

Credit Options

Let SP be the spread between the yield of a risky bond and the yield of a risk-free one. The payoff of a credit spread option at its expiration is equal to

$$payoff = SP \times \mod ified\ duration \times notional\ value \tag{8.84}$$

We do not resort here to the max function because SP is necessarily positive. The price of this option is obtained as usual, that is,

$$C = e^{-r(T-\tau)} E^Q \left(payoff \right) \tag{8.85}$$

where T is the date of expiration of the option and $E^Q(.)$ is the operator for the computation of a risk-neutral expectation.

We assume that a bank has granted a loan whose risk is equivalent to that of the risky bond that is used to value the option. If the loan depreciates, the bank will recover, in totality or in part, this loss because the yield spread that serves to value the option will have increased.

The spread that serves to value the option may also be equal to the difference between yields of two bonds of different risk, i.e., $(SP_1 - SP_2)$. The payoff of the credit option is then equal to

$$payoff = MAX\,(SP_1 - SP_2, 0) \times modified\ duration \times notional\ value \quad (8.86)$$

Moreover, a default put allows selling a risky obligation to a predetermined strike if there is default. The option payoff is thus

$$payoff = strike \times I(EC) \quad (8.87)$$

where $I(EC)$ is the indicator function, which takes a value of 1 if there is default and 0 otherwise. If there is no default, the bank loses the premium. A default put is thus like an insurance policy.

In addition, an exchange option allows exchanging a risky bond B^* against a given amount of a risk-free bond. The payoff of such an option is equal to

$$payoff = \left(qB - B^*\right)^+ \quad (8.88)$$

where B is the value of the risk-free bond and B^* is the value of the risky bond and $q < 1$.

Credit Forwards

A credit forward is a contract written on a bond that serves as benchmark for a loan. Assume that a bank has granted a three-year loan and it hedges its credit risk by writing a contract where the term spread K_F, the exercise rate, is 2 percent. The bond yield that serves as benchmark for the loan is SP. At expiration, the payoff of this contract is

$$payoff = notional\ value \times \left(S_{PT} - K_F\right) \times modified\ duration \quad (8.89)$$

The payoff of the counterparty is the opposite of the bank's payoff. If the loan granted by the bank is perfectly correlated to the bond that serves as benchmark in the forward contract, the credit risk of the bank is perfectly hedged. If the risk of the firm has increased during the loan life, then $(S_{PT} - K_F) > 0$ and therefore the contract is in the money at its expiration. However, the bank will have to pay its counterparty if $(S_{PT} - K_F) < 0$ at the contract expiration, but, according to the payoff equation, this amount is restricted to

$$notional\ value \times K_F \times modified\ duration \qquad (8.90)$$

Cuthbertson and Nitzsche (2001) note that, paradoxically, for a credit forward, the payoff for the seller is similar to that of a long position in a put.

Loan Securitization and Credit Linked Notes

Securitization in the United States has been practiced for numerous decades, which consists of transforming loans not having a liquid secondary market (as long as this secondary market exists) into liquid securities. This technique pools these loans and issues units to finance them, similar to shares in a mutual fund.

Securitization is particularly widespread in the mortgage sector. We divide mortgage funds in risk tranches to segment according to customer groups. Securitization consists of loan categories such as personal and commercial loans, which do not have a liquid market and can also be securitized. Note that securitized assets are considered off balance sheet by banks.

Credit linked notes are a securitization category that do not give rise to the removal of loans from balance sheets. The banks decide to securitize a loan category by issuing counterparty credit-linked notes. The yield of these notes is proportional to the risk borne by the investor. The owner of a credit-linked note assumes the entire amount of default risk of the securitized asset and is ready to suffer a capital loss in the case of the default by the bank's customer.

Jorion (2007) gives an example of another type of credit note. The investor acquiring a credit-linked note pays its nominal value. A trustee invests the collected funds in first-grade assets and takes a short position in a credit default swap. The yield of these assets is a spread over LIBOR amounting to *Y percent*. Moreover, the return of the CDS is an additional premium of *X percent*. A bank that wants to hedge itself against a credit risk may have been issued this swap. The total return of the investor is LIBOR $+ Y\% + X\%$. In counterparty of this accrued return, the investor is ready to suffer a capital loss in the case of default. Credit-linked notes may be exposed to more than one credit risk, and their return may be increased by resorting to leverage.

OTHER APPROACHES TO CREDIT RISK

The Moody's KMV Model

The KMV model is structural and was inspired by the Merton model. This model calculates the default distance with regards to a barrier triggering the default. The principal input of the KMV model is the expected frequency of default.

The J. P. Morgan's E2C Model (Equity to Credit)

This model is also in line with the Merton model. As the KMV model, it focuses on the expected probability of default. By incorporating the density function of default, it can compute the premiums on credit swaps.

RiskMetrics, CreditMetrics, and CrashMetrics

As proposed by J. P. Morgan, the RiskMetrics model focuses on the computation of the VaR parameters, while the purpose of CreditMetrics is for analyzing default risk. Its methodology allows computing the risk related to a securities portfolio. Furthermore, CrashMetrics studies extreme risk scenarios that may plague a portfolio.

CONCLUSION

Credit derivatives may have allowed banks to go through the high-tech market bubble observed at the beginning of the new millennium. Without these derivatives, many bank bankruptcies may have occurred. Credit derivatives efficiently transfer credit risk to the agents willing to accept the risk. Before the advent of credit derivatives, there were very few instruments to transfer credit risk. Credit letters and bankers acceptances were then the only instruments that could provide a protection against credit risk. The widespread development of credit instruments since the 1990s has given rise to a great improvement of transfer of risks related to payment default.

Compared to the B&S differential equation, the differential equation of a credit derivative incorporates an interest rate higher than the risk-free rate. Hence, this is its major difference when compared to the B&S model. In a structural model, the interest rate is shifted by a probability of default while in a reduced form model it is shifted by the hazard rate. This gives way to higher values for credit calls than for plain-vanilla ones, while the opposite relation holds true for puts. It is well known that the replicating portfolio for a call is formed by a long position in the underlying stock and a short position in bonds. The short position in bonds protects the call in case of ruin (Gatheral, 2006, p. 76). The opposite reasoning holds for the put.

It remains that the theory of credit risk is still in search of a risk measure that accounts appropriately for extreme risks, i.e., tails risk. The integration of the theory of stochastic dominance with these risk measures promises to attain this objective. Because the distribution of credit losses is very asymmetric and leptokurtic, the Markowitz theory, based on the mean-variance trade-off, is inappropriate to study credit risk. More research by both academics and practitioners should be attributed to the credit risk sector.

REFERENCES

Black, F. and Cox, J.C. (1976) Valuing Corporate Securities: Some Effects of Bond Indenture Provisions. *Journal of Finance,* 31(2): 351–367.

Black F. and Scholes, M. (1973) The Pricing of Options and Corporate Liabilities. *Journal of Political Economy,* 81(3): 637–654.

Black F., Derman, E., and Toy, W. (1990) A One-Factor Model of Interest Rates and Its Application to Treasury Bond Options. *Financial Analysts Journal,* 46(1): 33–39.

Cox, J., Ross, S., and Rubinstein, M. (1979) Option Pricing: A Simplified Approach, *Journal of Financial Economics*, 7(3): 229–264.

Cuthbertson, K. and Nitzsche, D. (2001) *Financial Engineering: Derivatives and Risk Management*, Hoboken, NJ: John Wiley & Sons.

Das, S.R., (2000) Interest Rate Modelling with Jump-Diffusion Processes. In: N. Jegadesh and B. Tuckman (eds), *Advanced Fixed-Income Valuation Tools*. Hoboken NJ: John Wiley & Sons.

Derman, E. and Taleb, N. (2005) The Illusion of Dynamic Delta Replication. *Quantitative Finance*, 5(4): 323–326.

Dixit, A. and Pindyck, R.S. (1994) *Investment under Uncertainty.*
    Princeton, NJ: Princeton University Press.

Duffie, G. (1999) Estimating the Price of Default Risk. *Review of
    Financial Studies*, 12(1): 197–226.

Gatheral, J. (2006) *The Volatility Surface: A Pratitioner's Guide.*
    Hoboken, NJ: John Wiley & Sons.

Haug, E.G. (1998) *Option Pricing Formulas.* Hoboken, NJ: John Wiley
    & Sons.

Haug, E.G. (1998) *The Complete Guide to Option Pricing Formulas.*
    New York: McGraw Hill.

Haug, E.G. (2006) *Derivatives: Models on Models.* Hoboken, NJ: John
    Wiley & Sons.

Haug, E.G. (2007) *Derivatives: Models on Models.* Chichester: John
    Wiley & Sons.

Haug, E.G. (2007) *Option Pricing Formulas.* Hoboken, NJ: John Wiley
    & Sons.

Haug, E.G. (2007) *The Complete Guide to Option Pricing Formulas,
    Second Edition.* New York: McGraw Hill.

Jorion, P. (2007) *Financial Risk Manager's Handbook, Third Edition.*
    Hoboken, NJ: John Wiley & Sons.

Kazemi, H., Schneeweis, T, and Gupta, R. (2004), Omega as a
    Performance Measure, *Journal of Performance Measurement*, 8(3):
    42–54.

Longstaff, F. and Schwartz, E.S. (1995) A Simple Approach to Valuing
    Risky Fixed and Floating Rate Debt. *The Journal of Finance*,
    50(3): 789–819.

Longstaff, F., Mithal, S., and Neis, E. (2003) The Credit Default Swap
    Market: Is Credit Protection Priced Correctly? USC FBE Finance
    Seminar, October 24, Los Angeles, CA.

Merton, R.C. (1974) On the Pricing of Corporate Debt: The Risk
    Structure of Interest Rates. *Journal of Finance*, 29(2): 449–470.

Merton, R. (1976) Option Pricing When Underlying Stock Returns Are Discontinuous. *Journal of Financial Economics,* 3(1–2): 125–144.

Merton, R. (1992) *Continuous-Time Finance.* Malden, MA: Blackwell.

Myrhe, H.M. (2003) Pricing Credit Derivatives. Working paper, Norwegian University of Science and Technology, Bergen.

Neftci, S.N. (2000) *An Introduction to the Mathematics of Financial Derivatives.* Burlington, MA: Academic Press.

Neftci, S.N. (2004) *Principles of Financial Engineering.* San Diego, CA: Elsevier Academic Press.

Racicot, F.É. and Théoret, R. (2005) *Traité de gestion de portefeuille: titres à revenus fixes et produits dérivés.* Presses de l'Université du Québec, Québec: Lévy.

Racicot, F.É. and Théoret, R. (2006) *Finance computationnelle et gestion des risques.* Levy, QC. Presses de l'Université du Québec.

Racicot, F.É. and Théoret, R. (2006) *Finance computationnelle et gestion des risques: Ingénierie financière avec applications Excel (Visual Basic) et MatLab.* Levy: Presses de l'Université du Québec.

Rouah, F.D. and Vainberg, G. (2007) *Option Pricing Models and Volatility Using Excel-VBA.* Hoboken, NJ: John Wiley & Sons.

Samuelson, P.A. (1965) Rational Theory of Warrant Pricing, *Industrial Management Review*, 6(1): 13–31.

Stuart, A. and Ord, J.K. (1994) *Kendall's Advanced Theory of Statistics. Volume 1: Distribution Theory.* London: Hodder Arnold Oxford University Press.

Vasicek, O. (1977) An Equilibrium Characterization of the Term Structure. *Journal of Financial Economics*, 5(2): 117–161.

Wilmott, P. (2000) *Paul Wilmott on Quantitative Finance.* Hoboken, NJ: John Wiley & Sons.

CHAPTER 9

Investigating the Link between Credit Default Swap Spreads and the U.S. Financial Market

Hayette Gatfaoui

ABSTRACT

We focus on the link prevailing between credit default swap spreads and the U.S. financial market. We apply linear and nonlinear regression methods to investigate the relationship between CDX spreads and Dow Jones Composite Index return. Specifically, we are concerned about the impact of the U.S. market index on CDX spreads. Do U.S. market changes impair CDX spread changes? Do CDX spreads move due to U.S. market changes? Our results are appealing insofar as U.S. market index return changes are a key determinant in explaining CDX spread levels. However, the joint reverse evolution of both CDX spread changes and index return changes is a fundamental factor in explaining the evolution of CDX spread changes.

INTRODUCTION

Academic and practical research has investigated various links between equity markets and credit markets during the last three decades [e.g., Abid and Naifar (2006), Bakshi et al. (2006), Das et al. (2006b), Hui et al. (2004), Stivers et al. (2002), and Vassalou and Xing (2004)]. The seminal work of Merton (1974) launched this research stream. More recently, Gatfaoui (2002) employs Merton's (1974) original framework to distinguish between systematic market-based and unsystematic market-based components in corporate bond spreads (i.e., credit risky assets) whereas Benos and Papanastasopoulos (2005) build a Merton-based hybrid model incorporating financial and accounting variables. Currently, academic research focuses on some equivalence between credit default swap spreads and credit spreads [i.e., corporate bond yields versus corresponding Treasury yields; see Blanco et al. (2005)]. Credit spreads are known as key determinants of default risk, whereas credit default swap (CDS) spreads are considered as both default risk and liquidity risk fundamentals[1] (Das and Hanouna, 2006a). However, CDS spreads and credit spreads are closely related as respective proxies of default risk (Longstaff et al., 2005). Moreover, Abid and Naifar (2005), Carr and Wu (2005), as well as Lin and Shyy (2003) highlight some link prevailing between equity market and CDS rates.

In the light of current and new research, we investigate the potential link between CDS spreads and a U.S. market index (as a proxy of U.S. financial market conditions) and specifically address two main questions. First, do U.S. market changes impair CDX spread changes? Second, do CDX spreads move due to U.S. market changes? These questions are fundamental insofar as credit risk management may have to be envisioned in the light of market risk impact. Thus, the significance of our study has some nonnegligible implications for scenario analysis as well as credit risk forecasting under the Basel II framework.

Our chapter is organized as follows. The first section describes the data under consideration and introduces related empirical facts as well as primary investigation. The next section investigates the possible impact of the U.S. financial market on CDS spreads using quantitative analysis. We then investigate linear as well as nonlinear links while using regression analysis. We demonstrate that both market price risk and market volatility risk impact CDS spreads. In the following section, we then establish a prevailing link while considering a joint risk structure within a linear framework. Specifically, we highlight the joint evolution of both market conditions and CDS spreads as a key determinant of CDS spread evolutions. Finally, we discuss future research extensions.

---

[1] Indeed, credit spreads may widen due to a degradation of liquidity conditions in credit markets.

DATA SET

We present the data set under consideration and investigate key statistical features and other related empirical facts.

Description

First, we consider as financial market data both the return of Dow Jones Composite Index (DJCI) expressed in basis points (i.e., R_DJCI), and the Chicago Board Options Exchange–Dow Jones Industrial Average (CBOE DJIA) Volatility Index (VXD).[2] Our financial market data are based on available closing prices. Second, we consider the spreads of eight Dow Jones CDX indexes (i.e., CDX spreads). Dow Jones CDX indexes are indexes aimed at tracking the CDS market as well as related liquidity. Corresponding spreads are expressed in basis points and computed as the difference between Dow Jones CDX rates and related London Interbank Offered Rate (LIBOR) rates (refer to http://www.markit.com for explanations). The set of Dow Jones CDX indexes is split into two groups. The first group refers to six Dow Jones North America credit derivative indexes, which relate to reference entities domiciled in North America. We label NA_IG, NA_IG_HVOL, NA_HY, NA_HY_BB, NA_HY_B, and NA_XO the investment grade, investment grade high volatility, high yield, BB-rated high yield, B-rated high yield, and crossover Dow Jones CDX indexes, respectively. Crossover NA_XO index refers to the fact that Standard & Poor's and Moody's rating agencies may differ across the ratings they assign to reference entities in the BB/Ba-BBB/Baa rating grades range. The second group refers to two Dow Jones Emerging Markets credit derivative indexes, which relate to entities domiciled either in Latin America, Eastern Europe, Middle East, Africa, or Asia. We label EM and EM_DIV the emerging markets and emerging markets diversified Dow Jones CDX indexes, respectively. Specifically, EM index focuses on sovereign entities, whereas EM_DIV focuses on both sovereign and corporate entities. Moreover, CDS IndexCo LLC members establish the weights of EM Dow Jones CDX index, whereas remaining Dow Jones CDX indexes are all equal-weighted indexes. Dow Jones CDX indexes are generally reviewed and updated on a semiannual basis. Finally, our daily data set is based on closing mid prices

---

[2] The CBOE DJIA Volatility Index illustrates investors' expectation about future stock market volatility.

(with regard to CDX indexes), and ranges from September 20, 2005 to August 14, 2006, a total of 225 observations per series.

Empirical Features

First, Table 9.1 displays some key descriptive statistics of our data set. Basically, our time series are all skewed and exhibit generally a negative excess kurtosis (i.e., leptokurtic time series) except for EM_DIV Dow Jones CDX index and R_DJCI return. In unreported results, we find that R_DJCI return is stationary whereas all Dow Jones CDX indexes are first-order integrated time series (i.e., Dow Jones CDX indexes are nonstationary, but their respective first-order differences are stationary). Other unreported results exhibit insignificant Kendall and Spearman correlation coefficients between Dow Jones CDX spreads and DJCI return at a 5 percent bilateral test level. To get a view, we display in Tables 9.2 and 9.3 Kendall and Spearman correlation coefficients of the first-order differences of our data set (i.e., daily changes). Correlation coefficients are generally significant at a 1 percent bilateral test level except for the correlation between NA_HY_BB CDX spread and DJCI return (5 percent significance level). By the way, we notice a negative correlation between CDX spread changes and DJCI return changes. Moreover, all CDX spread daily changes are positively correlated with VXD daily changes, whereas DJCI return changes are negatively correlated with VXD changes.

T A B L E   9.1

Descriptive statistics for data (expressed in basis points)

CDX Index	Median	Skewness	Excess Kurtosis
EM	154.7300	−0.1584	−0.4742
EM_DIV	102.1300	0.7123	0.7566
NA_HY_BB	240.4400	−0.3275	−0.6396
NA_HY_B	310.6200	0.0117	−0.3855
NA_HY	344.1000	0.4284	−0.1431
NA_IG_HVOL	89.1900	−0.1817	−0.9118
NA_IG	44.2200	−0.2183	−0.5853
NA_XO	211.5600	−0.3938	−0.7453
R_DJCI	6.5810	0.1164	0.4459
VXD	11.8900	1.2163	1.5888

TABLE 9.2

Kendall and (Spearman) correlation matrix for first-order differences of data

CDX Index	EM	EM_DIV	NA_HY_BB	NA_HY_B	NA_HY	NA_IG_HVOL	NA_IG	NA_XO	R_DJCI
EM	1.0000	0.5773	0.1998	0.2582	0.2951	0.3196	0.3117	0.2996	−0.2451
EM_DIV	(0.7518)	1.0000	0.1240	0.1965	0.2360	0.2431	0.2356	0.1853	−0.1593
NA_HY_BB	(0.2841)	(0.1803)	1.0000	0.6374	0.5998	0.4739	0.3982	0.4850	−0.1053
NA_HY_B	(0.3636)	(0.2916)	(0.8059)	1.0000	0.6390	0.4693	0.4661	0.5192	−0.1240
NA_HY	(0.4185)	(0.3453)	(0.7765)	(0.8167)	1.0000	0.5324	0.4895	0.5520	−0.1574
NA_IG_HVOL	(0.4452)	(0.3518)	(0.6546)	(0.6429)	(0.7130)	1.0000	0.7159	0.6154	−0.1754
NA_IG	(0.4352)	(0.3465)	(0.5521)	(0.6325)	(0.6575)	(0.8871)	1.0000	0.5579	−0.1611
NA_XO	(0.4250)	(0.2708)	(0.6563)	(0.6933)	(0.7242)	(0.7907)	(0.7305)	1.0000	−0.1557
R_DJCI	(−0.3584)	(−0.2363)	(−0.1541)	(−0.1827)	(−0.2315)	(−0.2535)	(−0.2375)	(−0.2282)	1.0000

TABLE 9.3

Kendall and Spearman correlations between daily changes of VXD and other data

CDX Index	Kendall	Spearman
EM	0.2076	0.2954
EM_DIV	0.1528	0.2230
NA_HY_BB	0.2060	0.2991
NA_HY_B	0.1348	0.2014
NA_HY	0.2051	0.2995
NA_IG_HVOL	0.2219	0.3203
NA_IG	0.1765	0.2628
NA_XO	0.1915	0.2744
R_DJCI	−0.1348	−0.1814

Second, as a preliminary investigation of the link prevailing between Dow Jones CDX indexes and DJCI returns, we introduce the following correlation index I^S_t for each time t ranging from 2 to 225 (i.e., 224 observations per series):[3]

$$I^S_t = \frac{\Delta S_t}{\Delta R \_ DJCI_t} \qquad (9.1)$$

where $\Delta S_t = S_t - S_{t-1}$ (i.e., first-order difference), and S_t is the Dow Jones CDX index spread (i.e., CDX spread) at time t. When I^S_t is positive, the Dow Jones CDX spread daily changes and the DJCI returns' daily changes exhibit the same sign (i.e., correlated evolution of Dow Jones CDX spreads and DJCI returns from day to day). When I^S_t is negative, the Dow Jones CDX spread daily changes and DJCI returns daily changes exhibit an opposite sign (i.e., reverse evolution of the Dow Jones CDX spreads and the DJCI return from day to day). Finally, when I^S_t is zero, we are unable to find a link between CDX spread daily changes and DJCI return daily changes (i.e., disconnected evolution of Dow Jones CDX spreads and DJCI return from day to day). Table 9.4 displays the proportion of observed positive, zero, and negative values of correlation index I^S_t over the time horizon.

---

[3] Dow Jones Composite Index return exhibits no zero-valued change from one day to another.

T A B L E   9.4

Proportion of correlation index values

Percentage	Proportion < 0	Proportion $= 0$	Proportion > 0
EM	65.6250	0.4464	33.9286
EM_DIV	58.0357	0.4464	41.5179
NA_HY_BB	53.5714	0.8929	45.5357
NA_HY_B	55.8036	0.4464	43.7500
NA_HY	58.0357	0.4464	41.5179
NA_IG_HVOL	57.1429	0.4464	42.4107
NA_IG	58.4821	0.8929	40.6250
NA_XO	58.0357	0.4464	41.5179

Namely, Prop. < 0, Prop. > 0, and Prop. $= 0$ refer to reverse, correlated, and noncorrelated joint evolution of Dow Jones CDX spreads and DJCI returns, respectively. The proportion of joint reverse daily changes in both CDX spreads and DJCI returns is far above the corresponding proportion of joint correlated daily changes. Consequently, CDX spreads and DJCI returns tend to evolve in a reverse way over the time horizon and on an average basis.

ECONOMETRIC STUDY

We investigate a potential linear and nonlinear link prevailing between CDX spreads and DJCI returns and resort to the classic regression methodology to achieve a two-step process. Namely, we run two different types of regressions to investigate two distinct kinds of influences of DJCI returns (i.e., financial market conditions) on CDX spreads (i.e., credit risk market). The first step investigates the impact of DJCI return changes on CDX spread changes, whereas the second step encompasses available information about equity volatility.

Impact of DJCI Return Changes

First, Gourieroux and Jasiak (2001) underline heavily nonlinearity patterns in financial markets. Hence, nonlinear structures in financial markets need to be acknowledged while studying related financial and economic phenomena. Therefore, our first step consists of a set of linear/nonlinear regressions linking daily changes in CDX spreads to daily changes in DJCI returns. We perform the following regressions for t ranging from 2 to 225:

$$\Delta S_t = a + b_1 \times \Delta R\_\text{DJCI}_t + \sum_{k=2}^{q} \left(b_k \times \Delta R\_\text{DJCI}_t^k \right) + e_t \qquad (9.2)$$

where a is a regression constant, $(b_1, \dots, b_q)$ are regression coefficients, (e_t) are regression residuals, and q describes the nonlinearity structure linking potentially CDX spread changes to DJCI return changes. The "optimal" regression models we obtained exhibited a lag q up to 9, and the results are summarized in Table 9.5. Regression adjusted R squares are generally very low. Though insignificant at a 5 percent Student test level, regression coefficient a is negative for all the CDX spread changes under consideration. However, regression coefficients b_k are all[4] negative and significant at a 5 percent Student test level. Consequently, we can clearly demonstrate a negative link between CDX spread changes and DJCI return changes over our time horizon. Moreover, except for NA_IG_HVOL, NA_IG, and NA_XO regressions,[5] regressions are sound insofar as Durbin Watson statistics (DW) indicate the nonexistence of first-order autocorrelations in residuals. For such regressions, we tested in unreported results for regression coefficients' stability, high-order autocorrelations in both residuals and squared residuals (e.g., Lagrange multiplier in a Breusch–Godfrey test), and heteroskedasticity in residuals (e.g., White test) and computed corresponding Ljung-Box statistics (i.e., white noise test). Finally, we found sound regression residuals.

Consequently, results exhibit the significance of DJCI return changes in explaining the level of CDX spread changes. However, DJCI return changes are far from explaining fully the evolution of CDX spread changes over our time horizon since corresponding regressions exhibit a generally low explanatory power.

Incorporating Equity Volatility

As a second step, we investigate some complementary information (i.e., potentially missing information in terms of equity volatility risk). For this

---

[4] Except coefficient b_9, which is almost zero.
[5] Those regressions exhibit a positive first-order correlation in corresponding residuals.

T A B L E   9.5

Regression models of CDX spread daily changes on DJCI return daily changes

Estimate (Student's t)	a	b_1	b_3	b_6	b_9	R^2(%)	DW
EM	−0.0570	−0.0161	—	−3.3300E−15	—	7.8251	1.7957
	(−0.1369)	(−4.5861)		(−3.5303)			
EM_DIV	−0.1052	−0.0077	—	—	2.7800E−23	4.4673	2.0323
	(−0.4488)	(−3.1060)			(2.1189)		
NA_HY_BB	−0.1618	—	−1.4700E−07	—	—	2.5164	1.7708
	(−0.4992)		(−3.5423)				
NA_HY_B	−0.196631	—	−1.15E−07	—	—	0.8349	1.9154
	(−0.5046)		(−2.2872)				
NA_HY	−0.1809	—	−1.6500E−07	—	—	1.1458	1.8026
	(−0.3611)		(−2.4993)				
NA_IG_HVOL	−0.0711	−0.0038	—	—	—	6.6567	1.6387
	(−0.6812)	(−4.0131)					
NA_IG	−0.0289	−0.0016	—	—	—	6.8371	1.6021
	(−0.6805)	(−3.5137)					
NA_XO	−0.1266	—	−1.5300E−07	—	—	3.4710	1.4057
	(−0.4319)		(−3.2053)				

purpose, we incorporate the daily changes of VXD volatility index as a proxy of equity volatility. Such an explanatory variable should bring complementary information in explaining CDX spread evolutions over time. Indeed, equity information (i.e., equity risk and equity uncertainty/volatility) appears to be necessary and useful for describing default risk fundamentals and more widely credit risk (Carr and Wu, 2005; Churm and Panigirtzoglou, 2005; Cremers et al., 2005).

We run the following regression models for t ranging from 2 to 225:

$$\Delta S_t = a + b_0 \times \Delta R\_DJCI_t + b_1 \times \Delta VXD_t + \sum_{k=2}^{q} \left(b_k \times \Delta VXD_t^k \right) + e_t \qquad (9.3)$$

where a is a regression constant, $(b_1, \ldots, b_q)$ are regression coefficients, (e_t) are regression residuals, and q describes the nonlinearity structure linking potentially CDX spread changes to VXD changes. Notice that VXD could be considered as some nonlinear transformation of DJCI returns. The optimal regression models we obtained exhibited a lag q up to 7, and the results are displayed in Table 9.6.

Table 9.6 exhibits first stable regression results through related DW statistics (i.e., no first-order autocorrelation in residuals) except for NA_XO index case. In unreported results, we checked for homoskedastic residuals (i.e., White test). Second, regression constant a is always negative and insignificant at a 5 percent Student test level. Third, b_k regression coefficients give us information about the average observed behavior of CDX spread changes over the studied time horizon. Those regression coefficients are significant at a 5 percent Student test level. When they are relevant in regressions, b_0 estimates are negative and illustrate a global reverse link between CDX spread daily changes and DJCI return daily changes over our time horizon. Differently, b_1 estimates are positive and highlight a global correlated joint evolution of CDX spread changes and VXD volatility index changes over our time horizon. Defining VXD daily changes ($(\Delta VXDt)$) as the key market volatility indicator, b_1 estimates allow for classifying CDX spreads as a function of their respective sensitivity to volatility risk. Under this assumption, NA_IG and NA_IG_HVOL indexes exhibit the lowest market volatility risk, whereas NA_HY exhibits the highest volatility risk.

Strikingly, b_3, b_5, and b_7 estimates are negative and illustrate a global reverse link between CDX spread changes and some nonlinear transformation of VXD volatility index changes over our time horizon. Finally, the explanatory power of regressions increases strongly with the incorporation of equity volatility information. Therefore, the complementary information brought by VXD volatility index allows for a better explanation of CDX spread evolutions over time in addition to DJCI return information.[6] Such a result is significant given its implications for risk management prospects. Indeed, not only is market price risk (as represented by DJCI return changes) important, but market volatility risk (as represented by VXD volatility index) is also more significant in explaining CDX spread evolutions. Focusing on the combination of risk factors explaining and driving CDX spreads' evolutions, we target a more detailed analysis in the next section.

---

[6] In unreported results, we remove the DJCI return's impact in the regressions where this explaining variable appears. However, results become poor and less significant insofar as the explanatory power of relevant regressions is strongly impaired.

TABLE 9.6

Regression models of CDX spread changes on both DJCI returns and VXD changes

Estimate (Student's t)	a	b_0	b_1	b_3	b_5	b_7	R^2(%)	DW
EM	−0.1893	−0.0128	2.3722	−0.1088	—	—	12.2604	1.8794
	(−0.4734)	(−3.0109)	(3.6105)	(−2.9352)				
EM_DIV	−0.1257	−0.0054	1.2615	−0.0638	—	—	8.7188	2.1411
	(−0.5498)	(−2.2011)	(3.5016)	(−3.1311)				
NA_HY_BB	−0.2088	—	2.2528	—	−0.0054	—	11.4519	1.9506
	(−0.6760)		(6.2287)		(−6.8292)			
NA_HY_B	−0.2472	—	2.2184	—	−0.0059	—	7.9273	2.1141
	(−0.6588)		(5.1411)		(−6.6237)			
NA_HY	−0.2432	—	3.0304	—	−0.0070	—	8.5268	1.9916
	(−0.5059)		(5.7207)		(−7.7087)			
NA_IG_HVOL	−0.0851	−0.0029	0.6839	—	−0.0015	—	15.7426	1.8023
	(−0.8546)	(−2.8325)	(5.1089)		(−4.7564)			
NA_IG	−0.0346	−0.0012	0.2651	—	−0.0006	—	15.0768	1.7624
	(−0.8453)	(−2.4133)	(4.1272)		(−3.9348)			
NA_XO	−0.1670	−0.0056	1.5299	—	—	−0.0001	9.8316	1.5220
	(−0.5882)	(−2.0197)	(4.0744)			(−4.7055)		

193

INVESTIGATING A JOINT EVOLUTION

Previous results support considering both market price risk and market volatility risk while explaining CDX spread evolutions over time. We construct an indicator based on a combination of both market price and market volatility risks, which summarizes jointly these two risk sources. We then demonstrate this indicator's impact on CDX spreads while resorting again to a linear regression methodology.

Linear Framework

Some authors like Carr and Wu (2005), Cremers et al. (2005), Luciano and Shoutens (2005) as well as Zhang et al. (2005), among others, recently advocated considering the joint behavior of market and credit data in determining default risk fundamentals. Indeed, two key factors among others explain CDX spread evolutions, namely, market price risk as represented by DJCI return changes and market volatility risk as represented by VXD volatility index in the previous section. We propose to embody those two risk sources in a dummy indicator $Dummy_t$. We define this indicator so that its value is unity only when simultaneously DJCI returns increase and CDX spreads decrease from one day to another. Hence, our dummy indicator is binary and defined as follows:

$$Dummy_t = \begin{cases} 1 & when \ \Delta R\_DJCI_t > 0 \ and \ \Delta S_t < 0 \\ 0 & else \end{cases} \qquad (9.4)$$

We choose this setting along with the results exposed in an earlier section. According to that section, the proportion of observed cases where CDX spread changes and DJCI return changes evolve jointly in a reverse way is far above the proportion of observed cases where CDX spread and DJCI return daily changes evolve jointly in a correlated manner. Moreover, Table 9.7 shows that there are more observed cases where we face jointly a CDX spreads' decrease with a DJCI return increase than cases where we face jointly a CDX spreads' increase with a DJCI return decrease.

Dummy indicator $Dummy_t$ takes into account not only the market price risk driving CDX spreads but the corresponding market volatility risk as well. The direction of changes in CDX spreads determines the sign

T A B L E   9.7

Proportions for joint behavior of CDX spread and DJCI return changes

Percentage	CDX Spreads Increase and DJCI Return Decreases	CDX Spreads Decrease and DJCI Return Increases
EM	31.2500	34.3750
EM_DIV	27.2321	30.8036
NA_HY_BB	25.4464	28.1250
NA_HY_B	24.1071	31.6964
NA_HY	26.3393	31.6964
NA_IG_HVOL	28.1250	29.0179
NA_IG	27.2321	31.2500
NA_XO	28.1250	29.9107

of corresponding changes, and the magnitude of variation of CDX spreads reflects corresponding volatility risk along with DJCI return daily changes (i.e., direction and magnitude of market changes).[7]

We then investigate the impact of the dummy indicator on CDX spread daily changes (i.e., CDS spreads' evolutions) while running the following regressions for time t ranging from 2 to 225:

$$\Delta S_t = a + b_1 \times Dummy_t + b_2 \times \Delta R\_DJCI_t^q + e_t \qquad (9.5)$$

where a is a regression constant, (b_1, b_2) are regression coefficients, (e_t) are regression residuals, and q describes the nonlinearity structure linking potentially CDX spread changes to DJCI return changes. Related results are provided in the next subsection.

Econometric Results

Concerning regression model (9.5), the optimal regression models obtained exhibited a lag q equal to 6 when DJCI return change was a relevant

---

[7] Indicator $Dummy_t$ is highly correlated with DJCI return changes (DR_DJCI_t). Indeed, Kendall/Spearman correlation coefficients range from 0.4653/0.5798 for NA_HY_BB index case to 0.5369/0.6690 for EM index case. Moreover, all correlation coefficients are significant at a 1 percent bilateral test level.

explanatory variable. When it is relevant, the power component of DJCI return change reflects some complementary nonlinearity structure in the financial market in addition to the joint behavior of both CDX spread and DJCI return changes. Corresponding regression results are summarized in Table 9.8.

First, except for NA_XO index case, regression residuals are stable insofar as they exhibit no first-order autocorrelation along with related DW statistics. In unreported results, we performed a White test ensuring homoskedasticity in residuals. Second, regression constant a is now always positive and significant at a 5 percent Student test level. Third, b_k regression coefficients provide us with information about the average observed behavior of CDX spread changes over the studied time horizon with regard to the joint behavior of CDX spread and DJCI return changes as well as a nonlinear transformation of DJCI return changes. Those regression coefficients are significant at a 5 percent Student test level.

Noticeably, b_1 estimates are negative and highlight a global reverse relationship between CDX spread changes and dummy indicator level over our time horizon. Moreover, the absolute level of b_1 estimates (i.e.,

T A B L E   9.8

Regression models of CDX spread changes on both DJCI return and VXD changes

Estimate (Student's t)	a	b_1	b_2	R^2 (%)	DW
EM	1.9355 (3.4961)	−5.9358 (−8.9185)	−2.0600E−15 (−2.5709)	19.3172	1.7845
EM_DIV	0.8101 (2.7056)	−3.0064 (−7.7103)	—	14.7044	2.0445
NA_HY_BB	0.9793 (2.4505)	−4.0512 (−7.4476)	—	13.4210	1.9068
NA_HY_B	1.2751 (2.5460)	−4.6389 (−7.2722)	—	13.2659	2.0018
NA_HY	1.7220 (2.6878)	−5.9974 (−7.2185)	—	13.3841	1.8584
NA_IG_HVOL	0.3770 (2.9933)	−1.5490 (−8.4673)	—	18.6589	1.8041
NA_IG	0.1749 (3.4990)	−0.6541 (−8.4060)	—	20.9582	1.7823
NA_XO	0.9114 (2.4535)	−3.4641 (−6.8919)	—	12.2852	*1.5202*

respective magnitude) allows for classifying CDX spreads' sensitivity to market volatility (i.e., to quantify market volatility risk). Namely, NA_IG and NA_IG_HVOL indexes exhibit the lowest volatility risk, whereas NA_HY index exhibits the highest volatility risk over our time horizon. Further, the nonlinear transformation of DJCI return changes is relevant only for EM index case. The corresponding b_2 estimate is negative and significant at a 5 percent Student test level. Therefore, NA_XO CDX spread changes exhibit a reverse evolution over time with comparison to the related nonlinear transformation of DJCI return changes.

Finally, adjusted R squares (R^2) are high as compared to regression results of earlier subsections. By the way, considering the average absolute error as a classification criterion, we can rank the regression models (9.2), (9.3), and (9.5) estimated in our study. Table 9.9 shows that model (9.5) seems to perform slightly better than models (9.2) and (9.3).[8] Such a result has an important significance insofar as the increased explanatory power and lower average absolute error underline a better understanding of fundamental drivers of CDX spread changes over time. Indeed, our dummy indicator allows for better catching fundamentals underlying CDX spreads' evolution along with market conditions. Therefore, the indicator of joint

T A B L E   9.9

Average absolute regression errors

Estimate	Model (9.2)	Model (9.3)	Model (9.5)
EM	4.0025	3.9061	3.6874
EM_DIV	2.4462	2.4161	2.2384
NA_HY_BB	3.1458	2.9442	2.9249
NA_HY_B	3.4297	3.3833	3.2709
NA_HY	4.2374	4.0385	4.0142
NA_IG_HVOL	1.0972	1.0427	0.9930
NA_IG	0.4400	0.4228	0.4087
NA_XO	2.7593	2.6618	2.6043

---

[8] In unreported results, we find a zero average value of regression residuals whatever the model under consideration. Moreover, ranking regression models as a decreasing function of their respective residuals' standard deviation yields model (9.2), model (9.3), and finally model (9.5). Therefore, regression model (9.5) exhibits the lowest residuals' standard deviation.

evolution of CDX spread and DJCI return daily changes allows for better explaining CDX spread changes over time than VXD volatility index does (even when it is combined with DJCI return information).

CONCLUSION

We investigate the link prevailing between CDS spreads and U.S. financial market conditions. We then use Dow Jones CDX spreads as proxies of CDS spreads, whereas we apply both Dow Jones Composite Index (DJCI) returns and CBOE DJIA volatility index (VXD) as proxies of U.S. market conditions.

As a first step, we exhibit the relevance of DJCI return changes in explaining CDX spread changes. However, such a key explanatory variable is insufficient to explain fully CDX spread evolutions. As a second step, we incorporate the equity volatility information embedded in VXD changes. We subsequently show the nonnegligible and valuable information brought by the VXD volatility index in explaining CDX spread evolutions in addition to DJCI returns. As a third step, from a different viewpoint, we consider the joint evolution of both CDX spread changes and DJCI return changes over time. Such a joint behavior is summarized in a dummy indicator competing with both DJCI returns and VXD determinants in terms of explaining CDX spread changes. The results are robust demonstrating that CDX spread evolutions must be studied jointly with market evolution. Consequently, explaining CDS spreads' evolution requires accounting for both market price risk and market volatility risk over time and analyzing jointly CDS spread changes, market price, and market volatility behaviors.

However, our study can be extended in two manners. First, one could define more precisely our dummy indicator by establishing a set of thresholds for possible levels of both CDX spread changes and DJCI return changes (i.e., a set of potential variation bounds for daily changes in order to scale the possible magnitude of those changes). Such a framework would allow for quantifying more precisely the market price and market volatility risks along with CDX spreads' evolution over time (i.e., joint market and credit risk evolution). Second, we focus on a linear framework to consider the joint risk structure of CDX spreads and DJCI returns. A relevant extension of our study should therefore focus explicitly on a nonlinear framework to characterize the dependence structure of both credit risk and market risk.

REFERENCES

Abid, F. and Naifar, N. (2005) The Determinants of Credit Default Swap Rates: An Explanatory Study. Working paper, Faculty of Business and Economics, University of Sfax, Tunisia.

Abid, F. and Naifar, N. (2006) Credit Default Swap Rates and Equity Volatility: A Nonlinear Relationship. *Journal of Risk Finance*, 7(4): 348–371.

Bakshi, G., Madan, D., and Zhang, F.X. (2006) Investigating the Role of Systematic and Firm-Specific Factors in Default Risk: Lessons from Empirically Evaluating Credit Risk Models. *Journal of Business*, 79(4): 1955–1987.

Benos, A. and Papanastasopoulos, G. (2005) Extending the Merton Model: A Hybrid Approach to Assessing Credit Quality. Working paper, Department of Economics, School of Management and Economics, University of Peloponnese, Greece.

Blanco, R., Brennan, S., and Marsh, I.W. (2005) An Empirical Analysis of the Dynamic Relation between Investment-Grade Bonds and Credit Default Swaps. *Journal of Finance*, 60(5): 2255–2281.

Carr, P. and Wu, L. (2005) Stock Options and Credit Default Swaps: A Joint Framework for Valuation and Estimation. Working paper, Zicklin School of Business, Baruch College, New York.

Churm, R. and Panigirtzoglou, N. (2005) Decomposing Credit Spreads. Working paper, No. 253, Bank of England.

Cremers, M., Driessen, J., Maenhout, P., and Weinbaum, D. (2005) Explaining the Level of Credit Spreads: Option-Implied Jump Risk Premia in a Firm Value Model. Working paper, Johnson Graduate School of Management, Cornell University, Ithaca, NY.

Das, S.R. and P. Hanouna. (2006a) Credit Default Swap Spreads. *Journal of Investment Management*, 4(3): 93–105.

Das, S.R., Freed, L., Geng, G., and Kapadia, N. (2006b) Correlated Default Risk. *Journal of Fixed Income*, Fall: 1–26.

Gatfaoui, H. (2002) Risk Disaggregation and Credit Risk Valuation in a Merton Framework. *Journal of Risk Finance*, 4(3): 27–42.

Gourieroux, C. and Jasiak, J. (2001) *Financial Econometrics: Problems, Models, and Methods*. Princeton, NJ: Princeton University Press.

Hui, C.H., Lo, C.F., and Huang, M.X. (2004) Estimation of Default Probability by Three-Factor Structural Model. *Financial Engineering Review*, 3(1): 40–46.

Lin, S.-Y. and Shyy, G. (2003) Credit Spreads, Default Correlations and CDO Tranching: New Evidence from CDS Quotes. Working paper, Department of Information Management, Ta Hwa Institute of Technology, Taiwan.

Longstaff, F. A., Neis, E., and Mithal, S. (2005) Corporate Yield Spreads: Default Risk or Liquidity? New Evidence from the Credit-Default Swap Market. *Journal of Finance*, 60(5): 2213–2253.

Luciano, E. and Shoutens, W. (2005) A Multivariate Jump-Driven Financial Asset Model. UCS Technical report 2005–02, U.C.S., K.U. Leuven, Belgium.

Merton, R.C. (1974) On the Pricing of Corporate Debt: The Risk Structure of Interest Rates. *Journal of Finance*, 29(2): 449–470.

Stivers, C., Sun, L., and Connolly, R. (2002) Stock Implied Volatility, Stock Turnover, and the Stock–Bond Return Relation. Working paper 2002–3a, Federal Reserve Bank of Atlanta

Vassalou, M. and Xing, Y. (2004) Default Risk in Equity Returns. *Journal of Finance*, 59(2): 831–868.

Zhang, B. Y., Zhou, H., and Zhu, H. (2005) Explaining Credit Default Swap Spreads with Equity Volatility and Jump Risks of Individual Firms. BIS working paper, No. 181, Monetary and Economic Department, Basel, Switzerland.

Design and Pricing of Collateralized Debt Obligations

CHAPTER 10

Design of Collateralized Debt Obligations: The Impact of Target Ratings on the First Loss Piece

Marc Gürtler, Martin Hibbeln, and Sven Olboeter

ABSTRACT

We analyze the design of collateralized debt obligations against the background of information asymmetries between the investors and the originating bank. These asymmetries can materially be influenced by the definition of the first loss piece if it is held by the bank. Based on different target ratings and various parameter settings, the optimal size of the first loss piece is determined via Monte Carlo simulation.

INTRODUCTION

In recent years collateralized debt obligations have become a very important vehicle to transfer credit risk of portfolios with defaultable assets. This importance is based on the variety of application areas and the different ways to structure a collateralized debt obligation (CDO). Thus, under the aspect of transferring credit risk, it is possible to perform a true sale of assets or to make use of credit derivatives while the assets remain on the balance sheet. Another application is to gain profits by the usage of arbitrage possibilities. The successful application of CDOs for the purposes mentioned above is dependent on the design of the CDOs. In this context the structure of CDOs is highly influenced by information asymmetries between the investors and the originating bank.

The design of a CDO mostly depends on the number and the size of the tranches. Number and size have to be chosen in a way to reduce information asymmetries regarding the issuers' interests and the interests of the potential investors. The first tranche, the so-called equity tranche, plays a very important role because it bears the first portfolio losses and thus it is the riskiest tranche. The reduction of information asymmetries can be achieved when the originator (bank) of the CDO retains the equity tranche. Under this condition, the size of the equity tranche and the rating of the first rated (mezzanine) tranche impart information to the investors about the quality of the securitized portfolio. Against this background, we analyze the impact of different target ratings on the size of the equity tranche under various parameter constellations (e.g., default probability, correlation, and loss given default).

The remainder of the article is organized as follows: The next section describes the design and application areas of CDOs. In the third section the structure of CDOs is motivated and different ways of reducing information asymmetries are shown. The size of the equity tranche under different parameter constellations is analyzed in the fourth section by the use of Monte Carlo simulations. The last section gives a short summary.

COLLATERALIZED DEBT OBLIGATIONS
Structure of CDOs

Collateralized debt obligations are financial instruments that securitize portfolios of defaultable assets. Possible underlying exposures comprise a variety of debt instruments including loans, bonds, or mortgages, just mentioning the most important assets. However, the universe of underlying assets of CDOs is much larger. Each asset with debt characteristics and credit risks can be part of a reference portfolio for a CDO transaction.[1] Some securitizations are named by the underlying assets like collateralized loan obligations (CLOs), collateralized bond obligations (CBOs) or collateralized mortgage obligations (CMOs). A CDO is suited for transferring

---

[1] Other well-known reference assets are credit cards, auto loans, and CDOs. The last are called CDOs of CDOs or CDO squared. See Goodman and Fabozzi (2002) and Smith (2004).

credit risk of a reference portfolio of the originator (e.g., a bank) to a so-called special-purpose vehicle (SPV). Usually the SPV is established only for CDO transaction and it is bankruptcy remote. That means that the SPV is not affected by bankruptcy or distress of the originator. The SPV buys the credit risk from the originator who wants to be protected against credit risk. To refinance this purchase, the SPV issues notes, which are linked to default losses of particular tranches with different risk characteristics and different ratings.

In the context of a CDO there are two possibilities of transferring credit risk: a true sale CDO and a synthetic CDO. A true sale CDO describes the primary form of a CDO. The originator pools defaultable assets to a portfolio and sells it to the SPV to be protected against the credit risk of the underlying assets. These assets are no longer on the balance sheet of the originator, and thus his risk is reduced. As mentioned above, the SPV issues tranches with different ratings to refinance the purchase of the portfolio. The design of the tranches is a specific feature. They differ in their participation in portfolio losses. The first tranche, often called *equity tranche* or *first loss piece* (FLP), bears the first losses of the portfolio. When the portfolio losses exceed the size of the equity tranche, it is eliminated and the second tranche bears the remaining losses. This tranche is canceled when losses exceed the size of the first and the second tranche and so on.[2] Figure 10.1 illustrates the risk participation of the different tranches, and Figure 10.2 illustrates the procedure of a true sale CDO.

As one can see, the equity tranche is the riskiest because it gets its interest payments after the administrative and management fees have been paid and the other tranches have been served. For this reason, investors would claim a very high spread for bearing such losses. Therefore, and for reducing information asymmetries, this piece is often retained by the originator. We will focus on this behavior in the next section. The second tranche is less risky, but the probability of suffering losses is higher than in the remaining tranches. Therefore, the credit spread is between the spreads for the first and the third tranche. The last tranche, called *senior tranche*, has the lowest credit spread, because there is only a very small probability of bearing portfolio losses. The tranche interests are paid by the cash flows of the underlying assets.

---

[2] See Goodman and Fabozzi (2002), p. 15, and Das (2005), p. 310.

F I G U R E   10.1

Risk participation of the different tranches

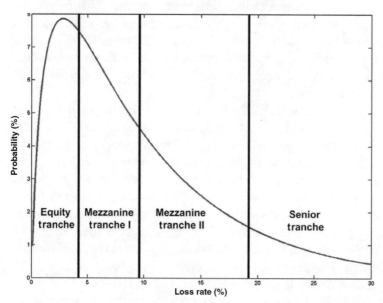

F I G U R E   10.2

Cash-flow structure of a true sale CDO transaction

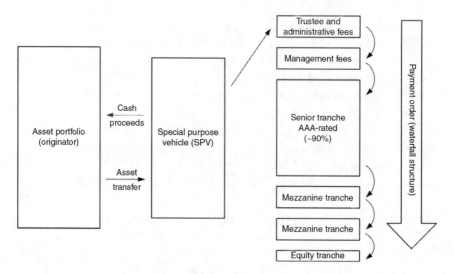

The structure of a synthetic CDO transaction is a little bit different from a true sale CDO transaction, although the relationship between the SPV and the investors as well as the creation of the tranches are the same. However, the connection between the originator and the SPV differs. There is no complete asset transfer from the originator to the SPV. Instead there is only an economic risk transfer, and the originator remains the owner of the assets. Delinking of ownership and economic risk is done using a credit derivative, namely, a credit default swap (CDS). A CDS can be interpreted as an insurance contract. The owner of a defaultable asset buys protection against a default of the underlying asset from the protection seller. The protection seller obtains a premium for taking these risks, and when a predefined default event triggers, the protection seller makes a default payment to the protection buyer. This payment typically replaces the incurred losses of the asset owner.

In a synthetic CDO the originator buys protection against defaults on the underlying portfolio from the SPV in the context of a CDS. There are no refinancing costs for the SPV because there is only a credit risk transfer and no asset transfer. It gets a CDS premium and issues tranches as in a true sale CDO transaction. The proceeds of these issues are invested in high-quality bonds like AAA-rated bonds or treasury bonds. These bonds serve as a collateral pool against claims from the CDS contract. As long as there are no defaults in the reference portfolio, the interests of the tranches are paid from the CDS premium and the interest payments from the collateral pool. In the event of a default in the underlying portfolio the incurred losses from the originator are eliminated by the SPV. The SPV sells assets from the collateral pool to clear the losses of the originator. After this payment there are less interest earnings from the collateral pool, and consequently, the SPV is not able to fulfill all claims of the tranche investors. As in the true sale transaction, the senior tranche gets its interest payment first, then the mezzanine tranche(s), and so on. If there are not enough interest earnings, the equity tranche (and possibly the tranches before the equity tranche too) gets just a fraction of its interests or nothing.[3] In Figure 10.3 the structure of a synthetic CDO is illustrated.

---

[3] See Goodman and Fabozzi (2002), p. 193, Das (2005), p. 328, and Tavakoli (2001), p. 237.

PART 3   Design and Pricing of Collateralized Debt Obligations

F I G U R E   10.3

Cash-flow structure of a synthetic CDO transaction

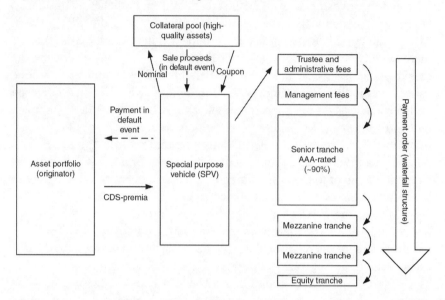

Calculation of Tranche Values

This section gives a short overview how tranche values are calculated. The cutoff points between the tranches are called *attachment* and *detachment points*, and they are denoted as fractions of portfolio loss. The attachment point of the equity tranche is 0 percent, and its detachment point is the attachment point of the second tranche. The cutoff points of the other tranches are given the same way. To calculate tranche losses, consider a CDO with k tranches and maturity T. The attachment point of tranche $k \in \{1, \dots, K\}$ is denoted by c_{k-1} and its detachment point by c_k. Tranche k is affected by losses if the relative portfolio loss exceeds c_{k-1}, and it is eliminated if the relative portfolio loss exceeds c_k. The portfolio loss rate L_t up to year t is calculated as

$$L_t = \sum_{j=1}^{t} l_j \qquad (10.1)$$

in which l_j describes the loss rate in year j based on the nominal portfolio value. The nominal value $V_{k,t}$ of tranche k at the initiation date of the CDO ($t = 0$) is given by

$$V_{k,0} = (c_k - c_{k-1}) \cdot V \tag{10.2}$$

and V denotes the nominal portfolio value. The calculation of the tranche value after the CDO issuance date depends on the incurred portfolio losses. The loss rate $L_{k,t}$ suffered by tranche k up to year t is determined as

$$L_{k,t} = \min\{L_t, c_k\} - \min\{L_t, c_{k-1}\} \tag{10.3}$$

The total loss of tranche k is achieved by multiplying $L_{k,t}$ with the portfolio value V. The calculation of the value $V_{k,t}$ of tranche k in year t is obtained as

$$V_{k,t} = V_{k,0} - L_{k,t} \cdot V \tag{10.4}$$

The tranche value is a decreasing function of the portfolio losses, and its value attains zero if the percentage portfolio loss exceeds the upper cutoff point c_k. Furthermore, one can see from Equations (10.3) and (10.4) that the first tranche, denoted by V_1, is affected first by portfolio losses. The senior tranche V_K will be hit by portfolio losses after all other tranches have been worthless. The basis of the interest payments to the investors of tranche k is its nominal value in the respective year. Thus, these payments may decrease until maturity of the CDO.

Areas of Application for CDOs

Collateralized debt obligations can be implemented for different reasons. First of all, they are used to reduce credit risk. As mentioned above, there are two ways of realization: true sale CDOs or synthetic CDOs. A true sale CDO transaction eliminates the assets from the balance sheet of the orig-inator, and the proceeds can be used to create new assets or to make new investments. Therefore, such a transaction can also be used for refinanc-ing purposes. Particularly banks with lower ratings will use true sale transactions to fund other activities. Funding or refinancing on the capital market can be expensive for such banks because they are confronted with high credit spreads. Therefore, a true sale of the portfolio can be the cheaper alternative. Banks with good ratings have low funding costs on the capital market. Probably, they will choose a true sale CDO transaction for other aspects rather than for refinancing purposes. Most banks will use a synthetic CDO transaction for risk reduction because it is less extensive and complex. Furthermore, the bank participates in the cash flows of the assets, and the relationship between the bank and its borrowers is still obtained.

Both types of CDOs are suited for reducing capital requirement. A true sale CDO eliminates the assets from the balance sheet of the originator. As a result, the regulatory capital can decrease dependent on the usage of the proceeds. An investment in treasury securities means a risk weight of 0 percent. In contrast to this reduction effect, an investment in risky assets can also increase the regulatory capital. The reduction of capital requirement with a synthetic CDO is a little bit different. The risk weight for the assets protected by a CDS is determined by the risk weight of the CDS counterparty. In a synthetic CDO this is the risk weight of the SPV. For the bank it is very important to know the investments of the SPV. As mentioned above, the proceeds of the issued notes are invested in high-quality assets that act as a collateral pool for absorbing defaults of the reference portfolio. The risk weights for high-quality assets are very low, implying a reduction of capital requirements for the originating bank.[4]

In recent years so-called arbitrage synthetic or arbitrage true sale CDO transactions have been initiated. The main focus of this CDO type is the creation of a positive difference between the spreads of the underlying portfolio and the spreads of the issued notes to gain arbitrage profits. As mentioned above, the originator of a CDO retains the equity tranche. The target of the originator is to maximize the excess spread that remains after the investors have been paid out. Because the spread payments to the investors are almost surely fixed, the excess spread can only be maximized by regular adjustments of the composition of the underlying portfolio. For this reason, the CDO manager has the possibility of changing the portfolio mixture. These CDOs are called *managed* CDOs because the CDO manager oversees the CDO transaction for the whole life of the CDO.[5] Arbitrage CDOs are the fastest growing segment on the CDO market.

---

[4] For further information, see Goodman and Fabozzi (2002), p. 203.

[5] The opposite of managed CDOs are so-called static CDOs. In this form the underlying portfolio is fixed at the beginning of the CDO transaction and thereafter not changed anymore. Further information about both kinds of CDOs can be found in Goodman and Fabozzi (2002) and Hawkins (2004).

Collateralized Loan Obligations versus CBO Transaction

There are some important differences between CLO and CBO transactions. The structure and the effort in creating a CLO are much more complex than in designing a CBO. In a loan contract the relationship between the lender (bank) and the borrower is closer than between a bond issuer and a bond holder. The content of a loan contract is part of the banking confidentiality. This complicates the sale of a loan by a bank because it needs the consent of the borrower for this transaction. In the case of an agreement the next step is the transfer of information about the contract from the loan seller to the loan purchaser.

At this time information asymmetries play a significant role. The loan seller knows all relevant information like payment history and reliability of the borrower. The potential new owner of the loan usually knows little about the borrower's characteristics; so he has to worry that the contract is a "lemon." As a result of his uncertainty, he is only willing to pay a price that is below the price under information symmetry. To reduce these information asymmetries, the loan seller has to set up a cash-flow process that reproduces the payment history of the contract to signal the reliability of the borrower. Thus, it is comprehensible that the sale of a loan contract is quite difficult and differs from a bond transfer. Most bonds are traded on capital markets. The buyer of a bond can get all relevant information from the capital market, and consequently, there are less information asymmetries and the purchase is arranged very quickly.

The information asymmetries are very important for the construction of a CLO and/or CBO. We will focus on this aspect in the next section. As mentioned above, the sale of a loan or a loan portfolio is much more difficult than the sale of a bond portfolio. If the bank is interested in transferring credit risk of a loan portfolio to reduce its capital requirement, a synthetic structure is the preferable procedure. This is supported by the setup of a lot of CDS contracts in the context of a CDO transaction. In some transactions the nominal value of the CDS contract is much lower than the nominal value of the securitized portfolio. An example is the C*Star Transaction of Citibank/Salomon Smith Barney. The underlying portfolio consisted of 4 billion euros corporate credit risk. Citibank retained a first loss position of 40 million euros and entered into a CDS with C*Star as the SPV. The nominal value of the CDS was 280 million euros, which was only 7 percent of the portfolio. The part was divided into three tranches in the context of a synthetic CDO. The remaining credit risk was covered by a CDS with an Organisation for Economic Cooperation and Development (OECD) bank.

To sum up, a true sale CLO transaction can be used for refinancing purposes or in situations where a bank wants to get these loans off balance sheet. Collateralized bond obligations, on the other hand, are suited for arbitrage purposes. For example, investment banks purchase bonds and pool them with the intent of creating tranches to benefit from the difference between the spread of the underlying bond portfolio and the spread of the tranches. Such a behavior can be interpreted as an active management to maximize the spread of the equity tranche that is held by the investment bank.

INFORMATION ASYMMETRIES IN CDO TRANSACTIONS
Pooling of Assets

The risk transfer in the context of a CDO transaction is always based on a reference portfolio of assets. It is also possible to transfer the risk using single-name credit derivatives contracts or selling each loan and bond separately. However, this is not the typical approach in reality. In his model, DeMarzo (2005) studies a market with an informed issuer and uninformed investors that have no ability to get information about the assets. He shows that under such conditions it is favorable for the issuer to sell securities individually because this maximizes his proceeds. The issuer can take advantage of his information advance to maximize the price and thus the payoff of every single security. The pooling of the assets diminishes this information advantage because there is only the chance to price the pooled assets as a whole but not on a single basis. DeMarzo calls this *information destruction* of pooling.

Gorton and Pennacchi (1990; 1993) consider a model with informed and uninformed traders. The uninformed traders suffer losses compared to the informed investors. Gorton and Pennachi show that the pooling of assets can reduce these losses because the information advantage of the informed investors is diminished. While pooling in the model of Gorton–Pennacchi is demand driven, Boot and Thakor (1993) consider a model with supply-driven pooling. They argue that the issuing firm can benefit from pooling because it can create information sensitive securities.

Another important aspect of pooling refers to the ability of creating new securities as in a CDO transaction. Pooling offers the originator or the owner of the pool an ability to construct securities with different risk characteristics. This is reasonable since some investors have special expectations or desires concerning risks of securities. That explains the existence of so-called single-tranche CDOs. They are created for special purposes of one or several investors. These investors advise their risk desires to an investment bank that sets up a pool of assets to satisfy these characteristics. Such a CDO includes only one tranche.[6]

Tranching and Its Implication

As mentioned in the previous section, the pooling of securities enables the owner of the pool to issue assets or notes with different risk characteristics. In the literature, tranching of an asset pool has been studied since the beginning of the 1990s. It allows the creation of information-sensitive and information-insensitive securities. Information-sensitive securities or tranches are more risky because there is a greater possibility of suffering losses. Informed investors will purchase these notes because they can appraise the risks assumed. These tranches almost always have a lower investment grade or a speculative grade rating, and consequently, they pay high interests. Thus, the informed investors can receive higher gains from their acquisition of information. Information-insensitive tranches will be bought by less informed investors. The ratings are usually AAA or AA, and the possibility of suffering losses is very low.[7] Hence, both types of investors are able to buy securities regarding their degree of information.

Another important aspect of tranching is the mitigation of a lemon problem. Selling a pool of assets as a whole can suggest a pool of low quality. Thus, the investors claim a higher credit spread, which can be avoided by dividing the pool into tranches with different risk levels. As we will see next, tranching is also a way to reduce information asymmetries.

Reduction of Information Asymmetries

The design of a CDO transaction is crucial because there are information asymmetries between the originator and the investors. The originator, respectively, the SPV, has all the information about the underlying portfolio,

---

[6] See Choudhry (2004), p. 214.
[7] See Gorton and Pennacchi (1990) and (1993), Boot and Thakor (1993), and DeMarzo (2005).

and they know the reason for the transaction under consideration. The investors on the other side do not know the occasion, and their information about the borrowers in the portfolio depends on the assets of the underlying portfolio. For a portfolio with publicly traded bonds the level of information is higher than for a loan portfolio because the investors in bonds are able to assess the underlying portfolio. In a CBO transaction the borrowers of the assets are often mentioned in the pre-sale and new-issue reports of the rating agencies. The issue and pricing of the tranches for such a CBO transaction is easy to implement.

A CLO transaction is quite different since the names of the borrowers and the payment structure of the loan contracts are only known by the originator and the SPV. The investors are not able to assess the underlying portfolio because they do not have enough information. Publicly available information includes the industry sectors and the type of loans of the underlying portfolio that are published in the pre-sale and new-issue reports of the rating agencies. To compensate for these information asymmetries, the investors claim for high premiums because there is an adverse selection problem. The investors can not observe the quality of the underlying loan portfolio and think that the bank just sells low-quality loans and retains the high-quality ones. This increases the estimated default risk of the different tranches and consequently the claimed spread. For this reason, the originator has an incentive to communicate the quality of the reference portfolio to the investors to reduce the spreads of the tranches.

The most important tranches in mitigating information asymmetries are the equity and the senior tranche. The originator aims at reducing the expenditure for the interest payments to the tranche holders. Therefore, he is interested in achieving a senior tranche with a AAA-rating that is as large as possible because this tranche is very information insensitive and thus the information asymmetry spread stemming from the lemon problem is very low. However, the use of a large high-quality senior tranche is limited in reducing information asymmetries. The remaining tranches are more or less information sensitive, and thus there is still some information asymmetry. Investors with information about the portfolio may be able to measure its quality with more or less certainty. These investors are disposed to buy the tranches of lower quality, but the values of these tranches are very information sensitive. Because they do not have all relevant information about the characteristics of the portfolio, they will claim a spread that is above the accurate spread for the case of information symmetry.

To mitigate the information asymmetries the originator can act as a "best informed" investor and retain the equity tranche and the FLP, respectively. The originator bears the first losses and makes the following tranches less information sensitive. The investors can interpret this signal as a quality characteristic of the portfolio. With their own information and the information about the size of the equity tranche, they are willing to accept a lower interest payment. Depending on the information status of the investors, the originator chooses the size of the equity tranche. If investors have good information and believe the quality of the portfolio is superior, then the originator can select a small equity tranche because investors can calculate the value of the different tranches correctly. Otherwise, if the investors have low information, the originator should choose a larger FLP to make the following tranches less information sensitive.

Besides the advantages of reduced information sensitivity for less informed investors, there is an additional benefit of retaining the FLP. As the bank can suffer high losses by holding the FLP, there is a big incentive to monitor the loans. This incentive is important because the bank is the only "investor" who is able to control (some of) and potentially react on the actions of the creditors. This monitoring can significantly reduce the losses, especially regarding the loss given default, because this allows quick reaction on financial distress. Further, it can be argued that the bank is more credible in negotiations with the creditor in the case of a suboptimal payment behavior because the bank has to represent a group of investors that does not have a relationship to the creditor.

Summarized we have established that a small FLP can serve as an indicator for a high-quality portfolio and a bigger one for a portfolio of lower quality.[8] In the next section we will analyze the size of the equity tranche by electing different parameter constellations (like high–low correlation, high–low probability at default, and different portfolio sizes). Before analyzing the size of the FLP, we will deal with another possibility of reducing information asymmetries.

Credit Enhancements

Information asymmetries can also be lowered by the insertion of credit enhancements. Credit enhancements are included in a CDO transaction to enhance the quality of the different tranches. Considering a pool with

---

[8] In the literature there are a lot of studies that focus on the equity tranche; see Franke and Krahnen (2005), p. 607, and Gale and Hellwig (1985), p. 650.

BBB-rated securities on average, inserting credit enhancements can increase the size of the AAA-rated tranche, which can be cheaper for the originator as we mentioned above. There are different types of enhancements. First of all, one can distinguish between external and internal credit enhancements. External credit enhancements are offered by third-party guarantees that provide protection against the first losses up to a specified level. The most common types are corporate guarantees, pool insurance and bond insurance.[9] Internal credit enhancements include the usage of the reserve funds that can be distinguished into excess servicing spread accounts and cash reserve funds. The former describes the cash or excess spread that remains after the tranche holders and fees have been paid. It is allocated into a reserve account that is established to absorb the first losses. Cash reserve funds result from the issuance proceeds. These are invested in a fund that invests in money market instruments.

Portfolio losses are first absorbed by selling parts of the cash reserve funds whereby it has the same function as the collateral pool in a synthetic CDO transaction. Another internal enhancement is denominated over collateralization (O/C). It is measured within a so-called coverage test. The O/C ratio is computed for every tranche by the principal par value of the collateral portfolio that is divided by the principal for the specified tranche plus the principal for all tranches senior to it. This ratio is compared to the required minimum ratio that is determined in the guidelines of the CDO. This ratio describes the downgrade barrier of a tranche. If the O/C ratio is below the required minimum ratio, the test fails. The CDO manager has to make sure that the required minimum ratio will be met as soon as possible. He can amortize parts of the tranche and the tranches senior to it. This reduces the tranche values and increases the O/C ratio. Otherwise, the tranche will be downgraded.[10] Another test is the interest coverage test (I/C). It has the same function as the O/C test. The only difference is that the interest payments of the collateral portfolio are compared to the interest payments of the considered tranche.

---

[9] See Goodman and Fabozzi (2002), pp. 86–87.
[10] See Bluhm et al. (2003), p. 246.

PORTFOLIO CONSTRUCTION AND THE SIZE OF THE FLP

Portfolio Modeling and Simulation Procedure

In order to analyze the design of CDOs (e.g., the size, the expected loss, and the loss given default of tranches), we first have to generate the portfolio loss distribution. Therefore, we use the well-known one-period one-factor setting like in Vasicek (1987).[11] In this model, the return of each obligor is driven by two components that realize at a future point in time T: a systematic part $\tilde{X}_T$ that influences all firms and a firm-specific (idiosyncratic) part $\tilde{\varepsilon}_{i,T}$.[12] Thus, the "normalized" asset returns[13] $\tilde{a}_{i,T}$ of each obligor $i \in \{1, \ldots, I\}$ in $t = T$ can be represented by the following model:

$$\tilde{a}_{i,T} = \sqrt{\rho_i}\, \tilde{x}_T + \sqrt{1 - \rho_i}\, \tilde{\varepsilon}_{i,T}, \tag{10.5}$$

in which $\tilde{X}_T \sim N(0, 1)$ and $\tilde{\varepsilon}_{i,T} \sim N(0, 1)$ are independently and identically normally distributed with mean 0 and standard deviation 1. In this model, the correlation structure of each firm i is represented by the firm-specific correlation $\sqrt{\rho_i}$ to the common factor. Hence, the correlation between two firms i, j can be expressed as $\sqrt{\rho_i} \cdot \sqrt{\rho_j}$ or simply as ρ for the case of a homogeneous correlation structure.

Furthermore, the probability of default of each obligor is exogenously given as PD_i.[14] Corresponding to formula (10.5), an obligor i defaults at $t = T$ when its normalized return falls below a default threshold $b_{i,T}$, which can be characterized by

$$\tilde{a}_{i,T} < b_{i,T} \Leftrightarrow \sqrt{\rho_i} \cdot \tilde{x}_T + \sqrt{1 - \rho_i} \cdot \tilde{\varepsilon}_{i,T} < b_{i,T}. \tag{10.6}$$

---

[11] See, e.g., Vasicek (1987; 1991; 2002) and Finger (1999; 2001).
[12] To keep track of the model, stochastic variables are marked with a tilde "~."
[13] The returns are normalized by subtracting the expected return and dividing the resulting term by the standard deviation in order to get standard normally distributed variables.
[14] The probability of default could either be determined by the institution itself or by a rating agency.

Against this background the threshold $b_{i,T}$ is determined by the exogenous specification of PD:[15]

$$PD_i = \text{prob}[\tilde{a}_{i,T} < b_{i,T}] = N(b_{i,T}) \Leftrightarrow b_{i,T} = N^{-1}(PD_i) \qquad (10.7)$$

To generate the portfolio loss distribution in this framework, it is common to use Monte Carlo simulations. Although there exist analytic approximations,[16] these results do not hold in general for real world credit portfolios, especially if one analyzes small subportfolios like the reference pool of a CDO.[17] The simulation engine performs the following steps: First, a realization of the systematic factor and i realizations of the idiosyncratic factors are drawn from standard normal distributions. Thus, the identical realization of the systematic factor is used for every obligor. Then, Equation (10.6) [under consideration of Equation (10.7)] is computed for each obligor to determine whether a default occurred. For each defaulted firm, the exposures are summed up to receive the total loss amount in this scenario.[18] This procedure is repeated frequently to obtain the loss distribution of the portfolio.

Collateralized Debt Obligation Construction

For our first analysis, we chose a homogeneous reference portfolio (Pool 1) with a maturity of five years for all credits. The reference pool will be modeled as described in the previous section. Particularly, there is only one payoff at the end of the maturity. The portfolio consists of $I = 1,000$ credits, each credit has a five-year probability of default PD = 2 percent, a loss given default LGD = 45 percent, and a correlation to the systematic factor $\rho = 20$ percent. After Monte Carlo simulations with 500,000 trials, we received the portfolio loss distribution presented in Figure 10.4.

---

[15] The term prob(A) stands for the probability of the occurrence of an uncertain event A. $N(.)$ characterizes the cumulative standard normal distribution and $N^{-1}(.)$ stands for the inverse of $N(.)$.

[16] The most famous is the asymptotic single risk factor (ASRF) approximation of Vasicek (1987) and Gordy (2003) that build the bottom of the Basel II framework. Wilde (2001) and Martin and Wilde (2002) derive approximation formulas for a finite number of obligors.

[17] Gürtler et al. (2008) determine the necessary number of obligors in credit portfolios, so that these approximation formulas are not critical. Dependent on the characteristics of the portfolio, they find, e.g., that for SME portfolios an effective number of up to 2,700 credits is needed—that means a concentration comparable to 2,700 homogeneous credits—to let the ASRF approximation be uncritical. This will usually not hold for typical CDOs.

[18] To get the net loss instead of the gross loss, the exposures have to be multiplied by the borrower-specific loss given default (LGD$_i$) and by 1 minus the recovery rate $(1 - RR_i)$, respectively.

F I G U R E   10.4

Loss distribution for a homogeneous portfolio with 1,000 credits, PD = 2%, LGD = 45%, computed with 500,000 trials

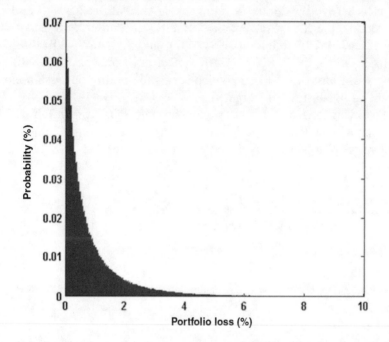

In an earlier section we argued that a bank should keep the FLP of
the CDO transaction to reduce problems resulting from asymmetric information between the bank and the investor. On the one hand, the bank
wants the FLP to be as small as possible because the bank wants to transfer its risk and to reduce the economic capital needed. On the other hand,
the spread stemming from information asymmetry is smaller when the
bank holds a big FLP and the sold tranches have a lower PD. There is no
obvious answer to the question of optimal size of the tranches and the
FLP. But it seems reasonable to assume that the bank wants to construct
tranches with a specific rating for a given reference pool and chooses
the size of each tranche optimally. In other words, the bank decides
that the tranche with the worst quality—apart from the FLP—shall have a
PD of, e.g., 10 percent, the next tranche a PD of 2 percent, and so on.
Thus, the "target rating" determines the tranche size and the size of the
first loss piece and not the other way around. This stays in contrast to
many examples in the literature, which use given attachment points of
say 3, 7, 10, and 20 percent and determine the PD, LGD and other ratios

of each tranche.[19] We believe that this approach better reflects many real-world transactions. Referring to some bigger CDO transactions (all mentioned reference pools have an amount between 1 and 5 billion euros), the tranches have the Moody's ratings Aaa/Aa2/A2/Baa2/Ba1 (London Wall 2002–2 Plc), Aaa/Aa2/A2/Baa2/Ba2/B3 (Promise XXS–2006–1), Aaa/A2/Baa2/Ba2/B2 (Geldilux-TS–2007), and Aaa/Aa2/A2/Baa2/Ba2/ B2 (CoSMO FINANCE 2007–1). Almost all rated tranches have ratings ending with 2 instead of 1 or 3, which seems to confirm our assumption of target ratings instead of "target size."

Following these transactions, we use the target PDs given in Table 10.1 for our simulations. These PDs correspond to the 5-year average cumulative default rates from Moodys with respect to the ratings Aaa/Aa2/A2/Baa2/ Ba2/B2.[20]

T A B L E   10.1

Target PDs of the CDO tranches

Tranche	Senior	A	B	C	D	E	FLP
Probability of Default	0.20%	0.45%	0.60%	1.80%	9.16%	28.45%	N.R.

Combining the loss distribution of Pool 1 (Figure 10.4) and the tranching of Table 10.1, we use Equation 10.3 to compute the relevant parameters of the tranches.

As can be seen in Table 10.2, there is a small probability that no default occurs in the FLP. Recalling that the expected loss (EL) of the reference portfolio is EL = 2% · 45% = 0.9%, we see that the first loss piece captures a bit more than the EL in this setting. It is interesting to notice that the Aaa-rated senior tranche has a size of more than 90 percent, even if all credits of the reference pool have a PD of 2 percent. Furthermore, the expected loss of almost all tranches is mainly driven by the corresponding PD. Only the expected loss of the senior tranche is significantly influenced by its small LGD.

We can also immediately construct the characteristics of the FLP if the lowest rated tranche shall have a target rating of Ba2 or Baa2 instead

---

[19] See, for example, Burtschell et al. (2005), Krahnen and Wilde (2006), or Rösch and Scheule (2006).
[20] See Moodys (2000).

T A B L E   10.2

Financial ratios of CDO tranches with respect to Pool 1

Tranche	Probability of Default	Attachment Point	Size	Expected Loss / Amount Total	Expected Loss / Amount Tranche	Loss Given Default
Senior	0.20%	8.91%	91.09%	0.004%	0.004%	2.23%
A	0.45%	7.34%	1.58%	0.005%	0.304%	67.64%
B	0.60%	6.80%	0.54%	0.003%	0.516%	86.02%
C	1.80%	4.82%	1.98%	0.021%	1.070%	59.42%
D	9.16%	2.34%	2.48%	0.108%	4.345%	47.44%
E	28.45%	0.99%	1.35%	0.225%	16.670%	58.59%
FLP	94.35%	0.00%	0.99%	0.533%	53.816%	57.04%

T A B L E   10.3

Effect of different target ratings (B2, Ba2, Baa2) for the first rated tranche

First Loss Pieces	Target Rating of the First Rated Tranche	Size	Expected Loss / Amount Total	Expected Loss / Amount Tranche	Loss Given Default
FLP (B2)	28.45% (B2)	0.99%	0.533%	53.816%	57.04%
FLP (Ba2)	9.16% (Ba2)	2.34%	0.758%	32.386%	34.32%
FLP (Baa2)	1.8% (Baa2)	4.82%	0.865%	17.972%	19.05%

of B2, because the other tranches are not influenced by this rearrangement (see Table 10.3). Since the target rating of the next tranche determines the characteristics of the FLP, we will identify the FLPs with their ratings. There should be no confusion about the name because the FLP itself gets no rating.

The corresponding probability distributions of the tranche losses for each of the constructed FLPs are plotted in Figure 10.5. In the first graph the tranche characteristics are heavily influenced by the probability of a full loss and thus by the rating of the next tranche. For bigger tranche sizes the loss distribution inside the tranche also becomes significant. As can be seen in the graphs, the mass of the distribution is more on the right side for the first graph, and it shifts to low losses in the later graphs. The

F I G U R E   10.5

Probability distribution of the tranche loss for the FLP compared for target rating B2 (top), Ba2 (middle), and Baa2 (bottom) of the next tranche

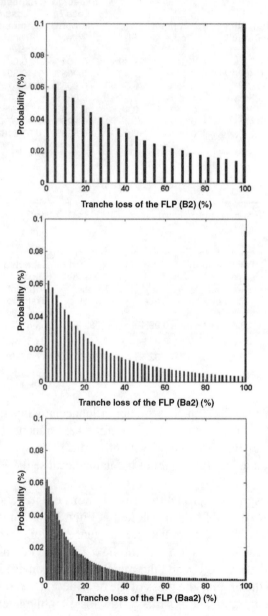

consequence is a small LGD of the FLP for high target ratings of the first rated tranche.

Sensitivity Analysis on the FLP

To gain a better understanding of the causal connections, we will modify several parameters of the reference pool and analyze the consequences, especially regarding the size of the FLP. Therefore, we use the definition of the first loss pieces for different target ratings of the next tranche from another section. In addition, the reference center is Pool 1 from that section (i.e., the key ratios are $I = 1,000$, PD = 2 percent, LGD = 45 percent, and $\rho = 20$ percent).

First, we vary the number of credits from $I = 1,000$ to $I = 100$ and to $I = 10,000$, respectively. For a decreasing number of credits, the size of the FLP is slightly decreasing only for FLP (B2) (see Table 10.3 and Table 10.4). On the contrary, if the bank chooses a better rating for the next tranche, it has to retain a bigger FLP for small reference pools.

T A B L E   10.4

Financial ratios of CDO tranches with $I = 100$ (top) and $I = 10,000$ (bottom)

Tranche	Probability of Default	Size	Expected Loss / Amount Total	Expected Loss / Amount Tranche	Loss Given Default
FLP (B2)	61.69%	0.90%	0.456%	50.667%	82.13%
FLP (Ba2)	61.69%	2.70%	0.762%	28.235%	45.77%
FLP (Baa2)	61.69%	5.40%	0.870%	16.104%	26.10%

Tranche	Probability of Default	Size	Expected Loss / Amount Total	Expected Loss / Amount Tranche	Loss Given Default
FLP (B2)	99.70%	1.00%	0.541%	54.139%	54.30%
FLP (Ba2)	99.70%	2.31%	0.759%	32.815%	32.91%
FLP (Baa2)	99.70%	4.79%	0.868%	18.103%	18.16%

Furthermore, the probability of no defaults is rising significantly for all target ratings for a decreasing number of credits, but the retained EL remains quite stable. Thus, the number of credits seems to be mainly relevant regarding the FLP size if there is a high target rating.

As can be seen in Table 10.5, a varying PD has a high impact on the size of the FLPs. In each considered case, the FLP is a multiple for the reference pool with higher PD. Thus, selling a riskier portfolio has to be paid by retaining a significantly bigger FLP. Consequently, the total amount of the expected loss for the FLP is significantly higher than for portfolios with small PDs.

T A B L E   10.5

Financial ratios of CDO tranches with PD = 1 percent (top) and PD = 5 percent (bottom)

Tranche	Probability of Default	Size	Expected Loss / Amount Total	Expected Loss / Amount Tranche	Loss Given Default
FLP (B2)	85.58%	0.45%	0.233%	51.809%	60.54%
FLP (Ba2)	85.58%	1.22%	0.361%	29.681%	34.68%
FLP (Baa2)	85.58%	2.75%	0.427%	15.539%	18.16%

Tranche	Probability of Default	Size	Expected Loss / Amount Total	Expected Loss / Amount Tranche	Loss Given Default
FLP (B2)	99.17%	2.70%	1.546%	57.247%	57.73%
FLP (Ba2)	99.17%	5.45%	2.010%	36.911%	37.22%
FLP (Baa2)	99.17%	9.72%	2.202%	22.657%	22.85%

The LGD also has a quite big impact on the size of the FLP (Table 10.6). Concretely, if the LGD is doubled, then the tranches need to be double sized to keep the target rating of the tranches. However, this is the only effect of a modification in LGD.

The effect of a change in correlation varies depending on the chosen target rating. We can find the highest impact in the Baa2-FLP (Table 10.7), whereas the impact in the case of lower target ratings is much smaller. It is interesting to notice that the B2-FLP is the only tranche that decreases

T A B L E   10.6

Financial ratios of CDO tranches with LGD = 30 percent (top) and LGD = 75 percent (bottom)

Tranche	Probability of Default	Size	Expected Loss / Amount Total	Expected Loss / Amount Tranche	Loss Given Default
FLP (B2)	94.35%	0.66%	0.355%	53.816%	57.04%
FLP (Ba2)	94.35%	1.56%	0.505%	32.386%	34.32%
FLP (Baa2)	94.35%	3.21%	0.577%	17.972%	19.05%

Tranche	Probability of Default	Size	Expected Loss / Amount Total	Expected Loss / Amount Tranche	Loss Given Default
FLP (B2)	94.35%	1.65%	0.888%	53.816%	57.04%
FLP (Ba2)	94.35%	3.90%	1.263%	32.386%	34.32%
FLP (Baa2)	94.35%	8.03%	1.442%	17.972%	19.05%

T A B L E   10.7

Financial ratios of CDO tranches with ρ = 10 percent (top) and ρ = 30 percent (bottom)

Tranche	Probability of Default	Size	Expected Loss / Amount Total	Expected Loss / Amount Tranche	Loss Given Default
FLP (B2)	99.21%	1.08%	0.674%	62.382%	62.88%
FLP (Ba2)	99.21%	1.94%	0.822%	42.478%	42.82%
FLP (Baa2)	99.21%	3.29%	0.883%	26.870%	27.08%

Tranche	Probability of Default	Size	Expected Loss / Amount Total	Expected Loss / Amount Tranche	Loss Given Default
FLP (B2)	85.72%	0.86%	0.408%	47.720%	55.67%
FLP (Ba2)	85.72%	2.57%	0.684%	26.683%	31.13%
FLP (Baa2)	85.72%	6.35%	0.846%	13.336%	15.56%

in size with high correlation. Thus, it seems favorable for the originating bank to choose a low target rating for the tranche behind the FLP if highly correlated credits are sold. Furthermore, the bank can transfer a high proportion of the EL through this transaction.

To conclude, the bank needs to retain only a small FLP if the PD and the LGD are low. The effect of changing the number of credits and the correlation depends on the concrete tranching design. Regarding the materiality of the effects on the FLP size, the PD is most relevant. However, if the bank chooses a low target rating of the tranche next to the FLP, a highly correlated portfolio seems to be most attractive for a bank. In this case it is possible to combine two aspired effects: The bank can keep a small FLP, and it can get rid of a big proportion of the bank's risks.

CONCLUSION

In this paper we analyzed the design of CDOs against the background of information asymmetries between the investors and the originating bank. These asymmetries can materially be influenced by the design of the FLP if the bank retains this position. The bank is usually interested in keeping a small FLP to transfer as much risk as possible, but the investors prefer that the bank retains a high amount as a positive signal because the bank is better informed about the quality of the creditors. In this environment we determine the impact of various parameters of the reference pool on the size of the first loss piece and give advice how the reference pool should be chosen and how the CDO should be structured.

We find that the tranches of typical real-world transactions are better explained by target ratings than by pre-assigned tranche sizes. Thus, for a given reference pool the originator first chooses the ratings of the tranches that correspond to the investors preferences. The necessary size of the tranches is determined as a resulting parameter. Based on these results, we compute the size of the equity tranche for typical target ratings via Monte Carlo simulation. The choice of a reference pool with high probability of default and low loss given default results in small FLPs that is favored by the originator but transfers low risks. The impact of varying the number of creditors is rather small in our analyses. For having both, transferring high risks and keeping a rather small FLP, the bank should choose a highly correlated reference pool and a low target rating for the first rated tranche.

REFERENCES

Bluhm, C., Overbeck, L., and Wagner, C. (2003) *An Introduction to Credit Risk Modeling*. London: Chapman & Hall/CRC.

Boot, A.W.A. and Thakor, A.V. (1993) Security Design. *Journal of Finance*, 48(4): 1349–1378.

Burtschell, X., Gregory, J., and Laurent, J.-P. (2005) A Comparative Analysis of CDO Pricing Models. Working paper.

Choudhry, M. (2004) Integrating Credit Derivatives and Securitisation Technology: The Collateralised Synthetic Obligation. In J. Gregory (ed.), *Credit Derivatives: The Definitive Guide*. London: Risk Books.

Das, S. (2005) Credit Derivatives: CDOs and Structured Credit Products. Singapore: John Wiley & Sons.

DeMarzo, P.M. (2005) The Pooling and Tranching of Securities: A Model of Informed Intermediation. *Review of Financial Studies*, 18(1): 1–35.

Finger, C.C. (1999) Conditional Approaches for CreditMetrics Portfolio Distributions. *CreditMetrics Monitor*, 4: 14–33.

Finger, C.C. (2001) The One-Factor CreditMetrics Model in the New Basel Capital Accord. *RiskMetrics Journal*, 2(1): 8–18.

Franke, G. and Krahnen, J.P. (2005) Default Risk Sharing between Banks and Markets: The Case of Collateralized Debt Obligation. In M. Carey and R. Stulz (eds.): *Risks of Financial Institutions*, Chicago, IL: National Bureau of Economic Research.

Gale, D. and Hellwig, M. (1985) Incentive-Compatible Debt Contracts: The One-Period Problem. *Review Economic Studies*, 52(4): 647–663.

Goodman, L.S. and Fabozzi, F.J. (2002) *Collateralized Debt Obligations: Structures and Analysis*. Hoboken, NJ: John Wiley & Sons.

Gordy, M.B. (2003) A Risk-Factor Model Foundation for Ratings-Based Bank Capital Rules. *Journal of Financial Intermediation*, 12(3): 199–232.

Gorton, G.B. and Pennacchi, G.G. (1990) Financial Intermediaries and Liquidity Creation. *Journal of Finance*, 45(1): 49–71.

Gorton, G.B. and Pennacchi, G.G. (1993) Security Baskets and Indexed-Linked Securities. *Journal of Business*, 66(1): 1–27.

Gürtler, M., Heithecker, D., and Hibbeln, M. (2008) Concentration Risk under Pillar 2: When Are Credit Portfolios Infinitely Fine Grained? *Kredit und Kapital* (forthcoming).

Hawkins, P. (2004). Synthetic Securitisation and Structured Portfolio Credit Derivatives. In J. Gregory (ed), *Credit Derivatives: The Definitive Guide.* London: Risk Books, pp. 169–192.

Krahnen, J.P. and Wilde, C. (2006) Risk Transfer with CDOs and Systematic Risk in Banking. Working paper, Goethe University, Frankfurt, Germany.

Martin, R., and Wilde, T. (2002) Idiosyncratic Credit Risk. *Risk*, 15(11): 123–128.

Moodys (2000) Historical Default Rates of Corporate Bond Issuers, 1920–1999. *Moodys Investors Service, Global Credit Research*, New York.

Rösch, D. and Scheule, H. (2006) Credit Rating Impact on CDO Evaluation. Working paper, University of Regensburg and University of Melbourne, Australia.

Smith, D. (2004). CDOs of CDOS: Art Eating Itself? In J. Gregory (ed.), *Credit Derivatives: The Definitive Guide.* London: Risk Books, pp. 257–279.

Tavakoli, J.M. (2001) Credit Derivatives and Synthetic Structures: A Guide to Instruments and Applications. Hoboken, NJ: John Wiley & Sons.

Vasicek, O.A. (1987) Probability of Loss on Loan Portfolio. KMV Corporation.

Vasicek, O.A. (1991) Limiting Loan Loss Probability Distribution. KMV Corporation.

Vasicek, O.A. (2002) Loan Portfolio Value. *Risk,* 15(12): 160–162.

Wilde, T. (2001) Probing Granularity. *Risk,* 14(8): 103–106.

CHAPTER 11

On the Pricing of Collateralized Debt Obligations

Raquel M. Gaspar and Thorsten Schmidt

ABSTRACT

This chapter addresses the pricing of two popular portfolio credit derivatives: first-to-default swaps and collateralized debt obligations. We use the recent model of Gaspar and Schmidt (2007) for the pricing of these portfolio credit derivatives. This approach combines general quadratic models for term structures with shot-noise models and therefore naturally solves a number of important issues in credit portfolio risk. First, resulting pricing formulas are in closed form, and therefore, the model implementation is straightforward. Second, this class of models is able to incorporate well-known features of credit risky markets: realistic default correlations, default clustering, and correlation between short-rate and credit spreads. Third, the recent turbulence in credit spreads caused by the U.S. subprime mortgage turmoil can be captured well.

INTRODUCTION

The demand for investments with higher returns in areas other than the stock market has increased enormously over the last decade. Investing in credit markets, investors take on credit risk in exchange for an attractive yield, and as a result methodologies for pricing and hedging credit derivatives as well as for risk management of credit risky assets became very important. The efforts of the Basel Committee are just one of many examples that substantiate this.

In the last years, credit markets developed at a tremendous speed, while at the same time the number of corporate defaults increased dramatically. It is therefore not surprising that the demand for credit derivatives is growing rapidly. Besides the liquidly traded single instruments, a number of portfolio products gained more and more attention recently. On one side, there is the demand of investors for investment possibilities in diversified portfolios and the search for new investment fields, while on the other side there is the difficulty of capturing dependencies between defaults. Modeling and estimating default dependencies is still an area of ongoing research, and the recent turbulence caused by the difficulties in the U.S. subprime mortgage markets confirm the necessity of developing suitable models.

The goal of this chapter is to propose a model for portfolio credit risk that is able to capture typical market effects, such as spread correlation and high default dependence leading to clustering of defaults and contagion effects. Moreover, the model still remains tractable and leads to a large number of explicit pricing results.

The most liquid single-name credit risky instrument is the so-called credit default swap. In this contract, a regularly paid, fixed spread is exchanged for a protection payment that covers the losses occurring at default of the underlying. For details, the reader may want to consider, e.g., Schönbucher (2003), Lando (2004), McNeil et al. (2005), or the survey by Schmidt and Stute (2004).

After a long success story of collateralized debt obligations (CDOs) in various forms, since four years there are a number of traded CDO indexes available that are traded at very high liquidity. The portfolio setup considered in this paper is a natural candidate for application in this area, and we provide all necessary tools in this article. For more information on CDOs, see Bluhm et al. (2003).

For illustration purposes, we consider here the case of the iTraxx.[1] This index has a number of different subindexes, and derivatives written on iTraxx are the most liquid on the credit market. We summarize the indexes and derivatives related to the iTraxx on Table 11.1.

---

[1] See www.itraxx.com.

T A B L E   11.1

iTraxx indexes and most liquid derivatives

Benchmark Indexes		
iTraxx Europe	iTraxx Europe HiVol	iTraxx crossover
(125 investment grade entities)	(30 highest spread entities from iTraxx Europe)	(50 sub-investment grade entities)
Sector Indexes		
Nonfinancials	Financials senior	Financials sub
(100 entities)	(25 entities)	(25 entities)
Derivatives		
Tranched iTraxx	iTraxx options	First-to-default swaps
(Five standardized tranches: 0–3%, 3–6%, 6–9%, 9–12%, 12–22%)	iTraxx Futures	(Baskets on: autos, consumer, energy, financials, industrials, hivol, crossover, diversified)

F I G U R E   11.1

Spreads of the iTraxx Europe w.r.t different maturities and w.r.t. standardized tranches

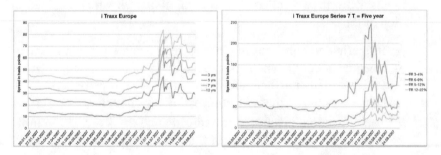

Figure 11.1 presents recent spreads on the iTraxx Europe with respect to (w.r.t.) different maturities and of the standardized tranches 3 to 6 percent, 6 to 9 percent, 9 to 12 percent, and 12 to 22 percent.

PORTFOLIO CREDIT DERIVATIVES

We start by introducing some notation required to deal with portfolio credit derivatives and then define exactly first-to-default swaps and CDOs.

We will deal with a basket of securities of K different entities subject to default risk. Each entity (for instance, a company) may default only once, and its default time is denoted by τ^k. The counting process counting *all* defaults is denoted by $N_t := \sum_{k=1}^{K} 1_{\{\tau^k \leq t\}}$. If a default of entity k happens, we denote the loss quota by q^k. The notional in the basket associated with entity k is denoted by M^k, $k = 1, \ldots, K$.

It is market standard to name the two exchanging counterparties of a credit derivative *protection seller* and *protection buyer*. The protection seller offers a protection payment on specific default events and during some time span, here denoted $[t_0, t_{N*}]$, while the protection buyer pays a periodic fee in exchange. The fee payment dates are due in advance and tend to rely on a fixed tenure structure $t_0, t_1, \ldots, t_{N*-1}$. As the protection buyer has only fixed payments, the payments due to him are also called *fixed leg*, while the payments of the protection seller are called *floating leg*.

First-to-Default Swaps

A *first-to-default swap* (FDS) is a contract that offers protection on the first default of a portfolio only. The FDS has an initiation date $t_0 < t_1$. If t_0 is in the future, the FDS is called *forward-starting FDS*. The FDS is characterized by the so-called *first-to-default spread*, which is fixed at initiation of the contract.

- If the first default occurred in $(t_{n-1}, t_n]$, then the protection seller pays the default payment at t_n. Assuming name k defaulted first[2] ($\tau^{1:k} = \tau^k$), then the default payment is $M^k q^k$. If no default happens until t_{N*}, the protection seller pays nothing.

- The protection buyer pays the spread at all dates $t_1, \ldots, t_{N*}$ until the maturity of the FDS or until the first default (whichever comes first).

The spread is chosen in such a way that entering the FDS is possible at zero cost. For the forward-starting FDS, such that its expected value at t_0 equals zero. Of course, after the spread is fixed, the value of the FDS changes. So the spread clearly depends on the current time, as agreements settled on different dates would originate different spreads. To emphasize this fact we write $S^{FD}(t)$.

---

[2] Throughout, we denote by $\tau^{1:K} < \ldots < \tau^{K:K}$ the *ordered default times*.

Collateralized Debt Obligations

A CDO is a security backed by a pool of credits from various reference entities. The *asset side* of the CDO is formed by the credits themselves, while traded on the market are issued notes (typically swaps) on *tranches* of the CDO. These tranches have different seniorities, building the *liability side* of the CDO. There are different types of CDOs, depending on the type of the underlying credits. If the underlying are loans, bonds, or mortgages, the CDO is named collateralized loan obligation, collateralized bond obligation, or mortgage-backed security, respectively. This article treats only so-called synthetic CDOs, where the underlying objects are credit default swaps (CDS). Particular kinds of this type of CDO are those written on the well-know credit indexes mentioned before. Swaps written on standardized tranches for these indexes are among the most liquid portfolio credit derivatives.

From now on we simply write CDO, while implicitly referring to synthetic CDOs. For further literature and other modeling approaches we refer to Bluhm and Overbeck (2006), Frey and Backhaus (2006), and Scherer (2007).

A CDO allocates interest income and principal repayments from a collateral pool of CDSs to a prioritized collection of CDO securities (tranches). While there are many variations, a standard prioritization scheme is simple subordination: *Senior* CDO notes are paid before *mezzanine; equity* is paid with any residual cash flow. Figure 11.2 clarifies the structure of a CDO.

In terms of notation, we consider a CDO with several tranches $i = 1, \ldots, I$. The tranches are separated according to fixed barriers, called attachment or detachment points, $b_0 < \cdots < b_I$. The general loss process of a CDO, describing the reduction in the face value of the whole underlying portfolio due to defaults, is given by $L(t) = \sum_{\tau^k \leq t} q^k M^k$. The loss of tranche i is, thus, given by

$$L^i(t) = \begin{cases} 0 & \text{if} \quad L(t) < b^{i-1} \\ L(t) - b^{i-1} & \text{if} \quad b^{i-1} \leq L(t) < b^i, \quad i = 1, \cdots, I \\ b^i - b^{i-1} & \text{if} \quad L(t) \geq b^i \end{cases}$$

Figure 11.3 illustrates the CDO setup with a possible loss path affecting various tranches.

FIGURE   11.2

Securitization procedure for CDOs

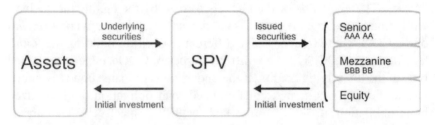

FIGURE   11.3

Tranches' losses in CDOs

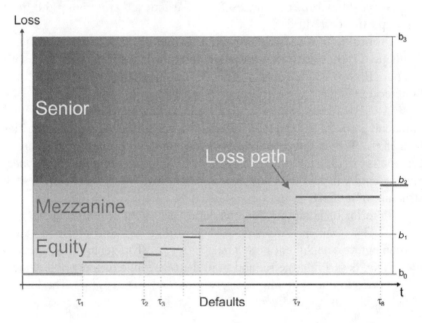

We now make standard normalizations and focus on the *pricing of tranches of CDOs*.

- The CDO offers notes on each tranche with par value 1. Recall that the attachment points of tranche i are b_{i-1} and b_i.
- At each intermediate time $t_0, \ldots, t_{N^*-1}$, the protection seller receives a coupon payment. The payment is on the remaining principal in the tranche, so that with fixed coupon S the payments due at t_n for tranche i are $S[t_n - t_{n-1}][b^i - L^i(t_n)]^+$.

- In exchange, the protection seller covers in $(t_{n-1}, t_n]$ occurring losses at, t_n, $n = 2, \ldots, N^*$. The protection payment, at t_n, for tranche i equals $L^i(t_n) - L^i(t_{n-1})$.

Note that coupon payments are exchanged at the beginning of each period, while the loss payments are due at the end of a period. Another critical point here is the reinvestment of the recovery payment. The default of an entity from the underlying pool leads to a nonpayment of the future coupons. The recovery payment has to be reinvested at the current market level and possibly gets a lower coupon. We assume that these missing future coupons are already included in the recovery amount q^k. This means that q^k is the actual recovery minus financing cost of the future coupons.

MODEL AND APPLICATIONS

This section considers the proposed model, which is a combination of general quadratic term structures and shot-noise processes. First, the model is motivated and the precise setup is given. Then the prices of FDSs as well as CDO tranches are derived. Thereafter, we discuss the important issue of obtaining realistic default correlations under the proposed model and finally we establish the link to credit indexes.

Motivation and Setup

We assume that the default times are doubly stochastic random times. This setup is also referred to conditionally independent default times. For an introduction to this topic we refer to McNeil et al. (2005) or Bielecki and Rutkowski (2002). Given this, we model the default intensity of each firm as a linear combination of General Quadratic Term Structure Models (GQTS) and shot noise processes.

Concretely, we consider an n-dimensional standard Brownian motion W and a state variable Z being the unique strong solution of $dZ_t = \alpha(t, Z_t)\, dt + \sigma(t, Z_t)\, dW_t$.

Here $\alpha: R_+ \times R^m \mapsto R^m$ and $\sigma: R_+ \times R^m \mapsto R^{n \times n}$ are such that

$$\alpha(t, z) = d(t) + E(t)z \tag{11.1}$$

$$\sigma(t, z)\sigma^*(t, z) = k_0(t) + \sum_{i=1}^{m} k_i(t)z_i + \sum_{i,j=1}^{m} z_i\, g_{ij}(t)z_j \tag{11.2}$$

with smooth functions $d : R_+ \mapsto R^m$, E, k_0, k_i, and $g_{ij}, i, j = 1, \ldots, m$ map R_+ to Here and in the following we will use $(\cdot)$ to denote transpose. $R^{m \times m}$. The risk-free short rate $(r_t)_{t \geq 0}$ is given by

$$r(t, Z_t) = Z_t^{\cdot} Q(t) Z_t + g^{\cdot}(t) Z_t + f(t) \qquad (11.3)$$

Q, g and f are smooth, mapping to R_+ to $R^{m \times m}$, R^m, and R. $Q(t)$ is symmetric for all t.

It is well-known that, under mild condition on the shape of the matrices k_i and $g_{i;j}$ [see Gaspar (2004) for further details on these conditions], the term structure of risk-free zero-coupon bond prices of exponential quadratic form

$$p(t, T) = \exp\left[A(t, T) + B^{\cdot}(t, T) Z_t + Z_t^{\cdot} C(t, T) Z_t \right] \qquad (11.4)$$

where (A, B, C, f, g, Q) solves the basic ordinary differential equation (ODE) system defined in the Appendix (Definition 11.A.1).

We now extend the default setup in Gaspar and Schmidt (2007) to the portfolio case. We assume that the default time of firm K, τ^k, is a doubly stochastic random time. Its intensity $(\lambda_t^k)_{t \geq 0}$ satisfies

$$\lambda_t^k = \mu_t^k + \varepsilon^k \mu_t^c \qquad (11.5)$$

The intensity of each firm depends on a firm specific term, μ^k, and a term common to all firms μ^c. All these expressions will have the same quadratic plus jump construction.

Specifically, we set $\mathbf{k} = \{1, \ldots, K\}$, and for each $k \in \mathbf{k} \cup \{c\}$, we take

$$\mu_t^k = \eta_t^k + J_t^k \quad \text{with} \quad J_t^k = \sum_{\tilde{\tau}_j^k \leq t} Y_j^k h^k(t - \tilde{\tau}_j^i),$$

$$\eta_t^k = Z_t^{\cdot} Q^k(t) Z_t + g^k(t)^{\cdot} Z_t + f^k(t) \qquad (11.6)$$

where Q^k, g^k, and f^k are smooth, mappings from R_+ to $R^{m \times m}$, R^m and R, respectively, and N^k are standard Poisson processes with intensity l^k. We denote the jumping times of N^k by $\tau^k{}_1, \tau^k{}_2, \ldots$ Finally, we assume that the risk-free short rate r is independent of the firm specific intensity μ^k, but not necessarily of the common intensity μ^c.

Intuitively, the modeling of a quadratic component and a shot-noise component leads to the intensity being driven by a predictable component (the quadratic part) as well as by an unpredictable component (the jump part). We note that both η^k and J^k are assumed to be strictly positive. This assumption is needed because μ is supposed to be an intensity. ε^k measures how sensitive is an entity to movements of the common factors. The higher ε_k is, the bigger is the dependence of the common default risk driven by μ^c. For intuition take $\varepsilon^i \equiv \varepsilon$. If μ^c jumps, then suddenly the default risk of all the assets increases a lot, and we will see numerous defaults. This can also be caused by a rise in the quadratic part to a high level, but then it is more or less predictable. The first effect causes some clustering similar to contagion effects, which means if one company defaults and others are closely related to this company, they are very likely to default also. The latter effect is more like a business cycle effect; so on bad days more companies default than on good days.

In the above setup, all necessary expressions for pricing relevant credit risky securities can be computed in closed form. We delegate the necessary formulas to the Appendix and refer to Gaspar and Schmidt (2007) for full proofs. At this point we only introduce a shorthand notation that will turn out extremely useful in the pricing formulas to follow.

For current time t, maturity T, and $\theta \in R$, we define[3]

$$S_\eta^k(\theta, t, T) := E^Q\left(\left. e^{-\int_t^T \theta \eta_s^k ds}\right|_{\mathbf{F}_t^W}\right) \qquad S_J^k(\theta, t, T) := E^Q\left(\left. e^{-\int_t^T \theta J_s^k ds}\right|_{\mathbf{F}_t^J}\right) \qquad (11.7)$$

$$\Gamma_\eta^k(\theta, t, T) := E^Q\left(\left. \theta \eta_T^k e^{-\int_t^T \theta \eta_s^k ds}\right|_{\mathbf{F}_t^W}\right)$$

$$(11.8)$$

$$\Gamma_J^k(\theta, t, T) := E^Q\left(\left. \theta J_T^k e^{-\int_t^T \theta J_s^k ds}\right|_{\mathbf{F}_t^J}\right)$$

---

[3] Throughout, denote by $\mathbf{F}^X$ the natural filtration generated by a generic process X. We classify the market information according to the following filtrations: $\mathbf{F}^W$ is the information about the *diffusion factors*; $\mathbf{F}^J$ is the information about the *jump factors*; the filtration $\mathbf{H}_t : = \sigma(1_{\{\tau > s\}} : 0 \le s \le t)$, information on the *default state*; $\mathbf{F}_t = \mathbf{F}^W{}_t \vee \mathbf{F}^J{}_t = \sigma(Z_s, J_s; 0 \le qs \le t)$, information about *all market factors;* and, $\mathbf{G}_t : = \mathbf{F}_t \vee \mathbf{H}_t$, the *total information*.

$$\bar{S}_{\eta}^{k}(\theta,t,T) := E^{\mathbf{Q}}\left(e^{-\int_{t}^{T} r_s + \theta \eta_s^k \, ds} \Bigg|_{\mathbf{F}_t^W} \right)$$

$$\bar{\Gamma}^{k}(\theta,t,T) := E^{\mathbf{Q}}\left(\theta \eta_T^k e^{-\int_{t}^{T} r_s + \theta \eta_s^k \, ds} \Bigg|_{\mathbf{F}_t^W} \right) \tag{11.9}$$

Independence between the diffusion and jump components leads to

$$S^{k}(\theta,t,T) := E^{\mathbf{Q}}\left(e^{-\int_{t}^{T} \theta \mu_s^k \, ds} \Bigg|_{\mathbf{F}_t^W} \right) = S_{\eta}^{k}(\theta,t,T)S_{j}^{k}(\theta,t,T) \tag{11.10}$$

$$\bar{S}^{k}(\theta,t,T) := E^{\mathbf{Q}}\left(e^{-\int_{t}^{T} r_s + \theta \mu_s^k \, ds} \Bigg|_{\mathbf{F}_t^W} \right) = \bar{S}_{\eta}^{k}(\theta,t,T)S_{j}^{k}(\theta,t,T) \tag{11.11}$$

$$\Gamma^{k}(\theta,t,T) := E^{\mathbf{Q}}\left(\theta \mu^k e^{-\int_{t}^{T} \theta \mu_s^k \, ds} \Bigg|_{\mathbf{F}_t^W} \right)$$

$$= \Gamma_{\eta}^{k}(\theta,t,T)S_{j}^{k}(\theta,t,T) + \Gamma_{j}^{k}(\theta,t,T)S_{\eta}^{k}(\theta,t,T) \tag{11.12}$$

$$\bar{\Gamma}^{k}(\theta,t,T) = E^{\mathbf{Q}}\left(\theta \mu^k e^{-\int_{t}^{T} r_s + \theta \mu_s^k \, ds} \Bigg|_{\mathbf{F}_t^W} \right)$$

$$= \bar{\Gamma}_{\eta}^{k}(\theta,t,T)S_{j}^{k}(\theta,t,T) + \Gamma_{j}^{k}(\theta,t,T)\bar{S}_{\eta}^{k}(\theta,t,T) \tag{11.13}$$

If $\theta = 1$, we use the shorthand notation (t, T) instead of $(1, t, T)$; e.g., we write $S^k(t, T)$ for $S^k(1, t, T)$.

In the above shorthand notation, for each entity $k = 1, \ldots, K$ and on $\{\tau^k > t\}$, we easily obtain the following:

- Implied survival probabilities:

$$\mathbf{Q}_{S}^{k}(t, T) = \mathbf{Q}(\tau^k > T \mid F_t) = S^k(t, T)S^c(\varepsilon^k, t, T)$$

- Prices of defaultable zero-coupon bonds:

$$\bar{P}_{0}^{k}(t, T) = E^{\mathbf{Q}}(\exp(-\int_{0}^{T} r_u \, du)1_{\{\tau^k > T\}} \mid_{\mathbf{F}_t}) = S^k(t, T)\bar{S}^c(\varepsilon^k, t, T)$$

- Prices of digitals (the price of a payoff of 1 unit of currency if the firm k defaults in) (t_{n-1}, t_n):

$$e^{*k}(t, t_{n-1}, t_n) = E^k(t, t_{n-1}, t_n)\bar{p}_o^k(t, t_{n-1}) - \bar{p}_o^k(t, t_n)$$

with E^k defined as in (11.22).

$$e^k(t, t_n) = \lim_{t_{n-1} \to t_n} \frac{1}{t_n - t_{n-1}} e^*(t, t_{n-1}, t_n) = \Gamma^k(t, t_n)\bar{S}^c(\varepsilon^k, t, t_n)$$
$$+ \bar{\Gamma}^c(\varepsilon^k, t, t_n)S^k(t, t_n)$$

Default Correlation and Clustering

It is often argued that in the framework used here, where the default times are conditionally independent, the resulting default correlation is not high enough. However, Duffie and Gârleanu (2001) have already showed that this is not the case. Especially through jumps or, more precisely, high peaks in the intensity, a high default correlation is induced. However, in their formulation the authors had the same parameter controlling the mean reversion speed of the diffusive as well as of the jump part. On the one hand, big jumps were necessary to induce high default correlation, but on the other hand, this lead to unrealistic mean reversion specifications for the diffusion part. In the framework presented above, this problem is solved, as the mean reversion speeds can be different.

The so-called default correlation is basically the correlation between the default indicators of two companies. Denote by $\mathbf{Q}_D^i$ the probability of company i defaulting in (t, T) and by $\mathbf{Q}_D^{i,j}(t, T)$ the probability that companies i and j default in (t, T). Using the building blocks, we can easily get the default correlation in closed form.

Lemma 11.1: *The default correlation of two different companies i and j is given by*

$$\rho^{i,j}(t,T) = \frac{S^i(t,T)S^j(t,T)\left[S^c(\varepsilon^i + \varepsilon^j, t, T) - S^c(\varepsilon^i, t, T)S^c(\varepsilon^j, t, T)\right]}{\sqrt{[1 - Q_S^i(t,T)][Q_S^i(t,T)Q_S^j(t,T)[1 - Q_S^j(t,T]}} \quad (11.14)$$

where $\mathbf{Q}_S^k(t, T)$, $k = i, j$ as previously defined.

To illustrate the capability of the model to capture sufficiently high default correlation, we present Figure 11.4 based on the concrete model supposed in Gaspar and Schmidt (2007). We refer to this article for further details.

Default correlation in a concrete model

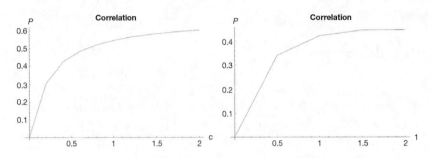

In the remaining part of the chapter we present the pricing results concerning portfolio credit derivatives under the quadratic–shot-noise model.

For notational simplicity we make the following *homogeneity assumption.*[4] However, the more general case is an immediate extension. Note that considering random, independent and identically distributed (i.i.d.) q^k lead to the same results when q is replaced by its expected value $E(q^k)$.

Assumption 11.2: *Assume that* $q^k = q$, $\varepsilon^k = \varepsilon$ *and* $M^k = M$ *for all* $1 \leq k \leq K$. Moreover the tenor structure is equidistant, i.e., $t_j = j\Delta$, $1 \leq j \leq N^*$.

First-to-Default Swaps

The following results rely on the distribution of the first default time, which is the minimum of all default times. The main result on FDS is Theorem 11.4. We start by computing the probability that the first default[5] occurs in $(t, T]$.

Lemma 11.3: *Consider a portfolio of K names, and assume no default has occurred up to time t. Furthermore suppose Assumption 11.2 holds. Then, the survival probability of the first default is given by*

$$\mathbf{Q}(\tau^{1:K} > T \mid_{\mathbf{F}_t}) = 1_{\{\tau^{1:K} > t\}} S^c(\varepsilon K, t, T) \prod_{k=1}^{K} S^k(t, T)$$

---

[4] All indexes mentioned previously are homogeneous portfolios. Still, it is straightforward to extend our CDO results to the inhomogeneous case, but formulas get rather involved.

[5] Proof is given in the Appendix.

Furthermore, the value of 1 unit of currency paid at T only if $\tau^{1:K} > T$ is given by

$$\bar{p}^{\text{FtD}}(t,T) := E^Q(\exp(-\int_t^T r_u \, du) 1_{\{\tau^{1:K} > T\}} \mid_{F_t}) = 1_{\{T_1 > t\}} \bar{S}^c(\varepsilon K, t, T) \prod_{l=1}^{K} S^k(t,T)$$

With the above result at hand the spread of a FDS is easily derived:

Theorem 11.4: *Consider a portfolio of K names, and assume no default has occurred up to time t. Then, the spread of the FDS is given by*

$$s^{\text{FD}}(t) = q \frac{\sum_{n=1}^{N^*} E^c(t, t_{n-1}, t_n) \bar{p}^{\text{FtD}}(t, t_{n-1}) - \bar{p}^{\text{FtD}}(t, t_n)}{\Delta \sum_{n=1}^{N^*} \bar{p}^{\text{FtD}}(t, t_n)}$$

with E^c defined as in Equation (11.22).

Collateralized Debt Obligations

Portfolio Loss Distributions

We start by computing the *distribution of portfolios losses* under both the martingale measure and the *T*-forward measure. This will serve as a building block for the pricing of CDOs. Given our setup, we can always conclude the unconditional distribution of the loss function *L*. However, for pricing and risk management it is necessary to consider *L* after some time passed, and we therefore will be interested in the *conditional* distribution of the loss function.

We note that, under Assumption 11.2, the loss process simplifies to $L(t) = qMN_t$.

It will be convenient to require the processes $(\lambda_t^k)_{t \geq 0}$, $k = 1, ..., K$, to be Markovian. In Gaspar and Schmidt (2007) it is shown that this is the case whenever $h^k(t) = a^k \exp(-b^k t)$ for all $k = 1, ..., K$. Using the Markovian property, Proposition 11.5 provides us the conditional distribution of *L*. However, before being able to handle defaulted and nondefaulted companies in a concise way, we need to introduce some more notation.

Denote by S_t the set which contains the indexes of assets not defaulted until *t*, the "survivors":

$$S_t := \{1 \leq k \leq K : \tau^k > t\}$$

In Proposition 11.5 we will fix the number of defaults in the interval $(t,T]$ and then sum over all possible combinations of defaults. We write $\Sigma_{K_n \in S_t}$ for the sum over all sets $\mathbf{k}_n = \{k_1, \ldots, k_n\}$ of size n with pairwise different elements and $k_1, \ldots, k_n \in S_t$. $\mathbf{k}_n$ represents the n companies that default in $(t, T]$. Given $\mathbf{k}_n$, the companies *not* defaulting are denoted by $S_t \setminus \mathbf{k}_n := \{1 \le l \le n : l \in S_t, l \in \mathbf{k}_n\}$.

Furthermore, we write $\{\tau^{k_n} \in (t, T)\}$ short for $\{\tau^{k_1} \in (t, T], \ldots, \tau^{k_n} \in (t, T]\}$.

Proposition 11.5: *Suppose Assumption 11.2 holds. Suppose the function* $h^k(x)$ *in Equation (11.6) is of the form* $a_k e^{-b_k x}$, $k \in \mathbf{k} \cup \{c\}$. *Then the* conditional distribution of the portfolio losses is given by

$$Q(L_T \le x \mid \mathbf{G}_t) = 1_{\{\tau^{S_t} > t\}} \sum_{n=0}^{K-N_t} \times$$

$$\left(1_{\{n \le x/qM - N_t\}} \times \sum_{\mathbf{k}_n \in S_t} \left\{ \begin{array}{l} S^c(\varepsilon(K - N_t - n), t, T)[\prod_{k \in S_t/\mathbf{k}_n} S^k(t,T)] \\ -S^c(\varepsilon(K - N_t), t, T)[\prod_{k \in S_t} S^k(t,T)] \end{array} \right\} \right)$$

where S^k *and* S^c *are as previously defined.*

Furthermore, if $t = 0$, the above expression gives the unconditional expectation, and the functions $h^k(x)$ need not have any special form.

Corollary 11.6: *Denote by* Q^T *the* **T**-*forward measure. Under the* assumptions of Proposition 11.5 we have that

$$Q(L_T \le x \mid \mathbf{G}_t) = 1_{\{\tau^{S_t} > t\}} \frac{1}{p(t,T)} \sum_{n=0}^{K-N_t} \times$$

$$\left(1_{\{n \le x/qM - N_t\}} \times \sum_{\mathbf{k}_n \in S_t} \left\{ \begin{array}{l} \overline{S}^c(\varepsilon(K - N_t - n), t, T)[\prod_{k \in S_t/\mathbf{k}_n} S^k(t,T)] \\ -\overline{S}^c(\varepsilon(K - N_t), t, T)[\prod_{k \in S_t} S^k(t,T)] \end{array} \right\} \right)$$

Link to Credit Indexes

In this section we draw the link between CDOs and the currently traded credit indexes tranches. We give pricing results for these tranche spreads using the quadratic–shot-noise model.

The iTraxx is effectively a portfolio of 125 single CDSs. To guarantee liquidity, the portfolio is reorganized (the so-called series) semiannually by a voting scheme, and entities whose rating fell below investment grade are removed in the new series.

The aim of this procedure is to guarantee that the underlying portfolio stays in a certain class of creditworthiness. The recovery of each entity is fixed and assumed to be zero. The mathematical setting for a credit index is as follows:

- Without loss of generality, we assume that the notional is 1.
- The credit index is on K names, each represented by a CDS with spread $s^i(t)$.
- All names are in the same credit class, so that the homogeneity Assumption 11.2 will hold.
- Especially, the single names have equal weight.

Recall that $N_t = \Sigma_{\tau^k \leq t}$ is the number of defaulted entities at time t. The payment stream of the credit index is as follows:

- *Fixed leg:* The spread is paid on the remaining notional, i.e., at each time t_n of the tenor $t_1, \ldots, t_{N^*-1}$ the payoff is

$$S\Delta \frac{K - N_{t_n}}{K}$$

- *Defaulting leg:* We assume the payments of default protection occur at the end of the defaulting period, i.e., the payments of the floating or protection leg in the interval $(t_{n-1}, t_n]$ due at $t_n : 2 \leq n \leq N^*$ are

$$\sum_{\tau^k \in (t_{n-1}, t_n]} (1-q) = (1-q)(N_{t_n} - N_{t_{n-1}})$$

Typically, the recovery in the traded indexes is set to zero, but for completeness we stay more general at this point.

Example 11.7: Connection of index spread with underlying CDS spreads.

Before any default happens and if the recovery is paid as in the underlying CDS, it is clear that the payment streams of the index are equivalent to the payment streams of the portfolio of the equally weighted underlying CDS (with spread denoted by S_i) and so the spread of the index is simply

$$S_t = \frac{1}{K} \sum_{k=1}^{K} s^k(t)$$

Now, if a default happens, the situation gets more complicated. One entity is removed and the index still pays the spread S. However, the spread of the portfolio with equally weighted CDS, where now the defaulting entity is removed, has a possibly different spread:

$$\frac{1}{K} \sum_{k=1}^{K} s^k(t) 1_{\{\tau^k > t\}}$$

For example, if $K = 2$ and $s^1 = 100$ and $s^2 = 200$, both constant, we obtain for the index spread 150, but after default of name 1, the portfolio with equal weights pays the spread 100, while the index pays the spread 75.

The above example shows that for pricing more effort has to be done.

Proposition 11.8: *The spread of a credit index on a pool of K entities, where Assumption 11.2 holds, computes to*

$$S_t = \overline{q} K \frac{\sum_{n=2}^{N^*} 1_{\{t_n \geq t\}} \sum_{k=1}^{K} e^{*k}(t, t_{n-1}, t_n)}{\Delta \sum_{t_n \geq t}^{t_{N^*-1}} \sum_{k=1}^{K} \overline{p}_0^k(t, t_n)} \tag{11.15}$$

Tranches on Credit Indexes

Finally, we have to determine the pricing of *tranches* of credit indexes. Investment in a tranche offers the possibility to separate between different credit qualities. Recall that the overall nominal was assumed to be 1. A tranche refers to an interval $(b_1, b_2) \subset [0, 1]$. Investing (selling protection) in a tranche is again done by a swap where the following payments are exchanged:

1. The investor receives at t_n, $1 \leq n \leq N^* - 1$ the payment

$$S \left(1_{\{L_{t_n} \leq b_1\}} + \frac{(b_2 - L_{t_n})^+}{b_2 - b_1} 1_{\{L_{t_n} > x_1\}} \right)$$

2. In turn, the investor has to cover eventual losses, i.e., pays at, t_n, $2 \leq n \leq N^*$,

$$\left[(b_2 - L_{t_{n-1}})^+ - (b_2 - L_{t_n})^+ \right] 1_{\{L_{t_n} > b_1\}}$$

It is cumbersome but not difficult to use Proposition 11.5 for pricing these expressions. However, under a quite common assumption in CDO analysis the pricing becomes rather straightforward.

Assumption 11.9: *Assume that the risk-free rate of interest is independent[6] from the default intensities $\lambda^k, 1 \leq k \leq K$.*

A special case is, of course, if the risk-free rate of interest is deterministic. If Assumption 11.9 holds, then the following result due to Filipović et al. (2007) is the key tool for pricing.

Let us define

$$
C(t, T, y) := E^Q \left(\exp\left(-\int_t^T r_u du \right) 1_{\{L_T < y\}} \bigg|_{G_t} \right) \tag{11.16}
$$

Proposition 11.10: *Suppose Assumption 11.9 holds. The par spread of tranche $(b_1, b_2]$ is given by*

$$
S(t, b_1, b_2) = \frac{\displaystyle\int_{b_1}^{b_2} \left(\begin{array}{l} p(t, t_1) 1_{\{L_t < y\}} - C(t, t_{N^*}, y) + \\[2mm] + \displaystyle\sum_{n=2}^{N^*-1} C(t, t_n, y)\left(1 - \frac{p(t, t_{n+1})}{p(t, t_n)} \right) \end{array} \right) dy}{\displaystyle\sum_{n=1}^{N^*-1} \frac{1}{b_2 - b_1} \int_{b_1}^{b_2} C(t, t_n, y)\, dy} \tag{11.17}
$$

where, $p(t, T)$ denotes the price at time t of a credit riskfree zero-coupon bond price with maturity T and C is as in (11.16).

Note that under the additional assumption of vanishing interest rates, the spread equals

$$
S(t, b_1, b_2) = \frac{\displaystyle\int_{b_1}^{b_2} (1_{\{L_t < y\}} - C(t, t_{N^*}, y))\, dy}{\displaystyle\sum_{n=1}^{N^*-1} \frac{1}{b_2 - b_1} \int_{b_1}^{b_2} C(t, t_n, y)\, dy}
$$

---

[6] In our setup, this means the Z components affecting the short rate of interest in Equation (11.3) are different from those affecting the quadratic part of the intensities η^k in Equation 11.6.

Given Proposition 11.10, it remains to compute $C(t, T, y)$, which under Assumption 11.9 becomes

$$C(t,T,y) = p(t,T)\mathbf{Q}^{\mathrm{T}}(L_T < y \,|_{\mathrm{G}_t})$$

However, both these distributions had been computed in Proposition 11.5 and Corollary 11.6; so the spread of a tranche is available. Note also that, as L takes values in the finite set $\{0, qM, \dots, KqM\}$, the integral in Equation (11.17) is simply a sum over at most $K + 1$ entries.

CONCLUSION

This chapter considers modeling of credit portfolio risk using a combination of general quadratic term structure models and shot-noise processes. This has a number of interesting features; in particular, the approach is able to capture spread risk as well as contagion on a reasonable level. The approach therefore seems very interesting for practical application in pricing and risk management of credit portfolios and credit portfolio derivatives such as CDOs. In particular, the turmoil caused by the U.S. subprime crisis showed credit spreads in liquidly traded credit indexes that are very similar to the suggested model. All necessary formulas are given in explicit form and therefore allow for fast implementation.

APPENDIX

Building Blocks in Closed Form

We start by defining three different types of ODE systems.

Definition 11.A.1 (Basic ODE System)

Denote $\mathbf{T} := \{(t, T) \in R^2 : 0 \le t \le T\}$ and consider functions, A, B, and on C on $\mathbf{T}$ with values in, R, R^m, and $R^{m \times m}$, respectively. For functions φ_1, φ_2, and φ_3 on $R+$ with values in R, R^m, and $R^{m \times m}$, respectively, we say that $(A, B, C, \varphi_1, \varphi_2, \varphi_3)$ solves the *basic ODE system* if

$$\frac{\partial A}{\partial t} + d^{\cdot}(t)B + \frac{1}{2}B^{\cdot}k_0(t)B + \mathrm{tr}\{Ck_0(t)\} = \varphi_1(t)$$

$$\frac{\partial B}{\partial t} + E^{\cdot}(t)B + 2Cd(t) + \frac{1}{2}\tilde{B}^{\cdot}K(t)B + 2Ck_0(t)B = \varphi_2(t) \quad (11.18)$$

$$\frac{\partial C}{\partial t} + CE(t) + E^{\cdot}(t)C + 2Ck_0(t)C + \frac{1}{2}\tilde{B}^{\cdot}G(t)\tilde{B} = \varphi_3(t)$$

subject to the boundary conditions $A(T, T) = 0$, $B(T, T) = 0$, $C(T, T) = 0$. A, B, and C should always be evaluated at (t, T). E, d, and k_0 are the functions from the above definitions [recall Equations (11.2) and (11.3)], while

$$\tilde{B} := \begin{pmatrix} B & 0 & \cdots & 0 \\ 0 & B & \cdots & 0 \\ \vdots & & \ddots & \\ 0 & \cdots & 0 & B \end{pmatrix}, K(t) = \begin{pmatrix} k_1(t) \\ \vdots \\ k_m(t) \end{pmatrix}, G(t) = \begin{pmatrix} g_{11}(t) & \cdots & g_{1m}(t) \\ \vdots & \ddots & \vdots \\ g_{m1}(t) & \cdots & g_{mm}(t) \end{pmatrix} \quad (11.19)$$

where we have $\tilde{B}$, $K(t) \in R^{m^2 \times m}$ and $G(t) \in R^{m^2 \times m^2}$.

Definition 11.A.2 (Interlinked ODE System)

Consider smooth functions $a, b, c, B, and C$ on $\mathbf{T}$ with values in R, R^m, $R^{m \times m}, R^m$, and $R^{m \times m}$ and smooth functions φ_1, φ_2, and φ_3 on R_+ with values in, R, R^m, and $R^{m \times m}$, respectively. We say that $(a, b, c, B, C, \varphi_1, \varphi_2, \varphi_3)$ solves the *interlinked ODE system* if it solves

$$\frac{\partial a}{\partial t} + d^{\boldsymbol{\cdot}}(t)b + B^{\boldsymbol{\cdot}}k_0(t)b + \operatorname{tr}\{ck_0(t)\} = 0$$

$$\frac{\partial b}{\partial t} + E^{\boldsymbol{\cdot}}(t)b + 2cd(t) + \frac{1}{2}\tilde{B}^{\boldsymbol{\cdot}}k_0(t)b + 2ck_0(t)B + 2Ck_0(t)b = 0 \quad (11.20)$$

$$\frac{\partial c}{\partial t} + cE(t) + E^{\boldsymbol{\cdot}}(t)c + 4Ck_0(t)c + \frac{1}{2}\tilde{B}^{\boldsymbol{\cdot}}G(t)\tilde{b} = 0$$

subject to the boundary conditions $a(T, T) = \varphi_1(T)$, $b(T, T) = \varphi_2(T)$, $c(T, T) = \varphi_3(T)$. a, b, c and B, C should always be evaluated at (t, T). E, d, and k_0 are the functions from Equation (11.3), while $[\tilde{B}, K \in R^{m^2 \times m}$ and $G \in R^{m^2 \times m^2}$ are as in Equation (11.19).

Definition 11.A.3 (Doubly Interlinked ODE System)

Denote $\mathbf{T}: = \{(t, t_{n-1}, t_n) \in R^3 : 0 \leq t \leq t_{n-1} \leq t_n\}$, and consider functions α, β, γ, on $\mathbf{T}$ with values in R, R^m, and $R^{m \times m}$, respectively. For functions, $\varphi_1, \bar{\varphi}_1, \varphi_2, \bar{\varphi}_2, \varphi_3, \bar{\varphi}_3$ on R^+ with values in, $R, R^m, R^m, R^{m \times m}$, and

$R^{m \times m}$, respectively, we say that $(\alpha, \beta, \gamma, \varphi_1, \varphi_2, \varphi_3, \bar{\varphi}_1, \bar{\varphi}_2, \bar{\varphi}_3)$ solves the *doubly interlinked ODE system* if

$$\frac{\partial \alpha}{\partial t} + d^{\cdot}(t)\beta + \frac{1}{2}\beta^{\cdot}k_0(t)\beta + \text{tr}\,\gamma k_0(t) + \beta^{\cdot}k_0(t)\bar{B} = 0$$

$$\frac{\partial \beta}{\partial t} + E^{\cdot}(t)\beta + 2\gamma d(t) + \frac{1}{2}\tilde{\beta}^{\cdot}K(t)\beta + 2\gamma k_0(t)\beta +$$

$$+ 2\bar{C}k_0(t)\beta + 2\gamma k_0(t)\bar{B} + \tilde{\beta}^{\cdot}K(t)\bar{B} = 0 \qquad (11.21)$$

$$\frac{\partial \gamma}{\partial t} + \gamma E(t) + E^{\cdot}(t)\gamma + 2\gamma k_0(t)\gamma + \frac{1}{2}\tilde{\beta}^{\cdot}G(t)\tilde{\beta} +$$

$$+ 4\bar{C}k_0(t)\gamma + \tilde{\bar{B}}^{\cdot}G(t)\tilde{\beta} = 0$$

subject to the boundary conditions $\alpha(t_{n-1}, t_{n-1}, t_n) = A(t_{n-1}, t_n)$, $\beta(t_{n-1}, t_{n-1}, t_n) = B(t_{n-1}, t_n)$, and $\gamma(t_{n-1}, t_{n-1}, t_n) = C(t_{n-1}, t_n)$ and where $(A, B, C, \varphi_1, \varphi_2, \varphi_3)$ and $(\bar{A}, \bar{B}, \bar{C}, \bar{\varphi}_1, \bar{\varphi}_2, \bar{\varphi}_3)$ both solve the basic ODE system in Equation (11.18). E, d, and k_0 are the functions from Equation (11.3), $\tilde{\beta}$, $K \in R^{m^2 \times m}$, and $\gamma \in R^{m^2 \times m^2}$. α, η, γ should be evaluated at (t, t_{n-1}, t_n) and $A, \bar{A}, B\,\bar{B}, C, \bar{C},$ at (t, t_{n-1}).

Theorem 11.A.4: *Let* $x = T - t$, *and consider* r *as in Equation (11.4),* J *and* η *as in (11.7), and* $\theta \in R$. *For (2) below we also require the existence of* $D^k(\theta, x)$ *and for (v) that* D^k *is bounded in some neighborhood of* x. *Then*

(i) $$S_\eta^k(\theta, t, T) := E^{\mathbf{Q}}\left(e^{-\int_t^T \theta \eta_s^k ds} \Big|_{\mathbf{F}_t^W} \right)$$

$$= \exp(A^k(\theta, t, T) + B^{k\cdot}(\theta, t, T)Z_t + Z_t^{\cdot}C^k(\theta, t, T)Z_t)$$

(ii) $$(S_J^k(\theta, t, T) := E^{\mathbf{Q}}\left(e^{-\int_t^T \theta^k J_s ds} \Big|_{\mathbf{F}_t^J} \right)$$

$$= \exp(\theta(\tilde{J}_t^k - \tilde{J}^k(t, T)) + lx[D^k(\theta, x) - 1])$$

(iii) $$\bar{S}_\eta^k(\theta, t, T) := E^{\mathbf{Q}}\left(e^{-\int_t^T r_s + \theta \eta_s^k ds} \Big|_{\mathbf{F}_t^W} \right)$$

$$= \exp(\bar{A}^k(\theta, t, T) + \bar{B}^{k\cdot}(\theta, t, T)Z_t + Z^{\cdot}(t)\bar{C}^k(\theta, t, T)Z_t)$$

(iv) $\Gamma_\eta^k(\theta,t,T) := E^Q\left(\theta\eta_T^k e^{-\int_t^{\cdot}\theta\eta_s^k ds}\Big|_{\mathbf{F}_t^W}\right)$

$$= \left[a^k(\theta,t,T) + b^{k\cdot}(\theta,t,T)Z_t + Z_t^\cdot c^k(\theta,t,T)Z_t\right]S_\eta(\theta,t,T)$$

(v) $\Gamma_J^k(\theta,t,T) := E^Q\left(\theta J_T^k e^{-\int_t^T \theta J_s^k ds}\Big|_{\mathbf{F}_t^J}\right)$

$$= S_J^k(\theta,t,T)\{\theta J^k(t,T) - l^k[D^k(\theta,x)(1-x)$$
$$- 1 + x\phi_Y^k(\theta H^k(x))]\}$$

(vi) $\overline{\Gamma}_\eta^k(\theta,t,T) := E^Q\left(\theta\eta_T^k e^{-\int_t^T r_s + \theta\eta_s^k ds}\Big|_{\mathbf{F}_t^W}\right)$

$$= \left[\begin{matrix}\overline{a}^k(\theta,t,T) + \overline{b}^{k\cdot}(\theta,t,T)Z_t \\ + Z_t^\cdot \overline{c}^k(\theta,t,T)Z_t\end{matrix}\right]\overline{S}_\eta^k(\theta,t,T)$$

where $(A^k, B^k, C^k, \theta f^k, \theta g^k, \theta Q^k)$ and $(\overline{A}^k, \overline{B}^k, \overline{C}^k, f + \theta f^k, g + \theta g^k, Q + \theta Q^k)$ solve the basic ODE system of Definition 11.A.1. $(a^k, b^k, c^k, B^k, C^k, \theta f^k, \theta g^k, \theta Q^k)$ and $(\overline{a}^k, \overline{b}^k, \overline{c}^k, \overline{B}^k, \overline{C}^k, \theta f^k, \theta g^k, \theta Q^k)$ solve the interlinked system of Definition 11.A.2.; and we have introduced the following notations $H^k(x) = \int_0^x h^k(u)du, \overline{J}^k(t,T) = \sum_{\overline{\tau}_1 \le t} Y_1^k H^k(T - \overline{\tau}_1), \phi_Y^k$ is the Laplace transform

of Y^k and $D^k(x) = \left[\int_0^1 \phi_Y^k(H^k(xu))du\right]$ with h^k, Y^k from Equation (11.6)

Furthermore,

(vii) $S^k(\theta,t,T) := E^Q\left(e^{-\int_t^T \theta\mu_s^k ds}\Big|_{\mathbf{F}_t}\right) = S_\eta^k(\theta,t,T)S_J^k(\theta,t,T)$

(viii) $\overline{S}^k(\theta,t,T) := E^Q\left(e^{-\int_t^T r_s + \theta\mu_s^k ds}\Big|_{\mathbf{F}_t}\right) = \overline{S}_\eta^k(\theta,t,T)S_J^k(\theta,t,T)$

(ix) $\Gamma^k(\theta,t,T) := E^Q\left(\theta\mu_T^k e^{-\int_t^T \theta\mu_s^k ds}\Big|_{\mathbf{F}_t}\right)$

$$= \Gamma_\eta^k(\theta,t,T)S_J^k(\theta,t,T) + \Gamma_J^k(\theta,t,T)S_\eta^k(\theta,t,T)$$

$$\overline{\Gamma}^k(\theta,t,T) := E^{\mathbf{Q}}\left(\left.\theta\mu_T^k e^{-\int_t^T r_s + \theta\mu_s^k ds}\right|_{\mathbf{F}_t}\right)$$

$$= \overline{\Gamma}_\eta^k(\theta,t,T)S_J(\theta,t,T) + \Gamma_j^k(\theta,t,T)\overline{S}_\eta^k(\theta,t,T)$$

Finally, we introduce one more shorthand notation.

Notation 11.A.5: For $k \in \mathbf{K} \cup \{c\}$ we define

$$E^k(\theta,t,t_{n-1},t_n) := \exp\left(\alpha^k(t,t_{n-1},t_n) + \beta^{k\cdot}(t,t_{n-1},t_n)Z_t \right.$$
$$\left. + Z_t^{\cdot}\gamma^k(t,t_{n-1},t_n)Z_t\right) \qquad (11.22)$$

where $(\alpha^k, \beta^k, \gamma^k, f, g, Q, \theta f, \theta g, \theta Q)$ solves the doubly interlinked ODE system in Equation (11.21) with f, g, Q as in Equation (11.4) and f, g, Q as in Equation (11.6). For $k = 1, \ldots K$ $\theta = \varepsilon$, while for $k = c$, $\theta = \varepsilon^K$.

Proofs and Auxiliary Results

Proof of Lemma 11.1: By the definition of $\rho^{i,j}$, we have

$$\rho^{i,j}(t,T) = \frac{\mathbf{Q}_D^{i,j}(t,T) - \mathbf{Q}_D^i(t,T)\mathbf{Q}_D^j(t,T)}{\sqrt{\mathbf{Q}_D^i(t,T)[1-\mathbf{Q}_D^i(t,T)]\mathbf{Q}_D^j(t,T)[1-\mathbf{Q}_D^j(t,T)]}}$$

where $\mathbf{Q}^{i,j}{}_D$ is the probability of joint default of the firms i, j until time T, given that none has defaulted until t. We can easily get

$$\mathbf{Q}_D^{i,j}(t,T) = E^{\mathbf{Q}}\left[\left.1_{\{\tau^i < T\}}1_{\{\tau^j < T\}}\right|_{\mathbf{G}_t}\right] = E^{\mathbf{Q}}\left(\left.\left(1 - e^{-\int_t^T \lambda_s^i ds}\right)\left(1 - e^{-\int_t^T \lambda_s^j ds}\right)\right|_{\mathbf{F}_t}\right)$$

$$= E^{\mathbf{Q}}\left(\left.\left(1 - e^{-\int_t^T \mu_s^i + \varepsilon^i \mu_s^c ds}\right)\left(1 - e^{-\int_t^T \mu_s^j + \varepsilon^j \mu_s^c ds}\right)\right|_{\mathbf{F}_t}\right)$$

$$= E^Q \left(1 - e^{-\int_t^T \mu_s^i + \varepsilon^i \mu_s^c ds} - e^{-\int_t^T \mu_s^j + \varepsilon^j \mu_s^c ds} + e^{-\int_t^T \mu_s^i + \mu_s^j + (\varepsilon^i + \varepsilon^j) \mu_s^c ds} \Bigg|_{F_t} \right)$$

$$= 1 - Q_S^i(t, T) - Q_S^j(t, T) + E^Q \left(e^{-\int_t^T \mu_s^i + \mu_s^j + (\varepsilon^i + \varepsilon^j) \mu_s^c ds} \Bigg|_{F_t} \right)$$

Using independence of μ^i, μ^j, and μ^c and $Q_S^k (t, T) = S^k (t, T) S^c (\varepsilon^k, t, T)$ for $k = 1, 2$, we obtain

$$Q_D^{i,j}(t, T) = 1 - [- S^i(t, T)S^c(\varepsilon^i, t, T)] - S^j(t, T)S^j(\varepsilon^k, t, T) + S^i(t, T)S^j(t, T) S^c(\varepsilon^i + \varepsilon^j, t, T).$$

The result follows from $Q_D^i (t, T) Q_D^j (t, T) = [1 - Q_S^i (t, T)] [1 - Q_S^j (t, T)] = 1 - Q_{,S}^i (t, T) - Q_S^j (t, T) + Q_S^i (t, T) Q_S^j (t, T)$ and again substituting Q_S^i and Q_S^j by its shorthand notation.

Proof of Lemma 11.3: The result is trivial on $\{\tau_1 \leq t\}$; so we consider $\{\tau_1 > t\}$ from now on. Then, by definition, $Q_S^{FtD} (t, T) = Q(\tau_1 > T \mid G_t)$. We start by conditioning on $\mu_{[t,T]}^c \vee G_t$. Recall that the default time of name k is denoted by τ_k. Then

$$Q\left(\tau_1 > T \mid \mu_{[t,T]}^c \vee G_t \right) = Q\left(\min(\tau_1, \tau_2, \cdots, \tau_K) > T \big| \mu_{[t,T]}^c \vee G_t \right)$$

$$= E^Q \left[1_{\{\tau_1 > T, \tau_2 > T, \cdots, \tau_K > T\}} \big| \mu_{[t,T]}^c \vee G_t) \right].$$

As $\tau_1, \ldots, \tau_K$ are independent, conditionally on $\mu^c{}_{[t,T]}$, the above expectation becomes

$$E^Q \left(\exp\left(-\sum_{k=1}^{\bar{K}} \int_t^T \lambda_s^k ds \right) \Bigg|_{\mu_{[t,T]}^c \vee F_t} \right) = e^{-\bar{K}\varepsilon \int_t^T \mu_s^c ds} \times$$

$$\times E^Q \left(\exp\left(-\sum_{k=1}^{\bar{K}} \int_t^T (J_s^k + \eta_s^k) ds \right) \Bigg|_{\mu_{[t,T]}^c \vee F_t} \right)$$

Hence, as $\eta^1, \ldots, \eta^{\bar{K}}, j^1, \ldots, J^K$ are mutually independent, we obtain

$$Q\left(\tau_1 > T \mid \mu_{[t, T]}^c \right) \vee G_t \right) = e^{-\varepsilon K \int_t^T \mu_s^c ds} \prod_{k=1}^K S^k(t, T)$$

It may be recalled that $S^k = S^k_\eta S^k_J$. Thus,

$$Q(\tau_1 > T \,|_{\mathbf{G}_t}) = E^Q \left(e^{-\varepsilon K \int_t^T \mu_s^c ds} \prod_{k=1}^K S^k(t,T) \Bigg|_{\mathbf{F}_t} \right) = S^c(\varepsilon \bar{K}, t, T) \prod_{k=1}^K S^k(t,T)$$

Using the same methodology with the fact that r is independent of μ^k for all $k \in \mathbf{k}$ but not of μ^c, this determines $\bar{p}^{\text{FtD}}(t, T)$.

Proof of Theorem 11.4: For ease of notation we write S_{FD} instead of S_{FD} (t). The value at time t of the fixed leg of the FDS follows from the results in Lemma 11.3:

$$E^Q \left[\sum_{n=1}^{N^*} e^{-\int_t^{t_n} r_s \, ds} s^{\text{FD}} 1_{\{\tau > t_n\}} |_{\mathbf{G}_t} \right] = s^{\text{FD}} \sum_{n=1}^{N^*} (t_n - t_{n-1}) \bar{p}^{\text{FtD}}(t, T_n)$$

For the pricing of the floating leg we need to compute

$$e^{\text{FD*}}(t, T_{n-1}, T_n) := E^Q \left(e^{-\int_t^{t_n} r_s ds} 1_{\{\tau^{1:K} \in (t_n, t_{n-1}]\}} \Bigg|_{\mathbf{G}_t} \right)$$

$$= E^Q \left(e^{-\int_t^{t_n} r_s ds} 1_{\{\tau^{1:K} > t_{n-1}\}} \Bigg|_{\mathbf{G}_t} \right) - E^Q \left(e^{-\int_t^{t_n} r_s ds} 1_{\{\tau^{1:K} > t_n\}} \Bigg|_{\mathbf{G}_t} \right)$$

where the second expectation equals $[\bar{p}^{\text{FtD}}(t, t_n)$. Furthermore, following the steps from Lemma 11.3, we can deduce[7]

$$E^Q \left(e^{-\int_t^{t_n} r_s ds} 1_{\{\tau^{1:K} > t_{n-1}\}} \Bigg|_{\mathbf{G}_t} \right) = E^Q \left(p(t_{n-1}, t_n) e^{-\int_t^{t_{n-1}} r_s ds} 1_{\{\tau^{1:K} > t_{n-1}\}} \Bigg|_{\mathbf{F}_t} \right)$$

$$= E^Q \left(p(t_{n-1}, t_n) e^{-\int_t^{t_{n-1}} [r_s + \varepsilon K \mu_s^c + \sum_{k=1}^K \mu_s^k] ds} \Bigg|_{\mathbf{F}_t} \right)$$

---

[7] Alternatively, in the conditionally independent approach the default intensity of the minimum of the default times is simply the sum over all intensities.

We write $\tilde{\mathbf{F}}_{t,tN^*}$ short for $\mathbf{F}_t \in \sigma(\mu^c{}_s, \mathbf{r}_s : t \leq s \leq t_{N^*})$. Conditioning on $\tilde{\mathbf{F}}$, we obtain

$$
E^{\mathbf{Q}}\left(p(t_{n-1}, t_n) e^{-\int_t^{t_{n-1}} [r_s + \varepsilon K \mu_s^c + \sum_{k=1}^K \mu_s^k] ds} \,\Big|\, \mathbf{F}_t \right)
$$

$$
= E^{\mathbf{Q}}\left(E^{\mathbf{Q}}\left(e^{-\sum_{k=1}^K \int_t^{t_{n-1}} \mu_s^k ds} \,\Big|\, \tilde{\mathbf{F}}_{t,t_{N^*}} \right) p(t_{n-1}, t_n) e^{-\int_t^{t_{n-1}} (r_s + \varepsilon \bar{K} \mu_s^c) ds} \,\Big|\, \mathbf{F}_t \right)
$$

Let us consider the inner expectation more closely. We have that $\eta^1, \ldots,$ η^k are independent of μ^c and r, so that

$$
E^{\mathbf{Q}}\left(e^{-\sum_{k=1}^{\bar{K}} \int_t^{t_{n-1}} \mu_s^k ds} \,\Big|\, \tilde{\mathbf{F}}_{t,t_{N^*}} \right) = E^{\mathbf{Q}}\left(e^{-\sum_{k=1}^{\bar{K}} \int_t^{t_{n-1}} \eta_s^k ds} \,\Big|\, \mathbf{F}_t \right) E^{\mathbf{Q}}\left(e^{-\int_t^{t_{n-1}} \sum_{k=1}^K J_s^k ds} \,\Big|\, \mathbf{F}_t \right)
$$

$$
= \prod_{k=1}^K S^k(t, t_{n-1})
$$

It may be recalled that $S^k = S^k{}_\eta S^k{}_J$. It remains to compute

$$
E^{\mathbf{Q}}\left(p(t_{n-1}, t_n) e^{-\int_t^{t_{n-1}} (r_s + \varepsilon K \eta_s^c) ds} \,\Big|\, \mathbf{F}_t \right) = \bar{S}_\eta^c(\varepsilon K, t, t_{n-1}) \exp\Big(\alpha^c(t, t_{n-1}, t_n) +
$$

$$
+ \beta^{c\bullet}(t, t_{n-1}, t_n) Z_t + Z_t^{\bullet} \gamma^c(t, t_{n-1}, t_n) Z_t \Big)
$$

The remaining part with J^c is given by $S^c{}_J$ such that by $\bar{S}^c = \bar{S}_\eta^c S_J^c$, the expression above equals

$$
\exp\Big(\alpha^c(t, t_n, t_{n-1}) + \beta^{c\bullet}(t, t_n, t_{n-1}) Z_t + Z_t^{\bullet} \gamma^c(t, t_n, t_{n-1}) Z_t \Big) \times
$$

$$
\times \underbrace{\bar{S}^c(\varepsilon \bar{K}, t, t_{n-1}) \prod_{k=1}^{\bar{K}} S^k(t, t_{n-1})}_{\bar{p}^{\mathrm{RD}}(t, t_{n-1})}
$$

where $\alpha,\ \beta,\ \gamma$ are as stated in Equation (11.22).

Proof of Theorem 11.5: The conditional distribution of L is given by

$$
Q(L_T \leq x \mid_{G_t}) = Q\left(L_T - L_t \leq x - L_t \mid_{G_t}\right) = Q\left(\left. \sum_{j=1}^{N_T - N_t} \xi_j \leq x - L_t \right|_{G_t}\right)
$$

$$
= Q\left(\left. \sum_{j=1}^{N_T - N_t} q^j \leq \frac{x - L_t}{M} \right|_{G_t}\right) = F_{q, N_T - N_t}\left(\frac{x - L_t}{M}\right)
$$

Recall that N is the counting process of *all* defaults. For the following, we first condition on μ^c. Then all individual defaults τ^k are independent and stem from independent Cox processes with (also independent) intensities $[\lambda^k(t)]_{t \leq 0}$, $k = 1, \ldots, K$. Observe that $N_T - N_t$ is not independent from N^8_t, but, it is not difficult to compute the conditional distribution. However, in contrast to the unconditional distribution, we need to distinguish which company defaults.

Using the Markovian nature of the processes μ^k, we need to determine

$$
Q\left(N_T - N_t = k \mid_{S_t, N_t, \mu^c_{[t, T]}, F_t}\right)
$$

We write $F_t := \sigma(S_t, N_t, \mu^c_{[t,T]}, F_t)$. In the above probability we will have k companies defaulting in $(t, T]$. Summing over all possible indexes was denoted by $\sum_{k_n \in S_t}$. Then

$$
Q\left[N_T - N_t = k \mid_{S_t, N_t, \mu^c_{[t,T]}, F_t}\right] = \sum_{k_n \in S_t} Q(\tau^{k_n} \in (t, T] \mid_{\tilde{F}_t}) Q(\tau^{S_t \setminus k_n} > T \mid_{\tilde{F}_t})
$$

Note that the survival probability of asset k is given by

$$
Q(\tau^k > T \mid_{\tilde{F}_t}) = Q\left(\left. \tau^k > T \right|_{1_{\{\tau^k > t\}}, \mu^c_{[t,T]}, F_t}\right)
$$

$$
= 1_{\{\tau^k > t\}} \exp\left(-\varepsilon \int_t^T \mu^c_s \, ds\right) \underbrace{E^Q\left(\exp(-\int_t^T \mu^k_s \, ds) \mid_{F_t}\right)}_{= S^k(t,T)}
$$

---

[8] For example, if all companies default before t (hence, $N_t = K$), it follows that $N_T - N_t = 0$.

The expectation on the right-hand side (RHS) is of the exponential quadratic from as given by (7) in Theorem 11.5. In the Markovian case, we can simplify even further. Furthermore, since conditionally on μ^c the defaults occur independently, we have

$$Q(\tau^{k_n} > T \,|_{\tilde{F}_t}) = 1_{\{\tau^{k_n} > t\}} \exp\left(-n\varepsilon \int_t^T \mu_s^c \, ds\right) \prod_{k \in k_n} S^k(t,T).$$

On $\{\tau^k > t\}$ we also have that $Q(\tau^k \in (t, T] \,|_{\tilde{F}_t}) = 1 - Q(\tau^k > T \,|_{\tilde{F}_t})$. Hence,

$$Q(N_T - N_t = n \,|_{\tilde{F}_t}) = \sum_{k_n \in S_t} \left(1 - e^{-n\varepsilon \int_t^T \mu_s^c \, ds} \prod_{k \in k_n} S^k(t,T)\right) \times$$

$$\times e^{-(K-N_t-n)\varepsilon \int_t^T \mu_s^c \, ds} \prod_{k \in S_t / k_n} S^k(t,T)$$

$$= \sum_{k_n \in S_t} \left[e^{-(K-N_t-n)\int_t^T \mu_s^c \, ds} \times \right.$$

$$\left. \times \prod_{k \in S_t / k_n} S^k(t,T) - e^{-\varepsilon(K-N_t)\int_t^T \mu_s^c \, ds} \prod_{k \in S_t} S^k(t,T) \right]$$

After we have done all calculation conditioned on μ^c, we finally have to consider the unconditional expectation.

This is, on $\{\tau^{S_t} > t\}$,

$$Q(N_T - N_t = n \,|_{S_t, N_t, F_t}) = \sum_{k_n \in S_t} \left[S^c(\varepsilon(K - N_t - n), t, T) \prod_{k \in S_t / k_n} S^k(t,T) \right.$$

$$\left. - S^c(\varepsilon(K - N_t), t, T) \prod_{k \in S_t} S^k(t,T) \right]$$

Proof of Corollary 11.6: Recall from Equation (11.5) that

$p(t, T) = \exp \{A(t, T) + B^{\bullet}(t, T)Z_t + Z_t^{\bullet} C(t, T)Z_t\}$. First, observe that

$$p(t,T)Q^T \left(L_T \le x \,|_{G_t} \right) = E^Q \left(e^{-\int_t^T r_s \, ds} 1_{\{L_T \le x\}} \,\bigg|_{G_t} \right)$$

We therefore just need to compute $E^{\mathbf{Q}}\left(\left.e^{-\int_t^T r_s ds} 1_{\{L_T \leq x\}}\right|_{\mathbf{G}_t}\right)$.

To this, let $\tilde{\mathbf{G}}_t := \sigma(\mathbf{S}_t, N_t, \mu_{[t,T]}^c, \mathbf{G}_t)$ and recall r has common factors, i.e., conditional on μ^c it is known. We thus have

$$E^{\mathbf{Q}}\left(\left.e^{-\int_t^T r_s ds} 1_{\{L_T \leq x\}}\right|_{\mathbf{G}_t}\right) = E^{\mathbf{Q}}\left(\left.e^{-\int_t^T r_s ds} E^{\mathbf{Q}}\left(1_{\{L_T \leq x\}}\big|_{\tilde{\mathbf{G}}_t}\right)\right|_{\mathbf{G}_t}\right)$$

$$= E^{\mathbf{Q}}\left(\left.e^{-\int_t^T r_s ds} \mathbf{Q}\left(L_T \leq x \big|_{\tilde{\mathbf{G}}_t}\right)\right|_{\mathbf{G}_t}\right)$$

For the inner expectation we may use Equation (11.29) to obtain that the above equals

$$E^{\mathbf{Q}}\left(e^{-\int_t^T r_s ds} \sum_{n=0}^{K-N_t} F_{q,n}\left(\frac{x - L_t}{M}\right) \sum_{\mathbf{k}_n \in \mathbf{S}_t}\left[e^{-\varepsilon(K-N_t-n)\int_t^T \mu_s^c ds}\right.\right.$$

$$\left.\left.\prod_{k \in \mathbf{S}_t/\mathbf{k}_n} S^k(t,T) - e^{-\varepsilon(K-N_t)\int_t^T \mu_s^c ds} \prod_{k \in \mathbf{S}_t} S^k(t,T)\right]\right|_{\mathbf{G}_t}\right)$$

Recalling the shorthand notation, we get

$$E^{\mathbf{Q}}\left(\left.e^{-\int_t^T r_s ds} e^{-\varepsilon(K-N_t-n)\int_t^T \mu_s^c ds}\right|_{\mathbf{G}_t}\right) = \bar{S}^c(\varepsilon(K - N_t - n), t, T)$$

Proof of Proposition 11.8: We start by determining the value of the index spread at a certain time t. The spread offered by the index is chosen such that fixed and defaulting legs are equal in value. We denote this spread by S_t. Using the above formulation, the value of the fixed leg at time t is

$$S_t \Delta K^{-1} \sum_{t_n \geq t}^{t_{N^*-1}} \frac{1}{K} \sum_{k=1}^K E^{\mathbf{Q}}\left(\left.e^{-\int_t^{t_n} r_u du} 1_{\{\tau^k > t_n\}}\right|\mathbf{G}_t\right)$$

where $\sum_{t_n \geq t}^{t_{N*-1}}$ is, more precisely, the sum over all $t_n \in \{t_1, \ldots, t_{N*-1}\}$ with $t_n \geq t$. The last expectation is equal to $\bar{p}^k{}_0(t, t_n)$, the appropriate zero recovery bond for the k th underlying. On the other side, the value of the floating leg equals

$$q\sum_{t_n \geq t}^{N^*} E^{\mathbf{Q}}\left(\left. \sum_{\tau^j \in (t_{n-1}, t_n)} e^{-\int_t^{t_n} r_u \, du} \right|_{\mathbf{G}_t} \right)$$

The expectation can be evaluated with the aid of e^* defined in Equation (11.15). From there it may be recalled that the value of 1 unit of currency, paid at t_n, when name k defaults in (t_{n-1}, t_n) was named $e^{*k}(t, t_{n-1}, t_n)$ and can be calculated in closed form. Thus, the value of the default leg is

$$q\sum_{t_n \geq t} E^{\mathbf{Q}}\left(\left. \sum_{\tau^j \in (t_{n-1}, t_n]} e^{-\int_t^{t_n} r_u \, du} \right|_{\mathbf{G}_t} \right) = q\sum_{t_n \geq t} \sum_{k=1}^{K} E^{\mathbf{Q}}\left(\left. e^{-\int_t^{t_n} r_u \, du} 1_{\{\tau^k \in (t_{n-1}, t_n]\}} \right|_{\mathbf{G}_t} \right)$$

$$= q\sum_{t_n \geq t} \sum_{k=1}^{K} e^{*k}(t, t_{n-1}, t_n)$$

REFERENCES

Bielecki, T. and Rutkowski, M. (2002) *Credit Risk: Modeling, Valuation and Hedging*. New York: Springer-Verlag.

Bluhm, C. and Overbeck, L. (2006) *Structured Credit Portfolio Analysis, Baskets & CDOs*. London: Chapman & Hall/CRC.

Bluhm, C., Overbeck, L., and Wagner, C. (2003). *Credit Risk Modeling*. London: Chapman & Hall/CRC.

Duffie, D. and Gârleanu, N. (2001) Risk and Valuation of Collateralized Debt Obligations. *Financial Analysts Journal*, (1): 41–59.

Filipović, D., Overbeck, L., and Schmidt, T. (2007) The Term Structure of CDO Losses. Working paper. University of Leipzig, Germany.

Frey, R. and Backhaus, J. (2006) Credit Derivatives in Models with Interacting Default Intensities: A Markovian Approach. Preprint, Department of Mathematics, University of Leipzig, Germany.

Gaspar, R.M. (2004) General Quadratic Term Structures for Bond, Futures and Forward Prices. Stockholm School of Economics, Working paper, *Series in Economics and Finance*, 559, Stockholm.

Gaspar, R.M. and Schmidt, T. (2007) Shot-Noise Quadratic Term Structure Models. Working paper. University of Leipzig, Germany.

Lando, D. (2004) *Credit Risk Modeling: Theory and Applications*. Princeton, NJ: Princeton University Press.

McNeil, A., Frey, R., and Embrechts, P. (2005) *Quantitative Risk Management: Concepts, Techniques and Tools*. Princeton, NJ: Princeton University Press.

Scherer, M. (2007). Tractable Multi-Firm Default Models Based on Discontinuous Processes. Ph.D. Thesis, University of Ulm, Germany.

Schmidt, T. and Stute, W (2004) Credit Risk—A Survey. *Contemporary Mathematics*, 36, 2:75–115.

Schönbucher, P. (2003). *Credit Derivates Pricing Models*. Hoboken, NJ: John Wiley & Sons.

CHAPTER 12

Pricing Forward-Starting Collateralized Debt Obligations Using Dynamic Copula Processes

Daniel Totouom and Margaret Armstrong

ABSTRACT

The rapid evolution of credit derivatives over recent years has led to the development of products such as forward-starting collateralized debt obligations, options on collateralized debt obligations, long and/or short collateralized debt obligation (CDO) portfolios, and leveraged super-senior tranches that require a dynamic model of portfolio losses over time in order to price them successfully. Tests such as those by Burtschell et al. (2005) have shown that the Clayton copula, which has lower tail dependence, is better at pricing CDO tranches than those with symmetric tails, such as the Gaussian copula. Using iTraxx spreads from April 2005 to July 2007, we show that experimental copulas for different series exhibit the classic ice cream cone shape of the Clayton copula but inverted. This is because upward movements in credit spreads are equivalent to downward movements in ratings.

INTRODUCTION

In this chapter we present our model for pricing CDO tranches based on a dynamic copula process with low tail dependence (Totouom and Armstrong, 2005; ibid., 2007a; ibid., 2007b) as a Levy process. We also develop a new gamma Ornstein–Uhlenbeck process that is mean reverting. Both dynamic copula models are calibrated to the single-name CDS, and they automatically reproduce the risk-neutral marginal default probabilities of each name and cumulative default probability in a consistent method, which is demonstrated using iTraxx. A formula for the asymptotic loss distribution, similar to Vasicek's formula, is derived simplifying the computations for a granular portfolio.[1]

From 2002 to 2007, major changes occurred in the credit derivatives industry whereby the liquidity of single-name CDS increased dramatically. Quotes are now available for standard tranches for reference baskets, iTraxx in Europe and CDX in North America, for the standard maturities of 3, 5, 7, and 10 years. Base correlation (McGinty et al., 2004) has become the industry standard for pricing CDOs. New types of derivatives including forward-starting CDOs, options on CDOs, long and/or short CDO portfolios, and leveraged super-senior tranches have been developed. A dynamic model of portfolio losses over time is required since static models such as base correlation are not suitable for pricing many of these new products.

Subprime Crisis in the United States and Abroad

Persistent rumors about the quality of subprime rated portfolios in the United States have been circulating since March 2007. Rising interest rates meant that some Americans were unable to make mortgage repayments and defaulted on their loans. In mid July it was announced that two Bear Stearns asset-backed (AB) funds based on these subprime mortgages were worthless, with other funds following suit. Banks that had invested heavily in this sector were obliged to sell assets to increase their liquidity, and the contagion spread to other sectors. This is reflected in the iTraxx S3 10-year indexes over the period from April 2005 to August 2007 (Figure 12.1). Note the asymmetry of movements in credit spreads where upward movements are more abrupt than downward ones.

---

[1] A granular portfolio is a diversified portfolio where each exposure represents only a small fraction of the portfolio.

FIGURE 12.1

Evolution of the major industrial sector indexs from April 2005 (during the GM–Ford crisis) until July 2007

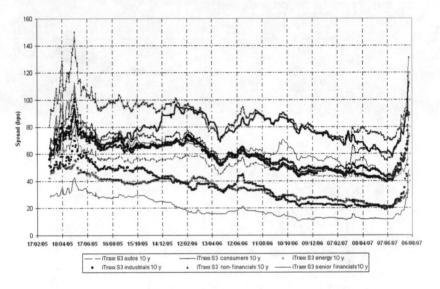

A majority of models for credit derivatives are based on the Gaussian copula and have symmetric upper and lower tails. When we compute the experimental copulas for the different sectors in the iTraxx index, asymmetric tail dependency is present. Figure 12.2 demonstrates this for the auto sector versus senior financials, for the period April 2005 to August 2007. The dots correspond to the first 100 days (i.e., the GM–Ford crisis in 2005), while the squares correspond to the 20 days up to August 6 (i.e., the subprime crisis). As upward movements in credit spreads are equivalent to drops in credit ratings, this is just the characteristic "ice-cream cone" shape of the Clayton copula turned upside down (cf Figure 12.3, left panel).

These findings regarding lower tail dependence in credit data are by no means new. Burtschell et al. (2005) carry out a comparative analysis of different models for pricing CDOs and conclude that the Clayton copula provides better results than models with symmetric tails, notably the Gaussian and Student's t. Our experimental results merely confirm that the Clayton is definitely more appropriate than the Gaussian.

The aim of this research project is to develop a new model for pricing CDO tranches based on a dynamic copula process with tail dependence.

Experimental copula for iTraxx S3 10-Year Auto versus iTraxx
S3 10-year senior financial showing the characteristic tail
dependency of credit indexes

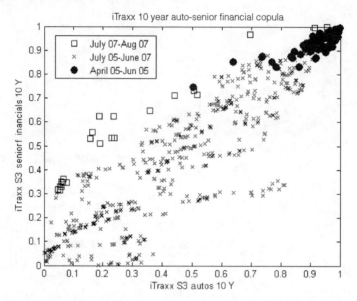

Clayton copula with parameter θ = 5 (left) and Gaussian
copula with ρ = 0.87 (right)

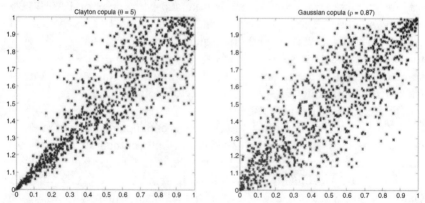

The Gaussian has symmetric tails; the clayton has lower tail dependence
(cf Figure 12.2).

The advantage of working with copulas is that it separates the question of modeling the marginal distribution of individual companies from that of modeling the correlation structure (dependence) between them. In previous work (Totouom and Armstrong, 2005; ibid., 2007a; ibid., 2007b), we presented a new approach for doing this. In this chapter we revisit this model reformulating it in terms of Levy processes, more specifically as a type of compound gamma process and then extend it to a mean-reverting gamma Ornstein–Uhlenbeck (OU) process.

   The chapter is organized as follows. In the next section we review the literature on Archimedean copulas (including the Clayton copula), highlighting the theoretical difficulties in developing multivariate copulas. We then review work on dynamic copulas, first for time series, then for continuous-time stochastic processes that include our earlier work. At the end of the section, we present an example on iTraxx to show how to calibrate the default probability using the single-name CDS data. This probability is used in both models as the threshold between default and survival for that name; hence, both models automatically reproduce the risk-neutral marginal default probabilities of each name and the cumulative default probability in a consistent fashion. The next section presents the compound gamma version of the dynamic copula model, while the following one presents the new gamma-OU process version. In the penultimate section we compare these two dynamic copula models. Proofs have been relegated to an appendix at the end of the chapter. A second appendix presents two methods for simulating gamma-OU processes. We finally conclude in the last section.

ARCHIMEDEAN COPULAS WITHIN THE CREDIT FRAMEWORK

Our overall objective is to develop a family of multivariate copula processes with different types of upper and lower tail dependence to reproduce the correlation smiles/skews observed in practice. We decide to work with Archimedean copulas because they encompass a wide range of types of tail dependence. Archimedean copulas are defined via a generator, f[2]:

---

[2] To avoid confusion, in this chapter we use φ for a Laplace transform and f for the generator of an Archimedean copula, whereas Nelsen (1994) uses φ for the generator of an Archimedean copula.

$$C(u_1, \ldots, u_n) = f^{-1}\left[f(u_1) + \cdots + f(u_n)\right] \qquad (12.1)$$

A vast literature exists on Archimedean copulas, with applications from a wide range of fields. However, when one looks more closely, a majority of studies examine only bivariate copulas and even less has been published on multivariate copulas. In the next section we explain the theoretical difficulties in extending from bivariate to trivariate and hence to multivariate copulas. Clearly, it is even more difficult to construct dynamic multivariate copula processes than static copulas. Our aim is to construct dynamic copula processes based on continuous stochastic processes.

Static Multivariate Copulas

The canonical textbook on copulas (Nelson, 1999) lists many bivariate Archimedean copulas (with one or more parameters) but since most are not strict 2-copulas no multivariate equivalent exists. The generators of strict copulas are related to specific Laplace transforms. For example, the generator for the Clayton copula corresponds to a gamma distribution with parameter $1/\theta$, and the Gumbel copula is related to an a-stable distribution. Nelsen (1999) provides several counter-examples to demonstrate how wrong "intuition" can be and how difficult it is to find multivariate copulas. The other major reference book (Joe, 1997) provides some results for the trivariate and quadrivariate cases. Furthermore, Lindskog (2000) also presents extensions and demonstrates the constraints on the parameter values in the nonexchangeable case. However, the above are all static copulas.

Dynamic Copulas Seen from a Time Series Point of View

Econometricians have developed dynamic copula models from a time series point of view. Patton (2003) develops an approach based on an ARMA-type process and applies it to foreign exchange data while Fermanian and Wegkamp (2004) extend Patton's approach. Duan (1995) and more recently Van den Goorbergh et al. (2005) use GARCH processes. A major shortcoming of these studies is their sole consideration of bivariate cases. Chen and Fan (2006) consider a class of semi-parametric copula-based multivariate dynamic models, which they apply to daily exchange rates. These models are not really suitable for pricing CDOs on large portfolios.

Berd et al. (2005) develop a more promising hybrid model in which the dynamics of the underlying latent variables are governed by a GARCH or a TARCH process. This has the advantage of producing aggregate return distributions that are asymmetric and clearly non-Gaussian. The authors use historical data on the S&P500 going back to 1962 as a proxy for market returns (pre and post 1990). While they mention using some market data (e.g., the level of hazard rates and the expected default probabilities) to calibrate parameters, they do not seem to use the available CDS data.

Dynamic Copula Processes

A handful of studies have tackled the question in continuous time. The earliest paper on copula processes seems to be produced by Darsow et al. (1992) who study Archimedean copulas and Markov processes from a theoretical point of view. Several authors have modelled credit risk dynamics using default intensities rather than default times. Rogge and Schonbucher (2003) develop a method for modeling dynamic portfolio credit risk based on Archimedean copulas. They provide some very useful results that link Archimedean copulas with Laplace transforms, and also a quick and efficient method for simulating realisations, not mentioned by Nelsen (1999). Following Madan's work on stock prices (Madan and Seneta, 1990; Madan and Milne, 1991) and that of Cariboni and Schoutens (2006) on the value of the firm, Joshi and Stacey (2005) used a gamma process when modeling default intensities and pricing CDOs and found that a double gamma process is required to match the base correlations observed in the market correctly. One disadvantage of working with intensities is that it requires calibrating the default functions for each of the names.

Anterior Work by Totouom and Armstrong (2005; 2007)

We use information from (Rogge and Schonbucher, 2003) as the starting point for our models. Let Y be a positive random variable whose Laplace transform is $\varphi(s)$ and let U_i be N uniform random variables on [0, 1] that are mutually independent and also independent of Y. Then the N random variables V_i, defined as

$$V_i = \varphi\left(\frac{-Ln(U_i)}{Y}\right) \qquad for\ i = 1, \ldots, N \qquad (12.2)$$

are uniform on [0, 1], and their cumulative distribution function is given

$$\text{Prob}\left(V_1 \le v_1, \ldots, V_N \le v_N\right) = \varphi\left(\sum_{i=1}^{N} \varphi^{-1}(v_i)\right) \qquad (12.3)$$

Consequently their multivariate copula is the Archimedean copula having φ^{-1} as its generator.

The extension from the static case to dynamic processes is straightforward. Let $Y(t)$ be a stochastic process that takes positive values. It represents the state of the economy. Let $\varphi_t(s)$ be its Laplace transform. Note that as $Y(t)$ need not be stationary, its distribution (and hence φ) depends on t. Let $U_i(t)$ be n mutually independent stochastic processes taking values that are uniform on [0,1]. As before, these must also be independent of $Y(t)$. The procedure for simulating the dynamic copula process $V_i(t)$ is simple. Simulate the processes $Y(t)$ and the $U_i(t)$. The copula process $V_i(t)$ is given by

$$V_i(t) = \varphi_t\left(\frac{-Ln\left(U_i(t)\right)}{Y(t)}\right) \text{ where } Y(t) > 0. \qquad (12.4)$$

At any given time t, the multivariate structure between $V_i(t)$ and $V_j(t)$ (for $I \ne j$) is just the Archimedean copula having φ_{t-1} as its generator. Similarly, a single name in a forward starting CDO will default during a time period $[t_{i-1}, t_j]$ if and only if

$$V_{t_{i-1}, t_i} = \varphi_{t_{i-1}, t_i}\left(-\frac{Ln\left(U_{t_i}\right)}{Y\left(t_i\right) - Y\left(t_{i-1}\right)}\right) \qquad (12.5)$$

Having simulated the value of the appropriate V, we determine whether that name has defaulted in that simulation by comparing its value to a threshold value determined for each name from the CDS spreads. The next section illustrates how to compute the threshold for the forward default probability but it is the same for standard default probabilities.

Example: how to calibrate the model to single name CDS data

Equation [5] gives the condition for a single name to default during the time period $[t_{i-1}, t_j]$. V_{t_{i-1}, t_j} is a latent variable; it cannot be observed directly. Let us assume, that the survival default probability of the company is given by:

$$S(t) = \exp\left(-\int_0^t \lambda(u)\, du\right) \qquad (12.6)$$

The forward default probability between during the time period $[t_{i-1}, t_i]$ is given by:

$$\mathrm{FwdDP}\left(t_{i-1},\ t_i\right) = 1 - \exp\left(-\int_{t_{i-1}}^{t_i} \lambda(u)\, du\right) \qquad (12.7)$$

The default event of a company is then defined by: $V_{t_{i-1}, t_i} <$ FwdDP (t_{i-1}, t_i), that is, if

$$\varphi_{t_{i-1}, t_i}\left(-\frac{\mathrm{Ln}\left(U_{t_i}\right)}{Y\left(t_i\right) - Y\left(t_{i-1}\right)}\right) < 1 - \exp\left(-\int_{t_{i-1}}^{t_i} \lambda(u)\, du\right) \qquad (12.8)$$

Our model is automatically calibrated to the forward default probability and hence to the cumulative probability. This is a desirable feature since the CDS spread or the forward CDS spread (which give the implied term structure) can have a wide range of shapes.

To illustrate the procedure we have taken the historical term structure of the probability of default for names in Moody's Baa2 ratings class because this is the average rating of CDO portfolios traded in the market. Any other class could have been used. Figure 12.4(a) compares the forward default probability produced by the forward dynamic copula (green: o) and the one extracted from idealized default probability term structure provided by Moody's for a Baa2 rating based on historical data (blue: +). Ten thousand MC simulations were used to compute the model. We can observe that with this many simulations convergence is present. Figure 12.4(b) compares the cumulative default probability produced by the forward dynamic copula (green: o) and the one extracted from idealized default probability term structure is provided by Moody's for a Baa2 rating based on historical data (blue: +).

(a) The forward default probability FwdPD $(t, t + 1\text{yr}) =$ $t - S(t + 1)/S(t)$; (b) the cumulative default probability of a Baa2 rating with dynamic copula (10,000 simulations)

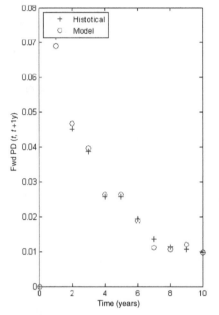

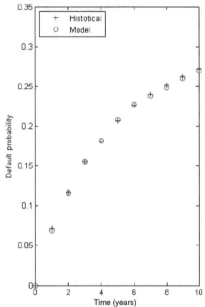

The forward default probability (circle) produced by the forward dynamic copula and the one extract from idealized default probability term structure provided by Moody's for a Baa2 rating based on historical data (cross)

The cumulative dafault probability (circle) produced by the forward dynamic copula and the one extract from idealized default probability term structure (cross)

DYNAMIC COPULAS FROM A LEVY PROCESS PERSPECTIVE

Definition of a Rescaled Compound Gamma Process

Let $X(t)$ be a stochastic process with independent increments having a gamma distribution whose first parameter takes a value equal to the corresponding increment of the gamma, $\alpha(t)$:

$$X(t+\delta t)-X(t)=\Gamma\big(\delta\alpha(t),1\big) \tag{12.9}$$

This is a type of compound gamma process. At time t, conditional on the realization of the gamma process, $X(t)$ has a gamma distribution $\Gamma(\alpha(t), 1)$. Figure 12.5 shows a typical realization of $\alpha(t)$ in red, together with two realizations of $X(t)$ based on this whereby its mean and variance are $a_1 a_2\, t$ and $a_1\, a_2\, t\,(1+a_2)$. In Appendix 1, we show that $X(t)$ is a Levy process. A rescaled compound gamma process, $Y(t)$, is obtained by dividing $X(t)$, by a positive deterministic function, $\beta(t)$, for $t>0$. The obvious candidates are $\beta(t)=1/t$ and $\beta(t)=\exp(-t)$ for the spot copula and $\beta(t)=$ constant for the forward-starting copula. Consequently

$$Y(t+\delta t)-Y(t)=\beta\left(t+\frac{\delta t}{2}\right)\delta X_t \tag{12.10}$$

$$Y(0)=0$$

F I G U R E   12.5

Simulation of a gamma process together with two realizations of the standard compound gamma process constructed using this realization of $\alpha(t)$

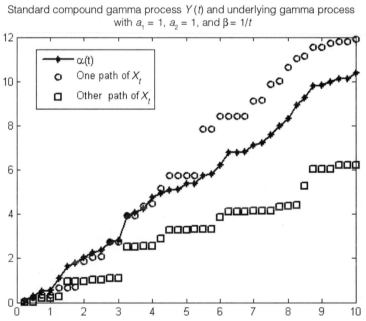

Standard compound gamma process $Y(t)$ and underlying gamma process with $a_1 = 1$, $a_2 = 1$, and $\beta = 1/t$

Because of the scaling property of the gamma process, $Y(t)$ has the following distribution

$$Y(t_n) = \sum_{i=1}^{n} \beta\left(t - \frac{\delta t_i}{2}\right) \times \Gamma\left(\alpha(\delta t_i), 1\right) \tag{12.11}$$

In continuous time, the process $Y(t)$ can be written as the integral of an increment of a Levy process: the compound gamma $X(t)$ times the continuous function $\alpha(t)$.

Moments of the Process $Y(t)$

As the increments are independent, the first two moments of $Y(t)$ are just

$$E\left(Y(t_n)\right) = a_1 \, a_2 \sum_{i=1}^{n} \beta\left(\frac{t_i + t_{i-1}}{2}\right) \delta t_i \tag{12.12}$$

$$\operatorname{Var}\left[Y(t_n)\right] = a_1 a_2 \left(1 + a_2\right) \sum_{i=1}^{n} \beta\left(\frac{t_i + t_{i-1}}{2}\right)^2 \delta t_i \tag{12.13}$$

Laplace Transform

The Laplace transform $\varphi(s)$, of $Y(t_n)$:

$$\varphi(s) = \prod_{i=1}^{n}\left[1 + a_2 \mathrm{Ln}\left(1 + s\beta\left(\frac{t_i + t_{i-1}}{2}\right)\right)\right]^{-a_1 \delta t_i} \tag{12.14}$$

is used in the construction and simulation of the $V_i(t)$. It is also important because it guarantees that the resulting copula is "strict" (see Nelsen, 1997) and hence the construction gives rise to a valid multivariate Archimedean copula. Furthermore, its continuous time limit will be used in the next section. Based on classical results on Riemann integral theory, the Riemann sums above converge to the integral below.

$$\lim_{\max\{\delta t_i\} \to 0^+} \varphi(s) = \exp\left(\exp\left(-\int_0^{t_n} a_1 Ln\left(1 + Ln\left(1 + s\beta(u)\right)a_2\right) du\right)\right) \tag{12.15}$$

Its moments can be obtained by differentiating and setting $s = 0$

$$\text{Mean} = a_1 a_2 \int_0^{t_n} \beta(u)\, du \qquad \text{Var} = a_1 a_2 \left(1 + a_2\right) \int_0^{t_n} \beta(u)^2\, du \qquad (12.16)$$

Default Only Occurs at Discrete Payment Dates

Although default events can occur at any time in practice, the legal contracts defining CDOs specify a finite set of n payment dates at which
default may occur. Consequently, the default time is the smallest time at
which the value of V_{t_{i-1}, t_i} falls below the threshold for that time interval:

$$\tau(t_n) = \inf \left\{ t_i < 0,\ i \leq n \quad \varphi_{t_{i-1}, t_i} \left(-\frac{\text{Ln}(U_{t_i})}{Y(t_i) - Y(t_{i-1})} \right) \right. $$
$$\left. < 1 - \exp\left(-\int_{t_{i-1}}^{t_i} \lambda(u)\, du \right) \right\}$$

$$(12.17)$$

In Appendix 1, we prove that $prob\ (\tau(t_n) = +\infty) = 0$.

Asymptotic Spot Loss Distribution with Bullet Exposure

Assume that the credit portfolio consists of N underlying credits whose
notionals are $P_i = P/N$, with fixed recovery rates are $R_i = R, (i = 1, \ldots, N)$.
The aggregate loss from today to time t is a fixed sum of random variables:

$$\text{Loss}_N(t) = \sum_{i=1}^{N} (1 - R_i) P_i\, 1_{(\tau_i \prec t)} = \frac{(1 - R)P}{N} \sum_{i=1}^{N} 1_{(\tau_i \prec t)} \qquad (12.18)$$

where $1_{\{\tau \prec t\}}$ is the indicator function for the default of the ith name. Its
Laplace transform is

$$E\left(\exp\left(-s\, \text{Loss}_N(t)\right) \right) = E\left(\prod_{i=1}^{N} \left(\left(1 - 1_{\{\tau_i \prec t\}}\right) + 1_{\{\tau_i \prec t\}} \eta^{1/N} \right) \right)$$

$$= E\left(\left[\left(1 - \eta^{1/N}\right) \exp\left(-Y_t \varphi_t^{-1} \left(\text{PD}(t)\right)\right) + 1 \right]^N \right)$$

$$(12.19)$$

where $\eta = \exp(-sN(1 - R)) > 0$. Since

$$\lim_{N \to +\infty} \left\{ N \left(\eta^{\frac{1}{N}} - 1 \right) \right\} = \left. \frac{\partial \eta^x}{\partial x} \right|_{x=0} = \mathrm{Ln}(\eta) = -sN(1-R) \quad (12.20)$$

$$\mathrm{Loss}_N(t)_{N \to +\infty} \approx P(1-R)\exp\left(-Y_t \varphi_t^{-1}(\mathrm{PD}(t))\right)$$

Asymptotic Forward Loss Distribution

We compute the aggregate loss from t to time T, assuming no default prior to time t. If k defaults had occurred in the portfolio, the analysis below would still hold, we need only replace N by $(N - k)$. The individual notional is independent of the number, k, of prior defaults. For simplicity, we only consider the case where we have zero defaults prior to time t. The Laplace transform of the forward loss distribution is

$$E\left(\exp\left(-s\,\mathrm{Loss}_N(t,T)\right)\right) = E\left(\left\{\left[1 - \exp\left(-(Y_T - Y_t)\varphi_{t,T}^{-1}(\mathrm{FwdPD}(t,T))\right)\right]\right.\right.$$
$$\left.\left. + \eta^{1/N}\exp\left(-(Y_T - Y_t)\varphi_{t,T}^{-1}(\mathrm{FwdPD}(t,T))\right)\right\}^N\right)$$

where

$$\mathrm{FwdPD}(t,T) = \frac{\mathrm{PD}(T) - \mathrm{PD}(t)}{1 - \mathrm{PD}(t)}$$

Hence,

$$E\left(\exp\left(-s\,\mathrm{Loss}_N(t,T)\right)\right) = E\left(\left[\left(1 - \eta^{1/N}\right)\exp\left(-(Y_T - Y_t)\varphi_{t,T}^{-1}(\mathrm{FwdPD}(t,T))\right) + 1\right]^N\right)$$

So its limit as N tends to infinity is

$$\mathrm{Loss}_N(t,T)_{N \to +\infty} \approx \mathbf{P}(1-\mathbf{R})\exp\left(-(Y_T - Y_t)\boldsymbol{\varphi}_{t,T}^{-1}(\mathrm{FwdPD}(t,T))\right) \quad (12.21)$$

The generator function of the forward copula $\varphi_{t-\delta t,\, t}\,(s)$ is the Laplace transform of the probability distribution of the forward compound gamma process $(Y_t - Y_{t-\delta t})$ with the filtration $F_{t-\delta t}$. The equation for the forward loss is quite similar to that for the spot loss. The difference is that the total notional of the portfolio from which it should be deducted, decreases whenever there is a loss.

DYNAMIC COPULAS BASED ON GAMMA-OU PROCESS

In this section we construct another building block for dynamic copulas but based on a gamma-OU process. This process is chosen (1) because a closed-form solution is known for its Laplace transform and (2) because it is a positive process and has been used for modeling stochastic spreads and interest rates. For example, Barndorff-Nielsen and Shephard (2001) applied it when modeling the stock market. In that case the volatility was modeled by an OU process driven by a subordinator. More recently this process was studied by Schoutens et al. (2003). Their results are impressive in terms of capturing the dynamics of the volatility of the stock prices. This has also been known to geostatisticians working in the earth sciences for many years. According to Chilès and Delfiner (1999, p.489), Matheron (1969) called this an *Ambartzumian* process after the Soviet mathematician of the same name.

Definition of Gamma-OU Process

We use the classical and tractable form of the gamma-OU process where the marginal distribution of the volatility is a gamma. Volatility can only jump upwards and subsequently decays exponentially. A co-movement effect between up jumps in volatility and (down) jumps in the stock price is also incorporated to make the price of the asset jump downwards when the volatility jumps upward. In the absence of a jump, the asset price process moves continuously, and the volatility decays also continuously. Other choices for OU processes can be made (e.g., the inverse Gaussian OU process, which is also tractable).

In Barndorff-Nielsen and Shephard (2001) the squared volatility follows a stochastic differential equation (SDE) of the form:

$$d\sigma^2(t) = -\lambda\sigma^2(t)\, dt + dz(\lambda t) \qquad (12.22)$$

where $\lambda \succ 0$ and $z = \{z_t, t \geq 0\}$ is a subordinator.

The risk-neutral dynamics of the log-price $Z_t = \mathrm{Ln}(S_t)$ are given by

$$dZ_t = \left[r - q - \lambda(\rho) - \frac{\sigma^2(t)}{2} \right] dt + \sigma(t)\, dW_t + \rho\, dz(\lambda t) \quad (12.23)$$

where $Z_0 = \mathrm{Ln}(S_0)$, $W = \{W_t, t \geq 0\}$ is a Brownian motion and is independent of the subordinator process $z = \{z_t, t \geq 0\}$. The parameter ρ controls the correlation between the volatility and the stock price dynamics.

In our case, the factor $Y(t)$ will be a gamma OU process; that is,

$$dX(t) = -\lambda X(t)\, dt + dz(\lambda t) \quad (12.24)$$

with $\lim_{t \to +\infty} Y(t) \equiv \Gamma(a_1, a_2)$, where $x \geq 0$.

$$f_{X(t), t \to +\infty}(x) = \frac{(a_1)^{a_2}}{\Gamma(a_2)} x^{a_2 - 1} \exp(-a_1 x) \quad (12.25)$$

This means that the Levy measure has zero drift and has the density

$$v^X(x) = \frac{a_2}{x} \exp(-a_1 x) \quad (12.26)$$

We can deduce that the Levy density of the Levy process $Z(t)$ has zero drift; its density is

$$v(x) = a_2 \exp(-a_1 x). \quad (12.27)$$

This Levy process is a compound Poisson subordinator with exponential jump size. Next we will analyze the integrated process

$$Y(t) = \int_0^t X(s)\, ds. \quad (12.28)$$

Based on the properties of non-Gaussian OU processes, we have the following:

$$Y(t) \equiv \int_0^t X(s)\,ds = \frac{y_0}{\lambda}\left(1 - \exp(-\lambda t)\right)$$

$$+ \frac{1}{\lambda}\int_0^t \left[1 - \exp(-\lambda(t-s))\right]dz(s) \tag{12.29}$$

$$Y(t) \equiv \int_0^t X(s)\,ds = \frac{1}{\lambda}\left[z(\lambda t) - X(t) + X(0)\right] \tag{12.30}$$

Laplace Transform of the Integrated Process

Cont and Tankov (2004) gave an explicit formula for the Laplace transform of a positive OU process, but we derive a different formulation here.

$$E\left[\exp(-uY(t))\right]$$

$$= \exp\left(-\frac{ux_0}{\lambda}\left[1 - \exp(-\lambda t)\right]\right.$$

$$\left. + \int_0^t l\left(\frac{u}{\lambda}\left[1 - \exp(-\lambda(t-s))\right]\right)ds\right) \tag{12.31}$$

where $l(u) = E\left(\exp(-uz(1))\right) = \dfrac{\lambda a_2 u}{(a_1 + u)}$

$$E\left(\exp(-uY(t))\right) = \exp\left(-\frac{ux_0}{\lambda}\left[1 - \exp(-\lambda t)\right]\right.$$

$$\left. -\frac{u\lambda a_2 t}{\lambda a_1 + u} + \frac{u\lambda a_2}{\lambda a_1 + u}\mathrm{Ln}\left(1 + \frac{u}{\lambda a_1}\left[1 - \exp(-\lambda t)\right]\right)\right)$$

The Laplace transform of the joint distribution is

$$
\begin{aligned}
E\Big(\exp\big(-uY(t)-vz(t)\big)\Big) \\
= \exp\bigg(-\frac{ux_0}{\lambda}\big[1-\exp(-\lambda t)\big] \\
+ \int_0^t l\Big(v+\frac{u}{\lambda}\big[1-\exp(-\lambda(t-s))\big]\Big)ds\bigg)
\end{aligned}
\tag{12.32}
$$

Simulating the Mean Reverting Gamma-OU Process

A mean reverting gamma-OU process can be seen as a classical mean reverting process where the stochastic part is driven by a compound Poisson process. The number of jumps is a Poisson counting process during the time interval, and their size follows an exponential distribution.

Two methods for simulating this process are provided in Appendix 2, and we adopt the first one. The background Levy process (BGLP) is as follows:

$$
BGLP_{t_n} = BGLP_{t_{n-1}} + \sum_{k=N_{t_{n-1}}+1}^{N_{t_n}} x_k \exp\big(-\lambda \delta t\, \tilde{u}_k\big)
\tag{12.33}
$$

Figure 12.6 shows the BGLP that is a compound Poisson process with an exponentially distributed jump size (above) with the corresponding gamma-OU process (below). The bottom panel of Figure 12.6 is stationary and a mean reverting distribution.

Building Blocks Based on Integrated Gamma-OU Process for Spot Copula

$$
\begin{aligned}
\varphi_t(s) = \exp\bigg(-\frac{sx_0}{\lambda}\big[1-\exp(-\lambda t)\big] - \frac{s\lambda a_2 t}{\lambda a_1 + s} + \frac{s\lambda a_2}{\lambda a_1 + s} \\
\mathrm{Ln}\Big(1+\frac{s}{\lambda a_1}\big[1-\exp(-\lambda t)\big]\Big)\bigg)
\end{aligned}
\tag{12.34}
$$

Background Levy process (above) and the mean reverting gamma OU process (below)

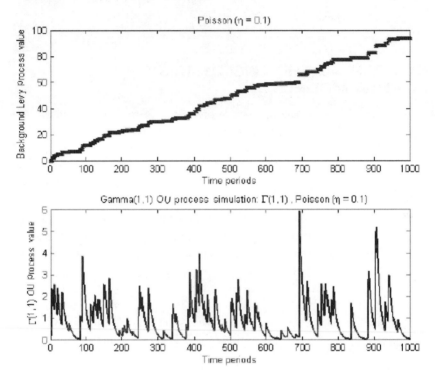

As usual, the marginal spot copula variable is given by

$$V_t = \varphi_t \left(-\frac{\mathrm{Ln}(U_t)}{Y(t)} \right) \qquad (12.35)$$

For the *forward dynamic copula*

$$
\begin{aligned}
\varphi_{t_0,t}(s) = \ & \exp\left(-\frac{sx_{t_0}}{\lambda}\left[1-\exp\left(-\lambda \times (t-t_0)\right)\right] - \frac{s\lambda a_2 (t-t_0)}{\lambda a_1 + s} \right) \\
& \times \exp\left(\frac{s\lambda a_2}{\lambda a_1 + s} \mathrm{Ln}\left(1 + \frac{s}{\lambda a_1}\left[1-\exp\left(-\lambda \times (t-t_0)\right)\right] \right) \right)
\end{aligned}
\qquad (12.36)
$$

Its copula variable is given by

$$V_{t_0, t} = \varphi_{t_0, t}\left(-\frac{\text{Ln}(U_t)}{Y(t) - Y(t_0)}\right) \qquad (12.37)$$

COMPARING THE TWO DYNAMIC COPULA MODELS

Two new models for dynamic copula processes were presented in the previous sections. In both cases the default probability for each name in the CDO is fitted by using the spread for the corresponding single-name CDS. Secondly, both processes use the gamma distribution to generate a copula with lower tail dependence (the classic ice-cream cone shape). Therefore, it would be difficult to distinguish between them using these two criteria, and readers will be wondering how to choose the appropriate one in practical cases. The key difference is in the symmetry/asymmetry of upward and downward movements. To illustrate this, Figures 12.7 and 12.8 present realizations of both processes: the compound gamma process and then the mean reverting gamma-OU process.

Note the asymmetry between sharp upswings and the exponential decline in the mean reverting OU process (Figure 12.8) compared to the symmetry in Figure 12.7. Figure 12.9 shows a realization with a shorter mean reversion time than Figure 12.6, but the asymmetry is maintained.

Looking back at the empirical copula for auto versus senior financial in iTraxx (Figure 12.2), we note the rapid rise as the subprime crisis (red points) started in 2007 compared to the slow decline as the GM–Ford crisis in 2005 wound down. This suggests that the second model may be more appropriate in this case. Clearly, further work would be required to prove this hypothesis.

CONCLUSION

Over the past 10 years the credit derivatives industry has evolved rapidly. The market-led development of many new products implies that new models have had to be created to price credit derivatives. The latest generation of derivatives such as forward-starting CDOs, options on CDOs, long and/or short CDO portfolios, and leveraged super-senior tranches

Simulation of a compound gamma process

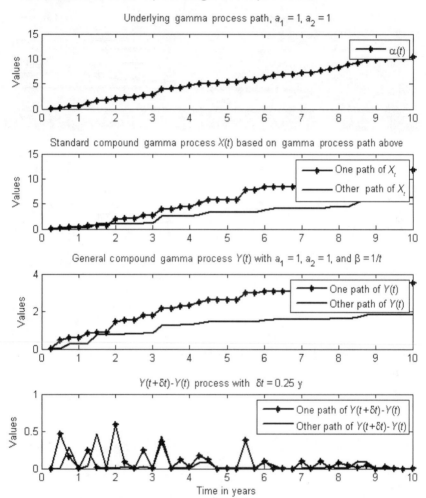

require a dynamic model of portfolio losses over time in order to price them successfully. The increased liquidity of the main CDS means that the default characteristics of single names can be extracted directly from them rather than having to be priced. Hence, the current challenge is to correctly price the correlation skew ("smile").

One possibility would be to use classical stochastic processes based on the Gaussian copula or Student's t. However, tests such as those by

F I G U R E   12.8

Mean reverting gamma OU process (mean reversion two years)

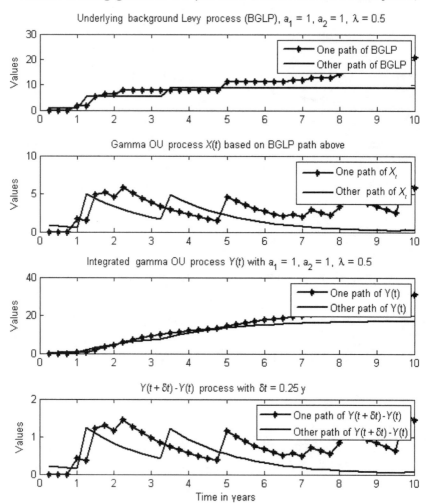

Burtschell et al. (2005) show that the Clayton copula, which has lower tail dependence, is better at pricing CDO tranches than those with symmetric tails, such as the Gaussian copula. We therefore decided to develop a dynamic copula model with lower tail dependence. The first difficulty we encountered was that while papers on bivariate copulas with tail dependence abound, very few of these models can be extended to multivariate

F I G U R E   12.9

Mean reverting gamma OU process (mean reversion
six months)

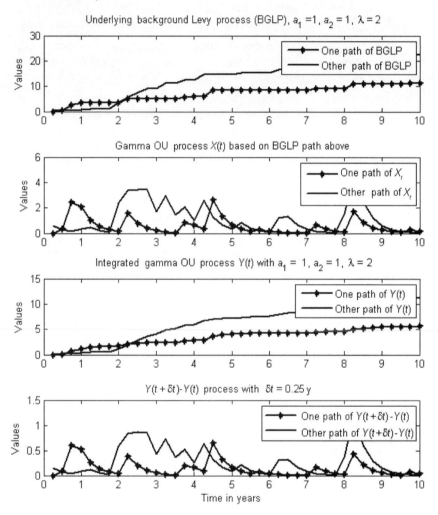

copulas. Archimedean copulas are certainly the most promising candidates, but these remain static models. Pricing forward-starting credit
derivatives calls for a dynamic approach. In Totouom and Armstrong
(2005; 2007) we proposed a dynamic copula process with low tail dependence similar to the Clayton copula.

This chapter was written in August 2007 when the subprime crisis was intense, giving us a unique opportunity to study the effect of a credit crisis on the shape of the experimental copulas. Using iTraxx spreads from April 2005 (the GM–Ford crisis) to July 2007, we show that the experimental copulas for different series exhibit the classic ice-cream cone shape of the Clayton copula but inverted. This is because upward movements in credit spreads are equivalent to downward movements in ratings. These findings confirm that it is vital to model the tail dependence.

Second, with hindsight we revisited our earlier model for pricing CDO tranches, but this time from a Levy process point of view. Seen from this angle, we develop a new gamma-OU process, which is of course mean reverting. Both dynamic copula models are calibrated to the single-name CDS; so they automatically reproduce the risk-neutral marginal default probabilities of each name and the cumulative default probability in a consistent way, which is demonstrated for an example on iTraxx.

In the last section we compared the two models. Both reproduce the single-name characteristics of the names in the CDO, and both copulas are lower tail dependent. What distinguishes between them? In fact, one key difference is that the mean reverting OU process is asymmetric. Upswings are much more abrupt than downward changes, which are a slow exponential decline. By looking back at the experimental copula for auto versus senior financials in the iTraxx S3, we postulate that the mean reverting OU process is more appropriate, but additional work is required to test this idea.

APPENDIX 1

Proposition 12.1: *If X(t) is a standard compound gamma process, then it is a Levy process.*

Proof: Following the line of reasoning in (Cont and Tankov, 2004), we prove that the standard compound process is a Levy process. The first two properties are obvious from the definition given earlier. By construction the process $(X_t)_{t \geq 0}$ is defined on (Ω, F, P):

$$\delta X_t \equiv X_{t+\delta t} - X_t = \Gamma\left(\delta\alpha(t), 1\right) \tag{12.38}$$

Since $\alpha(t)$ is a gamma process with independent increments, for $i \neq j$ the increments $\alpha(t_i) - \alpha(t_{i-1})$ and $\alpha(t_j) - \alpha(t_{j-1})$ are independent and so are $(X_{t_i} - X_{t_{i-1}})$ and $X_{t_j} - X_{t_{j-1}}$.

We show that the increments are stationary. The increment $X_{t+h} - X_t$ has the gamma distribution $\Gamma(\alpha(t+h) - \alpha(t), 1)$, while the corresponding increment of the α process has the following gamma distribution:

$$\alpha(t+h) - \alpha(t) \equiv \Gamma(a_1 h, a_2) \tag{12.39a}$$

Consequently the increments have a compound gamma distribution:

$$X_{t+h} - X_t \equiv \Gamma(\Gamma(a_1 h, a_2), 1) \tag{12.39b}$$

whose parameters depend on the time difference h but not on t itself. So the stationary increment $X_{t+h} - X_t$ does not depend on t.

Stochastic Continuity

In order to prove that $\forall\, \varepsilon > 0, \lim_{h \to 0} P\left(|X_{t+h} - X_t| \geq \varepsilon\right) = 0,$ we compute the Laplace transform of $|X_{t+h} - X_t| = X_{t+h} - X_t$:

$$E\left(\exp\left(-s|X_{t+h} - X_t|\right)\right) = E\left(\exp\left(-s\left(X_{t+h} - X_t\right)\right)\right)$$

$$= E\left[\exp\left(-s\Gamma\left(\Gamma(a_1 h, a_2), 1\right)\right)\right] \quad a_1 \geq 0, a_2 \geq 0$$

$$= E_{\Gamma(a_1 h, a_2)}\left(\exp\left(-s\left(\Gamma\left(\Gamma(u, 1), 1\right)\right)\right) \middle/ \Gamma(a_1 h, a_2) = u\right)$$

$$= \exp\left(-a_1 h\, \mathrm{Ln}\left(1 + \mathrm{Ln}(1+s)a_2\right)\right)$$

$\forall s \geq 0, \forall h > 0,$

$$\lim_{h \to 0}\left\{E\left(\exp\left(-s|X_{t+h} - X_t|\right)\right)\right\} = \lim_{h \to 0}$$

$$\left\{\exp\left(-a_1 h\, \mathrm{Ln}\left(1 + \mathrm{Ln}(1+s)a_2\right)\right)\right\} = 1$$

Therefore

$$\forall \varepsilon > 0, \lim_{h \to 0} P\left(|X_{t+h} - X_t| \geq \varepsilon\right) = 0 \tag{12.40}$$

Lemma 12.2: $\Pr\{\tau(t_n) = +\infty\} = 0$.

Proof: Since $V_{t_{i-1,si}}$ is a uniform variable on $[0, 1]$ at any given time, we only need to show that in at least one interval $[t_{i-1}, t_i]$, the probability of default is different from zero. $t_n < +\infty$, and hence,

$$\forall i \in \{1, ..., n\}, 0 < 1 - \exp\left(-\int_{t_{i-1}}^{t_i} \lambda(u)\, du\right) < 1.$$

Let k_q be the maximum of the forward default probabilities on the intervals $[t_{i-1}, t_i]$:

$$k_q = \max_{i \in \{1,...,n\}}\left\{1 - \exp\left(-\int_{t_{i-1}}^{t_i} \lambda(u)\, du\right)\right\}$$

$$= 1 - \exp\left(-\int_{t_{q-1}}^{t_q} \lambda(u)\, du\right) \Rightarrow 0 \prec k_q \prec 1 \tag{12.41}$$

Since $V_{t_{i-1,}}i$ is a uniform on $[0, 1]$,

$$\tau(t_n) = +\infty \; \forall i \in \{1, ..., n\},$$

$$\text{prob}\left(\varphi_{t_{i-1,}\, t_i}\left(-\frac{\text{Ln}(U_{t_i})}{Y(t_i) - Y(t_{i-1})}\right) < 1 - \exp\left(-\int_{t_{i-1}}^{t_i} \lambda(u)\, du\right)\right) = 0$$

but

$$\text{prob}V_{t_{q-1,}\, t_q} = \varphi_{t_{q-1,}\, tq}\left(-\frac{\text{Ln}(U_{t_q})}{\left(Y(t_q) - Y(t_{q-1})\right)}\right) \prec 1 - \exp\left(-\int_{t_{q-1}}^{t_q} \lambda(u)\, du\right)$$

$$= 1 - \exp\left(-\int_{t_{q-1}}^{t_q} \lambda(u)\, du\right) \neq 0 \tag{12.42}$$

Hence, prob $\{\tau(t_n) = +\infty\} = 0$.

APPENDIX 2: SIMULATING THE GAMMA-OU PROCESS

The gamma-OU process is as follows:

$$dY(t) = -\lambda Y(t)\,dt + dz(\lambda t) \tag{12.43}$$

with $\lim\limits_{x \to +\infty} Y(t) \equiv \Gamma(a_1, a_2)$. The integrated process is given by the following formula:

$$
\begin{aligned}
\tilde{Y}(t) \equiv \int_0^t Y(s)\,ds &= \frac{y_0}{\lambda}\big[1 - \exp(-\lambda t)\big] \\
&+ \frac{1}{\lambda}\int_0^t \big[1 - \exp(-\lambda(t-s))\big]\,dz(s)
\end{aligned}
\tag{12.44}
$$

Method 12.1

To simulate the gamma-OU process in discrete time $t_n = n\,\delta t, n = 1, 2, 3, \ldots,$ we first simulate a Poisson process $N = \{N_t, t \geq 0\}$ with intensity parameter λa_1 at the same time points. Then, with the convention that an empty sum equals zero,

$$
\begin{aligned}
y_{t_n} &= (1 - \lambda \delta t)y_{t_{n-1}} + \sum_{k=N_{t_{n-1}}+1}^{N_{t_n}} x_k \exp(-\lambda \times \delta t \times \tilde{u}_k) \\
&\underset{t_n \to +\infty}{\mathrm{Lim}}\{y_{t_n}\} = \Gamma(a_1, a_2)
\end{aligned}
\tag{12.45}
$$

$$u_k, \tilde{u}_k \ uniform\ [0,1] \qquad x_k = -\frac{Ln(u_k)}{a_2}, \qquad N(t)\ \ Poisson\ \ \lambda a_1 t$$

Method 12.2

Based on the result below, we will simulate the integrated gamma-OU process

$$\exp(-\lambda t)\int_0^t \exp(\lambda s)\,d\alpha(\lambda s) = \frac{1}{a_2}\exp(-\lambda t)\sum_{i=1}^{N(1)} Ln\left(\frac{1}{c_i}\right)\exp(\lambda t r_i) \tag{12.46}$$

With marginal distribution $\Gamma(a_1, a_2)$, r_i *uniform* $[0, 1]$, $N(t)$ *Poisson* $\lambda a_1 t$, $c_i, c_i \prec c_{i_{+1}} \leq 1$ *are arrvial times of the Poisson process:*

$$\tilde{Y}(t) \equiv \frac{y_0}{\lambda}\left[1 - \exp(-\lambda t)\right] + \frac{1}{a_2}\frac{1}{\lambda}\sum_{i=1}^{N(1)} Ln\left(\frac{1}{c_i}\right)\exp\left(\lambda t(1 - r_i)\right) \qquad (12.47)$$

The BGLP is given by the following formula:

$$\text{BGLP}_{t_n} = \text{BGLP}_{t_{n-1}} + \frac{1}{a_2}\frac{1}{\lambda}\sum_{i=1}^{N(1)} Ln\left(\frac{1}{c_i}\right)\exp\left(\lambda t(1 - r_i)\right) \qquad (12.48)$$

REFERENCES

Barndorff-Nielsen, O.E. and Shephard, N. (2001) Non-Gaussian Ornstein: Uhlenbeck-Based Models and Some of Their Uses in Financial Economics. *Journal of the Royal Statistical Society*, Series B 63, 167–241.

Berd, A., Engle, R., and Voronov, A. (2005) The Underlying Dynamics of Credit Correlations. Working paper, Stern School of Business, New York.

Burtschell, X., Gregory, J., and Laurent, J.P (2005) A Comparative Analysis of CDO Pricing Models. Working paper, ISFA Actuarial School, University of Lyon and BNP Paribas, Paris.

Cariboni, J. .and Schoutens, W. (2006) Jumps in Intensity Models. Working paper, Catholic University of Louvain, Belgium.

Carr, P., Geman, H., Madan, D.H., and Yor, M. (2001) Stochastic Volatility for Levy Processes. Prepublications du Laboratoire de Probabilités et Modèles Aléatoires 645, Universités de Paris (6 & Paris 7), Paris.

Chen, X. and Fan, Y. (2006) Estimation and Model Selection of Semi-parametric Copula-Based Multivariate Dynamic Models under Copula Misspecification, *Journal of Econometrics*, 135(1–2): 125–154.

Chilès, J.P and Delfiner, P. (1999) *Geostatistics: Modeling Spatial Uncertainty.* Hoboken, NJ: John Wiley & Sons.

Cont, R. and Tankov, P. (2004) Financial Modelling with Jump Processes. London: Chapman & Hall/CRC.

Darsow W.F., Nguyen, B., and Olsen, E.T. (1992) Copulas and Markov Processes. *Illinois Journal of Mathematics,* 36(4): 600–642.

Duan, J.-C. (1995) The GARCH Option Pricing Model. *Mathematical Finance,* 5(1):13–32

Fermanian, J-D, and Wegkamp, M. (2004). Time Dependent Copulas. Working paper, available at www.crest.fr/pageperso/fermanian/cond_copula10.pdf.

Joe, H. (1997) Multivariate Models and Dependence Concepts. *Monographs on Statistics and Applied Probability*, Vol. 37, London: Chapman & Hall.

Joshi, M. and Stacey, A. (2005) Intensity Gamma: A New Approach to Pricing Portfolio Credit Derivatives. Working paper, University of Melbourne, Melbourne, Australia.

Lindskog, F. (2000) Modeling Dependence with Copulas and Applications to Risk Management. Masters Thesis, ETH Zurich, Switzerland.

Matheron, G. (1969) Les Processus d'Ambarzoumian et leur Application en Géologie. Technical Report N-131, Centre de Géostatistique, Fontainebleau, France.

McGinty, L., Bernstein, E., Ahulwalia, R., and Watts, M. (2004) Introducing Base Correlation Credit Derivatives Strategy, J.P. Morgan, New York.

Nelsen, R.B. (1999) *Introduction to Copulas.* New York: Springer.

Patton, A.J. (2003) Modeling Asymmetric Exchange Rate Dependence. Discussion paper 01–09, University of California, San Diego, CA.

Rogge, E. and Schonbucher, P. (2003) Modelling Dynamic Portfolio Credit Risk. Working Paper, ETH Zurich, Switzerland.

Schoutens, W., Simonsy, E., and Tistaertz, J. (2003) A Perfect Calibration! Now What? Working paper, available at www.globalriskguard.com/resources/deriv/fwd_2.pdf.

Totouom, D. and Armstrong, M. (2005) Dynamic Copula Processes: A New Way of Modeling CDO Tranches. Working paper, at www.cerna.ensmp.fr/Documents/DTT-MA-DynamicCopula.pdf.

Totouom, D. and Armstrong, M. (2007a) Dynamic Copula Processes: A New Way of Modeling CDO Tranches. *Advances in Econometrics*. Working paper. CERNA, Ecole des Mines de Paris.

Totouom, D. and Armstrong, M. (2007b) Dynamic Copulas Processes and Forward Starting Credit Derivatives. Working paper, Cerna, Ecole des Mines de Paris, Paris.

Van den Goorbergh, R.W.J., Genest, C., and Werker, B.J.M. (2005) Bivariate Option Pricing Using Dynamic Copula Models. *Insurance: Mathematics and Economics,* 37(1): 101–114.

Identifying Systemic and Idiosyncratic Risk from Standardized Single-Tranche Collateralized Debt Obligations

Jorge A. Chan-Lau and Yinqiu Lu

ABSTRACT

Systemic risk remains a major concern to policy makers since widespread defaults in the corporate and financial sectors could pose substantial costs to society. Forward-looking measures and/or indicators of systemic default risk are, thus, needed to identify potential vulnerability buildups in advance. We fill this gap by explaining how to construct idiosyncratic and systemic default risk indicators using the information embedded into single-tranche standardized collateralized debt obligations (STCDOs) referencing credit derivatives indexes. As an illustration, both risk indicators are constructed for the European corporate sector using midprice quotes for STCDOs referencing the iTraxx Europe index.

INTRODUCTION

Systemic risk is a major concern for those in charge of ensuring financial stability. While the default of an isolated corporation or financial institution could be very costly, as experienced in the recent defaults of Delphi,

Enron, and Worldcom in the United States, it may not have a major impact on other corporations and institutions. Increased financial integration across markets and institutions, however, suggests that single defaults could trigger a second round of defaults. The possibility of such an event was highlighted dramatically during the collapse of Long Term Capital Management, a large highly leveraged hedge fund, in 1998.

Therefore, the assessment of systemic risk remains a major policy challenge. Fortunately, the rapid growth of the credit derivatives market during the past years has opened a window to the market views on systemic risk. According to the British Bankers Association, the notional amount in the global credit derivatives market amounted to about $5 trillion in 2005, up from less than $1 trillion five years ago. In contrast to other over-the-counter derivatives markets such as the swaps market, not only the notional amount of credit derivatives products has increased rapidly but also the complexity of the contracts.

Some of the most complex derivatives products can be broadly categorized as portfolio products, since their payoffs are associated with the default loss distribution of a pool of reference contracts. The reference contracts can be loans, corporate and sovereign bonds, plain-vanilla credit default swaps, or a combination of these. Thus, the price of these contracts should partly reflect market participant views on the probability of observing multiple defaults in the reference pool of contracts.

Among portfolio products, the most popular portfolio contract is the collateralized debt obligation (CDO). In a CDO, the cash flows associated to the reference portfolio are sold to investors in different tranches. Each tranche has a different default risk profile as the subordinated tranches bear the first losses associated with the defaults in the reference portfolio.

In this paper we construct idiosyncratic and systemic risk indicators for Europe using price information on the default loss distribution implied by the prices of different tranches of STCDOs. Single-tranche standardized collateralized debt obligations reference standard credit derivatives indexes in Europe and the United States. Each regional credit derivatives index references a broad pool of the largest corporate issuers in the region and, hence, incorporates market views on the loss distribution of the region's corporate sector. Because tranche prices react differently to idiosyncratic and systemic risk depending on its degree of loss subordination, it is possible to extract the different risk components from tranche prices.

The rest of this chapter is structured as follows. We provide background information on STCDOs in the second section. The reader already familiar with these concepts may want to jump ahead to the third section, which describes the data and empirical method used to extract the idiosyncratic and systemic risk components. Conclusions and future work are then discussed.

A BRIEF PRIMER ON CDOS

A CDO is an investment vehicle that issues notes to investors to raise funds that are invested in a portfolio of risky financial assets. The CDO market has been one of the fastest-growing segments of the credit derivatives market. For instance, the issuance of cash CDOs in the United States increased to $137 billion in 2005 from $91 billion in 2004, while the outstanding notional amount of single-tranche CDOs almost doubled during the same period (Figures 13.1 and 13.2). The market itself has witnessed the evolution of several types of CDOs with each one reflecting an increasingly sophisticated demand from investors and the emergence of new financial products.

F I G U R E   13.1

U.S. cash CDO issuance (in million U.S. dollars)

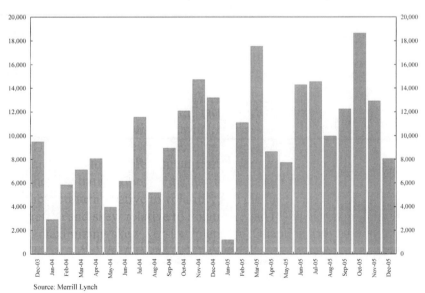

Source: Merrill Lynch

F I G U R E   13.2

Global single-tranche synthetic CDO national outstanding amount (in billion U.S. dollars)

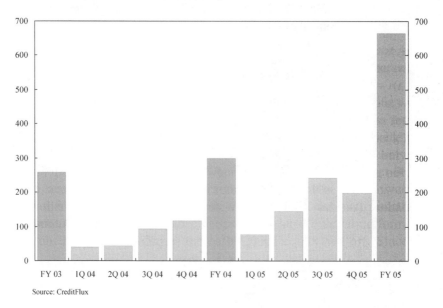

Source: CreditFlux

Synthetic CDOs

Rapid growth and liquidity in the credit derivatives market has led to a second type of CDO, the synthetic CDO. Instead of referencing assets that can generate cash flows, synthetic CDOs reference credit derivatives, usually credit default swaps (CDSs).[1] The special-purpose vehicle (SPV) associated to a synthetic CDO sells a portfolio of CDSs to the arranger and then uses the CDS premiums to pay investors.[2]

Synthetic CDOs can have funded or unfunded structures, with the SPV playing different roles depending on the CDO structure. In a funded synthetic CDO, as with a cash CDO, the investors have to pay the principal at the inception of the deal. The SPV uses the principal to buy collateral. Therefore, if an asset that is linked to one or some of the CDSs in the

---

[1] Credit default swaps work as an insurance against credit risks. The seller of a CDS contract agrees to insure a credit risk in exchange of regular premiums paid by the buyer.

[2] Selling a CDS is equivalent to buying the underlying bond to which the CDS is linked but without having to provide the up-front price of the bond.

portfolio defaults, the SPV uses the collateral to make a payment to the arranger. Therefore, the main role of the SPV is to collect collateral and to guarantee the bankruptcy remoteness of the CDOs. In an unfunded synthetic CDO, which is developed from the funded ones, the arranger directly sells a portfolio of CDSs in the market. The premium collected is shared by the CDO investors, who bear the potential losses of the CDS portfolio. Since investors are not required to fund the structure by paying the principal at the inception of the deal, no collateral is needed in an unfunded synthetic CDO.

Single-Tranche CDOs

More recently, the market has witnessed the emergence of STCDOs. In a synthetic CDO, all tranches, from equity to super-senior, have to be sold in order to finalize the deal. If one tranche cannot be sold, the deal cannot be completed no matter how marketable the rest of the tranches are. Owing to the difficulty of marketing synthetic CDOs, arrangers have begun to offer STCDOs.

In a STCDO, only one tranche is sold to the investor. The investor is exposed to potential losses as specified by the attachment points of the tranche. For example, an investor in a 3- to 7-percent mezzanine tranche is required to pay the arranger for losses in excess of 3 percent of the portfolio, but the investor's liability is limited to 7 percent of the portfolio losses. Because the arranger is implicitly holding the unsold tranches of the portfolio, it has to hedge its credit exposure by selling protection on the single names comprising the portfolio; that is, the arranger delta hedges its exposure selling single-name CDSs.

Standardized Single-Tranche CDOs on Credit Derivatives Indexes

In the past two years, a standardized STCDO market has emerged following the creation of two major CDS indexes: the Dow Jones CDX in the United States and the iTraxx in Europe, Asia, and Australia. The CDX investment grade (IG) is composed of equally weighted most liquid CDSs linked to 125 investment grade companies in the United States. Similarly, the iTraxx Europe index is composed of the most liquid CDSs of top 125 investment grade companies in Europe. The single-tranche standardized attachment points are 0–3, 3–7, 7–10, 10–15, and 15–30 for STCDOs referencing the

A single-tranche CDO structure

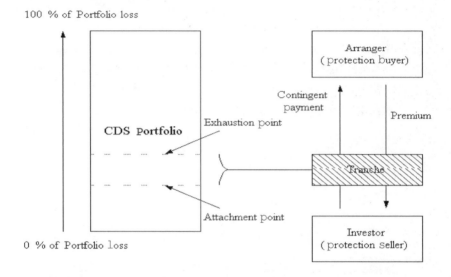

CDX IG, and 0–3, 3–6, 6–9, 9–12, and 12–22 for those contracts referencing the iTraxx Europe.[3]

The difference between arrangers (buyers of protection) and investors (sellers of protection) is blurred in the STCDO market, as the market allows them to enter either short or long credit positions. Market makers provide liquidity to the market as they stand ready to buy protections from protection sellers and sell them to protection buyers. Prices of the STCDO tranches are the market clearing equilibrium prices. A typical STCDO structure is shown in Figure 13.3.

DEFAULT PROBABILITY AND DEFAULT CORRELATION IN STCDOs

In a STCDO, both the protection buyer and the protection seller need to hedge the risks arising from changes in the default probability of a single company in the portfolio, and from changes in the default correlation of the portfolio. Changes in the default probability of the company affect the price (or spread) of the linked CDS and affect the value of the reference portfolio.

[3] See Amato and Gyntelberg (2005) for a comprehensive discussion of standardized STCDO on credit derivatives indexes.

The investors then have to calculate the hedge position for each CDS in the portfolio by computing the sensitivity of the tranche to changes in the underlying CDS spreads. The value of a STCDO depends on the assumed default correlation. While the value of the whole reference portfolio is not affected by changes in default correlation when spreads remain unchanged, the loss distribution is. Default correlation, therefore, affects the probability that losses could potentially reach the subordination level of the tranche.

Let's analyze in a qualitative way how the price of STCDO tranches react to changes in default probability and default correlation.[4] Intuitively, a change in the default probability of a single issuer or a group of issuers will have a similar impact on the prices of STCDO tranches. For instance, an increase in default probabilities of one or some companies in the portfolio causes price increases for both junior and senior tranches since the overall default probability increase makes default protection more valuable. Conversely, a decrease in default probabilities will make default protection cheaper, pushing tranche prices down.

Prices of different tranches react differently to changes in default correlation. As the default correlation when default probabilities are unchanged increases, the loss distribution of the portfolio spreads out, and the probability of extreme events, that is, the occurence of either a few or a large number of defaults, increases. Correspondingly, the probability of experiencing either very low or very high losses increases. In the case of the equity tranche, the higher probability of experiencing only few defaults implies limited losses to the tranche holders. Thus, the spread of the equity tranche, or price of equity protection, falls. That's why in the market jargon, selling protection on an equity tranche is equivalent to a "long" correlation position—as correlation increases, the mark-to-market value of the long position on the equity tranche increases.

In the case of the super-senior tranche, the increased probability of very high losses due to the increase in correlation implies an increased likelihood that losses could exceed the subordination point of the tranche. Thus, the price of protection on super-senior tranches increases. Hence, selling protection on a super-senior tranche is equivalent to a "short" correlation position—when correlation increases, the long position on the tranche suffers mark-to-market losses. It should be noted that the default correlation does not affect the expected losses in the portfolio; it only leads to a wider distribution.

---

[4] For a technical discussion, see Duffie and Garleanu (2001) and Gibson (2004)

F I G U R E   13.4

The impact of default correlation on the portfolio loss
distribution

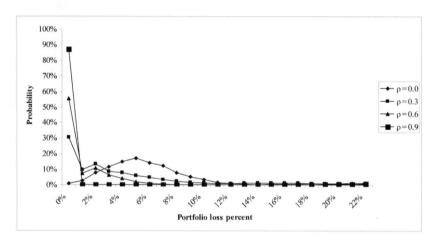

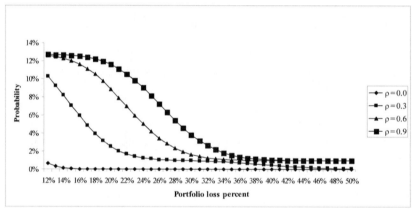

Source: Authors' calculations.

We use a made-up portfolio containing 100 names with the same
default probability to illustrate the relationship between the default correlation and the portfolio loss. The result is shown in Figure 13.4. The first
part of the figure shows the impact of the correlation on the portfolio loss
distribution. As the figure shows, as the default correlation (ρ) increases,
the probability of the zero portfolio loss increases, which makes the long

position on the equity tranche more valuable. The second part shows the probability of losses at or above the level displayed on the x (horizontal) axis. As the default correlation increases, the probability of large portfolio losses also increases, which reduces the value of the long position on the super-senior tranches.

IDIOSYNCRATIC AND SYSTEMIC RISK IN STCDO TRANCHES

Changes in the default probability and default correlation can be linked, respectively, with idiosyncratic and systematic risk factors. Idiosyncratic risk is company specific; so we observe that changes in the creditworthiness of a company are reflected in the changes of its default probability. In contrast, the default correlation reflects the systematic risk of the macro environment in which companies operate. Even if default probabilities remain constant, a change in the default correlation will change the probability of experiencing a large number of defaults. Therefore, increases in default correlation correspond to increases in systemic risk.

In other words, using the market prices on STCDO tranches, we can track the idiosyncratic and systematic risk in the portfolio. Namely, the price of equity and super-senior tranches should react similarly to changes in idiosyncratic risk. In contrast, the prices of these two tranches should move in opposite directions in response to changes in systemic risk. Hence, the price comovements of the equity and super-senior tranches allow us to identify: idiosyncratic risk or systemic risk.

DATA AND EMPIRICAL FRAMEWORK
Data

We exploit the qualitative response of the equity and super-senior tranches to idiosyncratic and systemic risk to identify idiosyncratic and systemic risk factors in the European corporate sector. We use price data for the traded tranches referencing the iTraxx Europe credit derivatives index. The index is constructed using a dealer liquidity poll, which is administered by the International Index Company (IIC). Each market maker submits to the IIC a list of investment grade companies incorporated in Europe with the highest CDS trading volume as measured over the previous six months. The companies in the index are ranked according to trading volumes—the one with the highest volume is ranked as number one.[5] Companies rated as BBB–Baa3 with negative outlook or below are excluded. The final portfolio consists of 125 companies by selecting the highest ranking issuers in each sector—10 autos, 30 consumers (15 cyclicals and 15 noncyclicals), 20 energy, 20 industrials, 20 telecoms, medias, and technologies (TMT), and 25 financials. Each company in the portfolio is weighted equally. The index is rolled over every six months by adding the next most liquid entities in the sector to replace the ones that defaulted, merged, or downgraded in the previous six months.

The summary statistics corresponding to quotes for five-year STCDO tranches referencing the iTraxx Europe index are shown in Table 13.1. The equity tranche (0–3) is quoted differently than the other three tranches, as investors receive an up-front fee, measured as a percent of the notional amount, and an annualized spread of 500 basis points (bps) paid quarterly during the life of the contract if no default happens. The other tranches pay investors a quarterly spread quoted in bps.

T A B L E   13.1

ITraxx tranches: Summary statistics, August 28, 2003 to May 16, 2005

	Attachment Points (percent)	Tranche Prices in (bps)*			
		Average	Minimum	Maximum	Standard Deviation
Tranches Equity	0–3	26.3	12.9	46.5	5.4
Junior mezzanine	3–6	182.6	84.6	330.0	56.6
Senior mezzanine	6–9	70.9	25.3	152.5	28.2
Super-senior	12–22	18.0	8.1	39.0	5.4

* Equity tranche prices quoted as an up-front percentage of the notional amount of the contract plus a 500 bps annualized spread paid quarterly.

Source: Authors' calculations

---

[5] The licensed market makers for iTraxx European indexes are ABN AMRO, Bank of America, Barclays Capital, Bayerische Landesbank, BBVA, Bear Stearns, BNP Paribas, CALYON, Citigroup, Commerzbank, CSFB, Deutsche Bank, Dresdner Kleinwort Wasserstein, Goldman Sachs, HSBC, HypoVereinsbank, ING, IXIS, J. P. Morgan, Lehman Brothers, Merrill Lynch, Morgan Stanley, Natexis Banques Populaires, Nomura, Royal Bank of Scotland, Santander, Sociéte Générale, TD Securities, and UBS.

T A B L E   13.2

ITraxx tranches: spreads correlations, August 28, 2003 to
May 16, 2005

	Attachment Points (percent)	Tranches			
		Equity	Junior Mezzanine	Senior Mezzanine	Super-senior
Tranches Equity	0–3	1.000			
Junior mezzanine	3–6	0.822	1.000		
Senior mezzanine	6– 9	0.774	0.976	1.000	
Super-senior	12–22	0.755	0.851	0.905	1.000

Sources: Authors' calculations

Principal Component Analysis

Principal component analysis (PCA) is used to reduce a set of correlated variables to a smaller set of uncorrelated variables and has been widely applied to analyze financial data.[6] Table 13.2 shows that this is the case for the iTraxx tranche spreads. Correlations range from 0.76 to 0.98, suggesting that it is proper to analyze the data using PCA.

The mechanics underlying the extraction of the principal components is relatively simple. Once the data is ordered in a matrix $Y_{n \times k}$, where n is the number of observations and k is the number of variables analyzed, the principal components correspond to the columns of the matrix $P_{k \times k}$ such that the variance of the transformed data $Z = P'Y$ is maximized subject to the constraint that $P'P = I$, where I is the identity matrix. Simple linear algebra shows that the principal components correspond to the eigenvectors associated to the characteristic vector λ, which solves the eigenequation $\Sigma - \lambda I = 0$, where is the variance–covariance matrix of Z. The results are presented in the next section.

RESULTS

Table 13.3 shows the coefficients associated with each principal component and the percentage of the variation explained by each component. The results presented there are robust to different specifications of the sample

---

[6] See Timm (2002) for a basic discussion of principal component analysis and Litterman and
   Scheinkman (1991) for an early application on modeling the term structure of interest rates.

T A B L E   13.3

Principal component cnalysis of iTraxx tranche spreads

	Principal Components Coefficients			
	First	Second	Third	Fourth
Equity	0.0007	−0.0012	−0.0069	−1.0000
Junior mezzanine	0.8950	−0.4391	−0.0787	0.0017
Senior mezzanine	0.4400	0.8395	0.3189	−0.0029
Super-senior	0.0740	0.3201	−0.9445	0.0062
Percent of variation explained	99.05	0.85	0.10	0.00

Source: Authors' calculations

period; so only the results corresponding to the full sample are reported. The results suggest that the first principal component explains most of the variation of the transformed data, while the contribution of the third and fourth components is negligible. The iTraxx spreads react positively to changes of the first principal component since its coefficients are all positive. The first principal component can be identified then with idiosyncratic risk factor in Europe, which accounts for most of the variation of the series. In contrast, the equity tranche coefficient of the second principal component has the opposite sign of the senior tranche coefficient, enabling us to identify it with the systemic risk factor.

After identifying the idiosyncratic and systemic risk components, it is possible to recover their time series behavior from the transformed data set Z, as shown in Figure 13.5. It should be borne in mind that these components are *forward-looking* risk measures, as they captured the market views on default risk going forward five years.

In the second half of 2004, systemic risk reacted to rapid increases of oil and commodity prices and uncertainty about the relative pace of interest rate tightening in the United States and European region. Idiosyncratic risk surged up in early 2004 following the bankruptcy of Parmalat, Italy's eighth largest industry group. Idiosyncratic and systemic risk rose together in May 2005 when hedge funds active in credit markets were forced to unwind their positions following the announcement of the ratings downgrade of General Motors and Ford. Mounting losses among hedge funds increased counterparty risk for the banks they were dealing

Idiosyncratic and systemic risk in Europe (normalized to 100 on 8/28/2003)

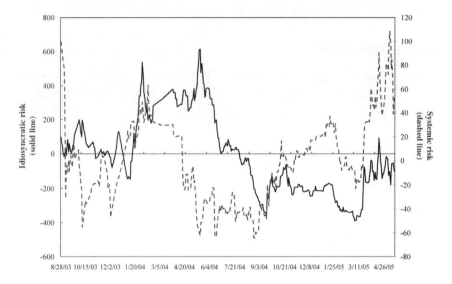

with and drove credit spreads up in the banking sector. Concerns about credit risk in the banking sector contributed to the simultaneous increase in systemic and idiosyncratic risk observed at the end of our sample.

CONCLUSION

We have presented a simple method for extracting measures of idiosyncratic and systemic risk from the prices of CDO tranches. The method relies on the different impact changes in idiosyncratic and systemic risk have on the tranches prices, and it was used to extract risk measures for the corporate sector in Europe. These forward-looking measures are useful to policy makers concerned about a buildup of risks that could potentially threaten financial stability. Going forward, there are a number of extensions that can be explored in future work. They include assessing the co-movements of idiosyncratic risk and systemic risk across emerging markets, Asia, Europe, and the United States and examining what the main economic determinants of both types of risk are with a view to predict their future evolution.

ACKNOWLEDGMENTS

This chapter benefited from comments by seminar participants at the Bank of Canada, the Bank for International Settlements, and Moody's KMV. Any errors or omissions are the authors' sole responsibility.

REFERENCES

Amato, J. and Gyntelberg, J. (2005) CDS Index Tranches and the Pricing of Credit Risk Correlations. *BIS Quarterly Review*, 3(1): 73–87.

Duffie, D. and Garleanu, N. (2001) Risk and Valuation of Collateralized Debt Obligations. *Financial Analysts Journal,* 57(1): 41–59.

Gibson, M. (2004) Understanding the Risk of Synthetic CDOs. Working paper, FEDS 2004–36, Washington: Board of Governors of the Federal Reserve.

J. P. Morgan (2004) Credit Correlation: A Guide. *Credit Derivatives Strategy*. New York.

Litterman, R. and Scheinkman, J. (1991) Common Factors Affecting Bond Returns. *Journal of Fixed Income* 1(1): 54–61.

Timm, N. (2002) *Applied Multivariate Analysis*. New York: Springer-Verlag.

CHAPTER 14

Default Contagion in Large Homogeneous Portfolios

Alexander Herbertsson

ABSTRACT

We study default contagion in large homogeneous credit portfolios. Using data from the iTraxx Europe series, two synthetic collateralized debt obligation (CDO) portfolios are calibrated against their tranche spreads, index credit default swap (CDS) spreads, and average CDS spreads, all with five-year maturity. After the calibrations, which render perfect fits, we investigate the implied expected ordered defaults times, implied default correlations, and implied multivariate default and survival distributions, for both ordered and unordered default times. Many of the numerical results differ substantially from the corresponding quantities in a smaller inhomogeneous CDS portfolio. Furthermore, the studies indicate that market CDO spreads imply extreme default clustering in upper tranches. The default contagion is introduced by letting individual intensities jump when other defaults occur but be constant between defaults. The model is translated into a Markov jump process. Using matrix-analytic methods derives expressions for the investigated quantities.

INTRODUCTION

In this paper we model dynamic credit dependence in a large homogeneous portfolio with default contagion. The approach is the same as in Herbertsson (2007a), where the author studies a smaller inhomogeneous credit portfolio; in Herbertsson and Rootzén (2006), where the authors focus on kth-to-default spreads; and in Herbertsson (2007b), where the same technique are applied to synthetic CDO tranches and index CDSs. Here we focus on multivariate default and survival distributions and related quantities in a large homogeneous portfolio. Many of the numerical results differ substantially from the corresponding quantities in a smaller inhomogeneous CDS portfolio. Default contagion in an intensity-based setting has been studied in, for example, Avellaneda and Wu (2001), (Bielecki et al. (2005), Bielecki and Rutkowski (2001), Bielecki et al. (2006), Collin-Dufresne et al. (2004), Davis and Esparragoza (2007), Davis and Lo (2001a; 2001b), Frey and Backhaus (2004), Frey and Backhaus (2006), Giesecke and Weber (2004; 2006), Jarrow and Yu (2001), Kraft and Steffensen (2007), Lando (2004), McNeil et al. (2005), Rogge and Schönbucher (2003), Schönbucher and Schubert (2001), and Yu (2007). The material in all these papers and books are related to the results discussed here.

The chapter is organized as follows. The following section gives the definition of the intensity-based model used in this chapter. This framework is then translated into a Markov jump process. In the next section we present formulas for multivariate default and survival distributions, marginal default distributions, default correlations, and expected default times. We then restate expressions, taken from Herbertsson (2007b), for our calibration instruments. These are synthetic CDO tranche spreads, index CDS spread, and average CDS spreads. A short description how to reduce the parameters space is then given. The subsequent section is then devoted to numerical investigations of several portfolio quantities, derived in an earlier section.

We use data from the iTraxx series and calibrate two homogeneous CDO portfolios against their CDO tranche spreads, index CDS spread, and the average CDS spreads. The maturity is five years and the fits are perfect. We then study the implied expected ordered defaults times, implied default correlations, and implied multivariate default and survival distributions, for both ordered and unordered default times. The numerical studies indicate that the market spreads imply extreme default clustering in upper tranches. The final section summarizes and discusses the results.

INTENSITY-BASED MODELS IN A HOMOGENEOUS MODEL REINTERPRETED AS MARKOV JUMP PROCESSES

The model we use in this chapter is a simplification of the one in Herbertsson (2007a) and Herbertsson and Rootzén (2006) to the case where the obligors are exchangeable. It is defined in terms of intensities and then reinterpreted as a Markov jump process. Closely following the cited references, for m exchangeable default times τ_1, τ_2, ..., τ_m, define the point process $N_{t,i} = 1_{\{\tau_i \le t\}}$ and introduce the filtrations

$$\mathfrak{F}_{t,i} = \sigma(N_{s,i}; s \le t) \qquad \mathfrak{F}_t = \bigvee_{i=1}^{m} \mathfrak{F}_{t,i}$$

Let $\lambda_{t,i}$ be the $\mathfrak{F}_t$ intensity of the point processes $N_{t,i}$, which we refer to as just *intensity* or *default intensity*. By exchangeability we have that all the intensities are the same $\lambda_{t,i} = \lambda$ if $\tau_i \ge t$ and $\lambda_{t,i} = 0$ if $\tau_i < t$. The model that we study is specified by

$$\lambda_t = a + \sum_{k=1}^{m-1} b_k 1_{\{T_k \le t\}} \tag{14.1}$$

where $\{T_k\}$ is the ordering of the default times $\{\tau_i\}$. Further, $a > 0$ and, b_1, b_2, ..., b_{m-1}, are constants such that λ_t is nonnegative. Thus, the default intensities are constant, except at the times when defaults occur: the parameter a is the base intensity for each obligor i, and given that $\tau_i > T_k$, then b_k is how much the default intensity for each remaining obligor jump at default number k in the portfolio. A positive b_k means that all remaining obligors are put at higher risk by the kth default in the portfolio, while a negative b_k means that the nondefaulted obligors in fact benefits from the kth default in the basket; finally, $b_k = 0$ if the remaining obligors are unaffected by the kth default.

Equation (14.1) determines the joint distribution of the default times. We will use the following observation, originally proved in Herbertsson (2007b), but restated here since it provides us with notation needed later on.

Proposition 14.1: *There exists a Markov jump process* $(Y_t)_{t \ge 0}$ *on a finite state space* $\mathbf{E} = \{0, 1, 2, ..., m\}$, *such that the stopping times*

$$T_k = \inf\{t > 0: Y_t = k\} \quad k = 1, 2, ..., m$$

are the ordering of m exchangeable stopping times τ_1, τ_2, ..., τ_m with intensities given by Equation (14.1). The generator $\boldsymbol{Q}$ to Y_t is given by

$$\boldsymbol{Q}_{k,k+1} = (m-k)\left(a + \sum_{j=1}^{k} b_j\right) \qquad \boldsymbol{Q}_{k,k} = -\boldsymbol{Q}_{k,k+1} \ \ for \ k = 0,1, \ldots, m-1$$

where the other entries in $\boldsymbol{Q}$ are zero. The Markov process always starts in $\{0\}$.

The states in $\mathbf{E}$ can be interpreted as the number of defaulted obligors in the portfolio. In the sequel, we let $\boldsymbol{\alpha} = (1, 0, \ldots, 0)$ denote the initial distribution on $\mathbf{E}$. Further, if k belongs to $\mathbf{E}$, then $\mathbf{e}_k$ denotes a column vector in $\Re^{m+1}$, where the entry at position k is 1 and the other entries are zero. From Markov theory we know that $P(Y_t = k) = \boldsymbol{\alpha}e^{\boldsymbol{Q}t}\mathbf{e}_k$, where $e^{\boldsymbol{Q}t}$ is the matrix exponential that has a closed-form expression in terms of the eigenvalue decomposition of $\boldsymbol{Q}$.

USING THE MATRIX-ANALYTIC APPROACH TO FIND MULTIVARIATE DEFAULT DISTRIBUTIONS AND RELATED QUANTITIES

In this section we derive formulas for multivariate default and survival distributions, for both ordered and unordered default times. The marginal survival distributions are then easily retrieved as special cases. Analytical formulas for the default correlations are given in the moments of the default times and the ordered default times are presented later in the following section.

The Multivariate Distributions

In this subsection we derive formulas for multivariate default and survival distributions for both ordered as well as unordered default times. We start with the latter. Let $\boldsymbol{M}_k$ and $\boldsymbol{N}_k$ be $(m + 1) \times (m + 1)$ diagonal matrices, defined by $(\boldsymbol{M}_k)_{j,j} = 1_{\{j<k\}}$ and $(\boldsymbol{N}_k)_{j,j} = 1_{\{j\geq k\}}$, where $(\boldsymbol{M}_k)_{j,j'} = (\boldsymbol{N}_k)_{j,j} = 0$ if $j \neq j'$. Note that $\boldsymbol{M}_k = \boldsymbol{I} - \boldsymbol{N}_k$. The following proposition is similar to Proposition 3.1 in Herbertsson (2007a).

Proposition 14.2: *Consider m obligors with default intensities given by Equation (14.1), and let $k_1 < \cdots < k_q$ be an increasing subsequence in $\{1, 2, \ldots, m\}$, where $1 \leq q \leq m$. Furthermore, let $t_1 < \cdots < t_q$. Then*

$$P\left(T_{k_1} > t_1, \ldots, T_{k_q} > t_q\right) = \boldsymbol{\alpha}\left(\prod_{i=1}^{q} e^{\mathbf{Q}(t_i - t_{i-1})} \boldsymbol{M}_{k_i}\right)\mathbf{1} \qquad (14.2)$$

and

$$P\left(T_{k_1} \leq t_1, \ldots, T_{k_q} \leq t_q\right) = \boldsymbol{\alpha}\left(\prod_{i=1}^{q} e^{\mathbf{Q}(t_i - t_{i-1})} \boldsymbol{N}_{k_i}\right)\mathbf{1} \qquad (14.3)$$

where $t_{i_0} = 0.$

Proof: By Proposition 14.1,

$$
\begin{aligned}
P\left(T_{k_1} > t_1, \ldots, T_{k_q} > t_q\right) &= P\left(Y_{t_1} < k_1, \ldots, Y_{t_q} < k_q\right)\\[4pt]
&= \sum_{j_1=0}^{k_1-1}\cdots\sum_{j_q=0}^{k_q-1} P\left(Y_0 = 0, Y_{t_1} = j_1, \ldots, Y_{t_q} = j_q\right)\\[4pt]
&= \sum_{j_1=0}^{k_1-1}\cdots\sum_{j_q=0}^{k_q-1} P(Y_0 = 0)P\left(Y_{t_1} = j_1 \big| Y_0 = 0\right)\cdots P\left(Y_{t_q} = j_q \big| Y_{t_{q-1}} = j_{q-1}\right)\\[4pt]
&= \sum_{j_1=0}^{k_1-1}\cdots\sum_{j_q=0}^{k_q-1} \boldsymbol{\alpha} e^{\mathbf{Q}t_1} \boldsymbol{e}_{j_1} \boldsymbol{e}_{j_1}^T e^{\mathbf{Q}(t_2-t_1)} \boldsymbol{e}_{j_2} \boldsymbol{e}_{j_2}^T e^{\mathbf{Q}(t_3-t_2)} \cdots \boldsymbol{e}_{j_{q-1}} \boldsymbol{e}_{j_{q-1}}^T e^{\mathbf{Q}(t_q-t_{q-1})} \boldsymbol{e}_{j_q}\\[4pt]
&= \boldsymbol{\alpha} e^{\mathbf{Q}t_1} \sum_{j_1=0}^{k_1-1}\left(\boldsymbol{e}_{j_1} \boldsymbol{e}_{j_1}^T\right) e^{\mathbf{Q}(t_2-t_1)} \sum_{j_2=0}^{k_2-1}\left(\boldsymbol{e}_{j_2} \boldsymbol{e}_{j_2}^T\right)\cdots e^{\mathbf{Q}(t_q-t_{q-1})} \sum_{j_q=0}^{k_q-1} \boldsymbol{e}_{j_q}\\[4pt]
&= \boldsymbol{\alpha} e^{\mathbf{Q}t_1} \boldsymbol{M}_{k_1} e^{\mathbf{Q}(t_2-t_1)} \boldsymbol{M}_{k_2} \cdots e^{\mathbf{Q}(t_q-t_{q-1})} \boldsymbol{M}_{k_q} \mathbf{1}
\end{aligned}
$$

which proves Equation (14.2). The third equality follows from the Markov property of Y_t, the fourth since Y_t is a homogeneous Markov process and that $P(Y_0 = 0) = 1$. The final equality is due to the definition of the matrix $\boldsymbol{M}_k$. Equation (14.3) is proved in the same way.

Finding joint distributions for $\{\tau_i\}$ in a homogeneous model with default intensities given by Equation (14.1) is a more complicated task than in an inhomogeneous model. For $1 \leq q \leq m$, fix a vector $t_1, \ldots, t_q \in \mathfrak{R}_+^q$. For a set of q distinct obligors $i_1, i_2, \ldots, i_q$, the probability $P(\tau_{i_1} \leq t_1, \ldots, \tau_{i_q} \leq t_q)$ is by exchangeability the same for any such distinct sequence of q obligors. Therefore, we will in this section, without loss of generality, only consider $P(\tau_1 \leq t_1, \ldots, \tau_q \leq t_q)$, where $t_1 \leq \cdots \leq t_q$ and similarly for $P(\tau_{i_1} > t_1, \ldots, \tau_{i_q} > t_q)$. To exemplify, we start with the following proposition, where we let $q = 2$ and $t_1 < t_2$.

Proposition 14.3: *Consider m obligors with default intensities given by Equation (14.1,) and let* $t_1 < t_2$. *Then*

$$P\left(\tau_1 \le t_1, \tau_2 \le t_2\right) = \frac{(m-2)!}{m!} \boldsymbol{\alpha} e^{Qt_1} \boldsymbol{n} + \frac{(m-2)!}{m!} \sum_{k_1=1}^{m} \sum_{k_2=k_1+1}^{m} \boldsymbol{\alpha} e^{Qt_1} N_{k_1} e^{Q(t_2-t_1)} N_{k_2} \boldsymbol{1} \quad (14.4)$$

where ***n*** *is a column vector in* $\Re^{m+1}$ *such that* $\mathbf{n}_j = j(j-1)/2$.

Proof: First, note that

$$
\begin{aligned}
P\left(\tau_1 \le t_1, \tau_2 \le t_2\right) &= \sum_{k_1=1}^{m} \sum_{k_2=1, k_2 \ne k_1}^{m} P\left(\tau_1 = T_{k_1}, \tau_2 = T_{k_2}, \tau_1 \le t_1, \tau_2 \le t_2\right) \\
&= \sum_{k_1=1}^{m} \sum_{k_2=1, k_2 \ne k_1}^{m} P\left(\tau_1 = T_{k_1}, \tau_2 = T_{k_2}, T_{k_1} \le t_1, T_{k_2} \le t_2\right) \\
&= \sum_{k_1=1}^{m} \sum_{k_2=1, k_2 \ne k_1}^{m} P\left(\tau_1 = T_{k_1}, \tau_2 = T_{k_2}\right) P\left(T_{k_1} \le t_1, T_{k_2} \le t_2\right) \\
&= \frac{(m-2)!}{m!} \sum_{k_1=1}^{m} \sum_{k_2=1, k_2 \ne k_1}^{m} P\left(T_{k_1} \le t_1, T_{k_2} \le t_2\right)
\end{aligned}
\quad (14.5)
$$

where the third and fourth equalities are due to the exchangeability in the portfolio. Now, if $k_1 < k_2$, then Proposition 14.2 renders $P(T_{k_1} \le t_1, T_{k_2} \le t_2) = \boldsymbol{\alpha} e^{Qt_1} N_{k_1} e^{Q(t_2-t_1)} N_{k_2} \boldsymbol{1}$. However, if $k_1 > k_2$, we can no longer use this argument. To see this, note that since $t_1 < t_2$ and $T_{k_1} > T_{k_2}$, we get

$$P(T_{k_1} \le t_1, T_{k_2} \le t_2) = P(T_{k_1} \le t_1) = \boldsymbol{\alpha} e^{Qt_1} N_{k_1} \boldsymbol{1} \ne \boldsymbol{\alpha} e^{Qt_1} N_{k_1} e^{Q(t_2-t_1)} N_{k_2} \boldsymbol{1}.$$

Hence,

$$
\begin{aligned}
\sum_{k_1=1}^{m} \sum_{k_2=1, k_2 \ne k_1}^{m} P\left(T_{k_1} \le t_1, T_{k_2} \le t_2\right) &= \sum_{k_1=1}^{m} \Bigg[\sum_{1 \le k_2 < k_1}^{m} P\left(T_{k_1} \le t_1, T_{k_2} \le t_2\right) \\
&\quad + \sum_{k_1 < k_2 \le m}^{m} P\left(T_{k_1} \le t_1, T_{k_2} \le t_2\right) \Bigg] \\
&= \sum_{k_1=1}^{m} \Bigg[\sum_{k_2=1}^{k_1-1} P\left(T_{k_1} \le t_1\right) \\
&\quad + \sum_{k_2=k_1+1}^{m} P\left(T_{k_1} \le t_1, T_{k_2} \le t_2\right) \Bigg]
\end{aligned}
$$

$$= \sum_{k_1=1}^{m}\left[(k_1-1)P\left(T_{k_1}\le t_1\right)\right.$$

$$\left.+ \sum_{k_2=k_1+1}^{m} P\left(T_{k_1}\le t_1, T_{k_2}\le t_2\right)\right]$$

$$= \sum_{k_1=1}^{m}(k_1-1)\boldsymbol{\alpha}e^{Qt_1}\boldsymbol{N}_{k_1}\mathbf{1}$$

$$+\sum_{k_1=1}^{m}\sum_{k_2=k_1+1}^{m}\boldsymbol{\alpha}e^{Qt_1}\boldsymbol{N}_{k_1}e^{Q(t_2-t_1)}\boldsymbol{N}_{k_2}\mathbf{1}$$

$$= \boldsymbol{\alpha}e^{Qt_1}\left[\sum_{k_1=1}^{m}(k_1-1)\boldsymbol{N}_{k_1}\right]\mathbf{1}$$

$$+\sum_{k_1=1}^{m}\sum_{k_2=k_1+1}^{m}\boldsymbol{\alpha}e^{Qt_1}\boldsymbol{N}_{k_1}e^{Q(t_2-t_1)}\boldsymbol{N}_{k_2}\mathbf{1}.$$

Note that the column vector $\mathbf{n} = \left[\sum_{k_1=1}^{m}(k_1-1)N_{K_1}\right]\mathbf{1}$ can be simplified according to

$$n_j = \sum_{k_1=1}^{m}(k_1-1)\left(N_{k_1}\mathbf{1}\right)_j = \sum_{k_1=1}^{m}(k_1-1)1_{(j\ge k_1)} = \sum_{k_1=1}^{j}(k_1-1) = \frac{j(j-1)}{2}.$$

Inserting the above expressions in Equation (14.5) renders Equation (14.4).

By using the same technique as in Proposition 14.3 we can state the following corollary.

Corollary 14.4: *Consider m obligors with default intensities given by Equation (14.1,) and let $t_1 < t_2$. Then*

$$P\left(\tau_1 > t_1, \tau_2 > t_2\right) = \frac{(m-2)!}{m!}\boldsymbol{\alpha}e^{Qt_2}\boldsymbol{m} + \frac{(m-2)!}{m!}\sum_{k_1=1}^{m}\sum_{k_2=k_1+1}^{m}\boldsymbol{\alpha}e^{Qt_1}\boldsymbol{M}_{k_1}e^{Q(t_2-t_1)}\boldsymbol{M}_{k_2}\mathbf{1} \quad (14.6)$$

*where **m** is a column vector in $\mathfrak{R}^{m+1}$ such that $\mathbf{m}_j = (m-j)(m-j-1)/2$.*

It is possible to generalize Proposition 14.3 and Corollary 14.4 to more than two default times. These expressions do not seem to be easily simplified. However, if $t_1 = \cdots = t_q = t$, we can find compact formulas.

Proposition 14.5: *Consider m obligors with default intensities as in Equation (14.1), and let q be a integer, where $1 \leq q \leq m$. Then*

$$P\left(\tau_1 \leq t, \ldots, \tau_q \leq t\right) = \alpha e^{Qt} d^{(q)} \qquad P\left(\tau_1 > t, \ldots, \tau_q > t\right) = \alpha e^{Qt} s^{(q)} \qquad (14.7)$$

where $d^{(q)}$ and $s^{(q)}$ are column vectors in $\Re^{m+1}$ defined by

$$d_j^{(q)} = \frac{\binom{j}{q}}{\binom{m}{q}} 1_{\{j \geq q\}} \qquad s_j^{(q)} = \frac{\binom{m-j}{q}}{\binom{m}{q}} 1_{\{j \leq m-q\}}. \qquad (14.8)$$

Proof: By Proposition 14.1,

$$\begin{aligned}
P\left(\tau_1 \leq t, \ldots, \tau_q \leq t\right) &= \sum_{j=q}^{m} P\left(\tau_1 \leq t, \ldots, \tau_q \leq t, Y_t = j\right) \\
&= \sum_{j=q}^{m} P\left(\tau_1 \leq t, \ldots, \tau_q \leq t \middle| Y_t = j\right) P\left(Y_t = j\right) \\
&= \sum_{j=q}^{m} \frac{\binom{j}{q}}{\binom{m}{q}} \alpha e^{Qt} e_j \\
&= \alpha e^{Qt} d^{(q)}
\end{aligned} \qquad (14.9)$$

where $d^{(q)}$ is a column vector in $\Re^{m+1}$ defined by $d_j^{(q)} = \binom{j}{q} / \binom{m}{q} 1_{\{j \geq q\}}$.

To motivate the third equality in Equation (14.9), note that $P(\tau_1 \leq t, \ldots, \tau_q \leq t | Y_t = j)$ is the probability that q specified obligors have defaulted before t given that exactly j obligors have defaulted until time t, where $j \geq q$. Since the portfolio consist of m obligors, and by exchangeability in the model, there are $\binom{m-q}{j-q}$ ways to choose a group of j obligors that contains our q specified obligors, where $j \geq q$. Further, there are $\binom{m}{j}$ ways to pick out a set containing j obligors. Hence,

$$P\left(\tau_1 \le t,\ldots,\tau_q \le t \middle| Y_t = j\right) = \frac{\dbinom{m-q}{j-q}}{\dbinom{m}{j}} = \frac{\dbinom{j}{q}}{\dbinom{m}{q}} \quad for \ j \ge q,$$

where the last equality follows from straightforward calculations. This proves the first equality in Equation 14.7. Next, by Proposition 14.1 again,

$$
\begin{aligned}
P\left(\tau_1 > t,\ldots,\tau_q > t\right) &= \sum_{j=0}^{m-q} P\left(\tau_1 > t,\ldots,\tau_q > t, Y_t = j\right)\\
&= \sum_{j=0}^{m-q} P\left(\tau_1 > t,\ldots,\tau_q > t \middle| Y_t = j\right) P\left(Y_t = j\right)\\
&= \sum_{j=0}^{m-q} \frac{\dbinom{m-j}{q}}{\dbinom{m}{q}}\, \boldsymbol{\alpha} e^{Qt} \mathbf{e}_j\\
&= \boldsymbol{\alpha} e^{Qt} \mathbf{s}^{(q)}
\end{aligned}
$$

(14.10)

where $\mathbf{s}^{(q)}$ is a column vector in $\mathfrak{R}^{m+1}$ defined by $\mathbf{s}^{(q)}_j = \dbinom{m-j}{q} \Big/ \dbinom{m}{q} \mathbf{1}_{\{j \le m-q\}}$.

To motivate the third equality in Equation (14.10), note that $P(\tau_1 > t,\ldots, \tau_q > t | Y_t = j)$ is the probability that q specified obligors have survived before t given that exactly $m - j$ obligors have survived until time t, where $m - j \ge q$. Since the portfolio consist of m obligors, and by exchangeability in the model, there are $\dbinom{m-q}{m-j-q}$ ways to choose a group of $m - j$ obligors that contains our q specified obligors, where $m - j \ge q$. Further, there are $\dbinom{m}{m-j}$ ways to pick out a set containing $m - j$ obligors. Hence,

$$P\left(\tau_1 > t,\ldots,\tau_q > t \middle| Y_t = j\right) = \frac{\dbinom{m-q}{m-j-q}}{\dbinom{m}{m-j}} = \frac{\dbinom{m-j}{q}}{\dbinom{m}{q}} \quad for \ j \le m-q,$$

where the last equality follows from straightforward calculations. This proves the second equality in Equation (14.7).

Note that the indicator functions $1_{\{j \geq q\}}$ and $1_{\{j \leq m-q\}}$ can be dropped in Equation (14.8) since

$$\binom{j}{q} = \frac{j(j-1)(j-2)\cdots(j-q+1)}{q!} = 0$$

for j = 0,1, ..., *q* − 1 and

$$\binom{m-j}{q} = \frac{(m-j)(m-j-1)(m-j-2)\cdots(m-j-q+1)}{q!} = 0$$

for $j = m, m - 1, \ldots, m - q + 1$. We can now check that Proposition 14.3 and Corollary 14.4 are consistent with Proposition 14.5. Letting $t_1 = t_2 = t$ in Equation (14.4) in Proposition 14.3 yields that

$$
\begin{aligned}
P(\tau_1 \leq t, \tau_2 \leq t) &= \frac{(m-2)!}{m!} \alpha e^{Qt} n + \frac{(m-2)!}{m!} \sum_{k_1=1}^{m} \sum_{k_2=k_1+1}^{m} \alpha e^{Qt} N_{k_1} N_{k_2} 1 \\
&= \frac{(m-2)!}{m!} \alpha e^{Qt} \left(n + \sum_{k_1=1}^{m} \sum_{k_2=k_1+1}^{m} N_{k_2} 1 \right) \\
&= \frac{(m-2)!}{m!} \alpha e^{Qt} (n+n) = \frac{1}{\binom{m}{2}} \alpha e^{Qt} n = \alpha e^{Qt} d^{(2)}
\end{aligned}
\tag{14.11}
$$

where the second equality follows from $N_{k_1} N_{k_2} = N_{k_2}$ since $k_2 > k_1$. To prove the third equality in Equation (14.11), note that

$$
\begin{aligned}
\left(\sum_{k_1=1}^{m} \sum_{k_2=k_1+1}^{m} N_{k_2} 1 \right)_j &= \sum_{k_1=1}^{m} \sum_{k_2=k_1+1}^{m} \left(N_{k_2} 1 \right)_j = \sum_{k_1=1}^{m} \sum_{k_2=k_1+1}^{m} 1_{\{j \geq k_2\}} = \sum_{k_1=1}^{m} \left(\sum_{k_2=k_1+1}^{j} 1 \right) 1_{\{j \geq k_1+1\}} \\
&= \sum_{k_1=1}^{m} (j - k_1) 1_{\{j \geq k_1\}} = \sum_{k_1=1}^{j} (j - k_1) = \frac{j(j-1)}{2} = n_j
\end{aligned}
$$

and the final equality in Equation (14.11) is due to the definition of $\mathbf{d}^{(q)}$ in Equation (14.8), $\mathbf{d}_j^{(q)} = \binom{j}{q} / \binom{m}{q}$, which for $q = 2$ implies that $\mathbf{d}^{(2)} = \mathbf{n} / \binom{m}{2}$. Hence, Proposition 14.3 is consistent with Proposition 14.5 for $q = 2$ an d the bivariate default distribution. Now, letting $t_1 = t_2 = t$ in Equation (14.6) in Corollary 14.4, we get

$$
\begin{aligned}
P\left(\tau_1 > t, \tau_2 > t\right) &= \frac{(m-2)!}{m!} \alpha e^{Qt} \mathbf{m} + \frac{(m-2)!}{m!} \sum_{k_1=1}^{m} \sum_{k_2=k_1+1}^{m} \alpha e^{Qt} \mathbf{M}_{k_1} \mathbf{M}_{k_2} \mathbf{1} \\
&= \frac{(m-2)!}{m!} \alpha e^{Qt} \left(\mathbf{m} + \sum_{k_1=1}^{m} \sum_{k_2=k_1+1}^{m} \mathbf{M}_{k_1} \mathbf{1} \right) \\
&= \frac{(m-2)!}{m!} \alpha e^{Qt} \left(\mathbf{m} + \mathbf{m} \right) = \frac{1}{\binom{m}{2}} \alpha e^{Qt} \mathbf{m} = \alpha e^{Qt} \mathbf{s}^{(2)}
\end{aligned}
\tag{14.12}
$$

where the second equality follows from $\mathbf{M}_{k_1} \mathbf{M}_{k_2} = \mathbf{M}_{k_1}$ since $k_2 > k_1$. To prove the third equality in Equation (14.12), note that

$$
\begin{aligned}
\left(\sum_{k_1=1}^{m} \sum_{k_2=k_1+1}^{m} \mathbf{M}_{k_1} \mathbf{1} \right)_j &= \left(\sum_{k_1=1}^{m} (m-k_1) \mathbf{M}_{k_1} \mathbf{1} \right)_j = \sum_{k_1=1}^{m} (m-k_1) \left(\mathbf{M}_{k_1} \mathbf{1} \right)_j = \sum_{k_1=1}^{m} (m-k_1) 1_{\{j < k_1\}} \\
&= \sum_{k_1=j+1}^{m} (m-k_1) = \frac{(m-j)(m-j-1)}{2} = m_j
\end{aligned}
$$

and the final equality in Equation (14.12) is due to the definition of $\mathbf{s}^{(q)}$ in Equation (14.8), $\mathbf{s}^{(q)}_j = \binom{m-j}{q} / \binom{m}{q}$, which for $q = 2$ implies that $\mathbf{s}^{(2)} = \mathbf{m} / \binom{m}{q}$. Hence, Corollary 14.4 is consistent with Proposition 14.5 for $q = 2$ and the bivariate survival distribution.

The Marginal Distributions

By Proposition 14.5 with $q = 1$, we get $P(\tau_i > t) = \boldsymbol{\alpha} e^{\boldsymbol{Q}^t} \mathbf{s}^{(1)}$, where $\mathbf{s}^{(1)}_j = (m - j)/m = 1 - j/m$. Furthermore, letting $\mathbf{m}^{(k)}$ denote $\mathbf{m}^{(k)} = M_k \mathbf{1}$, then Proposition 14.2, with $q = 1$ for any $1 \le k \le m$, renders that, $P(T_k > t) = \boldsymbol{\alpha} e^{\boldsymbol{Q}^t} \mathbf{m}^{(k)}$, where $\mathbf{m}^{(k)}_j = 1_{\{j < k\}}$.

The Default Correlations

In this subsection we use Proposition 14.5 to give expressions for pairwise default correlations between two different obligors belonging to a homogeneous portfolio of m obligors satisfying Equation (14.1). By exchangeability, $\mathrm{Corr}(1_{\{\tau_i \le t\}}, 1_{\{\tau_j \le t\}})$ is the same for all pairs $i \ne j$, and therefore, we write $\rho(t)$ to denote $\mathrm{Corr}(1_{\{\tau_i \le t\}}, 1_{\{\tau_j \le t\}})$.

Lemma 14.6: *Consider m obligors with default intensities as in Equation (14.1).*

$$\rho(t) = \frac{\boldsymbol{\alpha} e^{\boldsymbol{Q}^t} \boldsymbol{d}^{(2)} - \left(\boldsymbol{\alpha} e^{\boldsymbol{Q}^t} \boldsymbol{d}^{(1)}\right)^2}{\boldsymbol{\alpha} e^{\boldsymbol{Q}^t} \boldsymbol{d}^{(1)} \left(1 - \boldsymbol{\alpha} e^{\boldsymbol{Q}^t} \boldsymbol{d}^{(1)}\right)}. \tag{14.13}$$

Proof: By exchangeability we have that $\mathrm{Var}(1_{\{\tau_i \le t\}}) = \mathrm{Var}(1_{\{\tau_j \le t\}})$. Further, using the definition of covariance and variance, we get that

$$Cov(1_{\{\tau_i \le t\}}, 1_{\{\tau_j \le t\}}) = \boldsymbol{P}(\tau_i \le t, \tau_j \le t) - P(\tau_i \le t)P(\tau_j \le t)$$
$$\mathrm{Var}(1_{\{\tau_i \le t\}}) = \boldsymbol{P}(\tau_i \le t)(1 - P(\tau_i \le t))$$

and by Proposition 14.5, $P(\tau_i \le t, \tau_j \le t) = \boldsymbol{\alpha} e^{\boldsymbol{Q}^t} \boldsymbol{d}^{(2)}$ and $P(\tau_i \le t) = \boldsymbol{\alpha} e^{\boldsymbol{Q}^t} \boldsymbol{d}^{(1)}$. Inserting this into the definition of correlation between two random variables yields Equation (14.13).

Expected Default Times

In this subsection we present formulas for the moments for default times and ordered default times. By construction, the intensity matrix Q for the Markov jump process (see Proposition 14.1) has the form

$$Q = \begin{pmatrix} \mathbf{T} & \mathbf{t} \\ \mathbf{0} & 0 \end{pmatrix}$$

where $\mathbf{t}$ is a column vector such that $\mathbf{t}_{m-1}$ is nonzero and $\mathbf{t}_k = 0$ for $k = 0$, $1, \ldots, m-2$, because the kth element $\mathbf{t}_k, k \leq m - 1$, is the intensity for the Markov jump process Y_t to jump from the state k to the absorbing state m. Furthermore, $\mathbf{T}$ is invertible since it is upper diagonal with strictly negative diagonal elements. The following lemma is standard.

Lemma 14.7: *Consider m obligors with default intensities as in Equation (14.1). Then*

$$E(\tau_i^n) = (-1)^n \, n! \, \tilde{\boldsymbol{\alpha}} \mathbf{T}^{-n} \tilde{\mathbf{s}}^{(1)} \quad E(T_k^n) = (-1)^n n! \, \tilde{\boldsymbol{\alpha}} \mathbf{T}^{-n} \tilde{\mathbf{m}}^{(k)}$$

for $n = 1, 2, 3, \ldots$, where $\tilde{\boldsymbol{\alpha}}, \tilde{\mathbf{s}}^{(1)}, \tilde{\mathbf{m}}^{(k)}$ are the restrictions of $\boldsymbol{\alpha}, \mathbf{s}^{(1)}, \mathbf{m}^{(k)}$ from $\mathbf{E}$ *to* $\mathbf{E} \setminus \{m\}$.

For a proof, see Lemma 3.8 in Herbertsson (2007a). The implied variances of the default times can now be computed as

$$\mathrm{Var}(T_k) = 2\tilde{\boldsymbol{\alpha}} \mathbf{T}^{-2} \tilde{\mathbf{m}}^{(k)} - (\tilde{\boldsymbol{\alpha}} \mathbf{T}^{-1} \tilde{\mathbf{m}}^{(k)})^2 \; for \; k = 1, 2, \ldots, m,$$

and in the same way $\mathrm{Var}(\tau_i) = 2\tilde{\boldsymbol{\alpha}} \mathbf{T}^{-2} \tilde{\mathbf{s}}^{(1)} - (\tilde{\boldsymbol{\alpha}} \mathbf{T}^{-1} \tilde{\mathbf{s}}^{(1)})^2$, which by the exchangeability is identical for all obligors.

Remark

The main message in this section is that under Equation (14.1), computations of multivariate default and survival distributions, marginal default distributions, default correlations, and so on have been reduced to compute the matrix exponential. Computing e^{Qt} efficiently for large state spaces is a numerical issue that requires special treatment [see Herbertsson and Rootzén (2006)]. For small state spaces, perhaps less then 150 states, there are many different methods to compute the matrix exponential ((Moeler and Loan, 1978; ibid., 2003). Most of them are straightforward to implement using standard mathematical software. Following Herbertsson (2007b), in this chapter we will use Padé approximation with scaling and squaring [see Moeler and Loan (1978)]. In the model Equation (14.1) with $m = 125$, this approach outperforms all other methods that we have tried, both in computational time and accuracy. The robustness of the Padé approximation with scaling and squaring has previously also been verified in Moeler and Loan (1978; 2003).

Finally, recall that e^{Qt} has a closed-form expression in terms of the eigenvalue decomposition of Q. Thus, if the eigenvalues of Q are distinct, and letting D be a diagonal matrix containing them, then $e^{Qt} = Ue^{Qt}U^{-1}$, where U is the matrix whose rows are the corresponding eigenvectors. In this chapter Q is upper diagonal; so the eigenvalues are given by its diagonal. It is therefore tempting to use this decomposition. However, the method is numerically unstable even for moderate sizes of m [see Moeler and Loan (1978)] since U is often ill-conditioned, making it difficult to compute its inverse U^{-1} without introducing large numerical errors.

CALIBRATING THE MODEL PARAMETERS AGAINST CDO TRANCHE SPREADS, INDEX CDS SPREADS, AND AVERAGE CDS SPREADS

In this section we discuss how to find the parameters in the model (14.1). First, we present formulas for the single-name CDS spread in this model. Then, we give expressions for CDO tranche spreads and index CDS spreads. Finally, the last section is devoted to a short description of how to calibrate the model spreads against the corresponding market spreads. In the sequel all computations are assumed to be under a risk-neutral martingale measure P. Typically, such a P exists if we rule out arbitrage opportunities. Further, we assume that the risk-free interest rate is a deterministic constant given by r.

The Single-Name CDS Spread

In this subsection we give a short description of a single-name CDS, which is one of our calibration instruments. Consider a obligor i with default time and τ_i recovery rate ϕ_i. A single-name CDS with maturity T, where the reference entity is obligor i, is a bilateral contract between two counterparties, A and B, where B promises to pay A the credit losses $1 - \phi_i$ at τ_i if obligor i defaults before time T. As compensation for this, A pays $R_i(T)\Delta_n$ to the protection seller B at $0 < t_1 < t_2 < \cdots < t_{n_T} = T$ or until $\tau_i < T$, where $\Delta_n = t_n - t_{n-1}$. If default happens for some $\tau_i \in [t_{n-1}, t_n]$, A will also pay B the accrued default premium up to τ_i. By exchangeability in the model Equation (14.1), τ_i has the same distribution for all obligors and $\phi_1 = \phi_2 = \cdots = \phi_m = \phi$, so $R_1(T) = R_2(T) = \cdots = R_m(T) = R(T)$. The CDS spread $R(T)$ is determined so that expected discounted cash flows between A and B are equal when the CDS contract is settled at $t = 0$. It is expressed in basis points per annum and independent of the nominal size protected. The closed-form expression for $R(T)$ is obtained by using the expression for $P(\tau_i > t)$. For ease of reference we exhibit the resulting formulas [proofs can be found in Herbertsson (2005) or (2007a)].

Proposition 14.8: *Consider m obligors that all satisfy Equation (14.1), and assume that the interest rate r is constant. Then, with notation as above,*

$$R(T) = \frac{(1-\phi)\alpha(A(0) - A(T))s^{(1)}}{\alpha\left(\sum_{n=1}^{n_T}\left[\Delta_n e^{Qt_n}e^{-rt_n} + C(t_{n-1}, t_n)\right]\right)s^{(1)}}$$

where $\mathbf{C}(s,t) = s(\mathbf{A}(t) - \mathbf{A}(s)) - \mathbf{B}(t) + \mathbf{B}(s)$ and $\mathbf{A}(t) = e^{Qt}(\mathbf{Q} - r\mathbf{I})^{-1}\mathbf{Q}e^{-rt}$ and

$$\mathbf{B}(t) = e^{Qt}(t\mathbf{I} + (\mathbf{Q} - r\mathbf{I})^{-1})(\mathbf{Q} - r\mathbf{I})^{-1}\mathbf{Q}e^{-rt}.$$

For more on the CDS contract, see, e.g., Felsenheimer et al. (2006), Herbertsson (2005; 2007a), or McNeil et al. (2005).

CDO Tranche Spreads and Index CDS Spreads

In this section we present formulas for CDO tranche spreads and index CDS spreads in a model given by Equation (14.1). These expressions are then used in the calibration of the model. Our outline is a shorter version of the one presented in Section 2 in Herbertsson (2007b). We restate it here in order to make our chapter self-contained.

A synthetic CDO is defined for a portfolio consisting of m single-name CDSs on obligors with default times $\tau_1, \tau_2, \ldots, \tau_m$ and recovery rates $\phi_1, \phi_2, \ldots, \phi_m$. It is standard to assume that the nominal values are the same for all obligors. Here we focus on the model Equation (14.1), where all obligors are exchangeable and thus $\phi_1 = \phi_2 = \cdots = \phi_m = \phi$. The credit loss L_t for this portfolio at time t, in percent of the nominal portfolio value at $t = 0$, is given by

$$L_t = \frac{1-\phi}{m}\sum_{i=1}^{m}1_{\{\tau_i \leq t\}} = \frac{1-\phi}{m}\sum_{k=1}^{m}1_{\{T_k \leq t\}} \tag{14.14}$$

where $\{T_k\}$ is the ordering of the default times $\{\tau_i\}$.

Recall that a CDO is specified by the attachment points $0 = k_0 < k_1 < \cdots < k_k = 1$ with corresponding tranches $[k_{k-1}, k_k]$. The financial instrument that constitutes tranche γ with maturity T is a bilateral contract where the protection seller B agrees to pay the protection buyer A, all losses that occur in the interval $[k_{k-1}, k_k]$ derived from L_t up to time T. The payments are made at the corresponding default times if they arrive before T, and at T the contract ends. As compensation for this, A pays B a periodic fee at $0 < t_1 < t_2 < \cdots < t_{n_T} = T$, given by $S_\gamma(T)(\Delta k_\gamma - L_t^{(\gamma)})\Delta_n$, where $\Delta k_\gamma = k_k - k_{k-1}$, $\Delta_n = t_n - t_{n-1}$, and $L_t^{(\gamma)} = (L_t - k_{k-1})1_{\{L_t \in [k_{k-1}, k_k]\}} + \Delta k_\gamma - L_t^{(\gamma)}$. Note that $\Delta k_\gamma - L_t^{(\gamma)}$ is what is left of the tranche γ at time t.

For upper tranches $\gamma > 1$, the tranche spread $S_\gamma(T)$ is determined so that the expected discounted cash flows between A and B are the same at $t = 0$. It is quoted in basis points per annum. Furthermore, for the first tranche, often denoted the *equity* tranche, $S_1(T)$ is set to 500 bp and a so-called *up-front* fee $S_1^{(u)}(T)$ is added to the protection payments so that the expected discounted cash flows between A and B are equal at $t = 0$. It is quoted in percent per annum. Note that the spreads $\{S_\gamma(T)\}$, $S_1^{(u)}(T)$ are independent of the nominal size of the portfolio.

Consider the same synthetic CDO as above. An index CDS with maturity T has almost the same structure as a corresponding CDO tranche, but with two main differences. First, the protection is on *all* credit losses that occur in the CDO portfolio up to time T; so in the protection leg, the tranche loss $L_t^{(\gamma)}$ is replaced by the total loss L_t. Second, in the premium leg, the index spread $S(T)$ is paid on a notional proportional to the number of obligors left in the portfolio at each payment date, that is, $1 - 1/m \sum_{k=1}^{m} 1_{\{T_k \leq t\}}$.

The rest of the contract has the same structure as a CDO tranche. Hence, the index CDS spread $S(T)$ is determined so that the expected value of cash flows between A and B are the same at $t = 0$.

From Proposition 14.1 and Equation (14.14) it is clear that the loss L_t can be represented as a functional of the Markov jump process Y_t, $L_t = L(Y_t)$ [see Lemma 5.2 in Herbertsson (2007b)]. The mapping L goes from $E = \{0, 1, 2, \ldots, m\}$ to all possible loss outcomes determined via Equation (14.4). For example, if $k = \{0, 1, 2, \ldots, m\}$, then $L(k) = (1 - \phi)/m$. In view of these observations, we state the following result, proved in Herbertsson (2007b).

Proposition 14.9: *Consider a synthetic CDO on a portfolio with obligors that satisfy Eqaution (14.1), and assume that the interest rate r is constant. Then, with notation as above,*

$$S_\gamma(T) = \frac{\left(\alpha e^{QT} e^{-rT} + \alpha R(0,T) r\right)\ell^{(\gamma)}}{\displaystyle\sum_{n=1}^{n_T} e^{-rt_n}\left(\Delta k_\gamma - \alpha e^{Qt_n}\ell^{(\gamma)}\right)\Delta_n} \qquad \gamma = 2,\ldots,\kappa \tag{14.15}$$

and

$$S_1^{(u)}(T) = \frac{1}{k_1}\left(\alpha e^{QT} e^{-rT} + \alpha R(0,T) r + 0.05\sum_{n=1}^{n_T}\alpha e^{Qt_n} e^{-rt_n}\Delta_n\right)\ell^{(1)} - $$
$$0.05\sum_{n=1}^{n_T} e^{-rt_n}\Delta_n. \tag{14.16}$$

Furthermore,

$$S_\gamma(T) = \frac{\left(\alpha e^{QT} e^{-rT} + \alpha R(0,T) r\right)\ell}{\displaystyle\sum_{n=1}^{n_T} e^{-rt_n}\left\{1 - \alpha e^{Qt_n}\ell\,\frac{1}{1-\phi}\right\}\Delta_n} \tag{14.17}$$

where

$$\mathbf{R}(0, T) = \int_0^{T}\alpha e^{(Q - r\mathbf{I})t}\, dt = (\alpha e^{QT} e^{-rT} - \mathbf{I})(\mathbf{Q} - r\mathbf{I})^{-1}.$$

Here $\ell^{(\gamma)}$ is a column vector in $\Re^{m+1}$, defined by

$$\ell_k^{(\gamma)} = \begin{cases} 0 & \text{if } k < n_l(k_{\gamma-1}) \\ k(1-\phi)/m - k_{\gamma-1} & \text{if } n_l(k_{\gamma-1}) \le k \le n_u(k_\gamma) \\ \Delta k_\gamma & \text{if } k > n_u(k_\gamma) \end{cases} \tag{14.18}$$

where $n_l(x) = \lceil xm/(1 - \phi)\rceil$ and $n_u(x) = \lfloor xm/(1 - \phi)\rfloor$. Finally, ℓ is a column vector in $\Re^{m+1}$, defined by $\ell_k = k(1 - \phi)/m$.

The Calibration

In this subsection we show how to calibrate the model Equation (14.1) against the credit instruments described in the previous subsections. Let $\mathbf{a} = (a, b_1, b_2, \cdots, b_{m-1})$ denote the m parameters in Equation (14.1). Furthermore, let $\{C_j(T; \mathbf{a})\}$ be the $\kappa + 2$ model spreads for the instruments used in the calibration. These are the average CDS spread $R(T; \mathbf{a})$, the index CDS spread $S(T; \mathbf{a})$, and the κ different CDO tranche spreads $\{S_\gamma(T; \mathbf{a})\}$, $S_1^{(u)}(T; \mathbf{a})$. We let $\{C_{j,M}(T)\}$ denote the corresponding market spreads. In $C_j(T; \mathbf{a})$ we have emphasized that the model spreads are functions of $\mathbf{a} = (a, b_1, b_2, \cdots, b_{m-1})$ but suppressed the dependence of interest rate, payment frequency, etc. The vector $\mathbf{a}$ is then obtained as

$$a = \underset{\hat{a}}{\arg\min} \sum_{j=1}^{\kappa+2} \left[C_j\left(T; \hat{\mathbf{a}}\right) - C_{j,M}\left(T\right) \right]^2 \qquad (14.19)$$

with the constraint that all elements in $\mathbf{a}$ are nonnegative. For a fixed maturity T, we use $\kappa = 5$ tranche spreads. This gives us seven market observations, while the model can contain up to $m = 125$ parameters. In order to reduce the number of unknown parameters to as many as the market observations, we make following assumption on the parameters b_k for $1 \leq k \leq m - 1$;

$$b_k = \begin{cases} b^{(1)} & \text{if } 1 \leq k < \mu_1 \\ b^{(2)} & \text{if } \mu_1 \leq k < \mu_2 \\ \vdots \\ b^{(6)} & \text{if } \mu_5 \leq k < \mu_6 \end{cases} \qquad (14.20)$$

where $1, \mu_1, \mu_2, \ldots, \mu_6$ is an partition of $\{1, 2, \ldots, m\}$. This means that all jumps in the intensity at the defaults $1, 2, \ldots, \mu_1 - 1$ are same and given by $b^{(1)}$, all jumps in the intensity at the defaults $\mu_1, \ldots, \mu_2 - 1$ are same and given by $b^{(2)}$, and so on. Hence, in Equation (14.19) we now minimize over the unknown vector $\mathbf{a} = (a, b^{(1)}, \cdots, b^{(6)})$.

NUMERICAL STUDIES

In this section we will, in a homogeneous CDO portfolio, study several quantities of importance in active credit portfolio management. In the next section we calibrate the portfolio against market data on CDO tranches, index CDSs, and average single-name CDS spreads. We then investigate the implied expected ordered default times, the implied default correlation, and finally various kinds of implied multivariate default and survival distributions, for both ordered as well as unordered default times.

Calibration of a Homogeneous Portfolio

In this section we calibrate our homogenous model against data on the iTraxx Europe series collected from Reuters for August 4th, 2004 (see Table 14.1) and November 28, 2006 (see Table 14.2). For each date, the data contains five different CDO tranche spreads with tranches [0, 3], [3, 6], [6, 9], [9, 12], and [12, 22], the index CDS spreads, and the average CDS spread. For the 2004–08–04 portfolio, we set the average CDS spread equal to (i.e., approximated by) the index CDS spread, as in Frey and Backhaus (2006) and Hull and White (2004). All maturities are for five years, and these instruments are used in the calibration described in the section The Calibration. The interest rate is set to 3 percent, the payment frequency is quarterly and the recovery rate is 40 percent.

We choose the partition $\mu_1, \mu_2, \ldots, \mu_6$ so that it roughly coincides with the number of defaults needed to reach the upper attachment point for each tranche (see Table 14.3). The sum of the absolute calibration error is 0.2562 bp for the 2004–08–04 case and 1.59 bp for the 2006–11–28 set;

T A B L E   14.1

iTraxx Europe August 4, 2004*

	Market	Model	Error (bp)	Error (%)
[0, 3]	27.6	27.6	0.0004514	1.635e–005
[3, 6]	168	168	0.003321	0.001977
[6, 9]	70	70.07	0.06661	0.09515
[9, 12]	43	42.91	0.09382	0.2182
[12, 22]	20	20.03	0.03304	0.1652
Index	42	41.99	0.01487	0.03542
Average CDS	42	41.96	0.04411	0.105
Sum abs.cal.err			0.2562 bp	

* The market and model spreads and the corresponding absolute errors are in both basis points (bp) and percent of the market spread. The [0, 3] spread is quoted in percent. All maturities are for five years.

T A B L E   14.2

iTraxx Europe Series 6, November 28, 2006*

	Market	Model	Error (bp)	Error (%)
[0, 3]	14.5	14.5	0.007266	0.0005011
[3, 6]	62.5	62.41	0.08523	0.1364
[6, 9]	18	18.1	0.09727	0.5404
[9, 12]	7	6.881	0.1193	1.704
[12, 22]	3	3.398	0.3979	13.26
Index	26	26.13	0.1299	0.4997
Average CDS	26.87	26.12	0.7535	2.804
Sum abs.cal.err			1.59 bp	

* The market and model spreads and the corresponding absolute errors are in both basis points (bp) and percent of the market spread. The [0, 3] spread is quoted in percent. All maturities are for five years.

T A B L E   14.3

The integers 1, μ_1, μ_2, ..., μ_6 are partitions of $\{1, 2, ..., m\}$ used in the models that generate the spreads in Tables 14.1 and 14.2

Partition	μ_1	μ_2	μ_3	μ_4	μ_5	μ_6
	7	13	19	25	46	125

so in both portfolios we can therefore speak of a perfect fit for $T = 5$ years (see Tables 14.1 and 14.2).

The numerical values of the calibrated parameters **a**, obtained via Equation (14.19), show that in both portfolios the parameters a, $b^{(1)}$, and $b^{(2)}$ are approximately in the same order while $b^{(3)}$ is around two times bigger for the 2004–08–04 case compared with the 2006–11–28 collection. However, the parameters $b^{(4)}$, $b^{(5)}$, and $b^{(6)}$ differ substantially between the two portfolios, and given the big difference among the corresponding market spreads, this may not come as a surprise. In the 2004–08–04 case, the variables $b^{(4)}$, $b^{(5)}$, and $b^{(6)}$ vary rather smoothly, while for the 2006–11–28 collection, the jump parameters virtually explode after default number 25 (see Table 14.4). This drastic increase of the jumps after the 26th default will have a big impact on the different distributions and other quantities, as will be seen in the next subsections.

T A B L E   14.4

The calibrated parameters that give the model spreads in
Tables 14.1 and 14.2

	a	$b^{(1)}$	$b^{(2)}$	$b^{(3)}$	$b^{(4)}$	$b^{(5)}$	$b^{(6)}$	
04/08/04	33.0	16.4	84.5	145	86.4	124	514	$\times 10^{-4}$
06/11/28	24.9	13.9	73.6	62.4	0.823	2162	4952	$\times 10^{-4}$

We want to remind the reader that the intensities are implied, or
so-called risk-neutral intensities, and measured under a risk-neutral martingale measure, which exists if we rule out arbitrage opportunities in
our model. Here *implied* is referring to the fact that the quantities are
retrieved from market data via a model. Recall that risk-neutral default
intensities are substantially larger than the real, socalled actuarial, default
probabilities.

The Implied Expected Ordered
Default Times

Given the implied distributions, we can compute important quantities for
a credit manager. In this subsection we study the expected ordered default
times $E(T_k)$ and their standard deviations. Further, the expected default
times $E(\tau_i)$, which by exchangeability are the same for all obligors,
are also computed. The formulas for all these quantities are given in an
earlier section.

In Figure 14.1, we note that the implied expected ordered default
times take values roughly between 3.5 years and 14 years. A striking feature
in the November 28, 2006 portfolio is that after the 25th default, the $E(T_k)$
cluster around 14 years. This is a consequence of the explosion in the jump
intensities for $k \geq 25$. Under the risk-neutral measure, implied by the market
data in Table 14.2, this clustering of $E(T_k)$ implies that we expect extreme
losses in year 13 and 14 for the November 28, 2006 portfolio. This is confirmed by computation of the loss probability [see Herbertsson (2007b)],
which renders $P(L_{15} > 11.52\%) = P(Y_{15} > 24) = 66.62\%$, where a loss of
11.52 percent corresponds to 24 defaults when the recovery is 40 percent.
As a matter of fact, $P(L_{15} = 60\%) = P(Y_{15} = 125) = 64.256\%$. Again, recall
that all computations are under the risk-neutral measure and should not be

F I G U R E   14.1

Implied expected ordered default times $E(T_k)$ for the August 2004 and November 2006 portfolios, where $k = 1, 2, \ldots, 125$ (left) and $k = 26, \ldots, 125$ (right, for November 28, 2006)

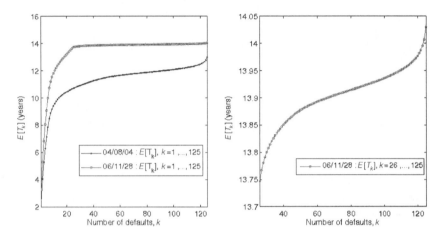

confused with real default probabilities and their expectations. These are likely to be substantially smaller for the loss probability and much bigger for the expected ordered default times. Since $\{T_k\}$ are strictly increasing, so are the $E(T_k)$.

It is interesting to note that the curves for the standard deviation of the T_k roughly have the same shape as for $E(T_k)$. Finally, the implied expected default times, which by the exchangeability are the same for all obligors i, have the values $E(\tau_i) = 11.21$, $StD(\tau_i) = 3.927$ for the August 4, 2004 portfolio and $E(\tau_i) = 13.38$, $StD(\tau_i) = 4.890$ for the November 28, 2006 portfolio (Figure 14.2).

The Implied Default Correlation

It may be of interest for a credit manager to have a quantitative grasp of the implied pairwise default correlation $\rho(t) = \text{Corr}(1_{\{\tau_i \leq t\}}, 1_{\{\tau_j \leq t\}})$ for two distinct obligors i, j, as function of time t. In this subsection, we study $\rho(t)$ in the calibrated portfolios in Table 14.1 and Table 14.2.

In the November 18, 2006 portfolio, we see that $\rho(t)$ is less than 2% when $t \leq 4$, but then starts to increase rapidly, first to 4% for $t = 4.5$, then to 77% for $t = 10$ and reaches 88 percent at $t = 15$ (Figure 14.3). After

Implied standard deviations StD(T_k) for the ordered default
times, where k = 1, 2, . . ., 125 (left) and k = 26, . . ., 125 (right)
for the November 28, 2006 portfolio

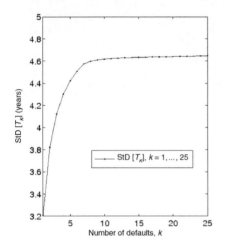
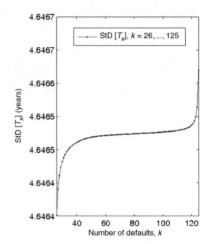

this drastic development, the implied default correlation flattens out and
converges to 91 percent as time increases against 30 years. The explosive
increase of $\rho(t)$ from 2 to 88 percent in the time interval [4.5, 15] is due
to the default contagion and is also consistent with the clustering of $\{T_k\}$
around $t = 14$. We also note that the implied default correlation for the
2004–08–04 portfolio follows an almost identical trend up to 8 years. This
is consistent with the jump-to-default parameters for the first 13 defaults,
which are in the same order as in November 28, 2006 case (see also Figure
14.1). Even though there is a big difference between the corresponding
contagious parameters for $k > 13$ in the two portfolios, the implied default
correlations never differ more than 10 to 12 percent during the first 30
years. Furthermore, the August 4, 2004 portfolio seems to have a global
maximum of 80.92 percent around 19 years, as seen in Figure 14.4.

We observe that implied default correlations around 90 percent,
which occur already for $t = 16$, are quite big. In Herbertsson (2007a) the
author studied implied default correlations in an inhomogeneous portfolio
consisting of 10 obligors and with very high five-year CDS-spread correlations. This gave rise to implied default correlations around 70 percent,
but first when $t \geq 95$ years. The corresponding correlation when $t = 15$
was around 12 percent [see Herbertsson (2007a)].

F I G U R E   14.3

Implied default correlation $\rho(t)=$ Corr $(1_{\{r_1 \le t\}}, 1_{\{r_1 \le t\}})$, $i \ne j$, as a function of time for the August 4, 2004 and the November 28, 2006 portfolios

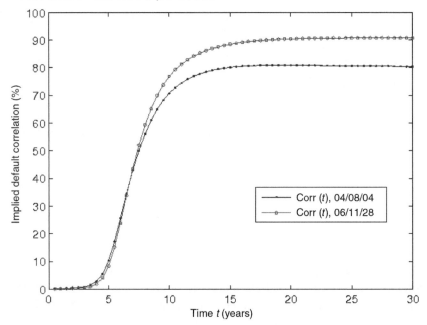

The Implied Multivariate Default and Survival Distributions

In this subsection we study the implied bivariate default and survival distributions, the implied survival and default distributions for a fixed t, and the joint implied survival and default distributions for the ordered default times. All computations are done with parameters obtained from the calibrated portfolio in Table 14.2. From Figures 14.5 and 14.6 we note some interesting features in the November 28, 2006 portfolio.

For example, the bivariate default distribution $P(\tau_1 \le t_1, \tau_2 \le t_2)$ is approximately constant on the lines (t_1, t_2), where t_1 is fixed and $6 < t_1 < t_2$. By exchangeability, this is also the case for the lines (t_1, t_2), where t_2 is fixed and $6 < t_2 < t_1$. Intuitively, this observation implies that the default events $\{\tau_i \le t_1\}$ and are $\{\tau_j \le t_2\}$ approximately independent for $(t_1, t_2) \in [6, \infty) \times [6, \infty)$. This property is not present in the region $(t_1, t_2) \in [0,6) \times [0, 6)$ (see Figure 14.7). It does not hold for the bivariate survival distribution $P(\tau_1 > t_1, \tau_2 > t_2)$ either.

F I G U R E   14.4

Implied default correlation $\rho(t) = \text{Corr}\,(1_{\{r_1 \leq t\}}, 1_{\{r_1 \leq t\}})$, $i \neq j$, as a function of time t, where $15 \leq t \leq 30$, for the August 4, 2004 portfolio

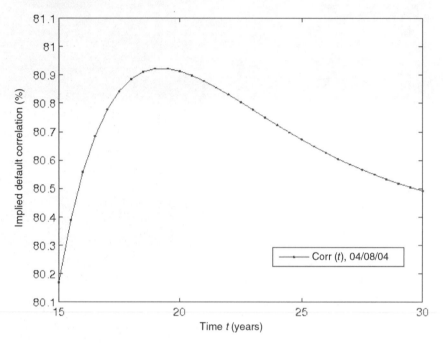

F I G U R E   14.5

Implied bivariate default (left) and survival (right) distribution for two obligors in the November 28, 2006 portfolio

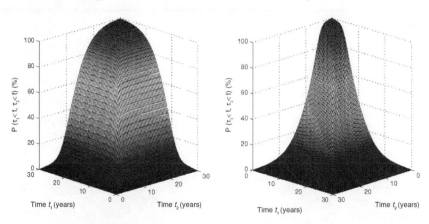

F I G U R E   14.6

Isolines for the implied bivariate default (left) and survival (right) distribution for two obligors in the November 28, 2006 portfolio

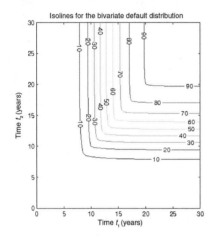
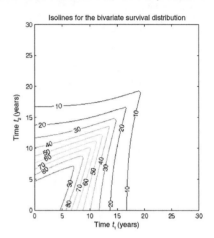

F I G U R E   14.7

Isolines for the implied bivariate default distributions, on the square [3.5, 5.5] × [3.5, 5.5], for two obligors in the November 28, 2006 portfolio

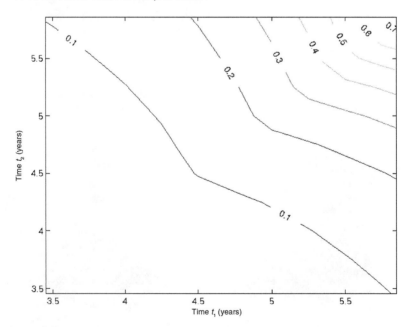

Figure 14.8 shows that $P(\tau_1 \leq t, \ldots, \tau_q \leq t)$ seems to be independent of q. Similarly, $P(T_k > t)$ appear to be unchanged for $k > 25$ (Figure 14.9). However, a closer study reveals that the computed survival distributions $P(T_k > t)$ are strictly increasing with k, as they should be, although this is on very narrow intervals (see Figure 14.10).

F I G U R E   14.8

Implied survival distributions $P(\tau_1 > t, \ldots, \tau_q > t)$ (left) and Default distribution $P(\tau_1 \leq t, \ldots, \tau_q \leq t)$ (right), as functions of q and time t, for the November 28, 2006 portfolio

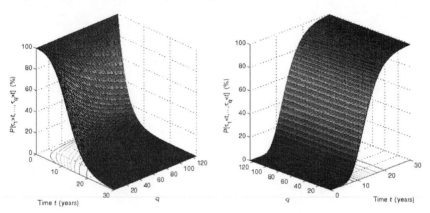

F I G U R E   14.9

Implied ordered survival distributions $P(T_k > t)$ (left) and its isolines (right) as functions of k and time t, for the November 28, 2006 portfolio

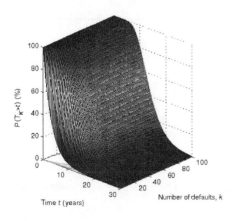
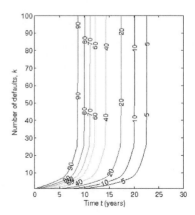

F I G U R E   14.10

Implied ordered survival distributions $P(T_k > t)$ for fixed t as a function of k, $k = 26, \ldots, 125$, for the November 28, 2006 portfolio

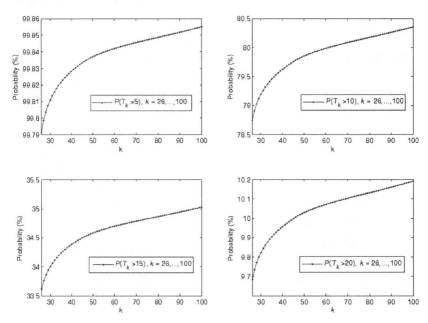

Table 14.5 shows that the effect of the default contagion is clear. For example, in the November 28, 2006 portfolio, $P(T_1 \leq 1, \ldots, T_{25} \leq 25) = 6\%$, while $P(T_1 \leq 14, \ldots, T_{25} \leq 38) = 95\%$; and $P(T_{101} \leq 1, \ldots, T_{125} \leq 25) = 0\%$, while $P(T_{101} \leq 14, \ldots, T_{125} \leq 38) = 57\%$. Furthermore, we also see some big differences between the two portfolios. For example, $P(T_1 > 1, \ldots, T_{25} > 25)$ and $P(T_{26} \leq 13.5, \ldots, T_{125} \leq 38.5)$ are 0.25, 2.3 percent and 80, 54 percent, respectively, for the 2004–08–04 and 2006–11–28 portfolio.

CONCLUSION

In this chapter we considered the intensity-based default contagion model (14.1), where the default intensity of one obligor is allowed to change when other firms default. The portfolio was homogenous so that all obligors were exchangeable. This implied that the individual intensives were expressed using the ordered default times. The model was translated into

T A B L E   14.5

Multivariate default (D) and survival (S) probabilities $P(T_{k1} \leq n \cdot t_1, \ldots, T_k \leq n \cdot t_q)$ and $P(T_{k1} > n \cdot t_1, \ldots, T_{k_q} > n \cdot t_q)$ (in percent), for the August 4, 2004 and November 28, 2006 portfolios, where $n = 0.25, 0.5, 0.75, 1$ for different sequences $k_1 < \cdots < k_q$ and $t_1 < \cdots < t_q$ with $k_j - k_{j-1}$ and $t_j - t_{j-1}$ constant for $j = 2, 3, \ldots, q$

$t_1, t_2, \ldots, t_q$	$k_1, k_2, \ldots, k_q$		$n = 0.25$	$n = 0.5$	$n = 0.75$	$n = 1$
1, 2, …, 25	1, 2, …, 25	D, 04	0.021	1	5.1	12
1, 2, …, 25	1, 2, …, 25	D, 06	0.0048	0.35	2.2	6
1, 2, …, 25	1, 2, …, 25	S, 04	84	25	2.9	0.25
1, 2, …, 25	1, 2, …, 25	S, 06	91	51	13	2.3
1, 2, …, 25	101, …, 125	D, 04	0	0	0	0
1, 2, …, 25	101, …, 125	D, 06	0	0	0	0
1, 2, …, 25	101, …, 125	S, 04	100	49	7.1	0.65
1, 2, …, 25	101, …, 125	S, 06	99	58	15	2.5
14, 15, …, 38	1, 2, …, 25	D, 04	11	68	93	99
14, 15, …, 38	1, 2, …, 25	D, 06	4.2	46	81	95
14, 15, …, 38	1, 2, …, 25	S, 04	22	1.7	0.052	0.0012
14, 15, …, 38	1, 2, …, 25	S, 06	33	6.7	0.62	0.039
14, 15, …, 38	101, …, 125	D, 04	0.00046	4.1	37	74
14, 15, …, 38	101, …, 125	D, 06	0.0022	2.6	24	57
14, 15, …, 38	101, …, 125	S, 04	84	6.4	0.16	0.0032
14, 15, …, 38	101, …, 125	S, 06	85	14	0.89	0.048
13.5, 13.75, …, 38.5	26, …, 125	D, 04	0.055	11	49	80
13.5, 13.75, …, 38.5	26, …, 125	D, 06	0.0027	2.4	22	54
13.5, 13.75, …, 38.5	26, …, 125	S, 04	81	5.8	0.14	0.0028
13.5, 13.75, …, 38.5	26, …, 125	S, 06	85	13	0.84	0.045

a Markov jump process. This made it possible to derive computationally tractable closed-form expressions for many quantities of importance in credit portfolio management.

In the above framework we calibrated two CDO portfolios containing 125 obligors, against market data for CDO tranches, index CDS, and average CDS spread. In both cases we obtained perfect fits. In the calibrated portfolios, we then studied the implied expected ordered default times, the implied default correlations, and the implied joint default and survival distributions for both ordered and unordered default times. Some of the results were surprising; others, not so. For example, in the November 28, 2006 portfolio, the bivariate default distributions revealed that the corresponding marginal events were approximately independent after 10 years.

The calibrated default intensities for the November 28, 2006 portfolio exploded after 25 defaults, which gave rise to heavy default clustering after 14 years (under the risk-neutral measure). This had profound effects on several of the studied quantities.

ACKNOWLEDGMENTS

Research supported by Jan Wallanders and Tom Hedelius Foundation. The author would like to thank Holger Rootzén, Catalin Starica, and Florin Maican for useful comments.

REFERENCES

Avellaneda, M. and Wu, L. (2001) Credit Contagion: Pricing Cross Country Risk in the Brady Debt Markets. *International Journal of Theoretical and Applied Finance,* 4(6): 921–939.

Bielecki, T.R., Crépey, S., Jeanblanc, M., and Rutkowski, M. (2005) Valuation of Basket Credit Derivatives in the Credit Migrations Environment. Working paper, Illinois Institute of Technology, Chicago, IL.

Bielecki, T.R. and Rutkowski, M. (2001) *Credit Risk: Modeling, Valuation and Hedging.* Berlin, Germany: Springer.

Bielecki, T.R., Vidozzi, A., and Vidozzi, L. (2006) An Efficent Approach to Valuation of Credit Basket Products and Rating Triggered Step-Up Bonds. Working paper, Illinois Institute of Technology, Chicago, IL.

Collin-Dufresne, P., Goldstein, R.S., and Hugonnier, J. (2004) A General Formula for Valuing Defaultable Securities. *Econometrica,* 72(5): 1377–1407.

Davis, M. and Esparragoza, J.C. (2007) Large Portfolio Credit Risk Modelling. *International Journal of Theoretical and applied Finance,* 10(4): 653–678

Davis, M. and Lo, V. (2001a) Infectious Defaults. *Quantitative Finance,* 1(4): 382–387.

Davis, M. and Lo, V. (2001b) Modelling Default Correlation in Bond
   Portfolios. In C. Alexander (ed), *Mastering Risk Volume 2:*
   Applications. Financial Times, Upper Saddle River, NJ: Prentice
   Hall, pp.141–151

Felsenheimer, J., Gisdakis, P. and Zaiser, M. (2006) *Active Credit*
   Portfolio Management. A practical Guide to Credit Risk
   Management. Weinheim, Whiley-VCH Verlag.

Frey, R. and Backhaus, J. (2004) Portfolio Credit Risk Models with
   Interacting Default Intensities: A Markovian Approach. Working
   paper, Department of Mathematics. University of Leipzig,
   Germany.

Frey, R. and Backhaus, J. (2006) Credit Derivatives in Models with
   Interacting Default Intensities: A Markovian Approach, Working
   paper, Department of Mathematics. University of Leipzig,
   Germany.

Giesecke, K. and Weber, S. (2004) Cyclical Correlation, Credit
   Contagion and Portfolio Losses, *Journal of Banking and Finance*,
   28(12): 3009–3036.

Giesecke, K. and Weber, S. (2006) Credit Contagion and Aggregate
   Losses, *Journal of Economic Dynamics and Control*, 30(5):
   741–767.

Herbertsson, A. (2005) Dynamic Dependence Modelling in Credit Risk.
   Licentiate Thesis, Department of Mathematics, Chalmers
   University of Technology, Göteborg.

Herbertsson, A. (2007a) Modelling Default Contagion Using Multivariate
   Phase-Type Distributions. Working paper, Department of Economics,
   Göteborg University.

Herbertsson, A. (2007b) Pricing synthetic CDO Tranches in a Model
   with Default Contagion Using the Matrix-Analytic Approach.
   Working paper, Department of Economics, Göteborg University.

Herbertsson, A. and Rootzén, H. (2006) Pricing kth-to-Default Swaps
   under Default Contagion: The Matrix-Analytic Approach. Working
   paper, Department of Economics, Göteborg University.

Hull, J. and White, A. (2004) Valuation of a CDO and an n-th to Default CDS without Monte Carlo Simulation. *Journal of Derivatives,* 12(2): 8–23.

Jarrow, R.A. and Yu, F. (2001) Counterparty Risk and the Pricing of Defaultable Securities. *Journal of Finance,* 56(5): 1765–1800.

Kraft, H. and Steffensen, M. (2007) Bankruptcy, Counterparty Risk and Contagion. *Review of Finance* 11(2):209–252.

Lando, D. (2004) *Credit Risk Modeling: Theory and Applications.* Princeton, NJ: Princeton University Press.

McNeil, A.J., Frey, R., and Embrechts, P. (2005) *Quantitative Risk Management.* Oxford, UK: Princeton University Press.

Moeler, C. and Loan, C.V. (1978) Nineteen Dubioius Ways to Compute the Exponential of a Matrix. *SIAM Review,* 20(4): 801–836.

Moeler, C. and Loan, C.V. (2003) Nineteen Dubioius Ways to Compute the Exponential of a Matrix, Twenty-Five Years Later. *SIAM Review,* 45(1): 3–49.

Rogge, E. and Schönbucher, P.J. (2003) Modelling Dynamic Portfolio Credit Risk. Working paper, Department of Mathematics, ETH, Zürich, Switzerland.

Schönbucher, P.J. and Schubert, D. (2001) Copula-Dependent Default Risk in Intensity Models. Working paper, Department of Statistics, Bonn University, Germany.

Yu, F. (2007) Correlated Defaults in Intensity-Based Models. *Mathematical Finance,* 17(2): 155–173.

PART FOUR

Asset Allocation and Credit Derivatives

CHAPTER 15

An Asset Allocation Problem with Credit Derivatives

Francesco Menoncin

ABSTRACT

We study the optimal portfolio for an investor maximizing the expected utility of his wealth at the time when a credit event occurs. The financial market contains (1) a riskless asset, (2) a stock, (3) a bond as a derivative on the stochastic interest rate, and (4) a credit derivative written on the stochastic default rate. With a default rate instantaneously uncorrelated with the interest rate but not independent of it, we demonstrate that the wealth invested in the credit derivative must be taken from the ordinary bond and the riskless asset proportionally to the duration of the bond and the credit derivative.

INTRODUCTION

We examine the asset allocation problem for an investor wanting to maximize the expected utility of his wealth when a credit event occurs. This problem is similar to that of an agent who maximizes the expected value of his final wealth during his lifetime. Such a problem can be traced back to the case of an infinitely living agent whose subjective discount factor is increased by his force of mortality [see Richard (1975) for the case of a deterministic force of mortality and Menoncin (2008) for a model with a stochastic force of mortality].

In order to find a closed-form solution for an optimal portfolio, the financial market is usually assumed to be complete (i.e., all contingent claims can be replicated with existing assets). When there is a stochastic default rate present, the completeness hypothesis becomes quite strong. In fact, in this case the financial market would be complete if it was possible to find a linear combination (portfolio) of financial assets able to replicate the stochastic behavior of the default rate. In this framework, a credit derivative whose price strongly depends on the underlying asset default rate helps to complete the financial market since it introduces the previously lacked link between financial and credit risk.

Some closed-form solutions for problems where the financial horizon is not stochastic have been found in the literature. In particular, we refer to the studies of Kim and Omberg (1996), Wachter (2002), Deelstra et al. (2000), Boulier et al. (2001), Zariphopoulou (2001), Menoncin (2002), and Chacko and Viceira (2005). In all these studies the market structure is as follows: (1) There is a stochastic state variable (the riskless interest rate or the risk premium) following the Vasičakcek (1977) model or the Cox et al. (1985) model, (2) there is a risky asset, and (3) a bond may exist. Numerous studies deal with a complete financial market (Wachter, 2002; Deelstra et al., 2000; and Boulier et al., 2001), while others address an incomplete market (Kim and Omberg, 1996; Menoncin 2002; Chacko and Viceira, 2005).

We investigate a perfectly competitive, arbitrage-free, and frictionless financial market containing two state variables and four assets. The state variables are (1) the stochastic riskless interest rate and (2) the stochastic default rate, while the assets are (1) a riskless asset that pays the riskless interest rate, (2) a stock, (3) a zero-coupon bond computed as a derivative on the riskless interest rate, and (4) a credit derivative that takes the form of a zero-coupon bond paying one monetary unit at the time a credit event occurs.

Our result shows that for any investor's risk aversion, the amount of money that must optimally be invested in the credit derivative is taken from both the bond and the riskless asset. If we call $\nabla_{L,r}$ and $\nabla_{B,r}$ the semi-elasticities (opposite of the duration) of the credit derivative and the bond respectively, then the optimal amount of wealth to be invested in the credit derivative must be taken from the wealth invested in the bond by the ratio $\nabla_{L,r}/\nabla_{B,r}$ and from the wealth invested in the riskless asset by the ratio $1 - \nabla_{L,r}/\nabla_{B,r}$.

A straight parallel between the credit derivatives and the derivatives on investors' lifetime can be easily done by comparing the results in this study with the results demonstrated in Menoncin (2008), where the role of a longevity bond in optimal portfolios is investigated. In fact, the actuarial and the financial literature often use the same stochastic processes for modeling the mortality rate and the default rate, respectively. Dahl (2004), for instance, shows how to find the price of any insurance contract when the force of mortality is stochastic and follows a Cox et al. (1985) process. The same process is used by Duffie and Singleton (2003) and Schmid (2004) for modeling the default rate when pricing assets subject to credit risk. In this chapter we use the dynamic programming technique. Since the financial market is complete, the so-called martingale approach [see Cox and Huang (1989; 1991)] leads to the very same result.

The rest of the chapter is structured as follows. We show the model and, in particular, we set the stochastic differential equations for the state variables (the spot riskless interest rate and the default rate) and the financial assets (the riskless asset, a zero-coupon bond, a stock, and a credit derivative). At the end of the next section we present the optimization problem for a representative investor. We then show the main result: the optimal portfolio computed for any (strictly increasing and concave) utility function. Next, the case for a hyperbolic absolute risk averse investor is investigated with all main demonstrations part of the Appendix.

THE MODEL
A General Framework

We assume that the entire financial market can be summarized by two vector stochastic processes describing the state variables and the asset prices. The vector $z \in \mathbb{R}^s$ contains all the relevant state variables (in our case they are the interest rate and the default rate), and it solves the differential equation

$$dz(t) = \underset{s \times 1}{\mu_z(t,z)}\, dt + \underset{s \times k}{\Omega'(t,z)} \underset{k \times 1}{dW} \qquad z(t_0) = z_0 \qquad (15.1)$$

where the prime denotes transposition and dW is a k-vector of independent Wiener processes.

A vector $A \in \mathbb{R}^n$ contains all the risky asset prices and solves the differential equation

$$\underset{n \times n}{I_A^{-1}} dA(t) = \underset{n \times 1}{\mu(t, z, A)} dt + \underset{n \times k}{\Sigma'(t, z, A)} \underset{k \times 1}{dW} \qquad A(t_0) = A_0 \quad (15.2)$$

where I_A is a diagonal matrix containing the elements of vector A.

Finally, on the financial market, there exists a riskless asset whose price $G(t)$ solves the deterministic differential equation $dG(t)/G(t) = r(t, z)dt$, $G(t_0) = 1$, where $r(t)$ is the spot instantaneously riskless interest rate, which may depend on other state variables (in many models the riskless interest rate is a state variable itself and does not depend on any other variable).

This financial market is complete if there exists one and only one vector ξ such that $\Sigma' \xi = \mu - r\mathbf{1}$, where $\mathbf{1}$ is a vector containing only 1s. Thus, according to Girsanov's theorem, if ξ satisfies the Novikov condition, then there exists a (martingale equivalent or riskless) probability measure (Q) such that

$$dW^Q = \xi \, dt + dW \qquad (15.3)$$

and under which the expected returns on all the risky assets on the financial market equate the riskless interest rate: $E_t^Q[I_A^{-1} dA] = r(t) \, dt$.

In the following sections we will present the two state variables ($s = 2$) interest rate and default rate, and the three risky assets ($n = 3$) a bond, a credit derivative, and a stock.

Interest Rate and Bond

The instantaneously riskless spot rate $r(t)$ is assumed to be stochastic. It follows the (one factor) stochastic differential equation

$$dr(t) = \mu_r(r, t) dt + \sigma_r(r, t) \, dw_r \qquad r(t_0) = r_0 \qquad (15.4)$$

Without any loss of generality we can assume σ_r to take only strictly positive values. The interest rates after Vasiček (1977) and Cox et al. (1985) are particular cases of Equation (15.4).[1]

---

[1] Even if we do not specify any particular functional form for μ_r and, σ_r, the usual conditions on drift and diffusion terms for the existence of a strong solution of the stochastic differential equation are assumed to hold.

Given this interest rate, the value of a riskless asset (G) on the financial market follows the differential equation

$$dG(t) = G(t)r(t)dt, \qquad G(0) = 1. \tag{15.5}$$

Furthermore, we assume that on the financial market there is a zero-coupon bond that pays one monetary unit at the expiration date (T). If the market is arbitrage free, then the value of this zero-coupon bond $B(t, T)$ is given by the expected present value of its future cash flow under the so-called martingale equivalent measure (Q). Thus, we can write

$$B(t,T) = \mathsf{E}_t^Q \left[e^{-\int_t^T r(s)ds} \right],$$

where E is the expected value operator and the subscript indicates that it is computed under the σ-algebra $\mathbf{F}_t$ generated by the entire financial market. The dynamics of $B(t, T)$ is

$$dB(t, T) = B(t, T)r(t)dt + \frac{\partial B(t, T)}{\partial r(t)} \sigma_r dW_r^Q,$$

and so, if we call ξ_r the market price for the interest rate risk, then we can finally write[2]

$$\frac{dB(t, T)}{B(t, T)} = \left(r(t) + \nabla_r^B \sigma_r \xi_r \right) dt + \nabla_r^B \sigma_r dW_r, \tag{15.6}$$

where

$$\nabla_{B,r} \equiv \frac{\partial B(t, T)}{\partial r(t)} \frac{1}{B(t, T)},$$

is the semi-elasticity of the bond price with respect to the interest rate and coincides with the opposite of the bond duration.

---

[2] We recall that, under the conditions of the Girsanov theorem, the process $dW_r^Q = \xi_r\, dt + dW_r$ is a Wiener process.

It is worth noting that if we want the bond to yield a higher return than the riskless asset, then the market price of risk must have the same sign as the product $\nabla_{B,r}\,\sigma_r$. Since we have already assumed $\sigma_r > 0$ and we know, by construction, that $\nabla_{B,r}$ is negative (since the bond negatively reacts to the shocks on the interest rate), then it must be true that $\xi_r < 0$.

Default Rate and Credit Derivative

Here, we call τ the time at which the credit event occurs. Thus, τ is a stochastic variable whose density function we call $\pi(t)$. Accordingly, we can define

$$\left(_t p_{t_0}\right) = 1 - \int_{t_0}^{t} \pi(s)\ ds \tag{15.7}$$

the probability that the credit event hasn't occurred yet in t given that it hadn't occurred yet in $t_0 \le t$ (i.e., the probability that the credit event does not happen between t_0 and t). We will refer to $(_t p_{t_0})$ as the *survival probability*.

If we differentiate Equation (15.7) with respect to time, we obtain that the relative change in the probability $(_t p_{t_0})$ is given by

$$\frac{d\left(_t p_{t_0}\right)}{\left(_t p_{t_0}\right)} = -\frac{\pi(t)}{\left(_t p_{t_0}\right)}\ dt \tag{15.8}$$

The ratio between $\pi(t)$ and $(_t p_{t_0})$ is called the *hazard rate*. In the actuarial literature, it is also called *force of mortality*. When the credit risk is studied, this ratio is called *default rate* and measures how many assets from t to $t + dt$ are subjected to a credit event relatively to the existing assets in t. We define the default rate as

$$\lambda(t) \equiv \frac{\pi(t)}{\left(_t p_{t_0}\right)}.$$

Accordingly, the probability $(_t p_{t_0})$ can be also computed by solving the ordinary differential Equation (15.8) with the natural boundary condition $(_{t_0} p_{t_0}) = 1$, i.e., the probability that a credit event does not occur in t_0 given that it has not happened until t_0 is actually 1. The solution of Equation (15.8) is

$$\left({}_{t}P_{t_0} \right) = e^{-\int_{t_0}^{t} \lambda(s)\,ds}. \tag{15.9}$$

We then examine the likely case when the default rate is stochastic. What we have presented so far remains unchanged except for Equation (15.9), which remains valid in expected value terms

$$\left({}_{t}P_{t_0} \right) = \mathrm{E}_{t_0}\left[e^{-\int_{t_0}^{t} \lambda(s,z)\,ds} \right]$$

where the default rate λ is now assumed to follow the stochastic process

$$d\lambda(t) = \mu_\lambda(t, r, \lambda)\,dt + \sigma_\lambda(t, r, \lambda)\,dW_\lambda \tag{15.10}$$

with dW_λ independent of dW_r. Accordingly, we assume that r and λ are instantaneously uncorrelated but not independent. In fact, μ_λ and σ_λ depend on r. In particular, we can assume that μ_λ is a positive function of r (when the interest rate becomes higher, the survival probability should decrease).

The value in t_0 of a zero-coupon bond paying one monetary unit in t and subjected to a credit risk is given by

$$B_d(t_0, t) = \mathrm{E}_{t_0}^{Q}\left[1 \cdot e^{-\int_{t_0}^{t} r(s)\,ds} \cdot e^{-\int_{t_0}^{t} \lambda(s)\,ds} \right]$$

Now, if the riskless interest rate $r(t)$ and the default rate $\lambda(t)$ are independent (which is very unlikely), then this equation can be simplified as

$$B_d(t_0, t) = \mathrm{E}_{t_0}^{Q}\left[e^{-\int_{t_0}^{t} r(s)\,ds} \right] \mathrm{E}_{t_0}^{Q}\left[e^{-\int_{t_0}^{t} \lambda(s)\,ds} \right] = B(t_0, t)\left({}_{t}P_{t_0} \right)^{Q}$$

where $B(t_0, t)$ is the value of a zero coupon that is not subjected to credit risk (nondefaultable bond) and $\left({}_{t}P_{t_0} \right)^{Q}$ is the survival probability computed under the riskless probability measure.

In this chapter we will not make the unlikely assumption that $r(t)$ and $\lambda(t)$ are independent.

There are numerous types of credit derivatives in financial markets. We now consider a vanilla derivative that pays one monetary unit when a credit event occurs and if it occurs before a given date T. Then, its value in t is given by

$$L(t,T) = E_t^Q \left[I_{\tau \leq T} \, e^{-\int_t^\tau r(u)du} + I_{\tau > T} \cdot 0 \right]$$

where I_E is the indicator function of the event ε (i.e., it is 1 if ε happens and 0 if it does not). The value L is an element of the vector $\mathbf{A}$ since L is assumed to be listed in the financial market we are taking into account.

If we compute the expected value with respect to τ by using its density function $\pi(t)$, we have

$$L(t,T) = E_t^Q \left[\int_t^\infty \pi(s) I_{\tau \leq T} \cdot e^{-\int_t^s r(u)du} ds \right] = E_t^Q \left[\int_t^T \pi(s) e^{-\int_t^s r(u)du} ds \right]. \quad (15.11)$$

This simplification allows us to see that such an asset can be interpreted as a coupon bond (expiring in T) whose (instantaneous) coupons are given by the density function of the credit event time τ. This implies that under the martingale equivalent measure, the value of the credit derivative follows (we neglect the functional dependences):[3]

$$dL = (rL - \pi)dt + \frac{\partial L}{\partial r} \sigma_r dW_r^Q + \frac{\partial L}{\partial \lambda} \sigma_\lambda dW_\lambda^Q$$

and, under the historical probability [by recalling the (15.3)],

$$dL = \left(rL - \pi + \frac{\partial L}{\partial r} \sigma_r \xi_r + \frac{\partial L}{\partial \lambda} \sigma_\lambda \xi_\lambda \right)dt + \frac{\partial L}{\partial r} \sigma_r dW_r + \frac{\partial L}{\partial \lambda} \sigma_\lambda dW_\lambda \quad (15.12)$$

where we have indicated with ξ_λ the market price of default risk.

If we call $\nabla_{L,r}$ and $\nabla_{L,\lambda}$ the semi-elasticities of L with respect to the interest rate and the default rate, respectively, i.e.,

---

[3] It is sufficient to apply Itô's lemma to Equation (15.11) and impose the nonarbitrage condition: Under Q the formula must be rescaled.

$$\nabla_{L,r} \equiv \frac{1}{L(t, T)} \frac{\partial L(t, T)}{\partial r}$$

$$\nabla_{L,\lambda} \equiv \frac{1}{L(t, T)} \frac{\partial L(t, T)}{\partial \lambda}$$

then we can write Equation (15.12) in terms of relative change in price L:

$$\frac{dL}{L} = \left(r - \frac{\pi}{L} + \nabla_{L,r} \sigma_r \xi_r + \nabla_{L,\lambda} \sigma_\lambda \xi_\lambda \right) dt + \nabla_{L,r} \sigma_r dW_r + \nabla_{L,\lambda} \sigma_\lambda dW_\lambda \quad (15.13)$$

The Stock Market and the Financial Market

Finally, in financial markets, we assume there is a stock whose price $S(t)$ follows the differential equation

$$\frac{dS(t)}{S(t)} = \left(r(t) + \sigma_{Sr}(t, S)\xi_r + \sigma_{S\lambda}(t, S)\xi_\lambda + \sigma_S(t, S)\xi_S \right) dt$$

$$+ \sigma_{Sr}(t, S)dW_r(t) + \sigma_{S\lambda}(t, S)dW_\lambda(t) + \sigma_S(t, S)dW_S(t) \quad (15.14)$$

where ξ_S is the stock-specific market price of risk. Here, we have assumed that S is instantaneoulsy correlated with L. In fact, by comparing Equations (5.13) and (15.14), we can immediately compute the covariance.

$$C\left[\frac{dL}{L}, \frac{dS}{S} \right] = \left(\nabla_{L,r} \sigma_r \sigma_{Sr} + \nabla_{L,\lambda} \sigma_\lambda \sigma_{S\lambda} \right) dt$$

The entire financial market can be summarized in a matrix form as follows. The state variables are

$$\underbrace{\begin{bmatrix} dr \\ d\lambda \end{bmatrix}}_{dz} = \underbrace{\begin{bmatrix} \mu_r \\ \mu_\lambda \end{bmatrix}}_{\mu_z} dt + \underbrace{\begin{bmatrix} \sigma_r & 0 & 0 \\ 0 & \sigma_\lambda & 0 \end{bmatrix}}_{\Omega'} \underbrace{\begin{bmatrix} dW_r \\ dW_\lambda \\ dW_S \end{bmatrix}}_{dW}, \quad (15.15)$$

and the risky asset prices are

$$
\underbrace{\begin{bmatrix} \frac{dS}{S} \\ \frac{dB}{B} \\ \frac{dL}{L} \end{bmatrix}}_{I_A^{-1}dA} = \underbrace{\begin{bmatrix} r + \sigma_{Sr}\xi_r + \sigma_{S\lambda}\xi_\lambda + \sigma_S\xi_S \\ r + \nabla_{B,r}\sigma_r\xi_r \\ r - \frac{\pi}{L} + \nabla_{L,r}\sigma_r\xi_r + \nabla_{L,\lambda}\sigma_\lambda\xi_\lambda \end{bmatrix}}_{\mu} dt
$$

$$
+ \underbrace{\begin{bmatrix} \sigma_{Sr} & \sigma_{S\lambda} & \sigma_S \\ \nabla_{B,r}\sigma_r & 0 & 0 \\ \nabla_{L,r}\sigma_r & \nabla_{L,\lambda}\sigma_\lambda & 0 \end{bmatrix}}_{\Sigma'} \underbrace{\begin{bmatrix} dW_r \\ dW_\lambda \\ dW_S \end{bmatrix}}_{dW}.
$$

(15.16)

This financial market is complete since there exists only one vector $\xi = [\xi_r \ \xi_\lambda \ \xi_S]$ such that

$$
\Sigma'\xi = \mu - r\mathbf{1}
$$

i.e., the matrix Σ is invertible.

Investor's Wealth and Optimization Problem

Let us call $w \in \mathbf{R}^n$ the vector containing the portfolio weights for the n risky assets in the economy described by Equations (15.1) and (15.2). If we call w_G the number of riskless assets held in the portfolio, then the investor's wealth $R(t)$ at each time t is given by

$$
R(t) = w'A(t) + w_G G(t)
$$

whose differential is (under the self-financing condition)

$$
dR(t) = w'dA(t) + w_G dG(t)
$$

If we take w_G from the static constraint and we plug it into the dynamic constraint, we obtain the usual dynamic behavior of investor's wealth

$$
dR(t) = \left\{ R(t)r(t, z) + w'I_A \left[\mu(t, z, A) - r(t, z)\mathbf{1} \right] \right\} dt
$$
$$
+ w'I_A \Sigma(t, z, A)' \, dW(t) \qquad \forall t < \tau
$$

(15.17)

Equation (15.17) is valid until a credit event occurs (in τ). Here, we assume that such a credit event coincides with the loss of the entire portfolio value with the exception of the riskless asset. This implies that when a credit event happens (in τ), the value of our remaining wealth ($\hat{R}$) just evolves according to

$$d\hat{R}(t) = \hat{R}(t)r(t, z)dt, \quad \forall t \geq \tau$$

In other words, we are assuming that all the risky assets are subjected to the same credit risk. This hypothesis seems to be less unlikely if we assume either that the portfolio just contains one risky asset or that it coincides with a market index.

Investor preferences are described by a utility function which is strictly increasing (more money is preferred to less money) and strictly concave (risk aversion) in wealth $U(R(t))$. The utility function is also assumed to verify the usual Inada's conditions: (1) There exists a nonnegative wealth level α for which the marginal utility is infinity:

$$\lim_{R \to \alpha^+} \frac{\partial U(R)}{\partial R} = +\infty,$$

and (2) the marginal utility for an infinite amount of wealth is zero:

$$\lim_{R \to +\infty} \frac{\partial U(R)}{\partial R} = 0.$$

As will be clearer in the following sections, the first condition prevents the optimal wealth from taking negative values. By suitably choosing $\mathbf{w}$, the investor maximizes the expected utility of his wealth at a given time horizon T unless a credit event occurs before (i.e., $\tau < T$). Thus, starting from t_0, if the credit event has occurred between t_0 and T (i.e., $t_0 < \tau \leq T$), then the investor's utility is given by $U(\hat{R}(\tau))$; if the credit event hasn't occurred from t_0 up to T, then the investor's utility is $U(R(T))$.

The optimization problem can be written as

$$\max_{w} E_{t_0} \left[I_{\tau \leq T} \cdot e^{-\rho(\tau - t_0)} U\left(\hat{R}(\tau)\right) + I_{\tau > T} \cdot e^{-\rho(T - t_0)} U\left(R(T)\right) \right],$$

where ρ is the (constant) subjective discount factor.[4] If we use the density function $\pi(t)$, we can write the objective function as

$$E_{t_0}\left[\int_{t_0}^{\infty}\pi(t, z)I_{t\leq T}e^{-\rho(t-t_0)}U\left(\hat{R}(t)\right)dt + \int_{t_0}^{\infty}\pi(t, z)I_{t>T}e^{-\rho(T-t_0)}U\left(R(T)\right)dt\right]$$

$$= E_{t_0}\left[\int_{t_0}^{T}\pi(t, z)e^{-\rho(t-t_0)}U\left(\hat{R}(t)\right)dt + e^{-\rho(T-t_0)}U\left(R(T)\right)\int_{T}^{\infty}\pi(t, z)dt\right]$$

$$= E_{t_0}\left[\underbrace{\int_{t_0}^{T}\pi(t, z)e^{-\rho(t-t_0)}U\left(\hat{R}(t)\right)dt}_{O_1}+\underbrace{U\left(R(T)\right)e^{-\rho(T-t_0)}e^{-\int_{t_0}^{T}\lambda(s,z)ds}}_{O_2}\right].$$

The objective function component O_1 does not depend on the control variable w and, accordingly, the optimization problem can be restated just in terms of O_2. Furthermore, since ρ is constant, we can divide O_2 by $e^{-\rho(T-t_0)}$, and finally write the problem as

$$\max_{w} E_{t_0}\left[U\left(R(T)\right)e^{-\int_{t_0}^{T}\lambda(s)ds}\right] \tag{15.18}$$

where the state variables z, A, and R follow the stochastic differential equations (15.15), (15.16), and (15.17), respectively.

THE OPTIMAL PORTFOLIO

A General Result

Without specifying any explicit form for the utility function we are able to find a general solution for the optimal asset allocation problem allowing us to present some first results.

Proposition 15.1: *Given the state variables described in Equations (15.15) to (15.17), the optimal portfolio solving (15.18) is*

---

[4] The results displayed in the paper do not change at all if the subjective discount factor is time dependent. Instead, the results are affected if ρ is assumed to be stochastic, but this hypothesis seems to be unlikely.

$$Sw_S^* = -\frac{J_R}{J_{RR}}\left(\frac{\xi_S}{\sigma_S} + \frac{\pi}{L}\frac{\sigma_{S\lambda}}{\nabla_{L,\lambda}\sigma_\lambda\sigma_S^2}\right),$$

$$Bw_B^* = -\frac{J_R}{J_{RR}}\frac{\xi_r}{\nabla_{B,r}\sigma_r} - \frac{\sigma_{Sr}}{\nabla_{B,r}\sigma_r}Sw_S^* - \frac{\nabla_{L,r}}{\nabla_{B,r}}Lw_L^* - \frac{1}{\nabla_{B,r}}\frac{J_{Rr}}{J_{RR}},$$

$$Lw_L^* = -\frac{J_R}{J_{RR}}\frac{1}{\nabla_{L,\lambda}\sigma_\lambda}\left(\xi_\lambda - \frac{\pi}{L}\frac{1}{\nabla_{L,\lambda}\sigma_\lambda}\right) - \frac{\sigma_{S\lambda}}{\nabla_{L,\lambda}\sigma_\lambda}Sw_S^* - \frac{1}{\nabla_{L,\lambda}}\frac{J_{R\lambda}}{J_{RR}}$$

where J(t, R, r, λ) is the value function of the problem (objective) such that

$$J\left(R,r,\,\lambda,\,T\right) = U\left(R(T)\right)e^{-\int_{t_0}^{T}\lambda(s)ds}$$

and the subscripts on it indicate partial derivatives.

Proof: See Appendix, where the elements of Σ, μ, and Ω are as in Equations (15.15) and (15.16).

The stock does not play any hedging role. In fact, the optimal amount of stock depends neither on J_{Rr} nor on $JR_{R\lambda}$, i.e., it is not affected by the changes in the state variables (r and λ). While we know that ξ_S and σ_S are positive parameters,[5] we do not know the signs of $\sigma_{S\lambda}$ and $\nabla_{L,\lambda}$. Accordingly, we are not able to conclude about the behavior of stock optimal weight with respect to changes in π.

The coefficient $\sigma_{sr}/(\sigma_r\nabla_{B,r})$ that can be found in the optimal bond weight coincides with the ratio between the covariance of stock and bond returns and the variance of bond return. In fact, we recall that

$$C\left[\frac{dS}{S},\frac{dB}{B}\right] = \sigma_{Sr}\sigma_r\nabla_{B,r}dt,$$

$$V\left[\frac{dB}{B}\right] = \sigma_r^2\nabla_{B,r}^2dt$$

---

[5] We also know that $-J_R/J_{RR}$ must be positive since J must be increasing and concave in R as the utility function.

and, in other words, $(\sigma_{sr}/\sigma_r \, \nabla_{B,r})$ coincides with the coefficient of the linear regression of dS/S with respect to dB/B.

In the same spirit of the preceding point, the term $\sigma_{S\lambda}/(\sigma_\lambda \, \nabla_{L,\lambda})$ is the coefficient of the linear regression of dS/S with respect to dL/L.

In order to explain the role of the coefficient $\nabla_{L,r}/\nabla_{B,r}$, let us take into account a portfolio (Π) that contains w_B bonds and w_L credit derivatives:

$$\Pi = w_L L + w_B B$$

This portfolio is hedged against interest rate changes if the derivative of Π with respect to r is zero:

$$w_L L \frac{\partial L}{\partial r} \frac{1}{L} + w_B B \frac{\partial B}{\partial r} \frac{1}{B} = 0$$

from which we have

$$\frac{w_B B}{w_L L} = -\frac{\nabla_{L,r}}{\nabla_{B,r}}$$

Accordingly, we can conclude that $\nabla_{L,r}/\nabla_{B,r}$ is the opposite of the so-called hedging ratio, which immunizes a portfolio formed by B and L against the changes in the interest rate r.

The optimal amount of money to invest in the credit derivative L must be taken from the wealth invested in the bond (by the ratio $\nabla_{L,r}/\nabla_{B,r}$) and from the wealth invested in the riskless asset (by the ratio $1 - \nabla_{L,r}/\nabla_{B,r}$). The ratio $\nabla_{L,r}/\nabla_{B,r}$ is equal to 1 (i.e., the wealth invested in the credit derivative is entirely taken from the bond) if the credit derivative and the bond have the same duration. This is the case, for instance, if λ and r are independent and both L and B have the same time to maturity.

Corollary 15.2: *If both the bond and the credit derivative have the same duration, then the optimal amount of money invested in the credit derivative is fully taken from the amount of money invested in the bond without changing either the stock weight or the riskless asset weight.*

Proof: If B and L have the same duration, then $\nabla_{L,r} = \nabla_{B,r}$. After substituting this equality in the optimal portfolio of Proposition 15.1, the result of the corollary immediately follows.

Remark 15.3: It is particularly relevant to stress that the form of the utility function does affect the amount of money that must be invested in the credit derivative but does not affect the way this investment is financed. Furthermore, this result is not affected by the dependence between r and λ.

The HARA Utility Case

Now, we take into account a hyperbolic absolute risk aversion utility function having the following form:

$$U\big(R(t)\big) = \frac{1}{1-\beta}\big(R(t) - \alpha\big)^{1-\beta}$$

where α could be thought of as the subsistence wealth (constant) level, i.e., a level below which the investor does not want his wealth to go. When optimizing the expected utility of wealth, the Inada's property

$$\lim_{R \to \alpha^+} \frac{\partial U(R)}{\partial R} = +\infty$$

prevents the optimal wealth from going below α. Accordingly, the investor receives utility only from the wealth exceeding the subsistence level α. The Arrow–Pratt relative risk aversion computed on such exceeding wealth is given by β, which must be positive in order for U to be both increasing and concave in wealth. If the relative risk aversion is computed on the wealth level R, then it is a hyperbolic function of wealth

$$-\frac{\big[\partial^2 U(R)/\partial R^2\big]R}{\partial U(R)/\partial R} = \beta \frac{R}{R-\alpha}$$

and accordingly, the function $U(R)$ is said to be a *hyperbolic absolute risk aversion* (HARA) utility.

We stress that this risk aversion is decreasing in wealth, i.e., richer investors have lower relative risk aversion. When the parameter α is zero, then we are in the case of a constant relative risk aversion, and the optimal wealth is prevented from becoming negative or zero but could take any very low level. When the parameter β is set to 1, the utility becomes a log function. In fact, since the result of the optimization problem does not change if we add a constant $(-1/(1-\beta))$ to the objective function, we have

$$\lim_{\beta \to 1} \frac{\left(R(t)-\alpha\right)^{1-\beta}-1}{1-\beta} = \ln\left(R(t)-\alpha\right)$$

With a HARA utility function the result stated in Proposition 15.1 can be rewritten as follows.

Proposition 15.4: *Given the state variables described in Equations (15.15) to (15.17), the optimal portfolio solving problem (15.18) with* $U(R)= (R-\alpha)^{1-\beta}\,(1-\beta)$

$$\frac{Sw_S^*}{R-\alpha B} = \frac{1}{\beta}\left(\frac{\xi_S}{\sigma_S} + \frac{\pi}{L}\frac{\sigma_{S\lambda}}{\sigma_\lambda \nabla_{L,\lambda}\sigma_S^2}\right),$$

$$\frac{Bw_B^* - \alpha B}{R-\alpha B} = \frac{1}{\beta}\frac{\sigma_{Sr}}{\sigma_r \nabla_{B,r}}\xi_r - \frac{\sigma_{Sr}}{\sigma_r \nabla_{B,r}}\frac{Sw_S^*}{R-\alpha B}$$

$$- \frac{\nabla_{L,r}}{\nabla_{B,r}}\frac{Lw_L^*}{R-\alpha B} + \frac{\nabla_{F,r}}{\nabla_{B,r}},$$

$$\frac{Lw_L^*}{R-\alpha B} = \frac{1}{\beta}\frac{1}{\sigma_\lambda \nabla_{L,\lambda}}\left(\xi_\lambda - \frac{\pi}{L}\frac{1}{\sigma_\lambda \nabla_{L,\lambda}}\right)$$

$$- \frac{\sigma_{S\lambda}}{\sigma_\lambda \nabla_{L,\lambda}}\frac{Sw_S^*}{R-\alpha B} + \frac{\nabla_{F,\lambda}}{\nabla_{L,\lambda}},$$

where $\Delta_{F,\,r}$ *and* $\Delta_{F,\,\lambda}$ *are the semi-elasticities of the following function F with respect to r and λ respectively:*

$$F\left(t,\,T,\,r,\,\lambda\right)=E_t^{Q_\beta}\left[e^{-\frac{1}{\beta}\int_t^T \lambda(s)ds}\,e^{-\frac{\beta-1}{\beta}\int_t^T\left[r(s)+\frac{1}{2}\frac{1}{\beta}\xi(s)'\xi(s)\right]ds}\right] \qquad (15.19)$$

$$dW^{Q_\beta} = \frac{\beta-1}{\beta}\xi dt + dW \tag{15.20}$$

Proof: See Appendix, where Σ, μ, and Ω must be substituted from Equations (15.15) and (15.16).

Here are some conclusions.

_____All optimal investments are computed as a percentage of wealth reduced by the present value of the minimum wealth (i.e., αB).

_____The optimal weight of bond is computed net of the minimum wealth present value (αB).

_____The coefficients $\Delta_{F,r}/\Delta_{B,r}$ and $\Delta_{F,\lambda}/\Delta_{L,\lambda}$ can be interpreted by the same arguments we have already used for the ratio $\Delta_{L,r}/\Delta_{B,r}$. Accordingly, $\Delta_{F,r}/\Delta_{B,r}$ is the hedging ratio for an interest rate immunized portfolio made by F and B, while $\Delta_{F,\lambda}/\Delta_{L,\lambda}$ is the hedging ratio for a default intensity immunized portfolio made by F and L.

In order to compute the optimal portfolio, the relevant wealth is given by the nominal wealth net of the present value of the minimum wealth (α) the investor wants to have at time T (his or her time horizon).

The function F coincides with the value of a zero-coupon paying one monetary unit in T and whose return in t is given by

$$\frac{1}{\beta}\lambda(t) + \frac{\beta-1}{\beta}\left[r(t) + \frac{1}{2}\frac{1}{\beta}\xi(t)'\,\xi(t)\right]$$

The value of this bond is computed under a new probability. In fact, as it is evident from Equation (15.19), the computation of the optimal portfolio implies the use of two probability measures: the martingale equivalent measure Q only depending on the financial market and the probability Q_β also depending on investor's preferences. For what concerns this second probability, there are two interesting limit cases:

$$\lim_{\beta\to 1} Q_\beta = P \tag{15.21}$$

$$\lim_{\beta\to\infty} Q_\beta = Q \tag{15.22}$$

This means that

1. For an agent described by a log utility function (with $\beta = 1$), the new probability Q_β coincides with the historical probability P.
2. For an infinitely risk averse investor (with $\beta \to \infty$), the new probability Q_β coincides with the riskless probability.

In these two cases, the optimal portfolio simplifies as shown in the following corollaries.

Corollary 15.5: *Given the optimization problem (15.18) and the behavior of the state variables (15.15) to (15.17), the optimal portfolio for a log investor (i.e., $\beta = 1$) is*

$$\frac{Sw_S^*}{R-\alpha B} = \frac{\xi_S}{\sigma_S} + \frac{\pi}{L}\frac{\sigma_{S\lambda}}{\sigma_\lambda \nabla_{L,\lambda}\sigma_S^2},$$

$$\frac{Bw_B^* - \alpha B}{R-\alpha B} = \frac{\sigma_{Sr}}{\sigma_r \nabla_{B,r}}\xi_r - \frac{\sigma_{Sr}}{\sigma_r \nabla_{B,r}}\frac{Sw_S^*}{R-\alpha B} - \frac{\nabla_{L,r}}{\nabla_{B,r}}\frac{Lw_L^*}{R-\alpha B},$$

$$\frac{Lw_L^*}{R-\alpha B} = \frac{1}{\sigma_\lambda \nabla_{L,\lambda}}\left(\xi_\lambda - \frac{\pi}{L}\frac{1}{\sigma_\lambda \nabla_{L,\lambda}}\right) - \frac{\sigma_{S\lambda}}{\sigma_\lambda \nabla_{L,\lambda}}\frac{Sw_S^*}{R-\alpha B} + \frac{1}{\nabla_{L,\lambda}}\frac{\partial(_T p_t)}{\partial\lambda}.$$

Proof: It is sufficient to substitute $\beta = 1$ in the results of Proposition 15.4. We stress that given Equation (15.21),

$$\lim_{\beta \to 1} E_t\left[e^{-\frac{1}{\beta}\int_t^T \lambda(s)ds} e^{-\frac{\beta-1}{\beta}\int_t^T \left(r(s)+\frac{1}{2}\frac{1}{\beta}\xi(s)'\xi(s)\right)ds}\right] = E_t\left[e^{-\int_t^T \lambda(s)ds}\right] = \left(_T p_t\right).$$

This result allows us to conclude that a log investor hedges against the changes in the survival probability due to the fluctuations in the default rate (λ). In fact, in this case, the investor does not care about the fluctuations in the interest rate (r). When there is no credit risk (i.e., the default rate is zero), the portfolio for a log investor does not contain any hedging component and therefore the investor is myopic. In fact, the only portfolio component that contains the investor's horizon T is ($_T P_t$).

Corollary 15.6: *Given the optimization problem (15.18) and the behavior of the state variables (15.15) to (15.17), the optimal portfolio for an infinitely risk averse investor (i.e., $\beta \to \infty$) is*

$$\frac{Sw_S^*}{R - \alpha B} = 0$$

$$\frac{Bw_B^* - \alpha B}{R - \alpha B} = 1$$

$$\frac{Lw_L^*}{R - \alpha B} = 0$$

Proof: It is sufficient to compute the limit of the results shown in Proposition 15.4 for β tending towards infinity. We stress that given Equation (15.22),

$$\lim_{\beta \to \infty} E_t^Q \left[e^{-\frac{1}{\beta} \int_t^T \lambda(s)ds} \, e^{-\frac{\beta-1}{\beta} \int_t^T \left(r(s) + \frac{1}{2}\frac{1}{\beta}\xi(s)'\xi(s) \right)ds} \right] = E_t^Q \left[e^{-\int_t^T r(s)ds} \right] = B(t,T),$$

and, accordingly, $\Delta_{F,r} = \Delta_{B,r}$ and $\Delta_{F,\lambda} = 0$.

This result allows us to conclude that an infinitely risk averse agent fully invests in a zero-coupon bond. In particular, such an investor neglects the default risk when computing the optimal portfolio. The same result is obtained by Wachter (2003). Here, we assume that the maturity of the zero coupon on the financial market coincides with the investor's horizon and only this case, the optimal bond weight is 1 (the entire wealth). If the bond maturity and the investor's horizon were different, the optimal bond weight would be given by the ratio between these two durations.

APPENDIX

The Optimal Portfolio

The Hamilton–Jacobi–Bellman Equation
The general problem can be written as

$$\max_w E_{t_0} \left[f(T,z) U(R(T)) \right]$$

$$dz = \mu_z(t,z)dt + \Omega(t,z)' dW,$$

$$dR = \left(Rr + w'I_A(\mu - r\mathbf{1}) \right)dt + w'I_A\Sigma'dW$$

(15.23)

where z is as in Equation (15.15) and Σ and μ are defined in Equation (15.16). Furthermore, $f\left(t,\, z\right) \equiv e^{-\int_{t_0}^{t} \lambda(s,z)ds}$. By using the stochastic dynamic programming technique (Merton 1969; ibid., 1970; ibid., 1971), the Hamiltonian of problem (15.23) is

$$H = J_R\Big[Rr + w'I_A\left(\mu - r\mathbf{1}\right)\Big] + \mu_z'J_z + \frac{1}{2}tr\left(\Omega'\Omega J_{zz}\right)$$

$$+ \frac{1}{2}w'I_A\Sigma'\Sigma I_A wJ_{RR} + w'I_A\Sigma'\Omega J_{zR},$$

where $J(t,\, R,\, z)$ is the value function (i.e., the indirect utility function solving the optimization problem) and the subscripts indicate partial derivatives. The first-order condition on H leads to

$$I_A w^* = -\frac{J_R}{J_{RR}}\left(\Sigma'\Sigma\right)^{-1}\left(\mu - r\mathbf{1}\right) - \frac{1}{J_{RR}}\left(\Sigma'\Sigma\right)^{-1}\Sigma'\Omega J_{zR},$$

and after substituting the value of matrices Σ, $(\mu - r\mathbf{1})$, and Ω as in Equations (15.15) and (15.16), we obtain the result stated in Proposition 15.1. Once the value w^* is substituted in the Hamiltonian, we obtain the so-called Hamilton–Jacobi–Bellman (HJB) partial differential equation:

$$0 = J_t + f\left(z,\, t\right)U\left(R(t)\right)$$

$$+ J_R Rr - \frac{1}{2}\frac{J_R^2}{J_{RR}}M'\left(\Sigma'\Sigma\right)^{-1}M$$

$$- \frac{J_R}{J_{RR}}M'\left(\Sigma'\Sigma\right)^{-1}\Sigma'\Omega J_{zR}$$

$$+ \mu_z'J_z + \frac{1}{2}tr\left(\Omega'\Omega J_{zz}\right)$$

$$- \frac{1}{2}\frac{1}{J_{RR}}J_{zR}'\Omega'\Sigma\left(\Sigma'\Sigma\right)^{-1}\Sigma'\Omega J_{zR}$$

whose boundary condition is

$$J\left(T,\, R,\, z\right) = U\left(R(T)\right)e^{-\int_{t_0}^{T} \lambda(s,z)ds}$$

The Solution for the HARA Utility

Now we define the guess function as

$$J(t, z, R) = F(t, z)^{\beta} \frac{1}{1-\beta} (R - H(t, z))^{1-\beta}$$

with the boundary conditions

$$F(T, z) = e^{-\frac{1}{\beta} \int_{t_0}^{T} \lambda(s) ds}, \tag{15.24}$$

$$H(T, z) = \alpha. \tag{15.25}$$

After substituting the partial derivatives of J into the HJB equation and doing some simplifications, we have

$$0 = \beta F^{\beta-1} (R - H)^{1-\beta} F_t - \frac{1}{2} \frac{\beta-1}{\beta} F^{\beta} (R - H)^{1-\beta} \xi'\xi$$

$$+ \beta F^{\beta-1} (R - H)^{1-\beta} \left(\mu_z' - \frac{\beta-1}{\beta} \xi'\Omega \right) F_z$$

$$+ \frac{1}{2} \beta F^{\beta-1} (R - H)^{1-\beta} tr(\Omega'\Omega F_{zz})$$

$$+ F^{\beta} (1-\beta)(R - H)^{1-\beta} r - F^{\beta} (1-\beta)(R - H)^{-\beta} H_t$$

$$+ F^{\beta} (1-\beta)(R - H)^{-\beta} Hr - (1-\beta) F^{\beta} (R - H)^{-\beta} \left(\mu_z' - \xi'\Omega \right) H_z$$

$$- \frac{1}{2} F^{\beta} (1-\beta)(R - H)^{-\beta} tr(\Omega'\Omega H_{zz})$$

$$+ \frac{1}{2} F^{\beta-2} (R - H)^{1-\beta} (-\beta)(1-\beta) F_z'\Omega' \left(I - \Sigma(\Sigma'\Sigma)^{-1} \Sigma' \right) \Omega F_z$$

$$+ F^{\beta-1} (R - H)^{-\beta} (-\beta)(1-\beta) F_z'\Omega' \left(I - \Sigma(\Sigma'\Sigma)^{-1} \Sigma' \right) \Omega H_z$$

$$+ \frac{1}{2} F^{\beta} (R - H)^{-\beta-1} (-\beta)(1-\beta) H_z'\Omega' \left(I - \Sigma(\Sigma'\Sigma)^{-1} \Sigma' \right) \Omega H_z$$

where I is the identity matrix. This equation can be disentangled into two differential equations: one containing the term $(R - H)^{-\beta}$ and the other containing the term $(R - H)^{1-\beta}$. If the market is complete, we have $I - \Sigma(\Sigma'\Sigma)^{-1}\Sigma' = 0$ and so

$$0 = F_t + \left(\mu_z' - \frac{\beta-1}{\beta}\xi'\Omega \right)F_z + \frac{1}{2}tr\left(\Omega'\Omega F_{zz}\right) - \frac{\beta-1}{\beta}\left(r + \frac{1}{2}\frac{1}{\beta}\xi'\xi \right)F,$$

$$0 = H_t + \left(\mu_z' - \xi'\Omega \right)H_z + \frac{1}{2}tr\left(\Omega'\Omega H_{zz}\right) - Hr.$$

Given the boundary conditions in Equations (15.24) and (15.25), the Feynman–Kaĉ formula [see, for instance, Øksendal (2003)] gives us

$$F\left(t,\,z\right)= E_t^{Q_\beta}\left[e^{-\frac{1}{\beta}\int_{t_0}^T \lambda(s)\,ds}\; e^{-\frac{\beta-1}{\beta}\int_t^T r(s)+\frac{1}{2}\frac{1}{\beta}\xi(s)'\xi(s)\,ds} \right]$$

$$= e^{-\frac{1}{\beta}\int_{t_0}^t \lambda(s)ds}E_t^{Q_\beta}\left[e^{-\int_t^T\left(\frac{1}{\beta}\lambda(s)+\frac{\beta-1}{\beta}r(s)+\frac{1}{2}\frac{\beta-1}{\beta^2}\xi(s)'\xi(s)\right)ds} \right],$$

$$H\left(t,\,z\right)= E_t^Q\left[\alpha e^{-\int_t^T r(s)ds} \right] = \alpha B\left(t,\,T\right)$$

where the new probability measure Q_β is such that

$$dW^{Q_\beta} = \frac{\beta-1}{\beta}\xi dt + dW.$$

The result of the proposition is obtained by substituting the form of function J into $I_A w^*$.

REFERENCES

Boulier, J.-F., Huang, S.J., and Taillard, G. (2001) Optimal Management under Stochastic Interest. *Insurance: Mathematics and Economics*, 28(2): 173–189.

Chacko, G. and Viceira, L.M. (2005) Dynamic Consumption and Portfolio Choice with Stochastic Volatility in Incomplete Markets. *The Review of Financial Studies*, 18(4): 1369–1402.

Cox, J.C. and Huang, C.F. (1989) Optimal Consumption and Portfolio Policies when Asset Prices Follow a Diffusion Process. *Journal of Economic Theory*, 49(1): 33–83.

Cox, J.C. and Huang, C.F. (1991) A Variational Problem Arising in Financial Economics. *Journal of Mathematical Economics*, 20(5): 465–487.

Cox, J. C., Ingersoll, Jr., J.E., and Ross, S. A. (1985) A Theory of the Term Structure of Interest Rates. *Econometrica*, 53(2): 385–407.

Dahl, M. (2004) Stochastic Mortality in Life Insurance: Market Reserves and Mortality-Linked Insurance Contracts. *Insurance: Mathematics and Economics*, 35(1): 113–136.

Deelstra, G., Grasselli, M. and Koehl, P.-F. (2000) Optimal Investment Strategies in a CIR Framework. *Journal of Applied Probability*, 37(4): 1–12.

Duffie, D. and Singleton, K.J. (2003) *Credit Risk—Pricing, Measurement, and Management*. Princeton University Press, Princeton, NJ.

Kim, T.S. and Omberg, E. (1996). Dynamic Nonmyopic Portfolio Behavior. *The Review of Financial Studies*, 9(1): 141–161.

Menoncin, F. (2002) Optimal Portfolio and Background Risk: An Exact and an Approximated Solution. *Insurance: Mathematics and Economics*, 31(2): 249–265.

Menoncin, F. (2008) The Role of Longevity Bonds in Optimal Portfolios. *Insurance: Mathematics and Economics*, 42(1): 343–358.

Merton, R.C. (1969) Lifetime Portfolio Selection under Uncertainty: the Continuous-Time Case. *Review of Economics and Statistics*, 51(3): 247–257.

Merton, R.C. (1970) A Dynamic General Equilibrium Model of the Asset Market and Its Application to the Pricing of the Capital Structure of the Firm. Working paper 497–70, A. P. Sloan School of Management, MIT, Cambridge, MA.

Merton, R.C. (1971) Optimum Consumption and Portfolio Rules in a Continuous-Time Model. *Journal of Economic Theory*, 3(4): 373–413.

Øksendal, B. (2003) *Stochastic Differential Equation: An Introduction with Applications*. New York: Springer.

Richard, S. (1975) Optimal Consumption, Portfolio and Life Insurance Rules for an Uncertain Lived Individual in a Continuous Time Model. *Journal of Financial Economics*, 2(2): 187–203.

Schmid, B. (2004) *Credit Risk Pricing Models: Theory and Practice*. New York: Springer.

Vasiček, O. (1977) An Equilibrium Characterization of the Term Structure. *Journal of Financial Economics*, 5(2): 177–188.

Wachter, J.A. (2002) Portfolio and Consumption Decisions under Mean-Reverting Returns: An Exact Solution for Complete Markets. *Journal of Financial and Quantitative Analysis*, 37(1): 63–91.

Wachter, J.A. (2003) Risk Aversion and Allocation to Long-Term Bonds. *Journal of Economic Theory*, 112(2): 325–333.

Zariphopoulou, T. (2001) A Solution Approach to Valuation with Unhedgeable Risks. *Finance and Stochastics*, 5(1): 61–82.

CHAPTER 16

Synthetic Collateralized-Debt-Obligation-Squared Pricing Methodologies

Dominique Guégan and Julien P. Houdain

ABSTRACT

We propose two different methodologies for the pricing of collateralized debt obligation (CDO), squared and by extension for the risk management of funds of CDO tranches. The first methodology is based on a drill-down approach, whereas the second one is based on a "correlation of correlation" approach. Our purpose is to be consistent with the inner CDOs' characteristics because of several issues that need to be addressed. The correlation "skew" of each underlying inner CDO must be reproduced. The outer correlation, the correlation of joint loss distributions, among the losses of the inner CDOs must be considered. The outer correlation, which can be interpreted as a global correlation skew, depends on the overlapping characteristics, the spread level and recovery rate assumptions for each credit in the portfolio, and the correlation structure among the credits. We demonstrate that these two methodologies can efficiently be used to price CDO squared and the risk management of funds of CDO tranches.

INTRODUCTION

Synthetic CDOs have been the principal growth engine for the credit derivatives market over the last few years. They create new, customized asset classes by permitting different investors to split the risk and return of an underlying portfolio of credit default swaps (CDSs). Multiple tranches of the underlying portfolio are issued offering investors various maturity and credit risk characteristics. Therefore, the striking feature to investors is determined by the underlying portfolio of CDSs and the regulations for partaking the risk and return. A synthetic CDO is often called a *correlation product* because it is a contract that refers to the default of more than one obligor. Investors of CDOs purchase correlation risk, or more precisely, joint default risk among numerous obligors. The fundamental portfolio loss distribution directly establishes the tranche cash flows and therefore the tranche valuation.

There are more complicated CDO structures that have been developed whereby each underlying credit risk is itself another CDO tranche or asset-backed security (ABS). These CDOs are usually referred to as *CDO squared* or *CDO of CDOs*, and are a growing part of the structured finance market. As a product type, CDO squared have been in existence since 1999 and have evolved in structure and collateral. More recently, deals have been structured as pure synthetic credit CDO squared. As synthetic single-tranche technology became extensively used, synthetic CDO squared started appearing around 2002. Default risk and correlation among the inner CDO credits, together with correlation among the inner CDO portfolios, impact the CDO squared premium. Thus, CDO squared are often called *correlation of correlation product*. A CDO squared can be assimilated as a fund of CDO tranches, but the major difference is that every asset in the CDO squared has subordination on its own, such as investors benefiting from two layers of subordination, which is not the case in a fund of CDO tranches.

In this chapter we will only focus on synthetic CDO squared, and the term *CDO squared* is devoted to a synthetic CDO squared. The CDO squared have recently gained popularity due to higher spreads than equally rated CDO tranches. The CDO squared have evolved as a result of the market's search for higher yields than synthetic CDO can provide. Therefore, CDO squared now fill an important space in the structured credit landscape and provide unique risk–return characteristics. Normally a CDO-squared structure will pay a greater yield for a specified rating to reflect the possibility of larger risk. Since the technology to price these structures is not very common, a CDO-squared deal can compensate the structurer with a high margin (hidden, though, as only the offer price is shown to the client). Patel (2005) states that "... for investors, the perceived attraction is simple: additional spread returns at a time when the structural arbitrage inherent in a standard synthetic CDO is less profitable. For example, single-A tranches of CDO squared paid around 5 to 10 basis points more than a similarly rated tranche from a straight synthetic CDO. Further down the capital structure, the difference was even marked more. CDO squared paid around 5 to 10 basis points more than a similarly rated tranche from a straight synthetic CDO. Further down the capital structure, the difference was even marked more."

From a quantitative point of view, the pricing of a CDO-squared tranche is a challenging exercise requiring advanced modeling. First of all, we need to define a methodology to calculate the loss distribution of each inner CDOs consistently with the market correlation "skew." We can find several models that reproduce very well or even perfectly selected market correlation skew for the different tranches of the same reference index [see Andersen et al. (2003), Andersen and Sidenius (2005), Guégan and Houdain (2005); Hull and White, (2004; 2005), Walker (2005; 2006), Burtschell et al. (2005), Li and Liang (2005); Albrecher et al. (2006)]. Note that the factor-based Gaussian copula model is now a standard market model. The CDS index tranches are traded using base correlations [see McGinty and Ahluwalia (2004)], and as described in Turc et al. (2005), bespoke tranches are quoted using a base correlation surface mapping.

Second, we must consider the joint distribution of losses across the inner CDOs, which in itself is a new dimension not considered in single-tranche pricing. Concerning the correlation between the inner CDO portfolios, the repetition of the same credit in several inner CDOs is an essential feature. Consequently, we have to model the correlation of defaults taking place across the various inner CDOs and take into account the overlap in this second modeling step. The literature regarding the modeling of CDO squared is not as developed as the single-tranche CDO modeling, but interesting ideas and results have been introduced and illustrated in Shelton (2004) and more recently in Li and Liang (2005). Nevertheless, the correlation-of-correlation approach proposed in Shelton (2004) does not consider the market correlation skew of the inner portfolio, whereas the approach proposed in Li and Liang (2005) is more developed and needs to be calibrated on the CDO-squared market correlation skew. However, the problem is that the CDO-squared correlation skew is not observable since there is not a standard and liquid market for synthetic

CDO-squared tranches. Only few major investment banks have agreed on a internally priced standard CDO-squared structure and compare it in terms of pricing results. The CDO-squared correlation skew is generated from this pricing but is not public information.

In this chapter, we propose two different approaches for CDO-squared pricing and for risk management of funds of CDO tranches. Indeed, even if the mark-to-market (MTM) of a fund of CDO tranches is equal to the weighted sum of the underlying tranches MTM, it is important from a risk management point of view to consider the joint distribution of losses across the underlying CDOs. Our first approach is based on a drill-down approach, whereas the second one is based on the correlation-of-correlation approach. Our purpose is to be consistent with inner CDOs characteristics in CDO-squared pricing. By characteristics we imply inner CDOs correlation skew, correlation between inner CDOs and the overlap between underlying credits.

The reminder of the chapter is organized as follows. In the first section we describe the main properties of synthetic CDO-squared structures. Then, we introduce our two different methodologies for the CDO-squared pricing, and we illustrate interesting numerical results. The last section concludes.

SYNTHETIC CDO-SQUARED STRUCTURES

The growth in synthetic CDO-squared transactions is traditionally leveraged single-tranche CDOs where the underlying assets are synthetic CDO tranches. As synthetic single-tranche technology became more extensively used, synthetic CDO squared started to appear around 2002. While the market for CDO squared was originally static,[1] a recent trend has been the emergence of actively managed transactions. The rapid growth of this market indicates that investors are accepting additional leverage and complexity to attain higher yields. In this section we present the most important specificities of synthetic CDO squared. A typical synthetic CDO squared references a portfolio, sometimes called *master* or *outer* CDO, consisting of single tranches of other synthetic CDOs called *baby* or *inner* CDOs. The CDO squared works by scrutinizing a portfolio of mezzanine tranches of synthetic CDOs. These deals are typically structured using

---

[1] Not managed transaction.

large pools of underlying credits; several existing deals have pools of 200 to 400 names. The underlying pool is used to produce a given number of inner CDOs. Most of the time, the inner CDOs are created only for the purpose of being included in the CDO squared. As Flanagan et al. (2005) state "... a bespoke inner tranche is carved out of each inner CDO, and together the inner tranches form the assets. On the liability side is the outer CDO, which is equal in size to the portfolio of inner tranches. Outer tranches of different risk (whether measured by rating or by spread) are created from the outer CDO for end investors." Given the limited universe of actively traded CDS, most CDO-squared deals have a structure where two or more inner CDOs reference some of the same credits. This overlap reduces diversification and tends to significantly alter the risk profile of a CDO squared. Intuitively, overlap is like perfect correlation.

If a reference credit defaults in the inner CDO portfolios, then the corresponding inner CDO tranches suffer losses or lose part of their subordination, depending on the amount of losses. Thus, if one or more of the CDO tranches suffer losses, losses flow into the outer CDO portfolio, then the tranche of the outer CDO suffers or loses part of its subordination, depending on the amount of losses in the outer CDO portfolio. In case subordination is reduced, the effect of the default is to reduce the MTM value of the outer tranche. In a typical CDO-squared structure, the amount of losses in the outer CDO depends not only on how many defaults occur but also in which inner CDO they occur. In a fungible CDO-squared structure, the subordination below all of the inner tranches must be exhausted before any of the inner tranches (and hence the outer portfolio) are affected. This is very similar to replacing the series of inner CDO mezzanine tranches by a series of equity tranches (comprising the mezzanine tranches and the subordination below them). The CDO squared and single-tranche CDOs are both tranched investments and are leveraged because once the subordination is eroded, both these products take the first loss from their respective reference portfolios. The CDO squared typically offer wider spreads versus like-rated single-tranche CDOs, which are primarily a function of the higher leverage.

SYNTHETIC CDO-SQUARED PRICING

"In order to price a CDO squared correctly there are several issues that need to be addressed. The correlation 'skew' of each underlying inner CDO must be reproduced. The outer correlation, the correlation of joint distribution, among the losses of the inner CDOs must be considered. The outer correlation, which can be interpreted as a global correlation 'skew', depends on the overlapping characteristics, the spread level for each credit in the portfolio, and the correlation structure among the credits" (Li and Liang, 2005, p. 22). In this section, we propose two different methodologies for the CDO-squared pricing. The first one is based on a drill-down approach, whereas the second one is based on a correlation-of-correlation approach. Our purpose is to include and to be consistent with inner CDOs characteristics in CDO-squared pricing. By characteristics we refer to inner CDOs correlation skew, correlation among inner CDOs, and overlap.

Portfolio and Tranche Loss Functions

Considering a CDO-squared structure with K inner CDOs. The underlying pool of assets is composed of n obligors with notional amount and recovery rate, respectively, equal to N_i^k and R_i with $1 \leq i \leq n$. For each inner CDO, the aggregate loss L^k, for a fixed k, $1 \leq k \leq K$, at time t is defined by

$$L_t^k = \sum_{i=1}^{n} N_i^k (1 - R_i) 1_{\tau_i \leq t} \tag{16.1}$$

where τ_i is the default time of the ith firm. If a certain percentage portfolio loss L_t^k occurs in the kth inner CDO, then for a tranche with attachment point B_k^- and detachment point B_k^+, we define the loss tranche function TL^k as

$$TL_t^{k/B_k^-, B_k^+} = \min[\max(L_t^k - B_k^-), B_k^+ - B_k^-]. \tag{16.2}$$

At any time t, this function, given any portfolio loss L_t^k, provides the corresponding loss suffered by the tranche holder. In order to evaluate the expected tranche loss, we need to use the tranche loss function and relate it to the experienced portfolio loss; thus, the tranche expected loss at a given time t is defined as follows:

$$E[TL_t^{k/B^-, B^+}] = \sum_{L_t^k} TL_t^{k/B^-, B^+} . P[Loss = L_t^k].$$

Considering an outer tranche with attachment point A^- and detachment point A^+, the expected outer tranche loss at a given time t is defined as follows:

$$E[TL_t^{A^-,A^+}] = \min\left[\max\left(\sum_{k=1}^{k} E\left[TL_t^{k/B^-,B^+} \right] - A^- \right), A^+ - A^- \right].$$

The Drill-Down Approach

This kind of approach has been introduced by rating agencies such as Standard and Poor's to evaluate the rating of an outer tranche CDO squared; we refer to Gilkes and Drexler (2003) for a complete description of their rating methodology. The underlying idea is to consider the underlying pool of assets of the CDO squared as one portfolio, to simulate correlated defaults in this portfolio, and then to transfer the inner CDO losses to the outer CDO portfolio. It is a well-known fact that rating and pricing models have similarities but also important differences. A rating model is based mainly on the credit notation of the underlying pool of assets, whereas a pricing model is driven most likely by the spreads observed in the market. In other words, the rating models are dependent on underlying firms' ratings and on their historically observed risk levels, whereas the pricing models are calibrated on a day-to-day basis to the market quotes and are dependent on underlying firms' CDS spreads.

We propose to merge the two different approaches in order to define a consistent model for the CDO-squared pricing. We divide our model in two steps. First, we use the synthetic CDO tranche pricing techniques and define an efficient way to capture the market correlation skew for each inner CDO tranches. Second, we use the drill-down technique to transfer the inner CDO losses to the outer CDO portfolio. The correlation modeling between each underlying credit is the key point that links the two steps of our model. We need to model this correlation consistently with both the market correlation skew and the drill-down technique.

Correlation Modeling

A standard approach used in the portfolio credit risk analysis and pricing is to make an assumption about the correlation between each pair of assets. Concerning single-tranche pricing, the standard market model is based on a Gaussian one-factor model associated with an assumption of constant correlation between pairs of assets, the base correlation. This correlation level is implied by the market and then interpolated for the pricing of bespoke single-tranche CDOs.

As regards to the standard approach, a problem comes when we want to determine the correlation level in the underlying pool of assets of a CDO squared. In that case, each inner CDO pool of assets will have a different constant pairwise correlation, and it will be impossible to link the different pools in terms of correlation. We propose the use of a full pairwise correlation matrix for the underlying pool of assets of the studied CDO squared. The idea in Andersen and Sidenius (2005) is to calculate a full correlation matrix and then to reduce it as a vector of factor loadings using the methodology based on the Frobenius norm proposed by Jackel (2005). Thus, we can use the vector of factor loadings in a one-factor model to calculate consistently the joint default probabilities of the underlying CDO-squared pool of assets.

Fitting the Inner Correlation Skew

Having a vector of factor loadings requires the selection of an efficient way to introduce the market correlation skew in the calculation of the joint default probabilities of the underlying CDO-squared pool of assets. We propose the use of the methodology introduced by Guégan and Houdain (2005). The underlying idea of this approach is to use the price quotes of the tranches available in the market to determine the implied normal inverse Gaussian (NIG) distribution of the common factor for a given input correlation level. The NIG distribution[2] has the remarkable property of being able to represent phenomena having heavy tails and/or being heavily skewed. In the standard market methodology, the distributions used in the factor model are Gaussian distributions, and the implied correlation of a tranche is calculated under these assumptions.

We use a different approach by fixing the correlation structure of the portfolio and the distribution of the idiosyncratic risk of each firm, and then we determine the implied NIG distribution of the common factor in the model. Using the properties of the NIG distribution, it is possible to fit the market quote of each tranche with the same correlation structure. Once

---

[2] The NIG distribution was introduced to investigate the properties of the returns from financial markets by Barndorff-Nielsen (1997). Since then, applications in CDO pricing have been reported in several papers: Guégan and Houdain (2005), Kalemanova et al. (2005), and Albrecher et al. (2006).

the implied NIG distribution of the common factor is calibrated to the tranche market quotes, we can use this same distribution to price any bespoke single-tranche CDO. It has been demonstrated that this method, using the implied NIG distribution of the common factor, seems to be one of best alternatives if we want to price a nonstandard or bespoke single-tranche CDO [for more details please refer to Guégan and Houdain (2005)]. We can now apply the same methodology to determine the joint default probabilities of the underlying pool of assets of the CDO squared consistently with a given market correlation skew. Nevertheless, we must highlight an important drawback of our model: We need to assume that the pricing of all the inner CDO tranches is driven by the same market correlation skew. This assumption is only relevant when the inner CDOs have the same kind of underlying pool of assets in terms of spread level and geographical allocation.

The Drill-Down Step

"The drill-down technique involves the simulation of correlated defaults of all credits in the CDO-squared reference pool. Simulated net losses are first passed through each inner tranche referencing a given underlying asset. Only when these net losses exceed the attachment point for that inner tranche, the excess net losses are passed on to the outer portfolio. The principal benefit of the drill-down approach is that each underlying name is explicitly linked to one or more inner CDO tranches" (*Business Wire*, 2004). Therefore, when we simulate a default for a given credit, this default or net loss impacts directly the inner CDO portfolios that are exposed to this credit, and we take the correlation between inner tranches into account.

Conditionally to the common factor, the defaults are independent, and thus we introduce the following procedure to calculate the expected outer tranche loss:

- Define a n-dimensional vector $\mathbf{p} = (P_1(z), P_2(z), ..., P_n(z))$, where Z is the common factor of the one-factor NIG model and $P_i(z)$ is the conditional default probability of the ith firm.
- Simulate a n-dimensional vector $\mathbf{u} = (u_1, u_2, ..., u_n)$ of univariate and independent random variables.
- Define a n-dimensional vector $\mathbf{d} = (d_1, d_2, ..., d_n)$ such as for $I = 1$ to n,

$$P_i(z) \geq u_i \leftrightarrow d_i = 1$$
$$P_i(z) \leq u_i \leftrightarrow d_i = 0$$

- For $I = 1$ to n, if $d_i = 1$ we consider that the ith firm defaults; so net losses are passed through each inner CDO portfolio referencing this firm and then to each inner CDO tranche using Equation (16.2), deriving $[TL_t^{k/B_i^-, B_i^+}/Z = z]$ conditional tranche loss of each inner CDO.
- Calculate the unconditional expected outer tranche loss:
$E[TL_t^{A^-, A^+}] = \int_{-\infty}^{\infty} E[TL_t^{A^-, A^+}/Z = z] \, \Phi(z) \, dz$
- Repeat the previous steps for each coupon payment date to determine the expected outer tranche loss term structure.
- Finally, calculate the outer tranche spread.

The key benefit of the drill-down approach is that correlation and overlap are modeled in an accurate and intuitive way, removing the need to estimate the correlation between pairs of inner CDO tranches, i.e., the outer correlation. However, we have to assume that all the inner CDOs prices are driven by the same market correlation skew.

The Correlation-of-Correlation Approach

Another methodology that should be proposed for CDO-squared pricing is the correlation-of-correlation approach. This approach is driven by the fact that similarly to compound options, which depend on "volatility of volatility," the value of CDO squared depends on the marginal loss distributions of each underlying inner CDO and their joint dependence, which is referred to as *correlation of correlation*. This approach is derived from the methodology using conditional normal approximation proposed in Shelton (2004). In this chapter, we add the possibility of including the correlation skew of each inner CDO. The underlying idea is to simulate correlated normal loss distributions and to use an appropriate transformation of these marginal distributions in order to price the outer tranche consistently with market correlation skew of each inner CDO.

Correlated Loss Distributions
Using Equation (16.1), we obtain the following exact expressions for the conditional mean and variance of the loss variable L_t^k:

$$\mu_{k/t}(z) = E[L_t^k / Z = z] = \sum_{i=1}^{N} N_i^k (1 - R^i)([1 - P_i(z)]) \qquad (16.3)$$

and

$$\sigma_{k/t}^2(z) = \Sigma (N_i^k)^2 (1 - R_i)^2 \, P_i(z)[1 - P_i(z)]$$

where Z is the common factor of a one-factor model and $P_i(z)$ is the conditional default probability of the ith firm. Then, conditioning on the random variable Z, we can compute the covariance of loss variables L_t^k and $L_t^{k'}$ with $1 \leq k, k' \leq K$:

$$\text{cov}(L_t^k, L_t^{k'} / Z = z) = \sum_{i=1}^{N} N_i^k N_i^{k'} (1 - R_i)^2 P_i(z)[1 - P_i(z)] \quad (16.4)$$

Thus, for each realization of the random variable Z, we can derive the covariance matrix of the inner loss variables. The loss distribution of the outer CDO is a function of the inner CDO's loss distributions. Subsequently, for each realization of the random variable Z, we calculate the conditional expected loss of the outer portfolio using Monte Carlo simulations.

Simulations of Correlated Loss Distributions

We simulate a wide range of multivariate distributions by choosing the marginal distributions and a suitable multivariate distribution function. While maintaining the underlying assumptions of the conditional normal approximation, we simulate correlated normal random variables. Because the structure of dependence among these normal random variables is driven by a covariance matrix, we use a multivariate Gaussian distribution function. More precisely, we define Σ as the covariance matrix of the inner loss distributions and use the following procedure:

- Define a K-dimensional vector $\mathbf{m} = (\mu_{1|t}(z); \mu_{2|t}(z); ...; \mu_{k|t}(z))$ using Equation (16.3).
- Simulate a K-dimensional vector $\mathbf{u} = (u_1; u_2; ...; u_k)$ of univariate and independent random variables.
- Compute $\mathbf{v}(\mathbf{u})$, where **1** is the Gaussian inverse function.
- Find a suitable decomposition D of Σ, such that $\Sigma = D \bullet D^T$.
- Set $\mathbf{x} = \mathbf{v}D + \mathbf{m}$.

Using this procedure, we then obtain

$$x = ([L_t^1 / Z = z], [L_t^2 / Z = z], ..., [L_t^K / Z = z]) \quad (16.5)$$

At this step, we have two possibilities:

- If the pricing of each inner CDO is not driven by the same market correlation skew, we have to transform the marginal distributions in order to be consistent with the market price of each inner CDO tranche. For this purpose we *use the procedure described in the correlation-of-correlation approach before using the following algorithm.*
- If we assume that the market correlation skew is the same for each inner CDO, then we can directly use the previous algorithm in a Monte Carlo simulation with M iterations:
  - From Equation (16.2), we derive $[TL_t^{k/B_k^-, B_k^+}/Z = z]$ conditional tranche loss of each inner CDO.
  - Calculate the conditional outer tranche loss:

$$[TL_t^{A^-, A} / Z = z] = \min[\max(\sum_{k=1}^{k}[TL_t^{k/B_k^-, B_k^+} / Z = z] - A^-), A^+ - A^-]$$

- Repeat the previous steps using a Monte Carlo simulation with M iterations to calculate $E[TL_t^{A^-, A^+}/Z = z]$, the conditional expected outer tranche loss.
- Calculate the unconditional expected outer tranche loss:

$$E[TL_t^{A^-, A^+}] = \int_{-\infty}^{\infty} E[TL_t^{A^-, A^+} / Z = z]\Phi(z)dz$$

- Repeat the previous steps for each coupon payment date to determine the expected outer tranche loss term structure.
- Finally, calculate the outer tranche spread.

Fitting the Inner Correlation Skew

As previously mentioned if the pricing of each inner CDO is not driven by the same market correlation skew, we have to transform the marginal distributions of the multivariate distribution function in order to be consistent with the market price of each inner CDO tranche. For this purpose we introduce the following procedure:

1. Define $(\Phi_{1,z}, \ldots, \Phi_{k,z})$ the cumulative density functions of the inner conditional loss distributions.

2. Then, using the conditional normal approximation, define
   $(\overline{\Phi}_{1,z}^{-1}, \ldots, \overline{\Phi}_{k,s}^{-1})$ the inverse cumulative density functions of the
   inner conditional loss distributions incorporating the appropriate
   market correlation skew for each inner CDO using the
   appropriate factor model and correlation assumptions.

3. Calculate $x = ([L_t^1/z], \ldots, [L_t^K/z])$ using Equation (16.5) such as
   for $k = 1$ to K, $[L_t^k/z] = \overline{\Phi}_{k,z}^{-1}(\Phi_{k,z}(L_t^k/z))$

Using this transformation step, we can derive the expected outer
tranche loss consistently with the market correlation skew of each inner
CDO. Nevertheless, we have to make an assumption concerning the outer
correlation by defining the factor model that is used to determine the correlation between the inner CDOs. This is the main drawback of the correlation-of-correlation approach.

Numerical Results

We compare the two previously described pricing methodologies by using
a structure that is common in the market. Thus, we consider a CDO-squared
structure with the following properties:

- Maturity date: 06/20/2012.
- Valuation date: 05/30/2007.
- Typical subordination structure.
- Five inner CDO tranches with attachment 5 percent and
  detachment 8 percent.
- Underlying pool of reference: 200 obligors.
- Each inner CDOs references to 75 equally weighted credits
- The average overlap in this structure is 20 percent.

We fit the correlation skew of the iTraxx (5Y) Series 7 using the
approach described in Guégan and Houdain (2005) based on a one-factor
model and an implied NIG distribution. Then we price each inner tranche
using the calibrated model. We also use this calibrated model to price the
CDO squared in the drill-down approach. Regarding the correlation-of-
correlation approach, we use a Gaussian one-factor model with a constant
correlation parameter to determine the outer correlation, and then we
include the iTraxx correlation skew in the inner CDOs using the calibrated
model. Therefore, we can compare the results for different levels of outer

correlation. We price several tranches among the structures of the outer portfolio using the drill-down and correlation-of-correlation approaches. We also re-price each inner tranche during the CDO-squared pricing in order to test that the pricing of the inner tranches is consistent. We illustrate our results in Table 16.1.

We can observe that the drill-down approach is consistent in terms of pricing for the inner tranches. Moreover, the pricing of the outer tranches is in line with the market expectations. The results obtained using the correlation-of-correlation approach are less consistent in terms of pricing for the inner tranches, which is certainly due to numerical errors in the interpolation of the cumulative loss distributions. Nevertheless, those prices are stable even if we change the outer correlation parameter. The pricing of the outer tranches is driven by the level of the outer correlation parameter. The results obtained for a level of outer correlation of 0.2 are similar to the results obtained using the drill-down approach.

We illustrate in Figure 16.1 the sensitivity of the outer tranches spreads to the level of outer correlation. The spread of the most junior outer tranches is a decreasing function of the level of outer correlation, the spread of the mezzanine outer tranches is flat, and the spread of the most senior tranches is an increasing function of the level of outer correlation. This is also in line with the market expectations.

CONCLUSION

We have introduced in this chapter two different methodologies for the synthetic CDO-squared pricing. These two methodologies should be used by a market participant who does not have access to the CDO-squared correlation skew information. We demonstrated that using these approaches a very good proxy for CDO-squared prices in the correlation market can be obtained. Nevertheless, we have to mention some theoretical drawbacks. The drill-down methodology is consistent with the outer correlation but assumes that prices of the inner tranches are driven by the same market correlation skew. The correlation-of-correlation approach is consistent with inner tranches pricing but not with the outer correlation. We illustrated that the outer tranche pricing should be very sensitive to the level of outer correlation when we use the correlation-of-correlation methodology. These two different methodologies can also be used to efficiently manage risk of a fund of CDOs whether we consider the correlation between the assets in

TABLE 16.1

Numerical results of the CDO and CDO-squared pricing*

Tranche	Att	Det	NIG Valorization	NIG & Drill-Down	Valorization Mapping	CC (0)	CC (0.1)	CC (0.2)	CC (0.3)	CC (0.4)	CC (0.5)	CC (0.6)	CC (0.7)	CC (0.8)	CC (0.9)	CC (1)
Inner 1	5	8	45	47	52	53	53	54	52	53	54	54	53	53	53	52
Inner 2	5	8	63	67	60	61	62	61	61	60	61	62	61	60	62	61
Inner 3	5	8	107	110	90	90	90	92	91	91	91	90	91	91	92	91
Inner 4	5	8	56	58	53	54	55	53	54	55	53	54	54	54	55	53
Inner 5	5	8	68	70	65	66	66	67	67	66	66	67	66	66	67	65
Outer	0	10	–	254	–	301	274	249	244	239	235	230	225	221	217	212
Outer	10	20	–	133	–	158	143	130	128	125	123	120	118	116	113	111
Outer	20	30	–	85	–	101	92	84	82	80	79	77	76	74	73	71
Outer	30	40	–	63	–	64	63	62	62	63	64	64	65	66	66	67
Outer	40	50	–	50	–	51	50	49	50	50	51	51	52	52	53	53
Outer	50	60	–	41	–	10	20	40	41	41	42	42	43	43	43	44
Outer	60	70	–	35	–	9	17	34	34	35	35	35	36	36	36	37
Outer	70	80	–	30	–	3	9	29	33	34	34	34	35	35	35	36
Outer	80	90	–	25	–	2	7	24	28	28	28	29	29	29	30	30
Outer	90	100	–	20	–	2	6	20	23	23	23	23	24	24	24	24
Outer	0	25	–	173	–	205	186	169	166	163	160	157	154	151	148	145
Outer	25	50	–	61	–	62	61	60	60	61	62	63	63	63	64	65
Outer	50	75	–	37	–	9	18	36	31	27	24	20	18	15	13	12
Outer	75	100	–	24	–	2	7	23	20	17	15	13	11	10	9	8

* Valuation date: 05/30/2006. Maturity date: 06/20/2012. CC(c) is equivalent to correlation-of-correlation with a constant outer correlation c.

F I G U R E   16.1

Sensitivity of the outer tranches spreads to the level of outer correlation

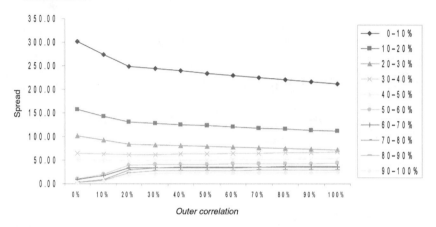

the fund. Therefore, we will calculate more realistic sensitivities than considering each asset separately.

REFERENCES

Albrecher, H, Ladoucette, S, and Schoutens, W. (2006), A Generic One-Factor Levy Model for Pricing Synthetic CDOs. Working paper, www.kuleuven.be.

Andersen, L., and Sidenius, J. (2005) Extensions to the Gaussian Copula: Random Recovery and Random Factor Loadings. *Journal of Credit Risk*, 1: 29–70.

Andersen, L., Sidenius, J., and Basu, S. (2003) All Your Hedges in One Basket. *RISK*, November: 67–72.

Barndorff-Nielsen, O.E. (1997) Normal Inverse Gaussian Processes and Stochastic Volatility Modelling. *Scandinavian Journal of Statistics*, 24: 1–13.

Burtschell, X., Gregory, J., and Laurent, J-P. (2005) Beyond the Gaussian Copula: Stochastic and Local Correlation, www.defaultrisk.com.

Flanagan, C., Ahluwalia, R., Graves, B., and Reardon, E. (2005) CDO
    Squareds—Valuing the Loss Cap. *Derivatives Week*, April 11, p. 1.

Gilkes K, and Drexler, M. (2003) Drill-Down Approach for Synthetic
    CDO Squared Transactions. Working paper, Standard & Poor's.

Guégan, D, and Houdain, J. (2005) Collateralized Debt Obligations Pricing
    and Factor Models: A New Methodology Using Normal Inverse
    Gaussian Distributions, www.defaultrisk.com/pp crdrv 93.htm.

Hull, J, and White, A. (2004) Valuation of a CDO and an *nth*-to-Default
    CDS without Monte Carlo Simulation. Working paper, University
    of Toronto.

Hull, J, and White, A. (2005) The Perfect Copula. Working paper,
    University of Toronto.

Jackel, P. (2005) Splitting the Core. Working paper, www.jaeckel.org.

Kalemanova, A, Schmid, B, and Werner, R. (2005) The Normal Inverse
    Gaussian Distribution for Synthetic CDO. Working paper,
    www.defaultrisk.com.

Li, D, and Liang, M. (2005) CDO squared Pricing Using Gaussian
    Mixture Model with Transformation of Loss Distribution, *Working
    Paper, www.defaultrisk.com*

Patel, N. (2005) The Challenge of CDO Squared. *Risk Magazine,* 18(3): 1.

Shelton, D. (2004) Back To Normal. Working paper, Citigroup, London.

Walker, M.B. (2005) An Incomplete-Market Model for Collateralized
    Debt Obligations. http://www.physics.utoronto.ca/qocmp/
    incompleteCDO.2005.10.05.pdf.

Walker, M.B. (2006) CDO Models Towards the Next Generation:
    Incomplete Markets and Term Structure. http://www.physics.
    utoronto.ca/qocmp/nextGenDefaultrisk.pdf.

CHAPTER 17

The Role of Credit and Credit Index Derivatives in Portfolio Management: Asset Allocation Issues and Opportunities

R. McFall Lamm, Jr.

ABSTRACT

Investors often regard fixed income as an amorphous asset class that is included in portfolios to mute risk. However, in recent years liquidity and the array of fixed-income instruments have expanded tremendously, and one can now generate equity-like returns in certain cases. Unfortunately, this comes at a cost—greater risk. This chapter evaluates the extent to which credit and credit derivatives should be used in building robust portfolios. The conclusion is that riskier credit—principally, high yield—adds significant performance value especially when allocations are managed actively. In contrast, employing credit index derivatives is less appealing.

INTRODUCTION

Investment managers often view credit exposure somewhat agnostically. The reason is that credit allocations historically have added little to overall portfolio performance when compared with stocks, hedge funds, private equity, and real estate. Consequently, debt instruments are often regarded as little more than augmented risk-free bond commitments and included in portfolios reluctantly as a method of smoothing portfolio volatility accrued from riskier investments. Of course, more aggressive professionals might add incremental high-yield exposure and perhaps even emerging market debt. However, the bulk of institutional fixed-income allocations are too often committed to the Lehman aggregate or a similar investment-grade benchmark with little afterthought.

However, when one digs deeper into credit—particularly high-yield debt—one discovers a fixed income subclass that has very attractive behavioral characteristics. These include equity-like returns over extended periods with substantially lower statistical risk than stocks. This comes with fairly low correlation versus both equities and investment-grade corporate debt since high yield follows a cycle that is at times out of phase with other assets. Furthermore, when viewed over an extended horizon, high yield provides significant downside protection compared with other assets due to price depreciation being offset by large income flows.

In this chapter, I critically evaluate the role of credit exposure in investment portfolios. I focus mainly on long-only high-yield exposure and, to a lesser extent, high-yield options as a mechanism for producing positive asymmetry in returns to meet the objectives of more risk-averse investors. While my approach is somewhat simplistic—only investment-grade and high-yield credits are added to a basic stock, bond, and cash asset universe—it is nonetheless adequate to support some basic conclusions.

The first section describes the basic performance properties of credits versus other assets. The second section then addresses the issue of how much credit exposure should be carried in portfolios. The third section explores the use of long call positions to inject positive asymmetry into portfolio returns. Fundamental active rules-based allocation—both for credits and equities—is then evaluated in the subsequent section with portfolio weights allowed to vary as market conditions evolve. The key conclusion is that high yield should play an important role in investment portfolios, especially when one varies credit exposure judiciously over the business cycle.

CREDIT MARKET PERFORMANCE

Investment-grade government, agency, corporate, and mortgage debt have performance characteristics that are well-known and need little elaboration. However, high yield is a less-explored, amorphous, and sometimes

misunderstood topic. One reason is that many institutions prohibit allocations to securities rated less than investment grade. This is paradoxical
since the same institutions frequently invest in hedge funds that not only
invest in high yield but even purchase bankrupt company debt. Therefore,
institutions that avoid high-yield securities are often investing by proxy
via allocations to "alternative" assets.

Figure 17.1 shows total returns for stocks [the Standard & Poor's
(S&P) 500], Treasuries, corporate bonds, high-yield securities, and three-
month Treasuries from January 1980 to June 2007.[1] The performance
record exhibits the classical asset paradigm—stocks outperform less risky
assets, and within the fixed-income universe, high-yield outperforms
investment-grade corporate debt, which in turn outperforms Treasuries.
The chart also illustrates that high yield possesses equity-like characteristics since downward movements in equity returns are often accompanied
with negative high-yield performance. That said, it is noteworthy that
high-yield returns were flat over the period 2000 to 2002 during the sharp
equity market sell-off.

F I G U R E   17.1

Selected asset returns, December 1979 to June 2007

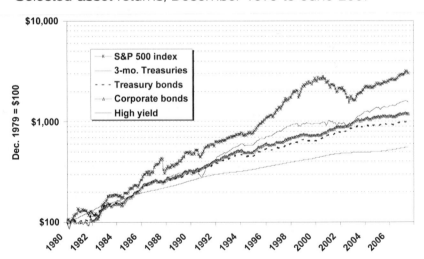

---

[1] For Treasuries I use the JP Morgan index while employing Merrill indexes for corporate bonds,
high yield (the "liquid 100" index), and three-month Treasuries.

T A B L E   17.1

Returns and performance metrics for various assets:
January 1980 through June 2007

Metric	S&P 500	Treasury (3-mo.)	Treasury bonds	Corp. bonds	High yield
Annual Compound Return	13.1%	6.4%	8.7%	9.4%	10.4%
Volatility (annualized)	14.8%	0.3%	5.8%	7.0%	8.7%
Skewness	−0.58*	1.35*	0.55*	0.68*	0.21
Kurtosis	2.59*	2.78*	3.32*	5.37*	4.91*
Jarque-Bera Test	93.8*	106.7*	152.2*	397.9*	333.1*
Sharpe Ratio	0.45	—	0.40	0.43	0.46
Correlations S&P 500	1.00	0.03	0.15	0.27	0.47
Treasury (3-month)		1.00	0.32	0.26	0.13
Treasury Bonds			1.00	0.94	0.48
Corporate Bonds				1.00	0.67
High Yield					1.00

Based on 330 months covering January 1980 to June 2007.

* Statistical significance with 99 percent confidence. The skew and kurtosis standard deviations are 0.135 and 0.269, respectively.

Of course, the cost of higher returns is greater volatility, the extent of which is reported in Table 17.1, where high-yield volatility is shown to lie between that of equities and investment-grade corporate debt. The same is true for higher moments—as reflected by skew and kurtosis—with high yield exhibiting asymmetry characteristics somewhere between stocks and corporate bonds.[2] However, the Sharpe ratio for high yield is slightly greater than other assets, but this may be attributable to the inclusion of data from the 1980s when high yield was beginning to surface as a distinctive fixed-income subclass. Also, when one examines correlations, the results confirm that high yield appears to offer diversification benefits by virtue of its position between equity and traditional fixed income.

---

[2] I define skew and kurtosis using standard normalized definitions as embedded in common spreadsheet functionality rather than the strict statistical usage.

THE ROLE OF RISKIER CREDIT IN INVESTMENT PORTFOLIOS

As for whether significant allocations to high yield are appropriate going forward, this clearly depends on one's expectations. However, as a starting point, it is convenient to employ "look back" analysis and derive optimal exposures retrospectively. I use monthly returns over the period from January 1980 through June 2007 to do this, initially by means of standard mean-variance analysis. While this ignores asymmetry in the underlying asset return streams, it avoids the problem of assigning arbitrary investor preferences for skew and kurtosis—an effort that would unlikely alter conclusions substantially given the fairly weak asymmetry pattern displayed in the past.

The results for various return-versus-risk combinations are presented in Figure 17.2 and indicate that high yield is a preferred asset. Indeed, high yield enters optimal portfolios at virtually all risk levels with the exception of very conservative and extremely aggressive portfolios, which tilt more to cash and equities, respectively. Importantly, allocations average more than 20 percent for portfolio volatility in the 7- to 12-percent range—bounds that encompass target and realized risk for typical institutional portfolios.

F I G U R E   17.2

Optimal retrospective portfolio weights

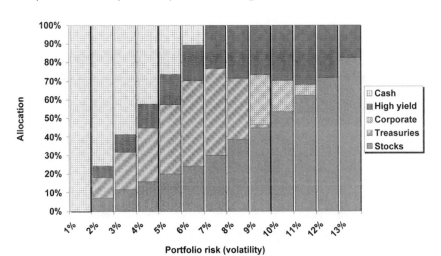

F I G U R E   17.3

Portfolio returns with/without high yield

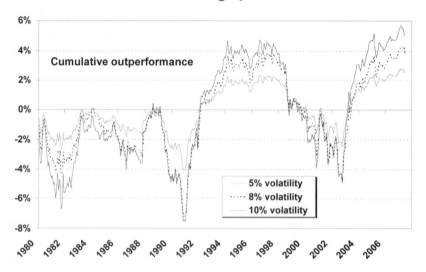

At the same time, the incremental returns added by including high yield in the investment universe are not very great, and the resulting outward push on the efficient frontier is limited. For example, when optimal portfolios with and without high yield are compared (in Figure 17.3), indications are that for the same risk, adding high yield increases cumulative returns only 3 to 5 percent over the period 1980 to June 2007.

Furthermore, much of this accumulates over the past few years after two decades where the record is nebulous. Adding only a fraction of a percent annually to investment performance might lead one to argue that including high yield does not appear to justify the effort. Perhaps this is why high yield is often avoided and investment managers typically devote modest effort to appraising its merits.

Even so, there are periods when high yield adds significantly to performance and other times when it detracts. In this regard, the time to avoid high yield is during economic weakness such as during the 1980 to 1982 U.S. recessions, 1990 to 1991, and in 2001 when high-yield exposure dampened portfolio returns. This suggests that, like equities, time-varying portfolio exposure to high yield may be more appropriate if one can anticipate business cycle fluctuations with any degree of precision.

USING INDEX DERIVATIVES TO ALTER PORTFOLIO ASYMMETRY PROPERTIES

In recent years much intellectual debate has centered on the efficacy of using mean-variance portfolio optimization as an analytical tool since it is conditional on normality and possesses other problems.[3] However, from an institutional perspective, the issue of nonnormality is greatly exaggerated since asymmetry is largely a function of periodicity. By this I mean that institutional allocation changes are often only considered infrequently (monthly or even quarterly). In contrast, excessive asymmetry typically is a short-term phenomenon occurring at high frequencies such as in daily and weekly returns and essentially vanishes at quarterly intervals. It is therefore disingenuous to fret about skew and kurtosis since asymmetry tends to "wash out" by the time performance reports arrive and rebalancing decisions are made. Low-frequency returns and moments are the relevant metric.

The "asymmetry fade" as frequency decreases is illustrated by the high-yield summary distribution statistics presented in Table 17.2. Daily and

T A B L E   17.2

High-Yield performance characteristics for different frequencies

Metric	Daily Returns from Jan. 1, 1988 to June 30, 2007				Monthly Returns Jan. 1981 to Dec. 2006		
	Days	Weeks	Mos.	Qtrs.	Mos.	Qtrs.	Years
Observations	4953	972	234	78	324	108	27
Annualized Return	9.5%	9.7%	9.6%	9.6%	10.7%	10.7%	10.7%
Annualized Volatility	3.6%	5.3%	7.0%	7.7%	8.7%	10.1%	11.4%
Skew	−1.56*	−0.71*	−0.48	0.23	0.20	0.39	0.84
Skew Standard Deviation	0.04	0.08	0.16	0.28	0.14	0.24	0.47
Kurtosis	17.40*	4.31*	3.29*	1.29	4.87*	3.13*	0.25
Kurt Standard Deviation	0.07	0.156	0.32	0.56	0.27	0.47	0.94
JB Test	64494*	834.3*	114.7*	6.05*	322.7*	46.7*	3.23

* Statistical significance with 99% confidence. Returns do not match exactly due to differences in days per month, weeks per year, and annualization factors.

---

[3] There is a long list of references on this subject but some of my favorites include Athayde and Flores (2004), Brooks and Kat (2002), Jean (1971; 1973), Lamm (2003; 2006), and Jondeau and Rockinger (2002; 2004).

weekly returns exhibit strong negative skew and fat tails that are statistically significant. This picture is largely reversed for monthly returns—which exhibit no statistically significant skew over the 1988 to 2007 horizon or the longer period 1981 to 2006. Similarly, quarterly returns exhibit no statistically significant asymmetry. That said, fat tails (excess kurtosis) are in evidence at virtually any frequency; that is why JB tests are affirmative.[4] The short conclusion is that high-frequency traders are the ones who need worry about negative asymmetry, while low-frequency decision makers should focus more on higher expected returns and volatility.

Nonetheless, low-frequency investors may be interested in injecting positive asymmetry into their performance stream to satisfy payout requirements or to avoid deficits that prompt unexpected top-ups.[5] The question then is whether positive asymmetry can be added without sacrificing too much in investment performance. I explore this issue—again via retrospective simulation—by allowing investments in the same pool of assets as before but adding equity and high-yield index calls to the admissible asset universe. I specifically consider the case where investors purchase calls at the beginning of the quarter and hold them to maturity with the position then rolled over at prevailing option prices upon quarter's end. This breaks the high correlation between delta-long exposure and the underlying assets, minimizes transactions costs versus monthly rolls, and fits more appropriately with a view of options as asymmetry modifiers.

Figure 17.4 shows the return stream for sequentially carried positions in out-of-the-money S&P and at-the-money high-yield calls.[6] The differences in returns are significant and reflect the fact that a significant portion of S&P performance arises from capital appreciation, while the opposite is true for high yield, where interest payments are the primary source of returns. Indeed, high-yield prices actually decline over the sample, so

---

[4] Also quite interesting is the fact that high-yield volatility increases as frequency declines— suggesting that longer horizon investors face greater risk than more active managers.

[5] While I presume positive asymmetry preference, some researchers assert that investors prefer negative return asymmetry. For example, see Kahneman and Tversky (1974; 1979) and Taleb (2004). Furthermore, there is a distinction between preferences for asymmetry in investment portfolio performance and taking asymmetry into account in building portfolios where individual managers exhibit asymmetric returns as discussed by Cremers et al. (2005).

[6] The S&P calls are 3 percent out of the money. Both are priced off trailing historical volatility corrected for smile and historical differences between actual vs. implied volatility.

F I G U R E   17.4

Equity and high-yield call returns

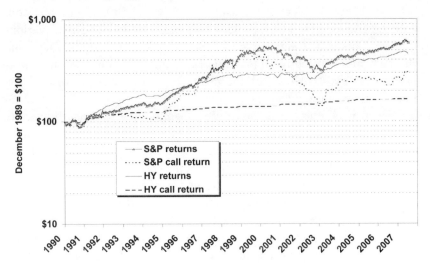

more than 100% of performance comes from interest payments. This is why high-yield calls struck at the money do not pay off as often as one might imagine.

As for whether long-only call exposure in a fixed-weight investment portfolio makes sense, the answer seems to be no—at least retrospectively. Indeed, optimizing over 1990 to mid 2007—the period over which there is sufficient daily data to price options—indicates that neither equity nor high-yield call positions enter efficient portfolios for any volatility target. This is primarily due to the fact that call returns are low relative to their volatility when compared with other assets.

Of course, if one focuses on skew as the relevant portfolio risk measure, the findings are quite different. Table 17.3 shows the results of constructing optimal portfolios for three cases: (1) The investor cares only about return relative to volatility; (2) the investor is concerned about both return and skew relative to volatility; and (3) the investor cares only about maximizing skew versus volatility.[7] Quantitatively, the investor's

---

[7] Note I drop kurtosis from consideration to simplify the analysis and to reflect the fact that one probably does not care too much if the upside tail is fat as long as there is positive skew in the return stream.

objective is simply to $\max_w E[U(W)] = \lambda r + \theta\sigma^2 + \gamma s^3$ for $r = w^T r$
(portfolio return), $\sigma^2 = w^T \Gamma w$ (portfolio variance), and $s^3 = w^T Sw \otimes w$,
(portfolio skew), subject to the usual positive weight and unit sum constraints. I use $[\lambda\ \gamma] = [1\ 0]$, $[0.95\ 0.05]$, and $[0\ 1]$ iterating over various
θ values. This is a straightforward hedonic approach and one may want
to impose more structure on the underlying utility function if such information is available. However, the main purpose here is to illustrate extremes and an intermediate case.

Table 17.3 reproduces the results of optimizing for volatilities of 6,
8, and 10 percent, while Figure 17.5 displays the return streams graphically. The key conclusion is that placing a large preference weight on
skew—that is, by carrying significant long call positions—involves a
considerable sacrifice in returns. The performance loss averages 3 to 4
percent annually—a very large price to pay to avoid sharp monthly drawdowns. This is especially true when one discovers that such short-term
protection fails to prevent participation in the large gradual performance
erosion that occurred during the early 2000s equity sell-off. Since the

T A B L E   17.3

Optimal portfolios for various risk preferences

Asset/ Metric	Volatility, 6%			Volatility, 8%			Volatility, 10%		
	Max Return	Blend	Max Skew	Max Return	Blend	Max Skew	Max Return	Blend	Max Skew
S&P	19%	—	—	35%	—	—	61%	—	—
S&P calls	—	24%	24%	—	31%	34%	—	41%	43%
Treas. bonds	—	35%	—	—	48%	19%	—	23%	34%
Corp. bonds	29%	—	—	—	—	—	—	16%	—
High yield	52%	13%	4%	65%	21%	39%	20%		
High yield calls	—	—	71%	—	—	47%	—	—	22%
3-mo. Treas.	—	28%	—	—	—	—	—	—	—
Return	9.3%	6.9%	4.6%	9.7%	7.8%	5.5%	10.5%	7.9%	6.4%
Skew	−.66*	.99*	1.18*	−.87*	.96*	1.07*	−.74*	0.98*	1.03*
Kurtosis	2.02*	2.31*	3.55*	2.70*	2.30*	2.74*	1.50*	2.37*	2.53*
JB test	35.8*	46.8*	111*	64.2*	46.4*	65.8*	20.1*	49.4*	56.5*

* Denotes 99% confidence.

F I G U R E   17.5

Downside protection cost: Portfolio performance with different objectives

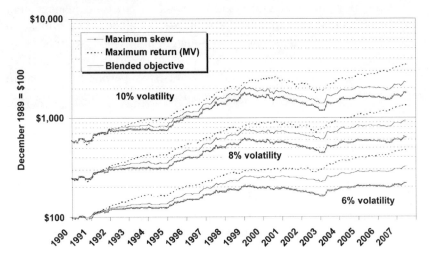

return stream for the maximally skewed portfolio is not much more than cash yield over the period, few investors are likely to find the cost acceptable. Even if one moves to the intermediate case where the investor has specific return, volatility, and skew preferences—the blended example— significant returns are given up with limited benefit other than escaping sharp short-term performance declines.

ALLOCATION VIA ACTIVE RULES

The analysis to this point presents a less than flattering view of riskier credits. Adding high yield to portfolios improves returns and behavioral characteristics in general, but not a lot. Furthermore, expanding the investment universe to include long calls on high yield—combined with admitting the same possibility for equities—can deliver a positively skewed return stream, but the performance sacrifice appears excessive.

However, these findings are based on the generally abstract case where investors hold fixed allocations through the investment horizon. In reality, most investors vary portfolio weights—although institutions are notorious for making only modest revisions over time that are often reactive and value destructive. Therefore, the more pertinent question is what role riskier credits might play in an active allocation world where decisions rationally take market fundamentals into account.

To explore the potential benefits of active portfolio management with time-varying weights, I apply a simple set of plausible allocation rules. I focus specifically on two long-held commonsense precepts. First, the investor overweights equities when earnings to price ratios (E/P) exceed long Treasury rates and underweights stocks when E/P ratios are less than rates. This is no more than the "Fed rule" except I employ one-month lagged E/P ratios and rates since they are known with certainty. The second rule is that the investor overweights high yield when default rates are less than the high-yield and/or Treasury spread and vice versa when the default rate is greater than the spread. These rules are somewhat antiquated ideas that were around in decades past and accepted by many professionals because they capture crude valuation relatives. As a result, the need for out-of-sample verification is muted since the 2000s constitute a reasonable test period. Retrospection, therefore, has greater merit.

The specific process I follow is a conditional sequence. First, I compare equity E/P ratios to the 10-year Treasury yield. If E/P is 1 percent or more above long rates, then the equity allocation is set at 70 percent. If E/P is 1 percent below long rates, the allocation is 50 percent. A 60-percent equity weight is the default for in-between values. After the equity weight is determined, the residual is allocated to "bonds" with 10 percent committed to high yield if spreads are 1 percent above default rates and 0 percent if spreads are less than 1 percent below. A 5-percent allocation to high yield is the default if neither of these conditions holds. The residual bond exposure is simply split half and half between Treasuries and corporate debt. Thus, bond exposure depends on the state of the equity market, and the high-yield allocation is a function of credit conditions. I make no effort to optimize the rules.

Table 17.4 shows the results of applying this methodology over the sample period, and Figure 17.6 presents the results graphically. Both compare active management to a passive portfolio with weights set exactly at the average exposure of the rules-based allocation. This represents a more "apples to apples" comparison than if a simple 60 percent stocks and 40 percent bonds comparison were made. Indications are that rules-based active management based on market fundamentals appears to add significant performance value—particularly in the later 1990s.

T A B L E   17.4

Active "rules-based" vs. passive portfolio performance

Metric	Active	Passive	Asset	Avg. Weight
Months	330	330	S&P	61%
Return	12.5%	11.9%	Treas. bonds	16%
Volatility	9.5%	9.8%	Corp. bonds	16%
Skew	−0.05	−0.21	High yield	7%
Kurtosis	0.76*	1.26*		100%
JB	8.39*	22.36*		

* Denotes 99% significance. The skew and kurtosis standard deviations are 0.13 and 0.27, respectively.

F I G U R E   17.6

Active rules-based allocation versus passive fixed weights

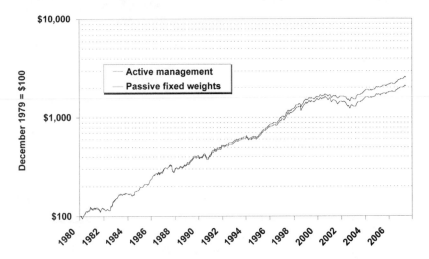

The actively managed portfolio (Figure 17.7) has a higher return (0.6 percent annually), lower volatility (9.5 vs. 9.8 percent), and lower kurtosis (0.76 vs. 1.26) compared with the passive fixed-weight portfolio. Both have statistically insignificant skew. Over the entire horizon the cumulative return for the actively managed portfolio is $2,574 on a $100 investment made in December 1979 versus $2,095 for passive holding. Importantly, while the actively managed portfolio experienced

F I G U R E   17.7

Active allocation weight changes

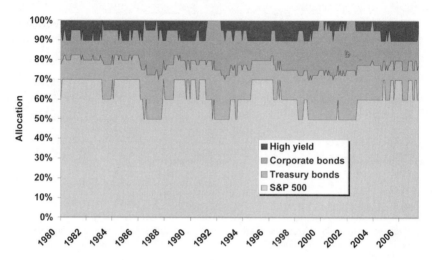

a drawdown during the early 2000s sell-off—15.7 percent from January 2001 to September 2002—this was much less than the 25 percent drawdown for the passive portfolio over the same period.

Interestingly, the conditional nature of the allocation process creates a situation where the credit rule is "tighter" than the equity rule. That is, the equity weight is changed 52 times over the 28-year sample—about twice a year—while the high-yield allocation changes 72 times—three times a year. This is because the high-yield allocation depends on equity exposure and every change in equity allocation affects the high-yield weight. Even so, two or three allocation shifts per year are not extreme by most standards.

Obviously, further calibration of these crude rules would improve the results. For example, instead of arbitrary 1 percent differences to define the bounds for a neutral allocation, one might use standard deviations. In addition, more complex valuation measures might be employed for equities such as price/book or profit margins. Furthermore, the weighting scheme could be liberalized to permit more extreme exposure. However, such modifications run the risk of "over-fitting" the model, which could negate intuitiveness and possibly mute future performance if applied ex post.

A critic would point out that while active management outperforms before the early 2000s, much of the added value takes place during the bubble blow-off when equity and high-yield allocations are low. This is a valid point, but even dropping these years leads to the same conclusion, although the differentials narrow. The counterargument is that imposing known rationale valuation principles in advance of the stock market sell-off would have provided significant protection and is likely to do so in the future when markets temporarily diverge due to excessive exuberance or overt despair.

CONCLUSION

Classic asset allocation treatises such as those by Campbell and Viceira (2002) and Fabozzi et. al. (2007) tend to focus on fixed-weight allocation and fuzzy stock and bond asset classes that are somewhat removed from reality. Similar comments can be made about active portfolio rebalancers, such as Grinhold and Kahn (1995). Even within the practitioner research realm, assets such as high yield are often ignored at the expense of more highly correlated equity subgroupings and pseudo-equity classes such as long/short hedge funds and private equity.

The evidence presented here suggests that riskier credits deserve a place in investment portfolios and, in this regard, high yield offers a valid performance enhancer. This is especially true when one adheres to elementary valuation rules in an active portfolio management context. Furthermore, using high-yield or equity index call options to achieve skewed return portfolios—a major concern of postmodern asset allocation experts—does not appear to make a lot of sense since downside protection costs appear to buy little more than short-term sell-off insulation while not avoiding prolonged periods of market weakness.

REFERENCES

Athayde, G.M., and Flores, R.G., Jr. (2004) Finding a Maximum Skewness Portfolio—A General Solution to Three-Moments Portfolio Choice. *Journal of Economic Dynamics and Control*, 28(6): 1335–1352.

Brooks, Chris, and Kat, Harry M. (2002) The Statistical Properties of Hedge Fund Return Index Returns and Their Implications for Investors. *The Journal of Alternative Investments,* 5(3): 26–44.

Campbell, John Y., and Viceira, Luis M. (2002) *Strategic Asset Allocation.* New York: Oxford University Press.

Cremers, Jan-Hein, Kritzman, Mark, and Page, Sebastian (2005) Optimal Hedge Fund Allocations: Do Higher Moments Matter? *Journal of Portfolio Management*, 32(1): 70–81.

Faboozzi, Frank J., Kolm, Peter N., Pachamanova, Dessislava A., and Focardi, Sergio M. (2007) *Robust Portfolio Optimization and Management.* Hoboken, NJ: John Wiley & Sons.

Grinold, Richard C., and Kahn, Ronald N. (1995) *Active Portfolio Management.* Chicago: Probis Publishing.

Jean, W.H. (1971) The Extension of Portfolio Analysis to Three or More Parameters. *Journal of Financial and Quantitative Analysis,* 6(5): 505–515.

Jean, W.H. (1973) More on Multidimensional Portfolio Analysis. *Journal of Financial and Quantitative Analysis*, 8(5): 475–490.

Kahneman, D. and Tversky, A. (1974) Judgment under Uncertainty: Heuristics and Biases. *Science*, 185: 1124–1131.

Kahneman, D. and Tversky, A. (1979) Prospect Theory: An Analysis of Decisions under Risk. *Econometrica*, 47(2): 263–291.

Jondeau, Eric and Rockinger, Michael (2002) The Allocation of Assets Under Higher Moments. Research paper, International Center for Financial Asset Management and Engineering, Geneva, December.

Jondeau, Eric and Rockinger, Michael (2004) Conditional Asset Allocation under Nonnormality: How Costly Is the Mean-Variance Criterion? Research paper, International Center for Financial Asset Management and Engineering, Geneva, December.

Lamm, R.M. (2003) Asymmetric Returns and Optimal Hedge Fund Portfolios, *Journal of Alternative Investments*, 6(4): 9–21.

Lamm, R.M. (2006) Blending Hedge Funds with Stock and Bond Portfolios: Investment Management in A New World. In Greg N.

Gregoriou and Dieter G. Kaiser (eds), *Hedge Funds and Managed Futures: A Handbook for Institutional Investors.* London: Risk Books, pp. 375–395.

Taleb, Nassim N. (2004) Bleed or Blowup? Why Do We Prefer Asymmetric Returns? *Journal of Behavioral Finance,* 5(1): 2–7.

INDEX

Page numbers followed by *f* or *t* indicate material contained in figures or tables, respectively.